The Twilight of the Nation State

Globalisation, Chaos and War

Prem Shankar Jha

Foreword by **Eric Hobsbawm**

Pluto Press
LONDON • ANN ARBOR, MI

First published 2006 by Pluto Press
345 Archway Road, London N6 5AA
and 839 Greene Street, Ann Arbor, MI 48106

www.plutobooks.com

British Library Cataloguing in Publication Data
A catalogue record for this book is available from the British Library

ISBN 0 7453 2530 0 hardback
ISBN 0 7453 2529 7 paperback

Library of Congress Cataloging in Publication Data applied for

10 9 8 7 6 5 4 3 2 1

Designed and produced for Pluto Press by
Sage Publications, B-42, Panchsheel Enclave, New Delhi 110 017
Typeset from disk by Star Compugraphics, Delhi
Printed in India by Chaman Enterprises, New Delhi

CONTENTS

FOREWORD

In the early years of the twenty-first century it is difficult to remember the optimism, not to say triumphalism, that followed the collapse of communism in the rich countries of the North. Where is Fukuyama's 'end of history'? Today even the politicians and ideologues of that region heavily qualify their forecasts of a peaceful and liberal future for a world which seems in obvious crisis. Yet the test of a book about the current situation of the globe is not whether it is hopeful or disenchanted, but whether it helps us understand it, that is to say, whether it shows a historical understanding of the present crisis. Prem Shankar Jha's strikingly intelligent, lucid and troubled book passes this test with flying colours. It is essential reading for the first decade of the third millennium.

He sees the present as the most recent of the major crises in the secular development of a by its very nature increasingly globalising capitalism. In his view we are living through the fourth time that capitalism has broken its economic, political and institutional 'container', in the course of a history which he traces back to the middle ages. As in the past, the end of each of its cycles of expansion has seen the destruction of institutions and prolonged conflict between and within states, and what has been called 'systemic chaos'. In Jha's view the violence released by these destructions has tended to increase with the global growth of the 'container'. He has no time for the comfortable reflection that we may hope to return to a bigger and better version of a globalised economy such as was familiar before 1914. Modern globalisation has an incomparably greater potential for destruction.

Each of the earlier phases, he argues, was associated with the hegemony of one major economic centre, linked since the seventeenth century to a historical innovation: the territorial 'nation state' within an international power system. Following what he sees as the era of medieval city-states, the economic hegemony of the Netherlands, and then of Britain, we are at the end of the 'American century'. But the acceleration of globalisation has gone beyond the relatively stable and flexible framework that capitalism generated—notably the nation state with its institutions and international system—and which allowed it to develop without explosion or implosion and to recover from the crises of the first half of the twentieth century. It does not function any longer. No clear alternative is in sight. Further destruction and a deeper chaos are to be expected before the internal and external contradictions of the current crisis of globalisation are overcome.

Unlike most works on globalisation, usually written in Europe or North America, Prem Shankar Jha's voice comes to us from India, the region which will probably be the core of the twenty-first century world, but whose spectacular development coincides with the 'systemic chaos' into which the global economy has been plunging since the onset of the present era of crisis in the 1970s. That is why he is more keenly aware of the problems created by the current phase of capitalist globalisation than the liberal economists who argue the virtues of the market, leave alone the brigades of business publicists.

The negative effects of globalisation on the developed countries, even the consequences of their de-industrialisation and the erosion of their welfare systems, are substantial but slow, and are moderated by their accumulated social wealth. Their earthquakes are tremors at the bottom end of the economic Richter scale. In the 'developing' world they are cataclysmic. When politicians and journalists in the European Union speak of economic crisis, they do not mean what Jha rightly calls the 'melt-down' of 1997–98, of whose South and East Asian manifestations he gives a vivid analysis. They do not mean the seismic explosions that have shaken Brazil, Mexico and Argentina since the 1980s, which were treated by Northern commentators chiefly as proofs of the immaturity of Third World businessmen and governments compared to those of the OECD.

An observer from a country like India is less likely than those in the rich countries to confuse the generally beneficial effects of industrialisation and techno-scientific progress with the much more problematic consequences of uncontrolled capitalist globalisation, notably the dramatic widening of the per capita income gap between the developed countries and most other countries—and, within almost all countries, the gap between the rich and the poor. Above all, he cannot but be constantly aware that phrases such as 'I am hungry' or 'I have no work' have a profoundly different meaning in countries with a mean per capita GDP of $25,000 than they do in countries where it is $500. After reading his book, even those of us from countries whose populations are still protected by the wealth and institutions of their past, should be aware of the forces globalisation generates that are impelling the world towards further destruction and darkness.

Eric Hobsbawm

Introduction

This book attempts to give shape to a widely shared and growing unease about the direction in which the world is moving. It argues—contrary to the belief that pervaded most of the intellectual debate about the future in the mid- and late 1990s, and which still survives in an attenuated form today—that the world is not moving towards order, peace and prosperity, but towards increasing disorder and violence. The largest and most power-ful nation the world has ever known, the United States, considers itself to be at war. This war is not being waged against a state, not even against a clan, a tribe, or a family, but against an abstract noun—*terrorism*, now short-ened to terror. To pursue this war, President George W. Bush has an-nounced that the US military will go wherever the terrorists reside, or are being spawned, in order to prevent the threat from reaching America's shores.[1] This is a recipe for war without end. The boundaries between war and peace are therefore being eliminated, side by side with the boundaries between nations. It is therefore hardly surprising that an opinion poll carried out in the weeks before Bush's second inauguration showed that 58 per cent of the people polled believed that his re-election had made the world less safe. Those who felt this way constituted a majority in 16 out of the 21 countries covered by the survey. Fear of an America ruled by Bush was strongest among its traditional allies: Germany, France, Britain, Italy, Canada, Mexico and Turkey. In short, precisely those who had the closest relations with the US in the past fear it the most today.[2]

My unease began almost a decade earlier, in 1995, when I spent half a year at the Centre for International Affairs (now the Weatherhead Center for International Affairs) at Harvard University. In those days Harvard was a heady place to be in. The Cold War was over and democracy was sweeping through the erstwhile communist countries and much of the post-colonial world. Trade barriers were going down, currencies were being released from the straitjacket of central bank control, and private capital was flooding into the erstwhile developing countries. It had already transformed a few of them into industrial giants within half a generation. There seemed to be no reason why it could not bring at least prosperity to the rest. Prosperity was releasing pressures for democratic reform in formerly authoritarian countries. A wonderful new world was therefore being born, and Harvard was a crucible, perhaps the single most important one, in which the ideas that would determine its shape were being forged.

In this euphoric atmosphere I found myself a bit of an odd man out. Till 1995 I had spent virtually my entire working life writing about India's political and economic development and its relations with its neighbours. This sudden plunge into the ferment of global ideas was the most electrifying experience of my life. But as I attended more and more seminars— on shock therapy versus gradualism in economic reform; state-society relations in a globalised world; the decline of the nation state and the resurgence of ethnicity; the origins of rogue and backlash states; the justification for and limits of military intervention in defence of human rights; China, the Balkans, US foreign policy after the Cold war, the break-up of the Soviet Empire, the crisis in Russia, the clash of civilisations and the end of history—I grew increasingly uneasy, not about what was being discussed but about what was being left unsaid. If there was anything I had learned from four decades of daily involvement with nation building in the largest and most complex democracy in the world, it was that the political and economic transformation of a society is never smooth. On the contrary, it tears apart existing relationships and creates great insecurity. It sets off struggles between different groups, as some try to increase their share of the cake while others struggle to retain theirs. This struggle in turn gives birth to new alliances that tilt the balance of political power and cause sudden and often counter-productive changes of policy. In the very first book I ever wrote, I had described the political struggle for power unleashed by economic development in India, and ascribed its very slow economic growth between 1956 and 1975 to the anti-growth policies that developed out of that struggle.[3] I also knew, from a lifetime's experience, just how powerful a force nationalism was. For better or for worse, it was the moving force behind the formation of modern states in the post-colonial world. The glib assumption that the nation state was headed for oblivion and that nationalism was destined to become a spent force seemed unreal, to say the least.

But at Harvard, although we were discussing social change, and advocating social engineering on an unprecedented scale, there was a worrying absence of concern for—and therefore of debate on—the perils of the transformation process itself. The underlying presumption in nearly all the discussions and lectures was that the transition the world was going through would be painless. Economic barriers would fall, the nation state would die and a global polity would replace it without too many hiccups along the way. There would be problems, of course, such as the ethno-national conflict let loose by the breakup of the Soviet empire, and the emergence of backlash ideologies and states. But these were aftershocks that would eventually die away. No one remembered, or showed an awareness of, the profound insight articulated by Karl Polanyi half a century earlier, that even potentially beneficial social change can destroy society if it occurs too fast.[4]

My unease crystallised into three articles written for *The Hindu*, in June and July 1995. In them I wrote:

> Discussions of international security after the Cold War are nearly always held within a particular framework of assumptions. These are, first, that the end of the Cold War has eliminated the potential for major global conflicts of the kind that led to the first and second World Wars, and the Cold War itself. Second, that the main sources of tension in future years will be sectarian and ethnic violence born out of a worldwide resurgence of such sentiments. Third, that since such conflicts tend to be localised, their resolution is essentially a local matter, preferably pursued bilaterally, or at the regional level. And fourth, that since the older industrialised countries of the West are not embroiled in these conflicts, they are qualified to act as referees, and suggest, or even decree solutions. These assumptions are flawed. Far from having been eradicated, the seeds of future global conflict have begun to sprout afresh. Neither the form nor the intensity of the conflict can be predicted at this stage. Nor can it be specified whether conflict will be primarily economic, or will spill over into a military confrontation. *What can safely be said, however, is that it will not be initiated by the ethnic-violence prone nations of the 'third world', or the flock of transitional, unstable regimes that have been hatched by the collapse of the Soviet Union, but by the industrialised nations of the West* (emphasis added).

This was written three years before Operation Desert Fox, in which two 'industrialised nations of the West' bombed Iraq incessantly for more than a year on the basis of pure, unfounded paranoia, and because they could do so with impunity; four years before NATO bombarded Serbia and Kosovo for two months; and six and eight years before the American and the Anglo-American invasions of Afghanistan and Iraq respectively.

Unlike Huntington, I did not locate the cause of conflict in a clash of cultures. I wrote,

> Ironically, the seeds of future global conflict lie buried in the very development that led to the emergence of a global marketplace, the collapse of the Soviet Union and the end of the Cold War. This is the (re-) emergence, not long after the Second World War, of technology as the driving force behind social and economic change. Technology has unified markets, through revolutions in information gathering and dissemination, brought transport costs down to a fraction of what they were in the fifties, and thereby created a global market.

Technology has also given countries the means to exploit that market. But since technology only thrives under conditions of fierce competition, it has also rung the death knell of economies that chose to shun competition. These were, notably, the centrally planned economies of the socialist countries.

Just as competition has promoted the growth of technology, technology has fostered the growth of competition. Today barriers to the movement of goods and services have all but disappeared. For the average company in an industrialised country, there are now literally no safe havens, no protected markets. To survive and prosper, it can harness newer and newer cost cutting technologies. Alternatively it can develop new products that meet consumer needs a shade better than the existing ones, and enjoy a temporary monopoly over their sale. But its third and easiest option is to exploit the huge and ever widening difference in real wage rates between the industrialised and developing countries. These differences are growing larger because in sharp contrast to the market for goods and services, and for capital, the international labour market is becoming more and more closed. Not only is the movement of labour severely constrained by consular prohibitions against immigration backed by deeply rooted cultural sanctions, but these barriers are being raised higher and higher all the time.

To harness cheap labour, Capital is moving to the countries where the Labour is located. When it does so, it does not create jobs in the country where the Capital and enterprise originated ... This has begun to pit a large section of the population of the capital-generating countries against the people of the capital-receiving countries ... Unlike the past, [the] unemployment [this has created] does not seem to be cyclical but stable. It has affected only certain types of people—mainly those who do not have a high degree of mental ability or education and who, in the past, found a secure niche in agriculture and semi-skilled industrial work. It is also putting a premium on having a young work force, for the young are able to adapt more easily to the integration of computers into the production process than the older generation of factory and office workers. As a result a large segment of society now feels that it has become a victim of changes over which it had no control, and which the government and ruling class did nothing to protect it from.

This is generating new social tensions in the industrialised countries, and a search for scapegoats among those hurt by the change. Racism, religious antagonism, and a new belligerent nationalism are all raising their heads ...

As the twentieth century draws to a close, it is difficult not to wonder whether the twenty-first will be a century of promise fulfilled or belied: whether it will see the fruits of industrial progress spread across the entire globe, or be wasted away in another even more devastating holocaust than the two that we have seen.[5]

These articles were to become the kernel of the present book. In the year or more that followed their publication, my dissatisfaction with existing studies of globalisation and its consequences continued to grow. A new form of disorder was spreading in a previously ordered world. The welfare state was under severe attack; the trade union movement was in retreat, and income differentials were widening rapidly in the industrialised countries. It seemed as if all the evils of early capitalism were being reborn. That led me to question whether globalisation was really a continuation of past trends in capitalism, or the birth of an entirely new economic epoch which stood in stark contradiction—in Marx's sense of the word—to the existing one.

In 1995, I sensed the potential for global conflict and suspected that the industrialised countries, far from being referees, were likely to be its initiators. But I had only a tentative idea of the shape that the conflict could take. The only cause I was able to identify was the growing social stress in the industrialised countries and the possibility that governments would try to turn outwards the anger that it generated among the dispossessed. I did not realise that transnational investment would create a powerful new motive to forcibly reshape and eventually destroy the Westphalian state system. I saw, hazily, that global economic integration was bound to be followed by political integration, but (in retrospect surprisingly) failed to see just how much resistance this would generate. I also did not make the connection that if the international state system collapsed in the face of overweening military power, terrorism was the only shape this resistance could take. In July 1995, when I returned to India, I had also not delved into the history of capitalism and therefore did not know that the sudden spread of disorder that the world was experiencing had happened on at least three earlier occasions and had generated prolonged cycles of disorder and violence. All that came much later.

In the years that followed, as I made repeated visits to the US, teaching or doing further research at Harvard and the University of Virginia, developments in the international economy and political system began to lift the haze that surrounded my understanding of the sources and nature of future conflict. The formal adoption of the Uruguay round of trade agreements, the establishment of the World Trade Organisation and the institutionalisation of cross retaliation as a tool for securing compliance showed that coercion had replaced consensus building as the prime tool for trade liberalisation. Operation Desert Fox in Iraq, the aerial bombing of Serbia and the invasion of Afghanistan and then of Iraq vindicated my initial surmise that the world would become more violent, and that large scale conflict would be initiated not by rogue or backlash states but by the self-appointed guardians of the international order.

The East Asian financial crisis and economic meltdown, and a succession of economic crises in weaker industrialised countries—Russia, Brazil, Argentina and Turkey—drew my attention to the similarities between unregulated global capitalism and early, unregulated industrial capitalism in Britain. What had previously happened within the confines of a single state seemed now to be happening across the globe. Finally the seemingly inexorable worsening of economic conditions in most of sub-Saharan Africa and the rise in the number of failed or failing states showed that globalisation did not necessarily have to spread to the whole world, and that some countries could get excluded. My attempts to make some sense of the madness that was spreading around the globe led me to examine the history of capitalism, and therefore to Hobsbawm, Arrighi, Wallerstein and Braudel.

Placing globalisation within the context of the development of capitalism has made me appreciate how much wishful thinking underlies the belief in human progress. Over the last 700 years, with the sole exception of the so-called 'Hundred Years' Peace from 1815 to 1914 in Europe, periods characterised by economic harmony, political stability and international peace have been far fewer than those characterised by turmoil, struggle and war. Many writers have been tempted to ascribe this to the innately aggressive nature of capitalism. Capitalism made exchange the predominant form of economic relationship, displacing older forms, such as reciprocity and redistribution. Reliance on exchange fostered the development of competition till it became the organising principle of society. Competition increased efficiency and multiplied wealth but also multiplied the number of losers and sharpened the conflict between them and the winners.

While not wrong, such an analysis places too much of the blame at capitalism's door. The roots of conflict lie not in capitalism but in the technological change that drives it. Since technological change is the inescapable product of mankind's intelligence, curiosity and propensity to innovate, it has been changing economic and political relationships for as long as human beings have lived on the earth. The history of humanity is therefore one of a continuous attempt to adjust. What makes capitalism as an overall system different from all previous epochs of history is that while old civilisations most certainly developed technology, changes in technology were not driven by profit. Once this happened human society slipped by degrees into a state of constant change. This took the control of social change out of the hands of human beings to an extent that had never been experienced before. It is therefore mankind's never-ending attempt to adjust to the change and limit its impact upon society that should be the prime focus of the humanities and social sciences. Scholars who study only the islands of peace that have punctuated this struggle and make light of the decades, even centuries, of disorder and violence, sorrow and misery that lie in between them are either utopian idealists, victims of selective amnesia or, more reprehensibly, purveyors of ideology.

This book attempts to study the disorder that has followed the 'golden age of capitalism' which spanned the third quarter of the last century. It is intended to warn readers that the transition the world is going through will not necessarily end in a new equilibrium—a new island of peace or golden age. On the contrary the disorder could easily deepen till it dismantles the entire edifice of civilised society. It is therefore imperative for decision-makers to recognise the threat and to take concerted action to evade it. The first step on that road is to abandon belief in the self-regulatory capacities of the market and the international political system. Concerted action requires multilateral decision making. The present drift towards unilateralism—towards a global empire backed by military force alone—therefore poses the most serious threat that the world has ever known.

The bulk of this book is devoted to tracing the globalisation of capitalism; its destruction of the institutions built during more than two centuries of nation state-based capitalism; the first, tentative steps in building institutions that will enable human society to cope with capitalism's stormy rebirth; and the threat that these infant institutions face from the USA's sudden and atavistic return to nineteenth-century hyper-nationalism. It is divided into four parts.

Chapters 1 and 2 present the alternate views of the future described above in greater detail and puts the rise of global capitalism in the historical framework of capitalism's earlier cycles of expansion. Chapters 3 to 7 describe the onset of systemic disorder in the industrialised countries and the international economic system. Chapters 8 to 12 describe the assault on, and dismantling of, the global political order established after the Treaty of Westphalia, and the inherent unsustainability (demonstrated by Iraq) of the American bid for Empire. Chapters 13 and 14 describe the crossroads at which the world stands poised, the acute pressures that seem destined to force it to continue down the road to nowhere, and the change of direction that is needed if a peaceful global society capable of reaping the benefits of technology and the information revolution is to emerge.

This book has taken me nine years to write. I have not kept, nor do I think I can reconstruct, an exhaustive list of all the authors to whom I am indebted for the formation of my views. I have therefore listed in the foot-notes only the works I have actually used, and the sources of my factual information. I have drawn especially heavily on the work of four great scholars: Fernand Braudel, Joseph Schumpeter, Karl Polanyi and Giovanni Arrighi. From Braudel this study borrows the profound insight that to turn its economic into political power, and then use the latter to propagate itself, capitalism needs not fixed but liquid, i.e., finance, capital.

It draws upon Braudel and Schumpeter to explain the sharp increases in profit that triggered long cycles of capital accumulation. These originated in an accretion of technological innovation that, every hundred to two hundred years, reached a critical mass and led to a 'gale of creative destruction' that wiped out a generation of fixed capital, substituting it with a new generation that was far more productive than the earlier one.[6]

It draws heavily on Arrighi to show that each expansion of capitalism has led to the economic and political reorganisation of a progressively larger area of the world, and this reorganisation has created the conditions for the birth of the next cycle of accumulation and the rise of a new hegemon. The origins of this paradox lie in the scissors movement of liquid capital accumulation and investment opportunities. As a 'gale of creative destruction' sets in, opportunities for the investment of liquid capital in new fixed capital equipment rise rapidly. As the new equipment replaces the old, the rate of profit rises and increases the rate of capital accumulation. But each replacement of the old generation of equipment, and older management practices with new, circumscribes the opportunities for further rapid increases in productivity. The rate of profit on future investment in fixed capital therefore begins to fall just as the rate of profit on existing investment reaches a peak. This creates an inexorable pressure for the mounting stocks of profit on past investment, i.e., of liquid capital, to find new investment opportunities. That is when capitalism assumes its hegemonistic form and begins to reorganise large parts of the world. This reorganisation is promoted with the aid of a 'legitimising ideology', but backed by the threat or use of force. During this phase, in all previous cycles of capitalism's expansion an increasing share of these profits have been loaned by the financial system to the state for use in 'rearmament'. So far, the end product of rearmament has invariably been war. Each cycle of capitalism has therefore given birth to long spells of violence, as the core cities and nations have sought to reorganise the periphery to augment and prolong the profitability of capital.

Lastly, this book draws on Polanyi to remind readers that it is necessary to slow down the onset of global capitalism if the world is to benefit from its unquestionable creative potential and not be destroyed by it. Through his examination of the rise of industrial capitalism in Britain, Polanyi demonstrated that capitalism tends to create 'a stark utopia' which human beings are unable to live with. They consequently band themselves to resist. This is the root cause of the tendency, noted by Arrighi, for the end of every cycle of capitalism's expansion and the beginning of the next to be heralded by domestic social unrest and rebellion.

This book ends with the warning that reifying the market and placing all of one's faith upon it to usher in a more prosperous and peaceful world could lead to the destruction of human civilisation. The twentieth century showed that the violence unleashed by the fourth cycle of capitalism's expansion had proved very nearly unmanageable. But the transition from British to American hegemony is dwarfed in scale by the transition that capitalism is making today. The future is inherently difficult to predict, but the possibility that the violence that it releases will prove unmanageable is too real to ignore. A frank recognition of the dangers it poses, and concerted international action to slow down the process and protect those who are hurt most severely by it will reduce the threat that civilisation faces. But that is precisely what the transnational corporations and the richest and most powerful nation on earth have set their faces against.

Notes

1. George W. Bush, 'The War on Terror', Speech at the National Defence University, Washington, 8 March 2005.
2. The poll of 21,953 people was conducted by the international polling firm Globescan, together with the Program on International Policy Attitudes (PIPA) at the University of Maryland. The survey team reports that polling, which included a sample of 1,000 Americans, was conducted from 15 November 2004 to 3 January 2005. In eight of the countries the sample was limited to major metropolitan areas. The margin of error per country ranged from ± 2.5 per cent to 4 per cent.
3. Prem Shankar Jha, *India: A Political Economy of Stagnation* (New Delhi, Oxford University Press, 1980).
4. Karl Polanyi, *The Great Transformation* (Boston, Beacon Press, 1957) Chapter 3.
5. Prem Shankar Jha, 'The Seeds of Future Conflict', *The Hindu*, 1 and 8 July 1995 (and a preliminary essay on 24 June 1995).
6. Fernand Braudel, *Civilisation and Capitalism, 15th to 18th Century. Vol. 1: The structures of Everyday Life*, (Collins/Fontana Press, 1988), pp. 402–4. Thus the European traders in the Mediterranean 'borrowed' triangular lateen sails from the Arabs (who got them from India) to replace their square rigged sails, and clinker-built hulls and inboard rudders from the ships of the Hanseatic League in the Baltic and the North Sea. These innovations increased the strength and stability of their ships and enabled them to sail closer to the wind. Venice, which was situated closest to the spices, silks and bullion of the Levant and Egypt, was the first city-state to take full advantage of the new technologies. But together with the compass, they enabled European explorers to open trade routes to India and the Far East, and to America, and thus to transform the political map of the world.

   In the same way, the emergence of Britain as the seat of the third expansion of capitalism can be traced to the accumulation of innovation during three periods of rapid technological and organisational change that culminated in the industrial revolution. A little over a century later, the development of a huge continental market, a spate of innovations in the organisation of industry and the internalisation of technological innovation in giant vertically integrated firms was responsible for the rise of America as the centre of the fourth cycle of capitalism's expansion. The accumulation of technological change in the transport and communications industries is the cause of the fifth.

1

Two Views of the Future

Human beings have been drawn to the idea of Utopia—a cessation of the struggle that characterises their lives, and a permanent state of well-being— in virtually every epoch of history. But only in the nineteenth century, when the industrial revolution created, for the first time, the possibility of producing enough wealth to permit all of humanity to rise above bare subsistence, did the discussion of Utopia move from the realm of the philosophical to the practical. Liberal political economists wrote at length about the 'stationary state'; and Karl Marx's 'classless society', which would follow a transitional 'dictatorship of the proletariat', was only Utopia in another guise. In his *Principles of Political Economy*, John Stuart Mill, who considered himself a socialist, wrote:

> I cannot, therefore, regard the stationary state of capital and wealth with the unaffected aversion so generally manifested towards it by political economists of the old school. I am inclined to believe that it would be, on the whole, a very considerable improvement on our present condition. I confess I am not charmed with the ideal of life held out by those who think that the normal state of human beings is that of struggling to get on; that the trampling, crushing, elbowing, and treading on each other's heels, which form the existing type of social life, are the most desirable lot of human kind, or anything but the disagreeable symptoms of one of the phases of industrial progress.[1]

Mill was reacting to the Manchester liberalism of economists like McCullough, whom he singled out in his essay for rebuttal. Today as capitalism enters yet another cycle of explosive growth and neo-liberal economics reigns supreme once again, it is not entirely surprising that the yearning for Utopia has resurfaced. This has been given a special sharp edge by the sheer horror and prolonged tension of the century that has just ended.

The philosopher Isaiah Berlin once described the twentieth century as 'the most terrible century in western History'.[2] This was if anything an understatement, for the twentieth century saw two developments that transformed the art of killing and led to slaughter on a scale that had never been imagined. The first was the application of technologies of mass production to war and the second was the application of the same techniques to the killing of civilians. The former led Germans to describe the First World War as the 'War of Mass Destruction'. The latter gave the English language a new word: genocide. Technology enabled human beings to streamline and dehumanise slaughter. 'We forget,' wrote Eric Hobsbawm, 'that the pogroms in Czarist Russia which (justifiably) outraged world opinion and drove Russian Jews across the Atlantic in their millions between 1881 and 1914, were small, almost negligible by the standards of modern massacre: the dead were counted in dozens, not hundreds, let alone millions.'[3] Half a century later the Nazi extermination camps took the lives of six million Jews, Gypsies and communists. Primo Levi, a survivor of the camps wrote, 'We who survived the Camps are not the true witnesses … We are those who, through prevarication, skill, or luck, never touched bottom. Those who have, and who have seen the face of the Gorgon, did not return, or returned wordless.'[4]

The death camps that Levi survived were set up when the twentieth century was less than half over. In the fifty years that followed, many more millions saw the face of the Gorgon in India and Pakistan, Myanmar, China, Indonesia, the Soviet Union, Central America, South Africa, Vietnam, Cambodia, Palestine, Bosnia, Rwanda, and countless other places where tens of thousands of human beings were exterminated without being accorded the courtesy of an epitaph in a history book. According to one estimate, between 1900 and the early 1990s, 187 million people had been killed, or allowed to die, by human decision. This was a tenth of the world's population at the beginning of the century.[5] But even this figure may be an underestimate, for it probably does not include the millions who died during the Cultural Revolution in China and the man-made famines that preceded it. And genocide, in the sense described above, has slowly become commonplace. While civilians made up roughly one in ten of those killed in armed conflicts at the beginning of the century, they accounted for nine out of ten deaths by its end.[6]

Will the twenty-first century be any more humane? In the early 1990s, as the Cold War ended, the yearning for Utopia burst forth once again. No one doubted that mankind had turned the darkest page in its history and that the future simply had to be a lot better than the immediate past. But a decade later that belief has worn thin. The world seems to be moving away from peace. The frequency of armed conflict, insurgency and attacks on ethnic minorities has increased dramatically. A decade of unnecessary economic sanctions, a pointless invasion and the death of thousands of Iraqis in the 'peace' that followed have brought Iraq to the verge of disintegration. Global terrorism, which had been ousted from Afghanistan, has found a new, far more congenial home in central Iraq. The Israeli-Palestinian conflict has plumbed depths of insensate hate that have never been visited before. The US has announced to the world that it is no longer bound by the rules laid down in the UN charter, and reserves the right to invade any country that it deems a present or future threat to its security. Suddenly the world is living in mortal fear of what the future might bring.

Despite the mounting chaos, the belief that these are only problems of transition and that the twenty-first century will eventually turn out to be much better than the twentieth refuses to die. This belief is fed by governments and think-tanks in the industrialised countries, in concert with tens of thousands of transnational corporations which now account for most of the economic activity in the industrialised world. These constitute an emerging international dominant class that is spreading its ideology and shaping the minds of the rest of the world with the help of the media. According to its catechism the debilitating Cold War is behind us, and the twenty-first century is likely to see humanity banish hunger and poverty and control all but a very few diseases. We can even dare to hope that it will, somehow, banish war.

This ideology feeds this hope by harping relentlessly upon two recent developments: the continuing technological revolution, and the apparent end of ideological conflict with the end of the Cold War. Technology has allowed human beings to gain a hitherto undreamed of control over their physical environment. The information and biotechnology revolutions are still gathering pace but have already extended the limits of the possible to a previously unimaginable degree. The information revolution is rapidly meshing together what had previously been separate national economies into a single global economy and the beginnings of what could become a system of global governance.

It admits that this process is not free from friction but has been accompanied by an increase in inequalities of income within the industrialised countries, and between the industrialised and all but a few developing countries. It has led to the reappearance of permanent, non-cyclical unemployment in the industrialised countries, and of a class of 'new poor', whose existence in the richest countries of the world mocks their claim of having built humanitarian and egalitarian societies. It has also caused an erosion of the international order that was built around the sovereignty of the modern state that emerged after the treaty of Westphalia in 1648.

But these are only problems of transition. Human ingenuity and adaptability will ensure that, notwithstanding occasional hiccups on the way, mankind will use its increasing mastery of nature and its vastly enhanced capacity to build and operate complex systems to improve the human condition. Its indispensable tool for doing all this is the market. The market encourages, indeed thrives upon, competition. Competition maximises efficiency. Efficiency maximises output. Output maximises well-being. Competition in the labour market more or less ensures that people earn according to their capability. As a result, a market economy is not only efficient but just. Since it is also self-regulating, human intervention, by the state, for instance, is largely unnecessary. The role of the state is to remove obstacles to the efficient functioning of the market, and to guard against its occasional failures. Mankind has thus entered the twenty-first century with not only the scientific power to eradicate its woes but a readymade mechanism that will enable it to do so. It is hardly surprising therefore that at least one vastly popular author of the early nineties, Francis Fukuyama, saw in this process the 'End of History' and the birth of a rather boring world.[7]

Fukuyama's celebrated essay 'The End of History', which was published in the summer of 1989,[8] gained instant fame and popularity because it fed the belief that Utopia was finally within mankind's grasp. But this belief also derived its intellectual legitimacy from another influential but less known work of the same period, Samuel Huntington's 'The Third Wave'.[9] Fukuyama used the term 'history' not as it is used in common parlance but in Hegel's sense of mankind's ideological evolution. The endpoint of this evolution, according to Fukuyama, was the 'universalisation of Western liberal democracy as the final form of human government'.

According to him, in the last two centuries international conflict had been driven, by and large, by ideology. The end of the eighteenth century and the first fifteen years of the nineteenth saw a struggle between nascent liberal democracy and the authoritarianism of entrenched monarchies. 'The twentieth century saw the developed world (again) descend into a paroxysm of ideological violence as liberalism contended first with the remnants of absolutism, then bolshevism and fascism, and finally an updated Marxism that threatened to lead to the ultimate apocalypse of nuclear war.' But the century closed with 'an unabashed victory of economic and political liberalism'. 'History' thus came to an end.

The corollary to Fukuyama's conclusion is that if war was fuelled largely by ideological conflict, the end of history meant the end of war. Fukuyama ended by speculating that if war were ever to resurface, it would probably be because mankind got bored with peace:

The end of History is a very sad time. The struggle for recognition, the willingness to risk one's life for a purely abstract goal, the worldwide ideological struggle that called forth daring, courage, imagination and idealism will be replaced
by economic calculations, the endless solving of technical problems, environmental concerns and the satisfaction of sophisticated consumer demands. In
the post-historical period there will be neither art nor philosophy, just the
perpetual caretaking of the museum of human history. Such nostalgia will continue to fuel conflict even in the post-historical world *for some time to come*
[emphasis added] ... perhaps this very prospect of centuries of boredom at the
end of history will serve to get history started again.

Huntington's 'The Third Wave' is much less well known, partly because
it was overtaken by his celebrated essay on 'The Clash of Civilisations'
only two years after it was published. But its main thesis was no less influential for policymakers in the early 1990s because it linked democracy,
economic development and the end of war in a single, coherent, causal
relationship. In brief, his thesis was that the period from 1974 to 1990 had
seen a 'third wave of democratisation'. No fewer than 34 countries had
switched from being authoritarian to democratic. That had happened even
before the bastions of communism came crumbling down.

This 'third wave' had been preceded by two others: the first between
1828 and 1926, and the second shorter wave from 1943 to 1962. While
Huntington was concerned mainly with explaining why democratisation
had occurred in waves, as a by-product of his analysis he pointed out not
only that democracies did not wage war against each other (for the obvious
reason that they were usually on the same side of the ideological fence)
but that most high-income countries were democracies. Huntington used
World Bank 1989 per capita GDP tables to show that while 21 out of 24
high-income countries[10] and 23 out of 53 middle-income countries were
democracies,[11] only two out of 42 low-income countries were democracies.[12] The moral was obvious: rising incomes would unleash democratic
forces in a country. As more and more countries became democratic, the
likelihood of major conflict would recede.

The belief that democracies do not fight each other is so much a part of
the western psyche that it is almost impossible to trace its origins. As far
back as the eighteenth century, Montesquieu, the French philosopher,
wrote in a book titled *The Spirit of the Laws*, 'Two nations who traffic with
each other become reciprocally dependent; for if one has an interest in
buying, the other has an interest in selling; and thus their union is founded
on their mutual necessities.' Montesquieu observed that international trade
had created an international 'Grand Republic', which was uniting merchants and trading nations across boundaries, and would surely 'lock in a

more peaceful world'.[13] A century later, when the industrial revolution was sweeping across Europe, not only had trade links deepened immeasurably, but they had been supplemented by cross-border investment. The savings of tens of thousands of people in one country were locked into fixed investments in another. War would therefore hurt both. In addition an entirely new player had entered the scene as a powerful force for peace. This was the shadowy network of international bankers whom Karl Polanyi called *Haute Finance*.

Polanyi wrote:

> The nineteenth century produced a phenomenon unheard of in the annals of western civilization, namely a hundred years of peace—1815–1914. Apart from the Crimean War, a more or less colonial event, England, France, Prussia, Austria, Italy and Russia were engaged in war among each other for altogether 18 months. A computation of comparable figures for the two preceding centuries gives an average of sixty to seventy years of major wars in each ... This triumph of pragmatic pacifism was certainly not the result of an absence of grave causes for conflict ... for an explanation of this amazing feat, we must seek some undisclosed powerful instrumentality at work in the new setting ... This anonymous factor was *Haute finance*. *Haute finance*, an institution *sui generis*, peculiar to the last third of the nineteenth and the first third of the twentieth century, functioned as the main link between the political and economic organization of the world in this period ... While the Concert of Europe acted only at intervals, *haute finance* functioned as a permanent agency of the most elastic kind. Independent of single governments, even the most powerful, it was in touch with all; independent of the Central banks, even the Bank of England, it was closely connected with them. There was intimate contact between finance and diplomacy; neither would consider any long range plan, whether peaceful or warlike, without making sure of the other's goodwill.[14]

Polanyi wrote his book during the Second World War, but he might have been describing the power of global finance capital today.

By the end of the first decade of the twentieth century, international trade had grown to the point where nations were selling almost one-tenth of all the merchandise they produced abroad. Their foreign direct investment added up to almost the same percentage.[15] The world, by which one means mostly the industrialised world, was so deeply intermeshed that war would create as many losers in the victorious countries as it would winners, and that was even before one counted the cost in lives and wanton destruction. These facts led Norman Angell to write a book, *The Great Illusion*, in the early years of the century, which declared that war itself had become obsolete. By a tragic irony, his book was published in 1910, only four years before the Great War.

Despite the fate   et with, the basic thesis propounded
by him has not lost   ty. Fifty million or more deaths in
two world wars undou   in burning it into people's minds.
In his Paul Henri Spaak   d in 1996, Ralf Dahrendorf remarked, 'Not only was th   ar fought and won in the name
of democracy and the rule   acy at home is about as solid
a guarantee against aggressi   n hope for. As a rule, democracies do not start wars.' D.   to point out that 'All the
way to monetary union one mc   ean integration has remained the desire to keep Germa.   cratic) fold ... Clearly
in this regard the post war hopes .   been fulfilled ...'[16]

And five decades after the Secon   mas Friedman has
made the same point in his book *The*   *Tree*.

> Today's version of Globalization—with ι   nic integration,
> digital integration, its ever widening conn   s and nations,
> its spreading of capitalist values and netwo   rners of the
> world ... makes for a much stronger web of   ign policy
> behaviour of the nations which are plugged i   increases
> the incentives for not making war, and it increa   war in
> more ways than in any previous era in modern h

The end of history worldview has been immense   reinforced by a spate
of optimistic literature on globalisation. Globalisation is leading to huge
and ever-expanding flows of capital from the industrialised nations, and
accelerating the growth of other nations till they catch up with the former.
Then they too begin to export capital to other capital-poor and labour-
rich countries, accelerating their growth in turn. This by no means incorrect
assessment of the impact of globalisation has been caught in the celebrated
paradigm of the flying geese, developed by writers like Kaname Akamatsu
and T. Ozawa.[18] This is already abolishing economic frontiers. In so doing,
it is steadily reducing the areas of autonomy of the sovereign state, and
presaging the end of the nation state. To quote Kenichi Ohmae, 'the glue
holding traditional nation states together at least in economic terms, has
begun to dissolve. Instead, Globalisation is linking not nations but cities
and industrial zones in different countries together in tight networks of
rising prosperity and shared interest that cut across national boundaries
to create region states.'[19]

Globalisation is also undermining the nation state through its impact
on politics. Satellite television and the internet revolution are linking people
in different countries directly without the mediation of the state. The latter
in particular has broken the state's monopoly of information and the power

this enables it to exercise over individuals. This is particularly true with respect to human rights. Today the concept of human security is slowly superseding that of national security.[20]

By far the most pervasive and comforting belief is that globalisation is not a new phenomenon. As Paul Krugman has pointed out, most economists date its onset to the 1840s, when railroads and steamships made the large-scale shipment of bulk goods possible.[21] All through the nineteenth century, the pace at which the cost of transport and communication fell rivalled the pace at which it has done so in the twentieth century. The steamship was as revolutionary a leap over the sailing ship as the airplane was over the steamship. The invention of the telegraph almost certainly speeded up communication by a higher multiple than the invention of the telephone over the telegraph. The internet bears the same relationship to the telephone as does the telephone to the telegraph. Thus, if globalisation is the child of technological evolution, then it has been going on for almost two hundred years. The integration of the global economy, measured by the ratio of trade and foreign investment to GDP, has also been rising continuously since the early 1800s. In fact, by these and several other yardsticks the world was more integrated in 1913 than it was in 1973, and not much less so than it is today. Globalisation is therefore a 'going back to the future'. It is the resumption of trends in the world economy that had existed for most of the nineteenth century but had been rudely disrupted by the hammer blows of the First World War, the depression of the thirties and the Second World War. In short, globalisation is taking the world back to the conditions that had given birth to the Hundred Years' Peace.

Over the years both Fukuyama and Huntington have been subjected to a good deal of criticism. Fukuyama's unabashed Hegelianism has drawn the most flak. Although he makes a token bow to Marx in one paragraph, the fact remains that although his two centuries of ideological conflict are also the two centuries of industrial capitalism, not once in his entire essay does he use the word 'capitalism' or explore the connection between its rise and conflict. For him all the battles for which people laid down their lives were over ideas. Another flaw is that Hegel had already set one date for the end of history, and that was 1806, when Napoleon defeated the Prussian monarchy at the Battle of Jena. One would have thought that two world wars and the Cold War would have invalidated Hegel's claim. But a French philosopher, Alexandre Kojeve, who died in 1958, resurrected Hegel's claim by stubbornly insisting that everything that followed 1806, including the two world wars was simply a working out, in the rest of 'humanity', of the ideological victory of 1806. Fukuyama used Kojeve's analysis to push Hegel's date forward to 1991. Critics were quick to point out the obvious flaw in his reasoning: how could Fukuyama be so sure that, like Hegel and Kojeve, he too would not be proved wrong?

Huntington's implied thesis too has come under damaging attack. In an article in *Foreign Affairs*, Edward Mansfield and Jack Snyder pointed out, on the basis of a 170-year statistical analysis of wars from 1811 to 1980, that the thesis that democracies did not go to war against each other needed to be heavily qualified. While stable democracies did indeed not, as a rule, go to war against each other, *neither did stable authoritarian regimes*. On the other hand democratising countries were more likely to go to war within a decade of their transition than those that had not undergone a change. Mansfield and Snyder were able to go one layer deeper and relate the type of democratic change with the chance of war. They found that freeing the choice of chief executive doubled the chance of war. Increasing the competitiveness of politics increased it by 90 per cent; weakening the chief executive increased it by 35 per cent. The longer the leap from autocracy to democracy, the greater the chance of war; likewise with increased mass participation. The reason, they surmised, was that democratisation tended to release powerful forces of nationalism and these increased the chances of conflict. The Napoleonic wars, the Franco-German war and the First World War itself could be traced to the rise of nationalist sentiment following democratisation in France and Germany.[22] The same, or at least similar, forces could be released by democratisation today.

Despite these and other inconsistencies, Fukuyama's and Huntington's 1989 theses have become the bedrock of liberal thinking about the post-Cold War world. Their most basic assumption is that democracies will never wage war on one another. The second is that as more and more countries become democratic, the areas of the world prone to conflict will diminish; and the third is that economic development automatically leads countries towards democracy. The final premise is that open market (i.e., capitalist) economies are the only ones likely to progressively raise their standards of living. Thus open market capitalist economic policies promote growth, which promotes democracy, which in turn promotes peace. Thomas Friedman has popularised it as his 'Golden Arches' theory of conflict prevention. 'No two countries that both had McDonald's,' he wrote in 1998, 'had fought a war against each other since each got its McDonalds.'[23]

For about three years after the fall of the Berlin wall, euphoria prevailed. The Cold War was over. The Gulf War had demonstrated the invincibility of the modern military technology possessed by the US. Power was securely in the hands of the major industrial democracies, and democracies did not go to war. The implosion of the Soviet Union and the helter-skelter rush of the formerly socialist countries towards market capitalism ensured that these countries would one day also join the community of peaceful nations. Where then was the need for the colossal stockpiles of weapons built up during the Cold War? The popular mood fully reflected this sentiment. Opinion polls carried out in the US between 1992 and 1995 showed a two-to-one majority in favour of cutting the budget deficit by reducing defence spending.[24] In his promises, President Clinton included a reduction in the size of American nuclear stockpiles and conventional forces, and a $20 billion programme to convert defence industries to civilian production—to turn swords into ploughshares.[25]

It was not long, however, before developments in the real world began to challenge some of the optimistic assumptions of the first post-Cold War years. To begin with, the end of the Cold War and the triumph of capitalism over communism did not lead to a reduction in wars and conflict in the world but seemingly to its opposite. Early in 1993, the *New York Times* published a list of countries in the throes of violent conflict. They numbered 48, and that was just a partial count![26] Three years later, by another count the number had risen to more than a hundred.[27] The dream of a new age for mankind began to go sour in other ways as well. Instead of making a smooth transition from socialist to market economies, the East European countries all collapsed into varying degrees of chaos. Their standards of living fell precipitately, income differentials widened, unemployment and crime grew by leaps and bounds, and, far from welcoming their newfound democratic freedoms, their older people in particular began to hanker for the 'good old days' of communism. By 1995 eight out of nine formerly socialist countries in Eastern Europe had voted the communists back into power or given them a majority in parliament.

Wars broke out all over the globe. One index of their rising frequency was the number of peacekeeping missions that the UN was asked to undertake. Between 1990 and 1992 it undertook 14 missions. This was the same number as it had undertaken in the previous 43 years.[28] This eruption of violence provoked Lawrence Eagleburger, then Deputy Secretary of State in the Bush (Sr.) administration to observe, 'For all its risks and uncertainties the Cold War was characterised by a remarkably stable and predictable set of relationships among the Great powers.'[29] As people began looking for explanations, another element in Fukuyama's thesis once again came in handy. This was the notion of lagged ideological evolution. For Hegel, history had ended in 1806 for the vanguard of humanity. For Kojeve, the two world wars, attendant upheavals and—one must presume by extension—colonial conquests, were merely a messy but unavoidable extension of the 'basic principles of the liberal state ... spatially, such that the various provinces of the human civilization were brought up to the level of its most advanced outposts.'[30] Fukuyama therefore predicted that wars would continue as some parts of the world continued to remain trapped 'in History', but die out as the rearguard of humanity caught up with the vanguard.

The powerful fascination that this thesis continues to exercise on people's minds was reflected in 2002 by Robert Kagan, a leading neo-conservative thinker and advocate of the invasion of Iraq, who chastised France and Germany for not joining the US and UK, by reminding them that

> Europe ... is entering a post-Historical paradise of peace and relative prosperity, the realisation of Kant's perpetual peace [because] the United States, meanwhile, remains mired in history, exercising power in an anarchic Hobbesian world where ... true security and the defense and promotion of the liberal order still depend on the possession and use of military might.[31]

Out of this view, and its corollary that the industrialised West represents the vanguard of humanity, has been born a belief that the resurgence of ethnicity and the wars that have been, or are being, fought on that account in the former Soviet Union, Turkey, Iraq, Iran, Afghanistan, South Asia and, above all, Africa are primitive and atavistic. The ideologies and beliefs that feed these conflicts, such as fundamentalism and nationalism, are irrational and doomed to extinction. The 'vanguard' societies have to bear with them, but if these conflicts threaten them, or threaten the consolidation of the liberal democratic system, they have a duty to intervene and prevent or control them. All such interventions are morally justified because no matter what pain they may inflict in the short run, and no matter how uncertain or unexpected their immediate outcome, they ultimately force the 'provinces' to catch up with the 'vanguard of humanity'. In short they force the former to be free. By an ironic twist of history, as noted by Anthony Giddens, liberalism in its hour of triumph is beginning to resemble more and more the totalitarian creeds that it vanquished.[32]

The Clash of Civilisations

The only powerful challenge to Fukuyama's thesis has come from Samuel Huntington's 'The Clash of Civilisations'. Written first as an article in 1993 and expanded three years later into a book,[33] Huntington's starting point, one suspects, was his discomfort with the messianic overtones in Fukuyama's 'End of History', particularly with its claim to universal validity. Implicit in it was the belief that in the end the world would become a single homogeneous entity. Cultural peculiarities, no less than political ones, would eventually get blended into a single featureless paste, while the global economy turned into a single completely intermeshed market.

Huntington believed this would never happen. Attempts to force such homogenisation and the resistance they provoked would draw the fault-lines of future global conflict.

He drew a distinction between modernisation, westernisation and universalisation. Societies were getting modernised, in the sense that they increasingly used much the same technologies as the western countries, and were developing political and economic institutions appropriate to the functioning of a modern state. But modernisation was not coterminous with westernisation, and the process was most certainly not producing 'a universal civilisation in any meaningful sense of the term'.

What was actually happening was that *culture*, i.e., what Huntington referred to more broadly as civilisation, remained outside the *modernisation* process in each country or group of countries, and provided the frame that gave it a distinct shape. Except in the most superficial sense, therefore, modernisation did not lead to the westernisation of non-western societies. The world that was emerging would therefore be a multi-civilisational one. At the same time, since economic power was shifting from the old industrial centres to a variety of new ones and was therefore much more evenly dispersed, it would also be a multipolar one. The core of his thesis therefore was that the 'West's universalist pretensions [will] increasingly bring it into conflict with other civilisations, most seriously with Islam and China ... At the local level "fault line wars" largely between Muslims and non-Muslims [will] generate "kin-country tallying" and [bring with it] the threat of broader escalation.' Huntington concluded that the survival of the West depended on Americans reaffirming their western identity on the one hand and the West accepting that their civilisation was unique but not universal. 'Avoidance of a global war of civilisations,' he concluded, 'depends on world leaders accepting, and cooperating to maintain, the multi-civilisational character of global politics.'[34]

It is easy to understand why Huntington's original article, which appeared in the summer 1993 issue of *Foreign Affairs*, has generated more discussion than any article published by the journal since George Kennan's 'X' article in the 1940s on containment of the Soviet Union. Huntington's hypothesis challenged virtually every premise of mainstream thinking of the post-Cold War years:

- Contrary to what Friedman and innumerable other writers thought, the world would not get completely McDonaldised. The presence of a McDonald's, an Avis or Hertz, a Coca Cola or Pepsi Cola in every country would not mean that everyone had become western, much less American.

- Cultural (civilisational) identities would not disappear, much less become western clones. In fact, onslaughts on them were more than likely to reinforce them.
- The nation state would therefore not disappear either. On the contrary the defence of cultural–civilisational identity would become a powerful new rationale for its continued existence.
- Backlash states were not transient, but the vanguard of the revolt against cultural homogenisation. Far from being recalcitrant or atavistic they embodied alternate views of humanity, which the 'provinces of human civilisation' simply would not give up.
- Intra-state ethnic conflict too might therefore not prove a transient phenomenon, to be contained by suppression or accommodation till the homogenising force of modernisation did away with the very rationale for separate identities.
- Thus, most important of all, intra-state conflict and localised war between states would not necessarily diminish in intensity and frequency over time, or become more amenable to control by the 'international system'. On the contrary, given a sufficient degree of pressure from western civilisation on others, what started out as a local conflict could snowball into a larger one between groups of culturally similar states.

To sum up, therefore, war as the twentieth century knew it had not become obsolete. To minimise the chance of its recurrence, the West needed to shed its messianism and to allow local conflicts to, as Luttwak puts it, burn themselves out.[35] It needed to shed the notion that all conflicts anywhere were threats to it because they threatened its 'values'. In terms of international relations theory Huntington made a powerful case for realism. It was hardly surprising that scholars of every other school, be they liberal, neo-liberal or social constructivist, felt obliged to attack his theories.

In 1993 Huntington's realist insights must have seemed unduly pessimistic. It was only two years since Operation Desert Storm. This had seen an unprecedented coalition of Christian countries rise to the defence of a small, highly conservative Islamic country, and forge a coalition with other conservative Muslim countries against one that, for all of its other faults, was the most secular, technologically advanced and, in a word, 'western' of them all. Saudi Arabia, the most rigidly fundamentalist and messianic Islamic country, had become a firm ally of the US. At the other side of the Asian landmass, China had opened its doors to foreign capital and was 'McDonaldising' itself with a fervour that few would have dreamed of a few years earlier.

But developments in the second half of the 90s, culminating in the '9/11' terrorist attacks in New York and Washington, vindicated at least the first part of his predictions. The Islamic backlash continued to grow. It subverted two states—Afghanistan and Sudan—and seemed on the way to subverting Pakistan in South Asia and Tajikistan in Central Asia. Another key country that could also fall prey to Islamic fundamentalism was Saudi Arabia. Were these states to go fundamentalist, an extreme Sunni-Wahhabi Islamic fundamentalism would embrace a vast chunk of contiguous territory stretching more than a thousand miles from the Indian border into central Asia. The ambitions of the fundamentalists did not stop there. They were active in Turkestan, Uzbekistan, Chechnya, Egypt, Algeria and the Philippines.[36]

China too had taken a direction that no one could have predicted. Clinton's state visit to Beijing in June 1998 had been the culmination of a six-year effort at constructive engagement. But in the very next year, following the bombing of the Chinese embassy in Belgrade by American bombers during the Kosovo 'war'—at precisely the moment when it was straining every nerve to get into the World Trade Organization—the Jiang Zemin government consciously embarked on a policy of internal repression, external bellicosity (towards Taiwan) and skilfully orchestrated anti-Americanism.

Prior to 9/11, the most telling proof of the soundness of Huntington's hypothesis had come from Indonesia. In that country, an overenthusiastic attempt by the IMF backed by the US treasury to hasten the pace of political and economic reform after the economic 'meltdown' of 1997 led to the ouster of Suharto in May 1998. The ensuing competition for power led to the surreptitious emergence, albeit on a small scale, of a brand of Islamic extremism that had been virtually unknown in the country till then. After the elections of 1999, this new brand of Islam allied itself increasingly with nationalism and won growing support within the army. As a result, clashes between Muslims and Christians erupted with increasing frequency across the country. This development also received a fillip from a separate and well intentioned effort to reverse the occupation of East Timor, which had taken place in 1975. Suharto had agreed to this in principle but had been dragging his feet over its implementation. His successor B.J. Habibie was far more forthcoming, but this was perceived by most Indonesians as a concession wrung out of him by the West during Indonesia's economic vulnerability. The fact that the Timorese were mainly Christians fed aspirations of independence in other mainly Christian islands and reinforced the Islamic backlash in the country. East Timor's separation from Indonesia after a much delayed referendum therefore widened the ethnic divide between Muslims and Christians. The simultaneous onset of the economic crisis, the ouster of Suharto and the acceptance of independence for East Timor therefore greatly weakened the Indonesian state, which had been trying to forge its identity as a unitary nation state. These developments combined to spawn a full fledged civil war in the western province of Aceh.

Despite its explanatory power, Huntington's thesis remains unsatisfactory on two counts. The first is that Huntington himself does not seem fully at ease with the full implications of his thesis. In particular he is unwilling to cross swords with American hegemonism. This is reflected by a contradiction of which he himself seems unaware. On the one hand he argues that global conflict, if it occurs, will be triggered by a civilisational offensive from the West. But on the other he argues that it is western civilisation that is under threat and needs to be defended (by America reaffirming its western identity). The offensive therefore is coming from the non-western civilisations. This defensive posture has made it relatively easy for the New Interventionists (to use Stedman's term) to co-opt his ideas into their 'End of History' project. What he is advocating is no different from what Madeleine Albright believes to be the prime goal of American foreign policy. In the end, all he has done is to provide one more argument for the West, and for America in particular, to maintain a strong defence posture and keep increasing its defence spending in real terms, while insisting that nations outside the perimeter of western civilisation reduce theirs.

The Thesis of this Book

This book presents a different, and far less optimistic, view of the future. Stated very simply it is this: technology, the information revolution in particular, does indeed have the power to transform the world for the better, and indeed, as Jeffrey Sachs has so eloquently argued, to end poverty in our lifetimes.[37] But this will not happen automatically, under the spur of market forces. It will only happen if there is deliberate human intervention to slow down the pace of economic transformation sufficiently to give the social, political and international institutions upon which civilisation depends time to adapt. Without such intervention, and particularly, if the pace of change is allowed to accelerate continuously under the spur of competition, it will overwhelm the institutions that human beings have built within and between nations to moderate conflict between the gainers and losers from change. The danger signal, that this has begun to happen, is hoisted when the social system starts to lose its capacity to generate self-equilibrating responses to new shocks. If the existing institutions are not given time to adapt to the new challenges, and if new institutions are not given time to develop, this process will end by destroying the world we know, without putting anything in its place.[38]

The potential for conflict, and therefore the need for conscious human intervention, arises from a profound asymmetry that lies at the very core of capitalism—while markets tend to restore economic equilibrium after each external shock, they are inherently blind to the distributive effects of their own working. Left to themselves they tend to widen income differences, as profits accumulate in some hands while labour-saving technology keeps incomes at the bottom of the pyramid from rising in equal measure. Competition also creates redundancy as technology and tastes change. Those who fail to keep up with their more efficient peers are driven out of business. Capitalism therefore constantly creates new gainers and new losers. But the market economy contains no mechanism for minimising or reconciling the conflict between the two.

In *The Age of Extremes* Eric Hobsbawm described the last three decades of the twentieth century as 'crisis decades' that saw the re-emergence of disorder in human society and concluded with the observation that he felt 'less reason to feel hopeful about the future than in the middle 80s.'[39] This book attempts to explore the causes of his instinctive pessimism. It suggests that the root cause of the growing disorder is that capitalism has burst the confines of the nation state, and is in the inexorable process of converting a large part (although as yet not quite the whole) of the globe into its new 'container'. The process is highly destructive and fraught with violence. This is the process that we refer to as globalisation.

Globalisation is perhaps the most extensively used word in the lexicon of the social sciences. It is also the least understood.[40] This is not surprising, because, unlike the natural sciences where the human observer is essentially outside the phenomenon being studied, in the social sciences the researcher is a part of it. Her/his perspective will therefore tend to be shaped by where the observer is located within the change being studied. One way to extricate oneself from this dilemma is to seek the help of history and see whether similar changes have occurred before and where they have led. That is the method that has been pursued in this book.

The concept of a 'container' for capitalism was devised by Fernand Braudel. It refers to the social, economic and political unit that is large enough to organise and contain all the interrelated functions of capitalism: finance, production and marketing. While the linkages that define this unit are primarily economic, the need for a secure environment within which to operate turns it into a political and military unit as well. Technology is the engine behind the relentless growth of capitalism's container over the past seven centuries, for each new development in technology enlarges the minimum economic scale of production.[41] This means that the minimum size of an *efficient* self-sustaining network of economic relations, i.e., of an efficient 'economy', has also grown in each cycle of capitalism's expansion, till it has, in the past quarter of a century, outgrown the political confines of even a very large nation state like the US.

This is not the first time that capitalism has burst its 'container'. Since its birth in the north Italian city states in the thirteenth century, capitalism has done this at least three times. In the first cycle Venice, Florence and Milan saw the rise of industrial capitalism and Genoa of finance capitalism. But the scale of capitalist production was small enough to be contained within the container of the city state.

The city state remained the container of capitalism during its second cycle of expansion when Holland and, more specifically, Amsterdam became its hub. But by the time capitalism made its next leap, it was too large to be contained within even a hybrid, nation-backed city state like Amsterdam, and needed to mould economic, technical and political relations in an entire nation state to turn it into its container. That 'container' proved to be England. But by the end of the nineteenth century, capitalism was outgrowing even the small nation state (which is what England really was) and required a large nation state as its container. The USA filled that need. Today, capitalism has out-grown the nation state altogether and is turning a large part of the globe into its container. That is the process that the world refers to as globalisation.

In each of its cycles of expansion, capitalism has gone through its own internal evolution, from early to mature to late capitalism. The early phase is typically one of increasing disorder. In it capitalism sets about destroying the social, economic and political institutions that had been created by human beings to serve its earlier incarnation. In the middle or mature phase of capitalism, new institutions develop that reflect society's attempt to harmonise the interests of the gainers and losers from competition. These become institutionalised, and often fossilised, in late capitalism.

The current cycle of expansion, from the nation to the globe, has brought it into direct conflict with the deeply embedded institutions of nation state-based capitalism. By far the most important conflict is with the nation state itself. This is the root cause of the social disorder that Hobsbawm referred to and the growing violence that is enveloping the world. What the world is going through is not without precedent. Growing disorder, eruptions of violence and decades of insecurity have accompanied each rebirth of capitalism in the past. Within states, it has triggered conflict between the new winners and new losers in society. Not just individuals, but entire classes of people that enjoyed an assured status, some degree of affluence and, above all, security, have been robbed of all three, and found themselves scrabbling frantically to retain their place in society. At the same time, ethnic, occupational and social groups, like the Jews of Europe, the Marwaris of India, and the Mafia in today's Russia, who were treated with condescension or reviled under the older dispensation, have suddenly shot up in status. Such dramatic changes are bound to be resisted and have often led to rebellion and bloodshed.

Internal disorder has therefore accompanied every expansion of capitalism. An early example was the Revolt of the Ciampi in Florence in 1378.[42] A similar revolt, of a suddenly impoverished and imperilled middle bourgeoisie—the Batavian rebellion—occurred in Holland in the closing stages of the Dutch cycle of capitalist expansion, a few years before the French revolution. Like the revolt of the Ciampi, it was ruthlessly crushed. In England, the rise of industrial capitalism led to a spontaneous revolt by the Luddites and more organised resistance by the Chartists. The formation of trade unions, the birth of socialism and eventually communism, and the triumph of the latter over large parts of Europe and Asia, were responses to the 'stark Utopia'[43] of industrial capitalism in the third and fourth cycles of expansion. Today as we enter the fifth, economic forces are once again attempting to recreate a stark Utopia, and so far there has been no coherent global response.

Capitalism's tendency to burst its container has also given rise to cycles of conflict between states and a remoulding of the international order at the end of each cycle. The Genoese cycle of capitalism was born out of an Italian 'hundred years war' between the northern city states. The Dutch cycle was born out of the Thirty Years' War and the preceding half-century long struggle of the Dutch against Spain. The British cycle emerged out of a spate of Anglo-French and Anglo-Dutch wars in the mid-eighteenth century, and the American cycle out of two world wars and intervening economic chaos. In every case, finance capital has been on the side of the 'revisionists', who have been bent upon changing power relations within the state system. This is because whenever capitalism has burst one container, it has looked immediately for the security of another. It is the search for security that has both shaped the container and given capitalism its innate aggressiveness.

The conflict between global and national capitalism is the root cause of the disorder that Hobsbawm has dubbed the 'crisis decades'. The regular recurrence of such conflict in all earlier cycles of capitalism's expansion led Giovanni Arrighi to give it a special name: Systemic Chaos. Systemic chaos arises when a political or economic system suddenly loses the capacity to generate equilibrating responses. This happens when 'conflict escalates beyond the threshold within which society is able to generate powerful countervailing tendencies', or adapt by developing new norms of behaviour and sets of rules without displacing the old.[44] On each occasion its arrival has been accompanied by a sudden loss of function of established institutions and relationships, confusion, anger, and eventually prolonged periods of violence. In each successive cycle the contradiction between the old and the new, between what was fashioned before and what has to be fashioned now, has become more pronounced and the conflict more intense. For as the size of the capitalist container has grown, it has enmeshed larger and larger numbers of people, living in an ever-expanding portion of the globe, in tightening webs of interdependence. This has raised their vulnerability to developments that they frequently do not understand and in any case cannot control. Violence is both a symptom and a product of that loss of control.

Today as capitalism embarks upon its fifth cycle of expansion, it is breaking the mould of the nation state altogether. In doing so it is beginning to generate enormous pressures for shattering the international state system that served a world of nation states. As a result, literally every human institution, from the welfare state to the nation state, is under assault because these institutions, which were till recently regarded as the crowning achievements of civil society, have become obstacles to the development of global capitalism. Globalisation is, therefore, anything but a 'return to the future'.

In every new cycle of expansion, the task of tearing down old political and economic institutions in order to build new ones has fallen upon one hegemonic power. During the first cycle of the growth of capitalism, the hegemonic power was Spain, in alliance with the widely dispersed Genoese banking 'nation'. In the second it was Amsterdam, allied to the House of Orange. In the third it was Britain, and in the fourth it was the US. In the fifth cycle too it is predominantly the US. What has still to be decided is whether the US will be able to exercise its hegemony alone or will be compelled to do so in concert with other major industrial powers, through organisations like NATO and the UN.

The twentieth century was exceptionally violent because disorder erupted not once but twice. The first time was when American hegemony replaced British hegemony in the final expansion of capitalism within the framework of the nation state. The second was during the 'crisis' decades', when capitalism burst the confines of the nation state. In contrast to the nineteenth century, therefore, conflict has been endemic in the twentieth century. Looking back, it is apparent that for the greater part of the twentieth century, mankind was not in control of its destiny. In only 40 of its years, roughly from 1900 to 1913 and from 1946 to 1973, did the world know comparative peace, stability *and a measure of tranquillity*. (But even the tranquillity of the first period was exceedingly fragile, for the peace upon which it depended was already unravelling.) The remaining 60 years were years of crisis and disorder in which human beings led fearful lives; in which they concentrated upon the present because the past was too terrible to remember, and the future too uncertain to contemplate.

Viewed against this dark background, the optimism that makes us instinctively believe that the next century can only be better is more a fervent hope than an expectation. For deep within us, we know that the current, fifth, cycle of capitalism's expansion has only just begun. It is still predominantly engaged in tearing down the institutions that served us so well in the past, not building the institutions we will need in the future. That challenge still lies ahead of us, and no one can be sure that humanity has the sagacity to meet it.

The purpose of this book is to trace the onset of Systemic Chaos resulting from the fifth cycle of expansion in some detail, and to warn that, far from having surmounted the challenge of co-existence, mankind is entering its most acute phase today. It traces systemic chaos to the early 1970s. That was the decade in which the technological change that had accumulated during the previous four decades began, quite suddenly, to render existing human institutions obsolete. The result was confusion and disorder as the existing division of labour in the world between industrialised and developing countries, in which the former produced manufactured products while the latter provided the raw materials, was turned on its head and time-honoured remedies for problems like recession and unemployment suddenly ceased to work. The disorder manifested itself first in the domestic economies of the highly industrialised (i.e., mature capitalist) nations. In short order it spread to the international economic system and, after the end of the Cold War, to the international political system. In the rise of global terrorism, the American response to it after the terrorist attacks of 11 September 2001, and the purposeless invasion of Iraq, we see that systemic chaos at a dangerously advanced stage.

Four years later, as terrorism spreads to new areas and becomes more deadly, and as tension mounts anew over Iran's presumed attempts to make nuclear weapons, it is apparent that the globalising world of today has no helmsman, and that its leaders, who fancy that they are in control of things, are emperors without clothes. W.H. Auden wrote in the thirties, 'We are lived by powers we pretend to understand.' That sums up the plight of humanity today.

Notes

1. John Stuart Mill, *Principles of Political Economy* (London, Longman, 1871), Vol. 2: 328–32.

2. Paola Agosti and Giovanna Borghese, *Mi pare un secolo: Ritratti e parole di centosei protagonisti del Novecento*. Quoted in Eric Hobsbawm, *The Age of Extremes* (Michael Joseph, 1994; Abacus, 1995).
3. Hobsbawm, *The Age of Extremes*, p. 13.
4. Agosti and Borghese, *Mi pare un secolo*.
5. Zbigniew Brzezhinsky, *Out of Control: Global Turmoil on the Eve of the Twenty-first Century* (Prentice Hall & IBD, 1993). Quoted by Hobsbawm, *The Age of Extremes*, p. 12.
6. International Commission on Intervention and State Sovereignty, 'The Responsibility to Protect' (Report presented to the United Nations General Assembly on 18 December 2001), p. 13.
7. Francis T. Fukuyama, 'The End of History', *National Interest*, Summer 1989.
8. Ibid.
9. Samuel Huntington, *The Third Wave. Democratization in the Late Twentieth Century* (University of Oklahoma Press, 1991).
10. The exceptions were the UAE, Saudi Arabia and Kuwait.
11. 25 were non-democratic and five were in transition.
12. Huntington, *The Third Wave*.
13. Quoted in Thomas Friedman, *The Lexus and the Olive Tree* (London, Harper Collins Publishers, 2000), p. 249.
14. Karl Polanyi, *The Great Transformation* (Boston, Beacon Press, 1957), pp. 5–10.
15. Dean Baker, Gerald Epstein and Robert Pollin (eds.), *Globalization and Progressive Economic Policy* (Cambridge University Press, 1998), Chapter 1, pp. 5, 9.
16. Ralf Dahrendorf, 'From Europe to Europe: A Story of Hope, Trial and Error' (Paul Henri Spaak Lecture, Harvard University, Centre For European Studies, 2 October 1996).
17. Friedman, *The Lexus and the Olive Tree*, p. 250.
18. T. Ozawa, *The Flying Geese Paradigm of FDI: Economic Development and Shifts in Competitiveness* (Colorado, Colorado State University, mimeo, 1995).
19. Kenichi Ohmae, *The End of the Nation State* (New York, The Free Press, 1995), p. 79.
20. Jessica T. Matthews, 'Power Shift', *Foreign Affairs*, January–February 1997, p. 51.
21. Paul Krugman, *Peddling Prosperity* (New York and London, W.W. Norton, 1994), p. 258.
22. Edward D. Mansfield and Jack Snyder, 'Democratization and War', *Foreign Affairs*, May–June 1995, pp. 79–97.
23. Thomas Friedman, *The Lexus and the Olive Tree*, p. 248.
24. Lawernce J. Korb, 'Our Overstuffed Armed Forces', *Foreign Affairs*, November–December 1995, pp. 22–35.
25. Address by President Clinton at a Westinghouse plant in Maryland. Quoted by Robert L. Borosage, 'Meeting real security needs', in Caplan and Feffer (eds.), *State of the Union 1994* (Westview Press, 1994), p. 65
26. Caplan and Feffer, 'Challenges of a New Era', in Caplan and Feffer (eds.), *State of the Union 1994* (Westview Press, 1994), p. 16.
27. Matthews, 'Power Shift', p. 51.
28. Stephen John Stedman, 'The New Interventionists' *Foreign Affairs*, January–February 1993, pp. 1–16.
29. Lawrence Eagleburger, Speech at Georgetown University. Speech at Georgetown University. Quoted by Caplan and Feffer, 'Challenges of a New Era', in Caplan and Feffer (eds.), *State of the Union 1994*, p. 15.
30. Fukuyama, 'End of History', p. 4.

31. Robert Kagan, 'Power and Weakness', *Policy Review*, 113, 18 November 2002. Available at: http://www.policyreview.org/JUN02/kagan.html.
32. Anthony Giddens, *Beyond Left and Right: The Future of Radical Politics* (Cambridge, UK, Polity Press, 1994), Chapters 1 and 2.
33. Samuel P. Huntington, *The Clash of Civilisations and the Remaking of the World Order* (New York, Simon and Schuster, 1996).
34. Ibid., pp. 20–21.
35. Edward Luttwak, 'Toward Post-Heroic Warfare', *Foreign Affairs*, May–June 1995, p. 111.
36. See *Los Angeles Times*, 'The Islamic Blowback', *Los Angeles Times*, 4, 5, 6 and 7 August 1996.
37. Jeffrey D. Sachs, *The End of Poverty: How We can Make It Happen in Our Lifetimes* (London, Penguin Books, 2005).
38. This profound insight was first provided by Karl Polanyi in his analysis of the reasons for the success of the industrial revolution in Britain. Polanyi pointed out that had the Tudor and early Stuart monarchies not resisted the commercialisation of agriculture and the wholesale displacement of tens of thousands of peasants from the land, the rate of displacement would have been so great that the poor would have overwhelmed the political system. The commercialisation process would then have ruined England instead of laying the foundation for its later rise and pre-eminence. The difference between Tudor England and the global polity today is that there is no global counter-part to the Tudor monarchy that can moderate to moderate the pace of global change (see Polanyi, *The Great Transformation*, pp. 33–40).
39. Hobsbawm, *The Age of Extremes*, p. 584
40. Despite being one of the most frequently used terms in the English language, 'global-isation' is very poorly understood. Although the word 'global' is about 400 years old, it was not turned into a verb or adjective ('globalise' or 'globalising') till around 1960. The *Economist*'s report on 4 April 1959, that 'Italy's "globalised" quota for the import of cars had increased', may well have been the first such use. Webster became the first dictionary to include the term globalisation in 1961, while the conservative Oxford English Dictionary held off till 1989 (Malcolm Waters, *Globalisation* [London, Routledge, 1995], p. 2). Since then there has been a flood of literature on globalisation. Despite this there is still no consensus on what globalisation is. The following set of definitions, picked almost at random, serves to illustrate this.
    Zygmunt Baumann, a well-known German philosopher defines or perhaps describes it as follows:

> Globalization is on everybody's lips; a fad word fast turning into a shibboleth, a magic incantation, a pass key meant to unlock the gates to all present and future mysteries. For some it is what we are bound to do if we wish to be happy; for others it is the cause of our unhappiness. For everybody, though it is the intractable fate of the world, an irreversible process ... The term 'time/space compression' encapsulates the ongoing multifaceted parameters of the Human condition (Zygmunt Baumann, *Globalization: The Human Consequences [European Perspectives]*, [Columbia University Press], pp. 1–2.).

According to Malcolm Waters, who has written one of the few books that tries to make sense of globalisation for students and non-academic readers, globalisation (working definition) is a social process in which the constraints of geography on social and cultural arrangements recede and in which people become aware that they are receding

(Waters, *Globalisation*, p. 3). It is a spread of western culture and capitalist society by forces that are beyond human control. He cites three views about when globalisation began:

a) It has been going on since the dawn of history but suddenly accelerated recently. When is 'sudden'? It could cover both the emergence of capitalism, i.e., the last 200 to 400 years, or the post-capitalist period, which dates roughly from 1980.

b) Globalisation is co-temporal with modernisation and the development of capitalism and that there has been a (still more) recent acceleration.

c) A recent phenomenon associated with other recent developments such as post-capitalism, post-modernism, and the disorganisation of capitalism.

Waters says the globalisation is basically the second of these points. He says that from the fifteenth-sixteenth centuries, globalisation was a linear, i.e., continuous, process. The date is significant because it coincides with the rise of the nation state and the first attempts to construct a national market. Waters explicitly rejects the third proposition (Waters, *Globalisation*).

Thomas Friedman, author of another bestseller, *The Lexus and the Olive Tree*, defines globalisation as follows:

it is the inevitable integration of markets, nation states and technologies to an extent never witnessed before—in a way that is enabling individuals, corporations and nation-states to reach around the world farther, faster, deeper, cheaper than ever before (Thomas Friedman, *The Lexus and the Olive Tree*, p. 9).

Manuel Castells, one of the most profound and thought-provoking analysts of the impact of globalisation on human society, defines it as the rise of informational capitalism.

Space and time, the material foundations of human experience have been transformed as the space of flows dominates the space of places and timeless time supercedes the clock time of the industrial era. (Manuel Castells, *Capitalism in the Information Age. Vol. III: The End of Millennium* [Basil Blackwell], p. 1).

Samir Amin characterises globalisation as the breakdown (not the continuation) of classical capitalism, which was characterised by two developments. The first was a polarisation of the world between the centre and the periphery. The second was the crystallisation of core industrial systems, which were, in his words, 'national and autocentered'. This second process went hand in hand with the construction of the 'national bourgeois', i.e., industrialised, nation state.

By contrast, he sees globalisation as the industrialisation of the periphery. This has taken place as part of the dismantling of auto-centred national production, and its reconstitution into an integrated international system of industrial production. In short the key difference is that *industrial production, which lay at the core of the classical capitalist organisation of society, has ceased to be national and has become international* (Samir Amin, *Capitalism in the Age of Globalisation* [Zed Books], pp. 1–2).

Amin apart, all the above definitions are imprecise. They all describe rather than define. They tell us the symptoms of globalisation, not its cause. All see it as a continuous process stretching back to at least the early nineteenth century, and in some cases implicitly a long way further back. By implication, therefore, they reject the idea that it is something new, or at most concede that incremental change in many fields has created a previously unforeseen synergy that has opened up new vistas for human progress.

Samir Amin is the only one of the above authors who sees globalisation as an overturning of national by global capitalism and therefore as a new epoch in human evolution. To use one of Karl Marx's terms, he sees a contradiction between national and international capitalism as systems for the organisation of society. This means that the one must necessarily destroy the other if it is to survive and flourish. What is on its way out is national capitalism. What is on its way in is world, or global, capitalism.

41. At least since the development of the water wheel which replaced human and animal power with mechanical power.

42. Giovanni Arrighi, *The Long Twentieth Century. Money, Power and the Origins of our Times* (London and New York, Verso, 1994), pp. 97–102. At its peak as a textiles centre, around the turn of the fourteenth century Florence had more than 300 workshops, employing 30,000 people (or about a third of Florence's population), and producing 100,000 or more pieces of cloth. But as local wages and costs rose, and transport links with northern Europe improved, new centres of production rose in northern Europe, and Florence began to import the coarser varieties of woollen cloth from the Brabant, Holland, England and France. Different classes were affected by, and reacted to, this change in different ways: Florentine industry graduated to processing the imported cloth and manufacturing cloth of a much higher quality, that found a ready market in the eastern Mediterranean and the Orient. A part of the working class therefore prospered as it produced higher-value-added goods. But the remainder found itself facing depressed wages and uncertainty of work. By 1338 the number of workshops had shrunk to 200 and output to between 70,000 and 80,000 pieces. By 1378, the year of the revolt, it had shrunk to 24,000 pieces of cloth, though admittedly of very fine quality. These changes thus led to the de-industrialisation of Florence, a rapid widening of income differences and a sharp rise in the insecurity of the poor. Unmediated by the state, whose merchants and bankers were doing as well or better than before, this 'stark Utopia' proved unbearable and led to revolt.

43. This famous phrase comes from Karl Polanyi, *The Great Transformation*, Chapter 1.

44. Arrighi, *Long Twentieth Century*, p. 30.

2

Four Cycles of Capital Accumulation

At the heart of this book resides the hypothesis that what the world calls 'globalisation' is the emergence of a higher 'order' of capitalism that is changing every human and social relationship and institution over the larger part of the world. This is not the first time since its birth approximately 700 years ago that there has been a sudden increase in the size of capitalism's container. It made a similar leap from the city to the nation state in the eighteenth century. It is making another incomparably larger one now.

The Origins of Capitalism

Both the origins and the sudden explosive expansions of capitalism can be traced to the uneven pace of technological change. The divorce of innovation from production that took place at the end of the nineteenth century and its centralisation in research institutes and laboratories has created the impression, now considered a truism, that technological change is incremental and continuous. This straight line is an invention. While change has not been absent in any epoch, the pace and the content of change has been profoundly uneven. The origins of capitalism lie in a major burst of technological change in the twelfth century, when wind- and water-mills spread throughout the European continent in a very short span of time. After that there was no similar technological leap for almost 700 years till the late eighteenth, nineteenth and twentieth centuries, when, in rapid succession, the harnessing of steam and electrical energy and, finally, the power of the internal combustion engine opened the way for a spate of complementary and induced technological change.[1] The third jump, centred on the rise of the intelligent machine, is a product of the second half of the twentieth century, and is going on as this is being written.

If technological progress has been uneven, then the changes it has wrought in the way people work and live have been even more so. This unevenness is fully reflected in the rise of capitalism. The emergence of capitalism as a mode of organising society probably became inevitable the moment human beings began to generate sustained surpluses that they wished to exchange for the surpluses of others. But while this was a necessary condition, it was not sufficient. Some surpluses have always existed within human society and have been exchanged for others through barter. Indeed it would have been impossible for the towns of antiquity to have come into being and grown had there been no agricultural surpluses to feed their inhabitants. Long-distance trade, i.e., trade between separate communities, is also almost as old as human civilisation. For the birth of capitalism though, one other condition had to be fulfilled: the surpluses had to come into being at the same time in a large number of places that were far removed from each other. This was possible only if there was a major technological change that affected an entire region comprised of many communities, or a substantial part of the world. The technological revolution of the twelfth century fulfilled this condition.

The tremendous increase in the surpluses generated in agriculture and industry can be judged by the rate at which new towns came into being. In the entire 800 years between 1150 and 1950, no other period came close to matching the number of towns that were founded between 1200 and 1400. As many as 200 towns were founded in a single decade between 1240 and 1250.[2] This burst of technological change gave rise to two major poles of industrial activity, one in the lowlands of northern Europe centred on cities like Bruges, Ypres, Thourot and Messines, and the other in Italy centred on cities like Genoa, Venice, Florence and Milan.[3]

Capitalism grew out of the need to transport and sell these surpluses in distant markets. Someone was needed who could pay the producer, finance the transport of the product to distant consumers, and recover the money from the buyer at the other end of the transaction. Ease and security of transport was the key to the successful disposal of the surpluses. Since transport was slow, the time a merchant needed in the Mediterranean trade of the twelfth and thirteenth centuries to complete one cycle of exchange and make his capital liquid once again could be as long as three years.[4] To bridge the time between purchase and sale, the merchant who engaged in this activity had to have liquid capital. Merchants too had existed as long as there had been long-distance trade. What turned the merchant into a capitalist in the modern sense of the word was the sharp rise in trade that followed the sudden increase in tradable surpluses. Technology altered the ratio between production for subsistence and local exchange through barter on the one hand and production for long-distance trade on the other, and gave birth to the capitalist in the modern sense of the term.

Since trade was fraught with considerable risk, the returns on the investment of capital in it had to be considerable. In a celebrated last will and testament written in 1423, which revealed the extent to which the spirit of what we now recognise as modern-day capitalism had permeated fifteenth-century Venice, the Doge of Venice, Mocenigo, estimated that the returns on the financing and conduct of trade amounted to 40 per cent on the value of goods exchanged. Drawing a significant distinction that suggested that financiers and traders were not always the same people, he estimated half to be trading profits and the other half to be interest on the capital invested in trade.[5] But 1423 was well after the profitability of the Eastern Mediterranean trade had reached its peak. In the second half of the fourteenth century the returns must have been higher still.

The increase in tradable surpluses and the consequent rise in the wealth and status of the merchant-capitalist initiated a profound change in the organisation of society and in the relations between cities and states. First, it facilitated the rise of towns, and their acquisition of pre-eminence over the countryside. In the twelfth to fourteenth centuries alone, more than 3,000 towns sprang up in Germany.[6] A similar but even more portentous revolution was taking place in Italy. Towns were centres of both industry and trade, but in the field of trade the inland towns were rapidly outstripped by the maritime ones. This was because many of the commonly traded goods—such as grain, timber, salt, minerals, and iron and steel—were low-value goods whose transport to distant consumption centres only made sense if it could be done in bulk, to keep their cost as low as possible. The sea provided the only mode of transport that fulfilled this requirement. In addition it was also by far the most secure mode of transport. This conferred a natural monopoly of trade on the maritime cities. Consequently it was in these cities that capitalism was born.

The high profits from maritime trade led to a shift of political power from inland to maritime cities and, more importantly, from large 'territorial' states to the rising maritime, capitalist cities. Within the former it also shifted from the traditional wielders of power—the monarchs and their representatives—to the new centres of power: the bands of merchant-financiers. Perhaps the best indicator of the former change is the size of the budget of various city and territorial states in 1423. In that year, not only was the budget of Venice several times larger than that of inland Italian cities such as Milan, Florence, Bologna, Ferrara and Monferrato, but it was larger than the budgets of major territorial states such as Burgundy, Spain, Portugal, France and England.[7]

City State Capitalism

Venice and Genoa

It was competition that turned capitalism into a political force. This forced the maritime cities in particular to convert their immense liquid capital resources into military and political power. They built up military power by hiring mercenaries and building powerful naval fleets, and they acquired political power by increasingly asserting their independence. Venice shrugged off its nominal allegiance to Byzantium, as did other emerging city states to the territorial states within which they lay. But the rise of several city states in Italy, in particular Venice, Genoa, Florence and Milan, led to a sharpening of rivalry, in which the four made a succession of shifting alliances with territorial states, and subjugated smaller urban and maritime cities and towns as they battled for supremacy. Thus Venice created a mainland zone under its control, the *Terraferma*, while Milan annexed Lombardy and Florence created Tuscany.

This struggle, dating roughly from the 1330s to the Peace of Lodi in 1454—and which Braudel has described as an Italian hundred years' war—was touched off by a levelling out and eventual decline in the rate of profit from investment in the eastern Mediterranean trade.[8] This was an inevitable outcome of the rise in the number of merchants and maritime cities engaged in the trade, and the absence of major technological change to push up tradable surpluses in line with the increase in the number of players.

In the absence of major, profit-increasing technological change, the ever-mounting surpluses of the new capitalist city states could not be reinvested in more trade, as the resulting competition would drive down the rate of profit still further. Venice invested the surplus in carving out a hinterland under its rule, thus becoming the archetype of the capitalist-territorial state of the future.

Genoa, which had fought Venice to control the eastern Mediterranean trade and lost, took a second route. As profits from trade declined,[9] Genoese merchants turned into bankers. As bankers they migrated to various cities across the length and breadth of Europe, from Antwerp in the north to Seville in the south. There the expatriate Genoese 'nation' of financiers first cooperated and later competed with other 'nations' like the Florentines and the Germans, and set up the first trans-European network of financiers, which, through bills of exchange, letters of credit and other financial instruments relieved traders (for a price) of the dangerous and onerous burden of carrying actual gold or silver coins long distances to the various fairs and markets where they bought and sold their wares. The financial innovation that enabled the Genoese to gain supremacy over their rivals was the invention of so-called 'good money' of a fixed value internationally in gold, against which all local currencies were traded. International contracts were denominated in this 'good money', and the Genoese pocketed the profits from arbitrage against local currencies. This network of international financiers and the multiplicity of financial instruments they created foreshadowed the emergence of *Haute Finance*, the network of international banking institutions that, among other things, played an important part in keeping the peace among industrialised nations four centuries later.

But in contrast to the merchant-capitalist rulers of Venice, the merchant-bankers of Genoa never succeeded in converting their nascent capitalist state into a territorial state. Instead, through more than a hundred years, during which Genoese bankers dominated European finance, Genoa needed, and actively looked for, support from major territorial states. It found such an ally in Spain. Having earlier established a near-monopoly over trade in the washed wool of Iberia, the Genoese diaspora 'nation' gradually became the bankers of the Spanish monarchy. What began as economic cooperation turned into a relationship of political exchange, in which the Genoese financed Spain's wars of expansion in Northern Europe, in exchange for a being granted a near-monopoly in the handling of the silver that was flowing into the country's coffers from America. Over the 80 years from 1566 to the Treaty of Westphalia in 1648, as Spain struggled to tame the Dutch, Genoese bankers converted the silver into bills of exchange (which could only be redeemed in gold) at their 'Piacenza' fairs in Italy, and transferred these to Antwerp where the Spanish army's payments (increasingly in gold) were centralised. In exchange Spain gave them *asientos* (contracts) that allowed them to take control of the silver that arrived in Seville and Cadiz.[10]

In the end it was the close connection that Genoese capital had forged with the Spanish empire that proved Genoa's undoing. Despite the inflow of specie from America, Spain's capacity to wage war was not limitless. Sooner or later it was bound to stretch itself too far. That point came in 1627 when the Spanish State became bankrupt and could not pay its debts. But even before this Genoa's success had already begun to undermine its dominance by attracting a host of other moneylenders into the sovereign-lending business. The Piacenza fairs had ceased to function five years earlier. After 1627, Genoese bankers began to look actively for other borrowers in order to diversify their lending. Genoa's place as the centre of the capitalist trading system in Europe was taken by Amsterdam, in the United Provinces of the Netherlands.

The United Provinces

Seen from the perspectives of a later age, the United Provinces seemed the least promising candidate among all countries in Europe for the role of a global economic hegemon. As late as 1650, it was a minuscule country with a population of a bare two million.[11] Its land was poor, being partly sand and partly marsh. Little of it was fit for agriculture, and there were no raw materials worth the name. Yet in the logic of capitalist accumulation these turned out to be advantages rather than handicaps. Because of the paucity of good soil, the cities had to rely from the very beginning on foreign trade to meet their need for foodgrains. This freed farmers to grow vegetables, fruit and other cash crops. The cash crops could only be sold in the towns. This created a very close link between the cities and the countryside, and a high level of urbanisation. In 1650 half the population of the United Provinces lived in towns. This was a far higher proportion than in any other country in Europe.

Dependence upon foreign trade for staples like grain, timber and salt gave the Dutch a powerful incentive to minimise shipping costs. The technological and managerial innovations that this need induced became the foundations of Dutch hegemony over the seas and therefore over long-distance trade and finance. The key was a series of changes in the design of ships that made them cheaper to build and even cheaper to operate, because they required fewer sailors for any given size of ship.[12] The resulting cost advantage enabled Dutch ships to wrest the Baltic trade from the merchants of the Hanseatic League—a loose confederation of between 70 and 170 German towns, which had acquired a stranglehold over trade in the Baltic and North Seas as early as the twelfth century. By the end of the sixteenth century the Dutch had completely replaced the German merchants of the Hansa.[13]

By the sixteenth century, five-sixths of the trade of the north Atlantic with the Iberian peninsula was also being carried in Dutch ships. These would bring wheat, rye, naval stores from the Baltic and the industrial products of northern Europe to Seville for export to America, and bring back salt, oil, wool, wine and, most important of all, silver.[14] This supremacy on the high seas was reflected by the size of the Dutch trading fleet. According to a French estimate of 1669, it consisted of around 6,000 twin- and triple-masted ships capable of making long voyages on the high seas. Braudel estimates that this amounted to at least 600,000 tonnes of shipping, with crews numbering at least 48,000. Although fantastic for the times, he does not consider the figure to be seriously exaggerated.[15] So great was the Dutch control of maritime commerce that although Spain was pitted against the United Provinces in the Thirty Years' War, by one of the ironies of history, much of the silver that was used to finance the Spanish army was carried to Antwerp in Dutch ships!

The port of Amsterdam became the nerve centre of this rapidly expanding commerce, displacing first Lubeck, the centre of the Hanseatic trade, and later Antwerp, the hub of Genoese financial activities in the Lowlands. A French guide published in 1701 spoke of Amsterdam's harbour containing 8,000 ships from all over the world. A traveller's account of 1738 gave the figure of 2,000 ships. Even the smaller figure attests to Amsterdam's commercial power.[16]

This power was based mainly upon the United Provinces' control over the supply of raw materials out of the Baltic seaboard countries to the rest of Europe and the control over the Iberian trade. But it was buttressed by the worldwide trading activities of the Dutch chartered companies. Of these the VOC (Verenigde Oost-Indische Compagnie), chartered in 1602, was the most successful. The trading companies immensely reinforced Amsterdam's position as the hub of the entrepôt trade between Europe and other parts of the world, in particular the East Indies. They did this by offering shippers in faraway places preferential access, safe warehousing and easy finance for their products at the sale point, while offering European traders access to these exotic goods at a convenient nearby location.

As finance is inseparable from trade, Amsterdam also developed into the financial hub of the Europe-centred world economy (in Braudel's sense of the term) of the seventeenth century. One can get an idea of the power of Dutch capitalism at the end of the fifteenth century from the fact that the seed capital of the VOC was ten times the size of the seed capital of the English East India Company, which was chartered by the English Crown in 1600. A contemporary observation serves to put Dutch financial power in perspective:

> If ten or twelve Businessmen of Amsterdam of the first rank meet for a banking operation, they can in a moment send circulating throughout Europe over two hundred million Florins in paper money, which is preferred to cash. There is no Sovereign who could do as much ... This credit is a power which ten or twelve businessmen will be able to exert over all the states in Europe, in complete independence of any authority.[17]

Despite the immense power of Amsterdam as the commercial and financial centre of the world economy of its day, there was an ephemeral quality to the Dutch hegemony, which made it very different from the Venetian or Genoese dominance that preceded it, and the British dominance which was to follow. This arose from the fact that Amsterdam was the last of the city-centred hubs of capitalism. Its dominance coincided with the rise of mercantilism and the consequent increase in the power of the territorial states. Thus, throughout the period of its pre-eminence, the policies dictated by its commercial interests were at odds with the policies that emerged from the territorial imperatives that governed the United Provinces as a whole. In practice this meant a fairly constant state of tension between the House of Orange (whose princes ruled five of the seven provinces and were conscious of the challenge posed by the rise of nation states around them) and Holland, which, thanks to the presence of Amsterdam within it, contributed more than half the United Provinces' revenue. This conflict of interests was triggered as much by differences over foreign policy as clashes over religion and other domestic matters. Thus one underlying cause of a serious clash in 1618 was a difference of opinion on whether or not to resume the war against Spain. Amsterdam, which had begun to ship grain, silver and other commodities to the Spanish troops in the southern Netherlands, was against the war, while the House of Orange was for it. The latter prevailed and war was resumed.[18]

The struggle was a protracted one, because it was born out a profound difference of opinion on the very goals of the state. The province of Holland, in which Amsterdam was situated, believed that the United Provinces should maintain peace with its neighbours to facilitate unrestricted trade with all, and concentrate on building a powerful navy to safeguard its merchant fleet. The territorially inclined provinces wanted, on the other hand, to build up the army in order to protect the United Provinces from their ever-dangerous neighbours. In the seventeenth century the interests of Amsterdam prevailed for the most part. As a result, during the Thirty Years' War it organised successive interventions by Denmark, Sweden and France, but followed a strictly defensive policy towards the Spanish, by building a string of forts and hiring mercenaries to discourage an invasion of the United Provinces. At the same time the United Provinces intervened to prevent wars from reaching decisive outcomes if these threatened its commercial interests. Thus it intervened in the Baltic to stop a war between Denmark and Sweden. Amsterdam also successfully opposed the Princes of Orange when they tried to conquer the Spanish Netherlands, because by that time a large part of the grain and bullion that fed the Spanish army was being carried in Dutch ships. For the same reason, the United Provinces also concluded a triple alliance with England and Sweden to halt the incursions of France into the Spanish Netherlands.

But as mercantilism gained strength throughout Europe, the territorial imperative gained the upper hand in the United Provinces. With the House of Orange striking alliances in territorial wars aimed at shoring up Dutch sovereignty, the merchants and financiers of Amsterdam found their commercial interests increasingly at odds with the territorial interests of the remaining provinces. They responded by ignoring the territorial imperative and carrying on business with whomsoever the profit motive dictated. Thus Dutch merchants and financiers invested in rival East Indies companies set up by Britain, Denmark, Sweden and France; invested in French privateering out of Dunkirk, despite the fact that many of the victims were Dutch ships; sold arms to the Portuguese when they were fighting the Dutch; and made payments via Amsterdam to French troops fighting in Italy against the Dutch and the English in the War of Spanish succession.[19]

Eventually it was a conventional 'territorial' alliance with France against England—reflected in assistance to Britain's American colonies to break free of the mother country—that sealed Amsterdam's fate. The British took their revenge by destroying the Dutch navy and soundly defeating the United Provinces in the war of 1782–83. The Treaty of Versailles in 1783 effectively spelt the end of Dutch pre-eminence, as also of the age of city-based capitalism. By then a large share of Dutch capital had forsaken Amsterdam and was carrying out its financial and entrepôt activities through London. Dutch merchants and financiers therefore continued to prosper, but Amsterdam declined.

State-based Capitalism—The English Long Century

For those studying the rise of global capitalism, an examination of the way in which capitalism leaped the confines of the city state and embraced the modern European state cannot fail to provoke a sense of déjà vu—exactly the same economic and technological forces were at work behind the jump as are at work today. One striking similarity is that the crucial change that made it possible was the emergence of national markets that conformed to the territorial boundaries of the modern European state. While the outlines of the European state system were more or less settled by the Treaty of Westphalia in 1648, even in the most economically advanced of the territorial states—Britain and France—the national market came into being only in the eighteenth century. In France it took more or less the entire century to create.

Traditional explanations of the rise of the national market have tended to focus on the destruction of internal barriers to the movement of goods, such as the multiplicity of toll barriers that bedevilled British and French roads. In this Britain had a sizeable lead on France, but as Braudel has shown, this explanation concentrates too much on the political forces that went into the making of the national market and underplays the economic factors.[20] The elimination of tolls was not the cause of the rise of the national market but its consequence. The primary cause was the continuing rise in productivity throughout the eighteenth century. This was the result of a string of technological innovations that took place throughout the century and led, especially in its second half, to an unprecedented surge in prosperity throughout Europe. These innovations were concentrated mainly in the textiles industry, but also, importantly, in steel and mining. The rise in productivity forced upon the producers a desperate need to enlarge the size of the market. This led to innovations that dramatically reduced transport costs. Britain again was the best placed to take the lead in this. Not only was it a relatively small area (compared to France), but it had taken the lead by allowing private investors to build toll-bearing turnpikes after 1663. Other investors built canals and the first half of the eighteenth century saw a canal building craze in the country. In France too, transport costs came down dramatically because of a spate of road building in the second half of the eighteenth century and a much more intensive use of the rivers and canals for internal transport.

The Role of the State

But economic pressures might not by themselves have succeeded in creating national markets if they had not had the sustained backing of the state. This sustained support emerged from the realisation in the territorial monarchies that their security and strength depended upon harnessing national economic forces and actors to the task of nation building. England was the first country to attempt this. It took two centuries to achieve the synthesis, but once its efforts were crowned with success it emerged as the most powerful centre of capitalist and territorial power that the world had ever known.

The architect of national capitalism was a powerful merchant and financier, Thomas Gresham. England had entered the reign of Queen Elizabeth I with her economy exhausted and her finances in a shambles. Henry VIII had emptied the treasury and plunged the country deep into debt to fight a succession of wars against the French in a fruitless attempt to regain the territories that England had once ruled across the channel. Expropriatory taxation had damaged the economy, and deficit financing had brought the intrinsic value of English currency down by almost two-thirds. English currency had ceased to be accepted for transactions and the 'nation' of English bankers and financiers preferred to operate out of Antwerp, then the hub of the Spanish empire in the north. British trade surpluses were therefore regularly invested in Genoese banks and went to finance the continued accumulation of capital in Iberian and Genoese hands.

Gresham advised the Queen at the very beginning of her reign that she had to create conditions in England that would make English merchants want to keep their money in England and make it work for the state. He advised her to stabilise the value of the currency. Queen Elizabeth accepted Gresham's advice. She paid off the Crown's internal debt by selling all the land that Henry VIII had expropriated from the monasteries. From the proceeds of Sir Francis Drake's privateering expeditions (estimated at £600,000) she paid off England's foreign debt and had enough left over to finance the Levant company, the first of England's chartered trading companies and the progenitor of the East India Company. Thereafter she not merely stabilised the currency, but restored it to its 'ancient and right standard' of 93 per cent silver content. Once the currency was stabilised in 1560–61, Gresham returned to England and set about building a bourse in London to compete with Antwerp's Commodity and Stock Exchange. In 1570 Queen Elizabeth visited the bourse and renamed it the Royal Exchange.

These enactments by the English Crown only set the stage for the rise of national capitalism and Britain's subsequent dominance. It was to be another two centuries before England displaced Amsterdam as the centre of the 'European World Economy'. Two more developments were needed for that to happen. The first was the emergence of England as by far the largest manufacturing nation in Europe. The second was the displacement of Amsterdam by London as the entrepôt and financial centre of Europe.[21]

England's industrialisation took place in three waves. The first occurred in the late fourteenth and early fifteenth centuries, when Edward III wooed and coerced weavers from Flanders into settling down in England to set up a woollen cloth weaving industry. The second wave occurred in the second half of the sixteenth and the first half of the seventeenth centuries, when entrepreneurs, financiers and artisans from Germany and other European countries migrated to England to get away from various religious wars. During this period the Crown passed a number of laws that were designed to slow down the displacement of farmers from the land, as land was enclosed to rear sheep for wool. This had the beneficial side effect of pushing capital and entrepreneurship into the manufacture of high-value products such as silk, glass, fine paper and, above all, armaments. The technology for these industries came in with the miners and craftsmen of the then more technically advanced countries of continental Europe.

The third wave occurred in the eighteenth and nineteenth centuries, when technological change became endogenous to British industry and its pace quickened. Productivity began to shoot up, first in the textiles industry and then in the mining and metallurgical industries. This was the Industrial Revolution, which greatly increased the need for raw materials and export markets. Thus it was probably inevitable that London, which was already by far the largest city in Europe, would displace Amsterdam as the entrepôt for the European world economy. But the shift from Amsterdam was facilitated by three economic crises in the United Provinces in 1763, 1773 and 1780, and the Batavian 'revolution' (of the Dutch middle classes) in 1780. These greatly weakened the Dutch economy and hastened a shift of Dutch capital to England that had already begun earlier. The defeat of the Dutch in the Anglo-Dutch war of 1781–83 sealed Amsterdam's decline and England's rise.[22]

The American Century

If the beginnings of the British 'Long Century' can be traced to the end of the Seven Years' War against France in 1763, the beginning of its end can be traced to the Great Depression of 1873–96. The former marks the commencement of a surge of prosperity that lasted for most of the rest of the century. It was during this period that the textiles industry was revolutionised by the development of Kay's flying shuttle (which increased the speed of handloom weaving manifold) and of the spinning jenny, Arkwright's water frame and Crompton's 'Mule', which increased productivity in the spinning industry tenfold.[23] It was also during this period that the English wrested supremacy over the high seas from the Dutch, and London replaced Amsterdam as the entrepôt and financial centre of the European world economy. Finally, it was during this period that the East India Company acquired the fabulously rich 'province' of Bengal in India, and began to ship back plunder and import surpluses, which at their peak amounted to just under a third of the British Gross National Savings.[24]

The sustained rise of British industrial and trading power in the nineteenth century is reflected by the rise in its consumption of raw cotton. This increased from 1.7 million pounds in the period 1737–40 to 50 million pounds (23,000 tons) in 1800 to over 800,000 tons (1800 million pounds) a year by 1900, an increase of over 1,000 times.[25] The growth of other industries paralleled the growth of cotton.[26]

However, some time after 1850, and more markedly during the 'Great Depression', British profit margins from investment in domestic industry began to fall.[27] The reason was that Europe as a whole had entered an era of cut-throat competition. Rising tariff walls in France, Germany, Russia and the US, and increasing competition from their manufactured exports in all markets including the British domestic market, combined with a deflationary shortage of gold as a backing for currency to push down prices on an average by a third between 1873 and 1896.[28] In a manner similar to the Genoese in the sixteenth century and the Dutch in the eighteenth century, British financiers began to shy away from investing still more in industry, and began instead to invest their ever-accumulating funds abroad, where the returns were higher.[29]

It was during this 'Great Depression' that the seeds of American hegemony—the coming American century—were sown. British capitalism was running out of steam because it was no longer capable of the structural changes that were needed to make further growth possible. As the productivity of machines and the economic scales of production grew progressively larger, the area that had to be brought under a common envelope of production and exchange—the container—grew too large for a single small island country to encompass. In short, national capitalism outgrew the British home market. This had begun to happen well before the Great Depression. For instance, Britain ceased to be self-sufficient in grain and flour as early as the decade of 1750–60.[30] Its cotton industry, which was always partly a re-export industry selling cloth to Europe, outgrew the absorptive capacity of both the home market and Europe at least as early as 1813, the year in which the British government lifted the ban on exports of finished cotton cloth to India.

In the same manner, production of capital goods for the domestic market had begun to yield diminishing returns in the 1840s. Thereafter an increasing proportion was exported to the rapidly expanding European and American markets. Between 1845–49 and 1870–75 British exports of iron and steel more than trebled, and exports of machinery increased by nine times. British exports were no longer confined to Europe and North America. During this period, export to South America, Australasia, the Middle East and Asia increased six-fold.[31]

Thus by the time of the Great Depression, Britain was the hub of a far-flung world economy that encompassed every continent and most countries of the world. But as in the case of Amsterdam a century or more earlier, the links that tied this economic 'empire' to the mother country were forged by trade. Even the rapid growth of British foreign investment from the 1860s onwards went mainly into the development of transport and communications infrastructure that was designed to facilitate a larger flow of raw materials to Britain and manufactures out of Britain, i.e., to further bolster trade. This reliance on foreign trade for the further growth of the home economy placed limits on the development of British capitalism, and hence upon the deepening of British hegemony, which only the United States was ultimately able to break.

The key constraint was the premium that a trade-driven economy placed upon the creation of a disarticulated trade, finance and industrial system, in which each of these sectors, and the enterprises in each sector, were largely independent of each other. Britain needed such a structure because heavy dependence on trade made its enterprises in industry and finance vulnerable to events in other countries that it could not control. British enterprises were therefore forced to be defensive and reactive. Faced with the prospect of adverse changes in markets or supplier countries, every enterprise had to be capable of formulating a survival strategy as quickly as possible. The choice of strategy hinged on the level of dependence upon imports from or exports to the affected country, and was therefore different for each enterprise. What is more, the need to compete made it necessary to conceal one's strategy from one's business rivals. These constraints put a limit on the degree of vertical integration that was possible within and between finance, manufacturing and marketing.[32]

This had a particularly constraining effect on British industry. Industry was the youngest of the three branches of British capitalism, for Britain had already established itself as the financial and entrepôt centre of the European world economy by the time the industrial revolution began in earnest. Thus finance was the most extroverted of the three branches of capital, with a wide range of clients all over the world. To find capital to grow, British industry had to offer terms that were more attractive than the terms that foreign borrowers could offer. Apart from raising the cost of borrowing, this also led to a lack of commitment in the banking system to the fate of British industry, which was strikingly at odds with the deep involvement of banks in the development of German and American industry.[33]

The extroversion of the British economy—and therefore its vulnerability to changes abroad—could only increase as it grew larger and became more international. This therefore imposed a natural limit to the growth of British capitalism, which could only be broken by a different form of growth, one that was less vulnerable to events abroad and therefore more susceptible to rational planning. That form of capitalist structure developed in America.

In sharp contrast to British enterprises, American firms were vertically integrated from a very early stage of their development. This resulted from the sheer size of the US, its distance from Europe, and its adoption of a protectionist policy from the early stages of its industrialisation. America had an abundance of natural resources and a continental market. Thus its capacity for inward-looking, autarchic development was far greater than that of Britain. Almost all the things that America needed, from the raw materials to the final, manufactured consumer products were available within the country. All it needed was the labour to farm the land, work the mines and man the machines. It ensured an adequate supply of this through massive immigration, mainly from Europe.

Its distance from Europe meant that transport costs to and from Britain—then the manufacturing centre of the world—were far greater than they were for manufacturers in Europe. This provided a natural protection to industry in the US, which was far greater than the protection that distance afforded to countries on the European continent.

Finally, throughout the nineteenth century and the first half of the twentieth century (except for a brief period in the 1830s), the American government maintained a policy of high tariff walls against European manufactures. Throughout this period American tariffs on manufactures seldom averaged less than 50 per cent, and for some of the time were as high as 60 per cent *ad valorem*.[34]

These three factors reinforced each other to make it profitable to concentrate every stage of production within the country. The rise of monopoly therefore took the form of vertical integration of stages of manufacture within a single enterprise. A similar vertical integration took place in the distribution trade, where the chain store, the mail-order house and the supermarket began to displace small, individually owned shops decades before they began to do so in Britain and Europe.

Vertical integration did not eliminate competition. What it did was to concentrate competition in the market for the final goods, especially consumer goods, while replacing competition with planning in the manufacture or procurement of intermediate goods. This made it possible to eliminate or reduce a host of 'transaction costs' by internalising them within a single organisational domain.[35] This lowered costs and increased efficiency by eliminating duplication and permitting streamlining and better use of a wide range of fixed assets. But it did more than that. Vertical integration freed suppliers of inputs from the need to look constantly for buyers, and the manufacturers of final goods from the need to shop around for alternative sources of supply. This made it possible to plan production a long way into the future, and to make investments in the technology, machinery and managerial changes needed to bring down costs and improve quality.[36] In sum, by replacing market forces with planning in the 'upstream' industries, vertical integration eliminated much of the uncertainty of the business environment that had made British capitalism defensive and incapable of growth beyond a point.

The vast size of the American home market and the high level of protection it enjoyed from foreign competition also made possible the other great managerial innovation of American capitalism: 'Fordist' mass production. Developed by Henry Ford in the 1920s, the assembly line virtually halved the cost of producing the Model-T automobile. But only the presence of a huge domestic market, capable of absorbing the increase in the output of cars and trucks made possible by mass production, made the heavy capital investment required by the assembly line economically viable.[37] Finally, American capitalism was the first to benefit from the surge of productivity that accompanied the switch from coal to oil as the primary source of energy. In the US this change began in the 1920s.

Capitalism and Conflict

Our brief survey of the rise of capitalism reveals two distinct trends that help us to understand the challenge that the transition from national to global capitalism poses to humanity. The first is that in each cycle—in each 'long century'—the 'containers of power' have grown inexorably larger.[38] The second is that each of the four 'long centuries' described above has been shorter than its predecessor. Depending upon what markers one chooses, the Genoese phase of city state-based capitalism can be said to have lasted for about 170–220 years, the Dutch phase for about 120–180 years, the British for 110–130 years, and the American for about 77–100 years. The oil price shock of the 1970s marked the beginning of the 'signal crisis' of American capitalism. In that decade the world entered what Hobsbawm called the 'crisis decades'. The 'crisis' was in fact the reappearance of 'Systemic Chaos', as the world entered a fifth, global cycle of capital accumulation.[39]

The compression of successive cycles of expansion has been caused by a steady acceleration in the pace of technological change. The combination of the two trends described above—the increasing scale of production and the consequently relentless expansion of capitalism's container, and the shorter time period in which the change has had to be completed—has put an evergrowing strain on human institutions and increased the violence of each transition.

As capitalism has grown in size and power with each succeeding 'cycle of accumulation', the systemic chaos preceding the rise of a new 'container of power' has grown deeper. Not surprisingly the conflict preceding the establishment of a new stable world order has also grown more intense. The systemic crisis that was unleashed in the northern Italian system of city states by the exhaustion of trading opportunities in the eastern Mediterranean led to what Braudel has dubbed the Italian 'hundred years' war'. This ended in 1454 with the Peace of Lodi, which stabilised the northern Italian city state system.

The systemic chaos that heralded the end of Genoese hegemony and the rise of the Dutch occurred in the early eighteenth century and culminated in the Thirty Years' War. During this period the Dutch, who had already been struggling to assert their freedom from Imperial Spain for 50 years, skilfully orchestrated a coalition of European states against Spain that made the war European in scale. This war, which saw the use of fully professional armies on both sides, involved far more soldiers and weaponry and was far more intense than the conflicts between the Italian city states two centuries earlier. Between 1550 and 1640, the number of soldiers mobilised by the great powers of Europe doubled and the cost of putting each soldier in the battlefield increased by five times. The huge increase in expenditure was financed in large part by extortionate taxation, which led to a sharp intensification of social conflict within the warring states.[40]

The onset of systemic chaos at the end of the Dutch cycle of accumulation saw a similar intensification of conflict and attendant social turmoil. France fought the Seven Years' War against England from 1756 to 1763; and a string of Anglo-Dutch wars took place, beginning in 1751 and ending in 1783. Both ended with the establishment of English ascendancy. But the social cost was high. England faced a revolt by its American colonies and eventually lost them; the United Provinces faced the Batavian rebellion, which was finally crushed by the House of Orange but cost Amsterdam its ascendancy within the United Provinces. Finally there was the French revolution, the rise of Napoleon, and the Napoleonic wars that convulsed Europe for two decades till the Congress of Vienna ushered in the Hundred Years' Peace in 1815.

Systemic chaos set in once again with the onset of the Great Depression in 1873. For a number of reasons, some of which were mentioned earlier, profits from agriculture and industry fell to 'unreasonably' low levels and set off an era of cut-throat competition between the industrialising European powers. France, Germany and Russia rapidly raised their tariffs in order to protect their domestic markets, and the US followed suit, leaving Britain the sole advocate and practitioner of free trade. Denied profitable avenues of investment in these sectors of the economy, bankers and financiers began to lend increasingly to governments, which in turn began to divert more and more of their resources to military spending. Starting in the 1880s, military spending began to grow rapidly. The total for Great Britain, France, Austria-Hungary, Germany, Russia and Italy rose from £132 million in 1880 to £205 million in 1900 and further to £397 million in 1914.[41] The militarisation of Europe eventually spilled over into the First World War, which cost 30 million lives. But the end of the war did not end the chaos that had overtaken Europe. The war discredited the European monarchies and left a vacuum in their place. This set off a struggle between communism and fascism to fill the space; this eventually led to the even more destructive Second World War. It was not till 1945–50 that a stable new international order, formed around two contending nations and ideologies, came into being.

However, this stability lasted for only a quarter of a century before capitalism outgrew the nation state and began to turn the globe into a single production and marketing centre. At the end of the 1960s and the beginning of the 1970s, capitalism's jump from the level of the nation to the level of the entire world began with a similar slump in the profit margins on investment and a decline in labour productivity. It took place not merely because revolutions in transport and information technology made it *possible*, but because falling profit margins from investment in the production of commodities made it *necessary*.

The accumulation of financial surpluses that occurred in the late 1960s and early 1970s found a ready outlet in the Vietnam war and, in the 1980s under President Reagan, in American rearmament to fight the 'Evil Empire' of the Soviet Union. These crisis decades have also seen the rate of killing, both of civilians and combatants, escalate even in the absence of a world war. The 1990s and the first years of the twenty-first century saw more military interventions than the entire period of the Cold War. If the experience of past cycles of capitalism's expansion is any pointer to the future, far from entering a period of widening peace, 'openness' and interdependence, the world once again seems headed for another period of increasing 'systemic chaos' and escalating violence.

As was pointed out in Chapter 1, in none of these cycles of capitalism's expansion did a new international order emerge spontaneously. The task of building it fell upon the city or country that had become capitalism's container. Success resulted in its emerging as the hegemonic power of the next cycle of capitalism—the next 'Long Century'. That is the endeavour upon which the US is embarked at the present moment.

Chapters 3 to 7 examine the onset of systemic chaos in the global economy in greater detail.

Notes

1. Fernand Braudel, *A History of Civilisations* (UK, Penguin Books, 1995), Chapter 18, p. 374. Braudel concedes that there were 'a multiplicity of small and often very ingenious technical inventions', but draws a distinction between these secondary innovations and the powerful thrust of primary innovations that increase the power at the command of human beings.
2. Fernand Braudel, *Civilization and Capitalism*, Vol. III: *The Perspective of the World* (Collins/Fontana Press, 1988), p. 93.
3. Ibid., p. 99.

4. Ibid., p. 376. For example, in the fifteenth century wool washed in Iberia was sent for weaving and finishing to the workshops of Spain. The finished woollen textiles were sent to Alexandria in modern-day Egypt to be exchanged for oriental goods, destined for sale in Florence and elsewhere in Europe. Another typical cycle of exchange went somewhat as follows: grain, timber, linen and woollen textiles would be transported by Venetian merchants to Egypt and the Levant, to be exchanged for spices, silks and fine cottons, drugs and gold. The silks would be taken to Byzantium to be exchanged further for oriental goods, which would be sold in Europe. The gold would be exchanged for silver, initially from northern Europe, and then in the sixteenth century from the Americas.

5. Ibid., p. 121, quoting Heinrich Kretschmayr. Mocenigo wrote his testament in 1423. His estimates were initially questioned, but accepted by later historians.

6. Ibid., p. 93.

7. Ibid., pp. 120–121. The comparison relates to the combined income of Venice city and the *Terraferma*, the area of the mainland that Venice conquered and controlled. On this basis, Venice with 1.5 million inhabitants had a budget of 1.65 million ducats, while France with 15 million inhabitants had a budget of 1 million ducats.

8. Fernand Braudel, *The Mediterranean and the Mediterranean World During the Age of Phillip II* (John Hopkins Press, 1976), quoted by Giovanni Arrighi, *The Long Twentieth Century. Money, Power and the Origins of our Times* (London and New York, Verso, 1994), pp. 90–96.

9. The total value of merchandise that passed through the port of Genoa dropped from 4,000,000 Genoese pounds in 1293 to 2,000,000 pounds in 1334, and seldom rose above that level during the second half of the century (Lauro Martines, *City States in Renaissance Italy*, London, The John Hopkins Press, 1988, quoted in Arrighi, *Long Twentieth Century*, p. 90).

10. Arrighi, *Long Twentieth Century*, pp. 131–132.

11. Braudel, *Civilization and Capitalism*, Vol. III: *The Structures of Everyday Life*, p. 184.

12. Ibid., pp. 190–193.

13. Ibid., p. 251. 2,000 Dutch ships entered the Baltic in 1597 for the purpose of trade.

14. Ibid., pp. 101, 207.

15. Ibid., p. 190.

16. Ibid., p. 182.

17. J. Accaras de Serionne: *Interets des nations de l'Europe developpes relativement au commerce 1766.* Quoted by Braudel, *Civilization and Capitalism*, Vol. III, p. 245.

18. Ibid., pp.194–195.

19. Ibid., pp. 203–206.

20. Ibid., pp. 289–292.

21. Arrighi, *Long Twentieth Century*, pp. 174–199.

22. Braudel, *Civilization and Capitalism, Vol. III*, pp. 266–276.

23. Ibid., pp. 566–567.

24. In the second half of the eighteenth century the Indian export surplus to Britain amounted to 2 per cent of its GDP. The national savings rate was estimated to be 7 per cent.

25. Braudel, *Civilization and Capitalism*, Vol. III, pp. 567, 571; Arrighi, *Long Twentieth Century*, p. 363, Fig. 9.

26. Eric Hobsbawm, *The Age of Revolution* (Vintage, 1962), p. 54.

27. Arrighi, *Long Twentieth Century*, p. 171.

28. David S. Landes, *The Unbound Prometheus. Technological Change and Industrial Development in Western Europe from 1750 to the Present* (Cambridge, Cambridge University Press, 1969), p. 231.

29. Jeffrey G. Williamson, *American Growth and the Balance of Payments 1820–1913. A Study of the Long Swing* (Chapel Hill: University of North Carolina Press, 1964), p. 207.

30. Braudel, *Civilization and Capitalism*, Vol. III, p. 559.

31. Eric Hobsbawm, *The Age of Capital* (New York: New American Library, 1979), pp. 38, 50–51.

32. Arrighi, *Long Twentieth Century*, pp. 239–240, 281–290.

33. Will Hutton, *The State We Are In* (London, Vintage Books, 1996).

34. Paul Bairoch, *Economics and World History: Myths and Paradoxes* (Chicago, The University of Chicago Press, 1993), pp. 30–38.

35. Richard Coase, 'The Nature of the Firm', *Economica*, 1937, pp. 386–405.

36. Alfred Chandler, *The Visible Hand: The Managerial Revolution in American Business* (Cambridge, Mass., The Belknap Press, 1977).

37. James P. Womack, Daniel T. Jones and Daniel Roos, *The Machine that Changed the World* (New York, Rawson Associates, Simon and Schuster, 1990).

38. Arrighi, *Long Twentieth Century*, pp. 217–218.

39. The longer periods encompassing each cycle are taken from Arrighi, *Long Twentieth Century*, pp. 217–218; Table 10, p. 364. The shorter periods refer to the period of political or financial dominance enjoyed by the hegemonic power in each cycle of capitalism's expansion.

40. Ibid., p. 42.

41. Eric Hobsbawm, *The Age of Empire 1875–1914* (New York: Pantheon Books, 1987), p. 350.

3

The Onset of Systemic Chaos

The first unmistakable signs of the end—what Arrighi called the 'signal crisis'—of capitalism grounded in the nation state came at the moment of the West's greatest triumph, its victory in the Cold War. Writing in *Foreign Affairs* in 1994, Charles Maier, Krupp Professor of European studies at Harvard University voiced an acute disquiet:

> How should one make sense of the malaise that currently sours public opinion in the countries of Europe, in Japan and North America? It reveals itself most saliently in tremendous electoral volatility as political parties are deserted for new formations and leaders ... And social cohesion apparently frays at a level even more basic than politics. Citizens become uneasy at the noticeable presence of the foreign-born, worry about the burden of welfare and the pool of jobs, and view imported mores, languages and religious manifestations as a threat to national identity ... No wonder that the common exhilaration that attended the collapse of Communism has largely dissipated. How difficult it is today to recover the spirit of the crowds of Leipzig or Wenceslaus square.[1]

Underlying the disillusionment was a profound confusion, almost a sense of betrayal. 'This is not how it was supposed to work', wrote Ethan Kapstein. 'For generations, students were taught that increasing trade and investment, coupled with technological change, would drive national productivity and create wealth.'[2] But, in a manner that was as inexplicable as it was frightening, the opposite seemed to be happening. At the peak of their economic power, after a century and a half of unimpeded growth and rising standards of living, the mature industrialised nations were facing problems that they thought they had left behind them forever. It was as if, quite suddenly, the very forces that were responsible for bringing them to the apogee of political power and economic well-being had betrayed them.

The Slowdown of Economic Growth

In truth, the 'signal crisis' had begun two decades earlier, and it had first manifested itself in the realm of economics. The economic crisis, which began what Hobsbawm termed the 'crisis decades', began in the early 1970s, after 25 years of the fastest economic growth that the industrialised countries had ever known. It only surfaced in the realm of politics at the end of the Cold War, which brought not peace but resurgent conflict, not triumph but disillusionment. Three developments conspired to create the disillusionment and sense of betrayal: a sharp and seemingly irreversible decline in the rate of growth of GDP and per capita productivity; the emergence of chronic, and rising unemployment—unemployment that was not caused by the contractionary phase of a trade cycle, but seemed there to stay; and an increasingly unequal distribution of income and wealth. The annual rate of growth of the Gross Domestic Product for the OECD as a whole fell from 4.9 per cent to 2.8 per cent between 1973 and 1979. The return of cheap oil in the 1980s did not however boost the growth rate, which fell further to 2.7 per cent between 1979 and 1989, and still further to 1.8 per cent between 1989 and 1994. The corresponding figures for the USA were 3.9 per cent between 1960 and 1973, 2.5 per cent between 1973 and 1979 (the period of the two oil shocks), 2.5 per cent between 1979 and 1989, and 2.1 per cent between 1989 and 1994.[3]

Table 3.1
The Slowdown of Growth in the Industrialised Countries

	Annual GDP Growth (Per Cent)			
Period	USA	Japan	Germany	OECD
1971–78	3.3	4.5	2.7	3.6
1979–94	2.2	3.5	2.2	2.7
1990–94	2.0	2.1	1.2	1.9

Source: OECD, Main Economic Indicators and Historical Statistics (Paris, OECD), 1995 and 2000.

The slowdown in the rate of growth was reflected in a sharp fall in the growth of labour productivity. The growth of value added per employee in the OECD countries fell from 4.4 per cent between 1960 and 1973 to 1.6 per cent between 1973 and 1979 and 1.5 per cent between 1979 and 1994.[4]

There was a parallel slowdown in the growth of total factor productivity, a measure that estimates the contribution of technology and better management practices to increasing the productivity of all factors of production.

Table 3.2
Growth of Labour Productivity in the OECD and Selected Countries

Period	Annual Growth in Labour Productivity (Per Cent)			
	USA	Japan	Germany (FR)	OECD
1960–73	2.2	8.3	4.5	4.4
1973–79	0.0	2.9	3.1	1.6
1979–94	0.8	2.5	0.9	1.5

Source: OECD, Main Economic Indicators (Paris, OECD), 1995.

Table 3.3
Growth in Total Factor Productivity in the OECD and Selected Countries

Period	Annual Growth in Total Factor Productivity (Per Cent)			
	USA	Japan	Germany (FR)	OECD
1960–73	1.6	5.6	2.6	2.9
1973–79	–0.4	1.3	1.8	0.6
1979–94	0.4	1.4	0.4	0.8

Distress in the Labour Market

Far more disturbing was the rise in chronic unemployment. The standard-ised unemployment rate as calculated by the OECD rose from an average of 3 per cent per annum between 1964 and 1973 to 4.9 per cent between 1974 and 1979, and further to 7.8 per cent in 1993. It fell to 6.5 per cent in 2001 at the end of the longest boom in post-war US history, and rose again to 7.1 per cent per annum in 2003.[5] But these bare statistics hide more than they reveal, for they do not capture the change in the nature of the employment that was available, the weakening of the bargaining power of workers and the consequent decline in their real wages, and the increasing feeling of defeat that was making more and more of them drop out of the workforce altogether, to return only for brief periods in the later stages of a cyclical upswing of economic activity.

Lawrence Mishel and Jared Bernstein estimated that even in 1989 (when the six-year American economic upswing of the 1980s peaked), although unemployment had formally dropped to 5.3 per cent, another 4.5 per cent of the working population was underemployed, i.e., they were working part-time against their will or had given up trying to find a job.[6] In 1991 the corresponding figures were 6.7 per cent and 5.3 per cent respectively. In sum, out of a workforce of 125.2 million, 15.2 million workers (or 12 per cent) were either unemployed, underemployed or had dropped out. No fewer than 1.025 million workers had dropped out of the labour market, while another 5.767 million were involuntary part-time workers.[7] Even in the middle of 1996, when the economic recovery had been under way for almost five years and the average US growth rate during the period had been over 3.5 per cent, unemployment and underemployment (including dropouts) had come down only to 10.1 per cent of the broad labour force. In absolute terms their number had dropped from 15.2 to 13.5 million.[8]

What is more, during the 1990s a structural change in the labour force that had begun in the 1980s became much more noticeable. In mid-1996, by a conservative estimate, fully 10 per cent of the employed labour force was working in 'contingent' and 'alternate' employment situations, i.e., either on lower pay for short assignments with little or no security and few benefits, or doing piece-work for lumpsum payments.

Conditions were similar, only worse, in Great Britain. In 1994, one in every four working age males was unemployed or idle.[9] More than one industrialised country has changed the definition of unemployment to exclude school leavers, and some other categories of people from being automatically counted as part of the employable workforce. In Britain, by an earlier definition, the proportion of the working population without jobs was not 10 per cent but 14 per cent in 1992. Another 1.5 million new jobs—for women—were part-time jobs.[10]

To capture the deteriorating quality of the labour market, Mishel and Bernstein devised the concept of 'labour market distress'. Those suffering from labour market distress in 1991 included workers earning poverty or below poverty-level wages[11] (22 per cent of the workforce between 25 and 64 years in age), discouraged workers who had left the workforce (1.8 per cent), those who had been involuntarily on part-time work for at least four weeks in the past year (5.8 per cent) and those who had been unemployed for at least four weeks (10.3 per cent). These added up to no less than 31.5 per cent of the prime age workforce. Add the 6 per cent unemployed and in 1991 not far short of two-fifths of the working population was experiencing mild to acute distress.[12]

Inequality, Insecurity and the Return of the Self-regulating Market

Growing distress in the labour market was accompanied by a rapid increase in the inequality of income distribution. This was most noticeable in the US and Britain, where neo-classical economic doctrines now reigned supreme. Overall, between 1980 and 1995, according to an OECD study, while the incomes of the top 10 per cent of income-earners rose by 8 per cent, those of the bottom 10 per cent fell by 18 per cent. In Britain the real incomes of the bottom 10 per cent of income-earners did admittedly rise by 13 per cent during this period, but that of the top 10 per cent rose by 48 per cent.[13] Most dramatic was the increase in the emoluments of the top managers of companies, especially their chief executives. In 1975 the average chief executive in America earned 35 times as much as the average production worker. In 1995 she earned 120 times as much.[14] In Britain the pay of executives rose by 50 per cent during the 1980s in real terms.[15] At the other end of the scale, the spread of incomes narrowed marginally in France and Germany, but seemingly at the cost of record levels of unemployment—10 per cent in Germany and 11 per cent in France. Britain alone seems to have had the worst of both worlds, with both a rapid growth of income inequalities and high unemployment.

Paul Krugman has described the change in income distribution that took place in the US after 1973 as the replacement of a picket fence with a step-ladder.[16] Dividing US families into quintiles, he pointed out that between 1947 and 1973, the real incomes of all five quintiles of American families, from the poorest 20 per cent to the richest, rose at almost exactly the same rate, of 2.6 to 2.8 per cent per annum. Thus a column graph depicting the annual rate of growth of real income for each quintile showed five columns of almost equal height, like the boards in a picket fence. Within this the incomes of the middle three quintiles rose slightly faster than that of the poorest and richest 20 per cent—reflecting the steady rise and consolidation of the American middle class that had been going on since the 1930s.[17]

Around 1974, however, the picture changed completely. The bottom 20 per cent suffered a decline in real incomes of 0.25 per cent per annum. The next poorest 20 per cent also suffered a decline in incomes, although at an almost imperceptible rate. The middle quintile (40 to 60 per cent) was the first to show some gain—an increase of about 0.3 per cent per annum. The 60 to 80 per cent quintile experienced an increase of about 0.7 per cent and the top quintile of 1.2 per cent per annum. The five columns thus look exactly like steps in a ladder. However, income differentials widened dramatically within the top 20 per cent as well. The top 1 per cent more than doubled its real income in this period, a gain of almost 4 per cent a year. In other words, while the growth of American real income slowed dramatically, that of the top one per cent accelerated to one and a half times the 1947–73 rate.

Detailed calculations by Mishel and Bernstein showed that average real family income grew in the USA from $18,100 in 1947 to $36,900 in 1973. But in the next 20 years it grew to only $38,400.[18] Almost the whole of this small increase in income resulted from the fact that in the 1990s there were many more families with two income-earners than there were in the 1950s. On an average, women worked 32 per cent more hours per year in

1993 than they were doing in 1973. This helped to offset a sharp drop in the real incomes of blue-collar workers and those without college degrees. Mishel and Bernstein divide the growth of income inequality into two phases. The defining development in the first phase (which began in the early 1980s) was that incomes fell for the bottom 60 per cent of families, while there was an extraordinary 63 per cent income growth for the top one per cent of families. This same disparity was also evident in wealth trends, as the wealth (i.e., ownership of assets) of the upper 1 per cent of families grew by 54 per cent while the net worth of the bottom 60 per cent of families actually declined.[19] The brunt of the fall in real wages was borne by high school graduates and dropouts. The former suffered an erosion of 12.7 per cent in their average real wages, while the latter group experienced an 18.2 per cent fall. However, during this period the wages of college graduates increased by 2.8 per cent.

From 1987, however, the US entered a second phase of income inequality. This time round, the white-collar workers and college graduates too felt the pain of declining real wages. The wages of college graduates fell by 3.1 per cent between 1987 and 1991. Men suffered more than women, experiencing a 4.9 per cent drop. The hourly wages of white-collar workers also fell by 3.5 per cent for men and 2.1 per cent for women between 1987 and 1991.[20] This was partly caused by difficulties that hit a number of service industries, especially finance and real estate, in the early 1990s, but a large part of the decline in wages resulted from 'restructuring'. Earlier restructuring hit mainly the blue-collar workers. From the late 1980s and early 1990s, as banks, train and airline reservations and accounting were computerised, it hit white-collar workers too. In the 1990s information technology replaced human beings with computers higher and higher up the corporate ladder. From making, sending and collecting bills and reconciling accounts, to dispensing cash at banks, to writing wills, divorce contracts, invoices and letters of credit, and to managing funds, maintaining charts and spread-sheets and taking decisions to buy and sell huge volumes of stock, computers began to do what humans used to till only a few years earlier. The result was large-scale white-collar redundancy. Corporate executives who had to fire hundreds of their colleagues began to coin euphemisms for what they were doing. Among the most popular was 'downsizing'.

Statistics cannot capture the change that has taken place in people's lives. A nationwide sample survey by the *New York Times* supplemented by extensive interviews and reports showed that while permanent layoffs used to take place only during recessions, in the 1990s they continued in the same large numbers during the first five years of the recovery that followed the short sharp recession of 1990–91. The survey also confirmed the trend of a deterioration of the white-collar job market, noted by Mishel and

Bernstein in the late 1980s. In the 1990s, workers with college degrees who had lost their jobs outnumbered in absolute terms those with high school diplomas or less. Most disturbing of all, those earning more than 50,000 dollars a year accounted for twice the share of those laid off as compared to the early 1980s.[21]

To put it briefly, computers were replacing competent middle managers, who performed important functions that did not require them to exercise a great deal of judgement and discretion. These were typically men and women in their forties and fifties, with families, mortgages on their homes, and children in private schools; in short, those in the throes of building the future not only for themselves but—in terms of new homes and a new generation of Americans—for the country. For them the ground on which they had stood for most of their lives turned into quicksand. The *New York Times*' sample survey showed that 19 million out of the 43 million who lost their jobs admitted that this had precipitated a major crisis in their lives. For most of them it had meant a loss of identity and self-respect, a re-definition of their relationships with peers who had escaped the axe (and gravitation towards others who had not), a withdrawal from community life, the forced sale of homes, the withdrawal of children from schools, and, in a disturbingly high proportion of cases, divorce and the break-up of the family.

As the *New York Times*' writers put it:

> The result is the most acute job insecurity since the Depression. And this in turn has produced an unrelenting angst that is shattering peoples' notions of work and self and the very promise of tomorrow ... The job apprehension has intruded everywhere, diluting self worth, splintering families, fragmenting communities, altering the chemistry of work places, roiling political agendas and rubbing salt on the very soul of the country.[22]

Hutton's description of contemporary Britain is equally poignant:

> One in three of the nation's children grows up in poverty. In 1991, one twenty-one year old in five was innumerate, one in seven was illiterate. The prison population is the highest in Europe ... The country is increasingly divided against itself with an arrogant officer class apparently indifferent to the other ranks it commands. This privileged class is favoured with education, jobs, housing and pensions. At the other end of the scale more and more people discover that they are the new working poor, or live off the state in semi-poverty. Their paths out of this situation are closing down as the world in which they are trapped becomes meaner, harder and more corrupting. In between are growing numbers of people who are insecure, fearful of losing their jobs in an age of permanent downsizing, cost-cutting and 'casualisation' and ever more worried about their ability to maintain a decent standard of living.[23]

These trends added up to a pattern that economic historians would have had no trouble in recognising. What Karl Polanyi had called the 'self-regulating market' was being reborn. Workers had lost their security. They were losing their place in society and once more becoming a 'factor of production'. And like the Manchester liberals of the first half of the nineteenth century, neo-liberal economists who lauded 'wage flexibility' had sided with the boardrooms of the giant corporations and forgotten the social costs. They were able to do so because the employers did not have to bear the cost. Workers who lost their jobs, on the other hand, often had to move to another town or locality to find a new one. In two-income families, now virtually the rule in America, this separated husbands from wives. In one-income families, it forced children to change schools. It therefore disrupted families and communities, as parents and children lost their friends. In extreme cases it ended by destroying the family. At the individual level, therefore, there is little wage flexibility—only the pain of displacement.

Neo-Classical Economics: A Refusal to Face the Truth

Chronic, non-cyclical unemployment was a new experience for the industrialised countries. Throughout the nearly two centuries of industrial capitalism, unemployment had been transient, caused by cyclical recessions. In fact, both in Europe and North America industrialisation had created a constant and seemingly insatiable demand for labour that had to be met through immigration. One result of this was a remarkable paucity of models in economic theory that explained the growth of employment, as opposed to the growth of production. Classical economics simply assumed that in the long run factor prices reflected their relative abundance or scarcity, and that the drive to maximise profits resulted in the development of technologies that made the fullest use of both. Full employment was a natural outcome of the equilibrium that was attained under conditions of perfect, or at least high, levels of competition. The chronic and rising levels of unemployment that remained through boom and bust therefore had economists at their wits' end trying to find an explanation.

Many economists pointed to the much lower rate of unemployment in the US as compared to the European Union (5.4 per cent against over 10.1 per cent for the EU in 1996), and claimed that the Europeans had only themselves to blame. Taking their cue from neo-classical economics, they argued that Europe's strong social legislation and highly organised trade unions had prevented the real wage rate from declining. Coining a new concept, the NAIRU—the Non-Accelerating Inflation Rate of

Unemployment—they claimed that the US had achieved the lowest rate of unemployment that was compatible with price stability (i.e., something close to full employment), because wages were far more flexible there than in any of the other industrialised countries. They buttressed this argument by pointing out that while the US may have erased 43 million jobs between 1979 and 1995, it had created no less than 70 million jobs during the same period. This was in dramatic contrast to Europe, where in most countries the unemployment rate has risen sharply despite an absolute decline or near-stagnation in the size of the labour force.

The argument that wage rigidity was at the bottom of Europe's woes, as well as of chronic unemployment in general, was endorsed by an OECD study which showed a clear, if weak, correlation between the flexibility of wages and the level of unemployment. The US, with the highest degree of inequality had the lowest growth of unemployment. Germany and France, where wage differentials actually decreased between 1980 and 1995, had the highest levels of unemployment.[24] The experience of the US since 1995 seemingly reinforced this finding. Fuelled by continuing strong growth, unemployment had fallen to a yearly average of 4.2 in 1999.[25] Wages however showed almost no tendency to rise, confirming that they had remained highly flexible.

But detailed surveys showed that the flexibility of wages in the US lauded by the OECD study was somewhat of a statistical abstraction. Truman Bewlay of the Harvard Business School found that despite the two recessions of the 1980s and early 1990s, American firms were not as a rule implementing wage freezes and cuts and not hiring the unemployed at lower wages. His survey of 183 employers in Connecticut in 1992 showed that they were reluctant to fire workers even during a recession because this demoralised the workforce and lowered its productivity. But they were also unwilling to hire new workers at lower wages, because 'a two-tier pay system would cause internal inequities which would be resented by new employees and hurt their morale.' The survey also found that the unemployed had great difficulty in finding new jobs even if they accepted a wage cut, because employers considered them over-qualified for the jobs that were available. Not only would this upset the internal hierarchy of rewards and skills, but the new employees would be among the first to leave when times improved and more jobs became available. As a result only employers who accepted a very high turnover of employees were ready to take such workers on. Most often these were temporary-work agencies.[26]

Bewlay's finding confirmed another finding by Michael Podgursky, based upon an analysis of the data collected by the US Bureau of Labour Statistics. Podgursky found that the main reason why two-thirds of those re-employed found themselves earning less than before was that almost half of them had to make do with part-time employment. 43 per cent of the blue-collar and 36 per cent of the white-collar workers could find only part-time work.[27] The illusion that the average wage rate had fallen arose because the proportion of the workforce in low-paid jobs had risen. Workers earned less when they shifted from the manufacturing sector to the services sector or switched involuntarily from full-time to part-time work, and when employers 'downsized' by firing senior employees and getting their work done by younger employees who earned a fraction of their salaries.[28]

De-industrialisation of the High-Wage Economies

Most of the distress in the labour market arose from two developments: a large-scale destruction of jobs in the manufacturing sector (often described as the hollowing-out of the industrialised economies) and the need to move out of manufacturing into the services sector to find alternate jobs. The distress did not arise because the share of employment in the manufacturing sector had gone down and that of services had gone up—this was an inevitable consequence of economic growth. According to the OECD job study, the share of employment in manufacturing began to fall in Germany in 1972, in France in 1973, in Finland in 1980, in Belgium as far back as 1961, in Italy in 1978, in the UK in 1962, and in the US around 1966. In Japan it reached a peak in 1973 and levelled off slightly below it in 1978.[29] However, with the exception of the UK, till the mid- to late 1970s (and in a few of the OECD countries till well into the 1980s), the decline in the industrial workforce was relative and not absolute. In practice this meant that workers who lost their jobs in industry because of technological change seldom had to shift out of the industrial sector to find new jobs. The change in the employment share of the two sectors took place because most of the new jobs were being created in the services sector.

On the other hand, distress arose in the mid- to late 1970s because the pattern changed: the job loss in manufacturing became absolute. Table 3.4 gives the number of workers employed in manufacturing in the larger industrialised and developing countries in 1980 and 1990.

Once employment in the manufacturing sector began to decline in absolute numbers, fewer and fewer of those who lost their jobs were able to find another within the manufacturing sector, and more and more of them had to settle for jobs in the services sector. With only a few exceptions, these were more poorly paid and less secure than the manufacturing jobs that the workers had lost. Finally, some of those laid off by industry could not find work in the tertiary sector either on any terms or terms that were acceptable to them. These workers either dropped out of the workforce

Table 3.4
Manufacturing Employment in Selected Industrialised Countries (in Thousands)

Country	1980	1990
France	5,103	4,243
Germany	7,229	7,119
Italy	3,333	2,858
Ireland	225	194
Spain	2,303	1,907
UK	6,462	4,785
USA	19,210	17,498

Source: Marlita A. Reddy (ed.), *Statistical Abstract of the World*, 2nd Edition (Detroit, Michigan, GALE, 1996).

or became unemployed. These facts were starkly revealed by two surveys of displaced workers carried out by Michael Podgursky, based upon the data gathered by the US Bureau of Labour Statistics in 1984 and 1986. The surveys showed that to find jobs, workers had to go out of industry altogether. In the nine industry categories tracked by the Bureau of Labour Statistics, *two-thirds of all re-employed workers were able to find jobs only by changing industries. And two thirds of these were able to find jobs only after accepting a large pay cut. The 1986 survey found that only 32 per cent of blue-collar and 39 per cent of white-collar workers had found equally (or better) paid jobs. At the other end of the spectrum, 17 and 15 per cent of them found themselves earning less than half their former wages.*[30]

Even if the neo-classical thesis on wage flexibility had been correct, it still evaded answering the key question: how had the US and Europe achieved very high rates of economic growth with very low rates of unemployment in conditions of equal or greater wage rigidity between 1945 and 1973? What had changed since then? What was the engine that had driven high economic growth in the earlier period but ceased quite suddenly to do so in the 70s? To this query economists had no ready answer.

Notes

1. Charles Maier, 'Democracy and its Discontents', *Foreign Affairs*, July/August 1994, pp. 48–64.
2. Ethan B. Kapstein, 'Workers and the World Economy', *Foreign Affairs*, May/June 1996, pp. 16–37.
3. OECD, *Historical Statistics* (Paris, OECD, 1996), p. 50, Table 3.1. Each of these periods happens to contain both an economic upswing and a downturn. Trade cycle effects have therefore been broadly netted out.
4. OECD, *Economic Outlook* (Paris, OECD, December 1995).
5. OECD, *Main Economic Indicators* (Paris: OECD, June 2004).

6. Lawrence Mishel and Jared Bernstein, *The State of Working America 1992–93* (Washington DC, Economic Policy Institute, 1993), pp. 5, 216–219.
7. Ibid.
8. Lawrence Mishel, Jared Bernstein and John Schmitt, *The State of Working America 1996–97* (Washington DC, Economic Policy Institute), p. 8.
9. Jonathan Wadsworth, 'Terrible Waste', *New Economy*, Vol. 1, Spring 1994; quoted in Will Hutton, *The State We Are In* (London, Vintage Books, 1996), p. 1.
10. Michael Barratt-Brown, *Models in Political Economy* (UK, Penguin Books, 1995), p. 78.
11. The poverty level is defined as being 40 per cent of the median wage level in the economy.
12. Mishel and Bernstein, *The State of Working America 1992–93*, p. 17.
13. *The Economist*, 'Survey of the World Economy', *The Economist*, 28 September 1996, p. 24.
14. Ibid.
15. Hutton, *The State We Are In*, p. 7.
16. Paul Krugman, *The Age of Diminished Expectations*, 3rd edition (Cambridge, Mass., MIT Press), p. 23.
17. This has been referred to by Claudia Goldin as 'The Great Compression'. Quoted by Krugman, ibid.
18. Mishel and Bernstein, *The State of Working America 1992–93*, p. 32.
19. Mishel and Bernstein, *The State of Working America 1992–93*, p. 15.
20. Ibid., p. 14.
21. Louis Uchitelle and N.R. Kleinfeld, in *The Downsizing of America. A Special Report* (New York, Times Books, 1996), p. 5.
22. Ibid., pp. 6–7.
23. Hutton, *The State We Are In*, pp. 2–3.
24. OECD, *OECD Jobs Study: Investment Productivity and Employment* (Paris: OECD). Reproduced in *The Economist*, 'Survey of the World Economy', p. 24. A chart showing the rise of income inequality is to be found in Mishel, Bernstein and Schmitt, *The State of Working America 1996–97*, p. 397.
25. US Bureau of Labour Statistics data: Employment status of civilian non-institutional population 1999.
26. Hutton, *The State We Are In*, p. 101. The research findings of the survey by Prof. Truman Bewlay of Harvard were presented to the Happiness Conference at the London School of Economics, November 1993.
27. Michael Podgursky, 'Job Displacement and Labour Market Adjustment: Evidence from the Displaced Worker Surveys', in R.M. Cyert and D.C. Mowery (eds.), *The Impact of Technological Change on Economic Growth* (Cambridge, MA, Ballinger Publishing Company, 1988). Cited in OECD, *OECD Jobs Study*, p. 47.
28. Podgursky, 'Job Displacement and Labour Market Adjustment', p. 47. Podgursky also found that:

   • 60 per cent of the workers laid off came from goods producing industries, although these industries accounted for only 34 per cent of the full-time adult workforce. Workers in durable goods industries made up 32 per cent of those laid off, although these industries employed only 15 per cent of the workforce. The 1984 survey showed that of the workers who had been laid off between 1979 and 1982, only 67 per cent of the blue-collar and 75 per cent of the white-collar workers had found employment by January 1984, i.e., two to five years later.

- 12 per cent of both groups had withdrawn from the workforce, and another 21 per cent of blue-collar and 13 per cent of white-collar workers remained unemployed.
- With the long economic upswing of the post-1983 years, the situation improved somewhat. The 1986 survey showed that 75 per cent of the blue-collar and 80 per cent of the white-collar workers laid off between 1981 and 1984 had found jobs. But that still left a quarter of the former and a fifth of the latter who had not. Podgursky found that in January 1984 the median duration of unemployment (for those that did find jobs) was 29.6 weeks for the blue-collar workers and 14.5 weeks for the white-collar workers. Despite the upswing that followed, these figures improved only marginally in 1986.

29. OECD, *OECD Jobs Study*, pp. 52–53, Chart 1.2.
30. See Podgursky, 'Job Displacement and Labour Market Adjustment', cited in OECD, *OECD Jobs Study*, p. 47.

4

Seven Explanations for the End of the Golden Age

The sudden and disconcerting changes in the economies of the industrialised countries set off a frantic search for explanations. Some, like minor actors in a Shakespearan play, came on stage, played their parts, and were seen no more. Others gained a wide measure of acceptance, but were either disproved or shown to be less than complete by future developments. No explanation did more than clutch at the coat-tails of a transformation that was too vast—and too much in the process of revealing itself—to be fully comprehended.

In all, no fewer than seven hypotheses were put forward to explain the onset of economic disorder described in the previous chapter. Two of these were specifically related to the US and reflected the effort of the Republicans to make political hay out of the Democrats' discomfiture during the Carter Presidency (1976–1980). Twenty years later these are of only historical interest, but for the record they were:

1. The slowdown in the growth of productivity was caused by the arrival of the post-war generation on the job market in the late 1960s and early 1970s. These young people simply did not want to work hard. They had been born into relative affluence, and were therefore much less highly motivated than their G.I. bill-educated fathers. A perceptible decline in educational standards and the beginnings of a social collapse compounded this.
2. It was caused by a loss of inclination to work and save, brought on by high taxation, inflation, and excessive regulation. All these made people discount the future very heavily over the present. This could be set right (and growth accelerated once more) only by lowering

taxation, especially of those with a capacity to save and invest, reducing the budget deficit and cutting down the size of government.

The sheer illogic of these arguments was exposed by Paul Krugman. Reducing taxes would increase the budget deficit. To offset this, the federal government would have to cut expenditure savagely. But since these cuts would reduce the incomes of the poor who are the main recipients of federal welfare grants and subsidies, and since the poor consume the greatest part of their income, this would reduce demand and lower the growth of output. That would narrow the tax base, and reduce tax revenues. The budget deficit would therefore either not decrease or decrease very little.[1] Whatever effect lower taxes had on the willingness to save and invest would therefore be swamped by the deflationary impact on demand. But the goal of the protagonists of these theories was political and not economic, and in achieving it they were eminently successful.

There were, however, five serious attempts to explain the simultaneous slowdown of growth and the rise of income inequality and unemployment in the industrialised world. These were:

1. It was a result of the sudden increase in petroleum prices in 1973 and again in 1979. By itself this hypothesis did not gain much credence among professional economists. But it was widely touted in the popular press in the late 1970s and early 1980s because it coincided with and sharpened the impact of other changes that had begun in the late 1960s.
2. The disorder was brought on by three simultaneous developments:

   - A squeeze on profits at the end of the 1960s caused by near full employment;
   - The breakdown of US hegemony in the international economy, which was reflected by its refusal to back its currency with gold in 1971 and its subsequent decision to delink the dollar from gold altogether; and, finally,
   - A shift of paradigm about the nature and function of the state.

The first development lowered the productivity of the worker (who had little to fear if he lost a particular job because he could always get another), even while it strengthened the trade unions. This gave rise to wage demands, squeezed profits, and slowed down investment. The second development triggered inflation during the 1970s. The third development led, in essence, to the replacement of full employment by the maintenance of price stability as the central goal of government policy.[2] This gave rise to an entire industry devoted to calculating the minimum rate of unemployment that was compatible with price stability. Their findings were enshrined as the NAIRU (Non-Accelerating Inflation Rate of Unemployment). This was believed to be around 6 per cent of the workforce for mature industrialised countries. The three developments led to the adoption of high interest rate policies that slowed down growth and permanently raised the level of unemployment.

3. The slowdown of growth in particular was an inevitable by-product of successful economic development. Economic growth leads to a decline in the share of industry—more specifically, manufacturing—in total employment. This happens first in proportionate but later in absolute terms. It also leads to a corresponding increase of employment in the services sector. Since labour productivity grows much more slowly in the services sector, this change of proportions brings down the overall rate of growth of labour productivity in the economy, and therefore the rate of growth of GDP. This happens without any slowdown in the rate of technological change. The mature industrial economies therefore simply needed to accept that their growth will slow down and remain slow.

4. The slowdown reflected an exhaustion of investment opportunities, as one Schumpeterian long wave of technological change in industry drew to an end and another had yet to set in. As a result, there was a fall in the return on capital, and a slowing down of investment.

5. The last—and, among liberal economists, least acceptable—explanation was that the all three adverse developments in the mature industrialised countries were the consequences of 'globalisation', a profound and not very well-understood change in the global economy that is still far from complete. The 'de-industrialisation' that the highly industrialised countries were experiencing went far beyond the natural decline in the share of industry in employment as described above. The decline of employment in manufacturing was not just relative but absolute. It was thus 'hollowing out' industry in these countries. The cause was a decline in the competitiveness of the manufactures of the OECD countries in relation to those being produced in the newly industrialised countries. This was reflected by rising trade deficits in the developed countries, a rapid and growing penetration of their markets by cheaply produced manufactures from the newly industrialised countries, and the emergence of structural, non-cyclical unemployment. This very same process was responsible for the near miraculous rates of growth experienced by East and Southeast Asia, and the high growth pockets in many Latin American countries. The engine behind both was not just technology,

as was frequently claimed, but a specific anomaly that did not exist in the nineteenth century. This was that while capital is as free to move across international boundaries as it had been in the nineteenth century, labour, which had also moved freely then, was no longer able to do so.

False Theories?

The Oil Price Shock and the Paradigm Shift

The oil price shock and the paradigm shift theories reinforced each other. By the late 1960s the industrialised countries had experienced, virtually uninterrupted for almost a quarter of a century, the highest rate of growth they had ever known. Unemployment levels were lower than they had ever been, and the job market had become very tight. Trade unions had grown in strength with the tightening of the labour market, and the high rates of growth of productivity and output had made it possible for employers to accommodate their demands without too much difficulty. But by the end of the 1960s in the US and the early 1970s in Europe, cost-push inflation brought on by strong trade union demands had become a serious problem. A recession was probably already on the way in 1973 when OPEC quadrupled oil prices for the first time. The immediate impact of the oil price hikes was to cause a sharp deterioration in the terms of trade of the OECD countries. The USA, which was importing 14 per cent of its oil in 1973, suffered the least, and Japan, which was almost entirely dependent for its energy on imported oil, suffered the most. Between 1973 and 1979, terms of trade worsened by an average of 6.4 per cent per annum for Japan, by 1.4 per cent per annum for Germany, and by 2.4 per cent for Italy.[3] As consumers were forced to pay more for oil, they spent less on other products. This deepened the recession of 1974. But higher oil prices also pushed up costs and therefore fed cost-push inflation from another direction. Since trade unions continued to press for higher wages in the face of rising costs of living, the result was a dual push on prices that pushed inflation still higher. On top of that, several governments tried to combat recession by using the Keynesian technique of pump priming, which had worked so well during the depression of the thirties. The three effects converged to give Europe and the US the highest rates of inflation they had ever experienced.

The 1973–74 recession turned out to be brief. The immediate decline in consumption caused by the rise in oil prices was partially offset by a sharp rise in exports to the oil exporting countries and a dramatic recovery of the industrialised countries' terms of trade. Their economies therefore began to respond from 1975 onwards, although at a very high cost in terms of inflation. It was an experience that the industrialised countries did not wish to repeat. The 1970s thus ended with the firm belief that Keynesian monetary policies had exacerbated stagflation.[4] This led to the paradigm shift from maintaining full employment to maintaining price stability, to which Marglin and Schorr traced the end of the Golden Age of capitalism. In 1979, when OPEC virtually quadrupled its oil prices again, the US reacted by adopting a tight money policy that raised prime interest rates to an unprecedented 16 per cent in 1980. Europe was forced to follow suit, and this plunged the mature industrialised countries into another sharp, and this time longer, recession that did not end till 1983 in the US and 1984 in Europe.

But in the end the oil price shock and the paradigm shift were unable to explain all the changes that were taking place. They explained the trade cycles of the decade after 1973, and the slowdown of productivity growth in the 1970s. But they were unable to explain why an equally dramatic decline in oil prices from $35 a barrel or more in 1981 to around $12 a barrel in 1986 and a six-year economic recovery from 1983 to 1989 did not reverse the rising trend in unemployment and income inequality and the progressive softening of the labour market.

The paradigm shift argument in particular raised several awkward questions that it could not answer. We know that the shift did take place. We also know that after the traumatic experience of inflation in the 1970s and early 1980s, few people were willing to go back to a situation where it could recur. But why did the willingness to sacrifice full employment at the altar of price stability not disappear when the collapse of oil prices in 1986 and the rise of chronic unemployment ended the conditions that had given birth to it? Why did the choice of price stability over employment become virtually a knee-jerk reflex among policymakers in all the OECD countries? What made price stability of such critical importance that governments were willing to live with 6–12 per cent unemployment rather than risk even mild inflation again? And why did breaking the power of the unions become the preferred way of achieving price stability? Something else was happening, which these explanations did not capture.

Slow Growth as a Product of Economic Maturity

The view that found the most general acceptance was that the slowdown in growth was an unavoidable by-product of economic maturity. In the US, this view was popularised by Paul Krugman in his book, *The Age of Diminished Expectations*.[5] The theory rested upon a statistical finding that has become a truism of economics. As nations industrialise, productivity

Table 4.1
Average Growth of Labour Productivity by Sectors for Six Countries (UK, USA, France, Germany, the Netherlands and Japan), 1913–87 (Annual Average Compound Growth Rate), and Level of Output per Person as Percentage of Average for the Whole Economy in 1987

Sector	1913–50	1950–73	1973–87	Output Level (1987)
Agriculture	1.1	5.9	3.5	70
Industry	1.2	5.6	2.5	120
Services	0.4	2.5	1.1	95

Source: Angus Maddison, 'Dynamic Forces in Capitalist Development. A Long-Run Comparative View (Oxford University Press, 1991), Tables 5.13 and 5.14, pp. 150–151.

grows far more slowly in the services sector than in industry and, for that matter, agriculture.

As a result, even when agricultural and industrial output increase solely because of rises in productivity, some part of the additional production can be distributed and utilised within the country only if more people are employed in the services sector. Over time, therefore, increases in *product-ivity* in the primary and secondary sectors of the economy lead to increases in *employment* in the tertiary sector. More and more of the labour force therefore comes to be employed in the latter. Thus, even when there is no fall in the rate of growth of productivity in any of the three sectors, the average labour productivity of the economy will fall, since it is the weighted average of the productivity in the three sectors.[6] The thesis of industrial maturity therefore more than suffices to explain the slowdown of industrial growth.

What it cannot explain is why slower growth should be accompanied by the emergence of permanent non-cyclical unemployment, or a widening gap in incomes, *for so long as productivity grows more slowly in the services sector than in the industrial (and agricultural) sector, maturity should lead to growing labour shortages and not to labour redundancy.*[7]

Development and Employment

This can be shown with the help of a simple model. Let us first assume that we are talking of a closed economy, i.e., one which indulges in no trade. So long as productivity rises faster in the material sectors of the economy than in services, there can be no unemployment, for the reason given above.[8] In the early stages of industrialisation, the demand for labour from manufacturing *and* the service industries will be met by labour released from agriculture and from domestic and personal service. To offset the drain of labour from the countryside, farmers will employ machines, thus automatically raising productivity in agriculture. Once all the valets, cooks and maids have become factory or office workers and the supply of labour in agriculture is exhausted, and if productivity in manufacturing keeps rising, the additional demand for labour from the *service* industries can only be met by allowing immigration. Even if technological progress in industry is so rapid that it actually throws some workers out of work, they will immediately find work in the services sector because, with lower productivity, more hands will be needed there than will be released by industry. What is more, the tightness of the labour market will ensure that workers in the services sector do not earn much less than their counterparts in industry.

Dropping the assumption of a closed economy and bringing the model closer to reality by introducing export and import trade does not alter its basic features as long as the trade is balanced. As the industrialised economy nears full employment, wage rates start to rise. Industries with a higher-value-added product can afford to pay more. They therefore start drawing away workers from industries with a lower-value-added product. Workers at the lower end of agriculture and the less sophisticated industries move to more sophisticated ones. The low-value-added products that cease to be produced are then imported and paid for with high-value-added products. Much the same thing happens in tradable services.

International trade is therefore no more than an import of the scarce factor of production embodied in goods and tradable services, and an export of the abundant factor of production in the same manner. International trade performs this function well so long as the factors of production are embodied in tradable goods. For example, raw materials and simple manufactures, which are usually produced with cheap labour, have been routinely exchanged for manufactured goods, to the benefit of both trading partners.

But most services are not tradable, for they are consumed the moment they are produced. They cannot therefore enter into international trade.[9] As a result, trade cannot fully make good the shortage of labour in a rapidly growing industrial economy. Even an open economy is therefore left with no option but to increase the workforce—specifically, the share of it employed in the services sector. It can do this by drawing a larger part of the population into the workforce, for instance by increasing the female labour force or drawing in school- and college-goers as part-time help. When even this does not suffice, immigration becomes unavoidable. This immigration takes place both legally and illegally, and both take place by design. A market rapidly develops for illegal immigrants because productivity at the lower end of the services sector is so low that illegal immigrants are the only people who are prepared to work at wages low enough to make the services viable.

The above model is a not inaccurate description of the conditions that existed in Europe and North America before 1973. As Table 4.1 shows, between 1950 and 1973 labour productivity in six large OECD countries (USA, Japan, Germany, France, UK and the Netherlands) grew by 5.9 and 5.6 per cent per annum in industry and agriculture respectively, but by only 2.5 per cent per annum in services. The unemployment rate during the latter part of this period (1964–73) was 2.7 per cent for the European Union and 4.7 per cent for the US.[10] During this period both Europe and the USA experienced high rates of immigration. Between 1965 and 1990 the percentage of population that was foreign-born rose from 6.0 per cent to 8.6 per cent in the US and Canada, and from 3.3 per cent to 5 per cent in Europe.[11] It was only after 1980—when it had become clear that the slowdown in OECD growth was not temporary, and unemployment rose to 7.2 per cent for the US (1980–89) and 9.3 per cent for the EU—that curbs on immigration began to be contemplated. In Europe the rate of immigration fell dramatically from 0.5 per cent per annum between 1970 and 1980 to 0.1 per cent between 1980 and 1985.[12]

The Schumpeterian Long Wave Hypothesis

Neo-liberals who have embraced globalisation with open arms have advanced another version of Krugman's 'grin and bear it' theory, but with an upward twist to its tail. Technological innovation moves in long waves. Ever since the industrial revolution, every 60 or 70 years a host of technical inventions in unrelated fields suddenly mesh together to bring about a dramatic jump in the range of possibilities open to mankind. This triggers a spate of derived technological change, or innovation, that pushes up human productivity at an electrifying pace. This spate of innovation makes tried and tested methods of production obsolete and threatens established enterprises with bankruptcy. The only way for them to survive is to junk perfectly sound existing machinery, install the new cutting-edge machines and adopt managerial and human resource training practices appropriate to their functioning. Those that fail to do so are driven out of business. Schumpeter called these bursts of innovation 'gales of creative destruction'.[13]

The next few decades see a widespread diffusion of the new innovation to less dynamic producers and from advanced to backward areas. All these result in a step up in the rate of growth of productivity and output that lasts for several decades. Eventually the impetus begins to flag. Most of the potential created by the original inventions has been exhausted.[14] Further increases in productivity come to depend more and more upon marginal improvements in existing applications of the new technologies. Inevitably the rate of growth of productivity slows down.

The period from roughly 1930 to 1950 saw a phenomenal burst of invention in very different fields. Coal was replaced by oil as a primary fuel; steam power was replaced by electricity as the motive force of manufacture; long distance telephone calls became possible; and commercial aviation made its debut. In the realm of medicine came the development of antibiotics. Perhaps most important of all, the very end of the 1920s saw the advent of 'Fordist' mass production, which brought down the price of manufacturing and assembling automobiles to a fraction of what it was under the older system of craft production. In the next 50 years these inventions were turned into innovation by industry, first in the US and after the war in Europe.

By the end of the 1960s, most of the juice had been sucked out of the wave of innovation that began in the late 1920s and 1930s. Oil had almost entirely replaced coal as the primary source of energy; the price of a transatlantic three minute phone call had come down (in 1990 dollars) from $250 in 1930 to $5 or thereabouts in 1980 (by the mid-90s it had fallen further to only about $2).[15] Air transport costs had virtually bottomed out by 1980 with the universal use of wide-bodied jets. Automobile design too was close to an optimum. Although improvements in efficiency and safety continued, they were no longer reflected in price. Most important of all, Fordism (i.e., assembly line techniques of mass production) had been fully absorbed not only by Europe but by the entire industrialised world. The only major development beyond Fordism took place in Japan, which led the world in the development of 'flexible' and 'lean' production and on this strength clawed its way into the front rank of industrialised countries. The decline in growth of productivity and output in the 1970s and 1980s reflected this 'technological exhaustion'.

But that long downswing is over. According to this theory, the world has entered a new Long Wave. This one is based upon developments in the fields of communication and information processing. Satellite communication has made it possible for people in a dozen countries to hold video conferences several times a day if necessary and coordinate decision-making on production and marketing in different parts of the world to an extent that was unthinkable only two decades ago. The development of the computer goes back to the Second World War. But the worldwide dissemination of this technology has followed a reduction in the cost of processing information by 10,000 times between 1975 and 1995 (and further dramatic declines since then).[16]

The combination of the computer and the satellite has created the internet. In September 1996 there were 30 computers to every 100 Americans.[17] In August 1999, there were 107.3 million internet users in Canada and the USA alone. According to one survey carried out in 1999, 62 per cent of the adult population of the US was likely to be connected through the internet in 2003.[18] But the actual growth was even faster. By May 2004, the 'digital media universe' in the US had gone up to more than 205 million users or about 80 per cent of all Americans, regardless of age.[19]

Neo-liberals ascribe the nine-year-long upswing in the US economy (from 1991 to the end of the century) to the percolation of the IT revolution into the workplace. The most recent estimates of labour productivity bear this out, for throughout the 1990s and especially since 1997, labour productivity in the US has risen at a rate that had not been witnessed for 30 years.[20] They frankly confess that they do not know what society will look like when the 'Transformation', as Peter Drucker calls it, is over.[21] They hold on nonetheless to the belief that whatever it will be like, it will be better than what society has been so far. As Giddens has pointed out, this blind faith in science and technology, and the necessary goodness of change is no more than a rebirth of radicalism. But this time the rebirth has taken place in the boardrooms of 'monopoly capital' and not the beer halls of the trade unionists. In the topsyturvy world of globalisation, Right has become Left, and Left has become Right.[22]

The slowdown of technological change in the 1970s explains the decline in the growth of total factor productivity in the same decade that was referred to in the previous chapter. But it is at best only part of the explanation, for it runs up against one insurmountable hurdle: most if not all the technological and managerial advances that accounted for the last long wave have occurred in (or been applied first in) manufacturing. So the exhaustion of one long wave and the beginning of another should have revealed itself first in the manufacturing industries. *But in the USA at least there was no slowdown of productivity growth worth the name in manufacturing after 1973.* Robert Z. Lawrence has pointed out in the US manufacturing productivity rose between 1979 and 1989 at exactly the same rate—2.7 per cent per annum—as it did between 1955 and 1973.[23] The significance of this apparent anomaly is discussed in greater detail below.

What the Schumpeterian hypothesis also cannot explain is why slow growth should have led to unemployment and rising income inequalities. It fails to surmount the same theoretical hurdle that the 'maturity' hypothesis faced, i.e., that so long as the growth of productivity in industry remains faster than in the services sector, even slower overall growth must get reflected in a tightening and not slackening of the labour market, for fewer people will be laid off in industry than will be needed to distribute and otherwise service the products of industry. There will therefore be a tendency for wages in the services sector to converge with those in industry, instead of diverging from them.

A False Presumption

To sum up therefore, all four theories examined above can explain the slow-down of growth in the 1970s. But none of them is able to explain the simultaneous rise of chronic (i.e., non-cyclical) unemployment and the widening of income inequalities after a century of convergence. It is there-fore necessary to look for another explanation. One possibility that has been overlooked so far is that there is something wrong with the question economists have been asking. All the economists who have studied the slowdown have assumed that chronic unemployment and widening of in-come inequalities were consequences of the slowdown of growth. They have therefore focused exclusively on finding an answer to 'The Slow Growth Mystery'. This assumption may be wrong. It is perfectly possible that while industrial maturity, technological exhaustion and the paradigm shift in economic policy from full employment to price stability have been responsible for the slower growth of output and productivity, the rise of unemployment and growing income inequality have been caused by some-thing entirely different. The rest of this chapter is devoted to showing that this is the explanation that most closely fits all the facts.

The De-industrialisation Thesis

That only hypothesis that explains all the three developments is the pro-gressive 'de-industrialisation' or 'hollowing out' of industry in the highly industrialised countries—a phenomenon that is a direct outcome of glob-alisation. The hollowing-out is a product specifically of trade with the newly industrialised countries, whose exports of manufactures—especially manufactures that require lower levels of skills in the workforce—are mak-ing heavy inroads into the domestic markets of the OECD countries. This is happening because capital is moving there to produce more cheaply what used to be previously produced at home. It is able to do so because labour-cost differences between industrialised and developing countries have increased on the one hand and transport costs have come tumbling down on the other. It has therefore become profitable to supply even home markets from offshore production sites where labour is cheap.

The 'de-industrialisation' thesis is two decades old. Concern about 'hol-lowing out' first surfaced in the United Kingdom.[24] The share of manu-facturing in total civilian employment fell very gradually from 38.4 per cent in 1960 to 34.6 per cent in 1974. But thereafter it plummeted to 26.2 per cent in 1983, and continued to fall rapidly to 20.2 per cent in 1993. In absolute terms employment in manufacturing fell from 7.1 million in 1971 to 4.5 million in June 1992.[25] While there was full employment in the UK in the 1950s, in 1983 three million people were out of work. The UK also experienced a fall in manufacturing output of 18 per cent between 1973 and 1982, against a rise of 15 per cent for the OECD countries as a whole. As a result of this, the bulk of the UK's increase in GDP of 2 per cent per annum came from the discovery of oil in the North Sea. The UK's non-oil GDP actually fell by 2 per cent between 1973 and 1983.[26]

The steep decline in manufacturing employment and output created a near panic in Britain. Michael Smith and Jane Renton captured this mood in *The Observer* in September 1992:

> Overall, Britain's manufacturing industry has been in continuous decline since 1979 with a litany of factory closures, company bankruptcies, and staff redundancies. Last week's retrenchment was merely the latest chapter. Productive capacity has been slashed, new investment has declined, and Britain, once the workshop of the world, now suffers a deficit in manufactured goods for the first time since the industrial revolution.[27]

In 1984, it seemed that the UK was a unique case. A decade later, with unemployment having remained at high levels throughout the 1980s in both Europe and North America, and not just labour productivity growth but total factor productivity growth having slowed down further, it had become apparent that whatever was happening was affecting all the highly industrialised countries.

Liberal economists do not deny that the share of industry is declining not only in employment but also in the gross output. They only deny that it is the cause of rising unemployment in the industrialised countries. A part of their resistance stems from confusion over the meaning of the word 'de-industrialisation'. In common usage the word refers to the reduction of industry's share of employment and the rise of that of services. But this, as Krugman, Lawrence and others have pointed out repeatedly, is a perfectly natural outcome of industrial maturity. So why blame globalisation?

The word is, however, also used to refer to a decline in industry's share of total output, i.e., of the GDP. Liberal economists also see nothing unusual about this because it too is an outcome of industrial maturity. However, in a book that appeared in 1989, two British economists, Robert Rowthorn and J.R. Wells, distinguished between what they called 'positive' de-industrialisation and 'negative' or 'pathological' de-industrialisation. They pointed out that the belief that industry's share of GDP always falls is based on calculations in current prices. In constant prices industry's share rises for a long time before it starts to fall. It is the fall in industry's share of GDP *in constant prices* that is 'pathological' de-industrialisation— the true hollowing-out of industry.

Rowthorn and Wells did not however link pathological de-industrialisation to the globalisation of manufacturing. This was because their analysis was confined to trying to find out what had gone so seriously wrong in the UK. They concluded that in the UK de-industrialisation resulted from the discovery of North Sea Oil, and simultaneous increases in agricultural productivity that reduced Britain's imports of foodstuffs. The two together pushed up the value of the pound against all other currencies to a level that made Britain's export of manufactures uncompetitive and opened large sections of the domestic market to imports.[28] However, their model of pathological de-industrialisation provides the starting point in establishing the link between globalisation and de-industrialisation.

Three Stages of Industrialisation

As explained earlier, modern economic growth starts with technological changes that sharply raise labour productivity in industry. This increases the output in the industrial sector. However the slower growth of productivity in the services sector makes it necessary to find labour from somewhere to meet its needs. In the earliest phase of industrialisation this comes from agriculture and from the traditional services sector, which includes a large component of domestic service. *The early phase of industrial development therefore sees, at the very least, a rise in the share of industry in the Gross Domestic Product, a rise in the share of the services sector in employment, and a fall in the share of agriculture both in GDP and in employment.* In practice, early industrialisation sees not only an increase in industry's share of output, but also of employment in its modern sector.

The second stage, or 'mature' industrialisation, is reached when agriculture's capacity to give up its workers has been exhausted, and population growth and increased labour participation can no longer meet the need for extra hands. The service sector's hunger for workers can then be satisfied only by immigration or by taking workers from industry. This is the stage that Rowthorn and Wells characterise as 'positive de-industrialisation'. *In this phase, the share of industry in the GDP in constant prices keeps rising or stays constant, but its share in employment starts to fall.*

It is only when the share of industry in not only employment but also output starts to fall that one reaches the third stage—that of negative or 'pathological' de-industrialisation. Studying changes in the share of output of the three sectors over time, Rowthorn and Wells came to a surprising conclusion. The widely held belief that the share of services in the national output must rise from a very early stage of industrialisation through all of its later stages was false. It was an illusion created by measuring changes in the structure of GDP in *current* and not *constant* prices. In current prices the share of services keeps rising because labour productivity rises far more slowly in this sector than in industry: between 1820 and 1989 its growth never exceeded two-fifths of the growth of labour productivity in industry.[29] However, since wage rates in the services are governed by the overall tightness of the labour market, they have never been as low as two-fifths of those in industry. As a result some part of the increase in labour productivity in manufacturing has gone to pay for an increase in wages of an expanding workforce in the services sector. This has resulted in a rise in the service sector's share of the national product in current prices.

However, in constant prices the picture is very different. After studying cross-section data for 100 countries and time series data for 18, Rowthorn and Wells concluded that the services sector tended to account for a fairly constant proportion of GDP through all stages of industrial development.[30] The share of industry, on the other hand, rose rapidly at first, then stabilised and finally declined. The stable relationship between increases in productivity in industry and agriculture on the one hand and services on the other provides the analytical frame for the model of negative de-industrialisation, derived from Rowthorn and Wells, given below.[31]

A Model of Negative De-industrialisation

Let us take a highly simplified model of an economy and examine what happens to it if there is a 50 per cent increase in productivity in industry, and a concomitant 20 per cent increase in productivity in services. We will first examine what happens when the economy is closed and there is no trade or foreign direct investment. Then we will examine what happens when there is trade. Lastly we will examine what happens when there are both trade and outward foreign direct investment. For the sake of simplicity, this analysis excludes the effect of trade cycles.

In the first case all the increase in industrial output *must* be distributed within the country. Thus the real increase in output in the services sector must equal the increase in output of industry.

Case 1: No Trade, No FDI

	Agriculture	Industry	Services	GDP
Before	10	40	50	100
After	10	60	70	140

The effect on employment of the above changes in output will be as follows:

1. There will be no change of employment in industry.
2. Ten out of the 20 extra units produced will be distributed by the *existing workers* in the service sector.

3. *New workers* will have to be found to distribute the 10 extra units. In other words, the number of workers in the service sector will rise by 10/60, i.e., one-sixth.
4. The share of industry in employment will fall, but its share of total output will rise from 40 per cent to 43 per cent.

Case 1 therefore conforms to Rowthorn and Wells' description of positive de-industrialisation.

Case 2: Balanced Trade, but No FDI

	Agriculture	Industry	Services	Total
Before	10	40	50	100
After	10	48 + 12 (e)	58 + 12 (i)	140

This is the classical open economy. Assume that exports consist only of manufactures and imports only of agricultural products. Assume that 8 of the 20 extra units produced by industry are consumed at home and 12 are exported. Against these 12 units of exports, the country imports 12 units of food and raw materials. These will have to be distributed in the country. Thanks to the 20 per cent rise in service sector productivity, 10 units (8 domestic plus 2 imports) will be handled by the existing workers in the service industries. New workers will be needed to distribute the remaining 10 units of imports. The number of workers will therefore rise by 10/60 of the original number, i.e., *exactly the same number as in the closed economy*.

The lesson to be drawn from Case 2 is that trade does not create unemployment so long as it is balanced. *But neither do increases in productivity create unemployment*. As long as productivity rises more slowly in services than in manufacturing (and agriculture), it can only increase the tightness in the labour market. To see what creates non-cyclical, permanent unemployment in a mature capitalist economy, we turn now to Case 3.

Case 3: When There is Both Trade and FDI in Manufacturing Industries

	Agriculture	Industry	Services	Total
Before	10	40	50	100
After	10	40 + 5 (e)	50 + 10 (i)	115

In this case, although industrial productivity has risen by 50 per cent, the domestic industrial output has risen by only 5 units, all of which are exported. The remaining 15 units worth of production capacity is allowed to go out of production. This can only happen if some of the existing industries or factories are no longer able to compete with manufactures from other countries even in the home market. The most common response by owners and managers to this failure to compete is to shift their industries abroad to places where they can produce more cheaply. The only return flow generated by this investment is dividends. It is assumed here that the dividends are 5 units and that these are used to finance additional imports. The overall effect on employment of such FDI abroad is as follows:

1. The 50 per cent rise in industrial productivity makes it possible to produce 60 units with the same number of workers, but only 45 units are produced of which 5 units are exported. The transfer of 15/60 units of productive capacity abroad means a decline in employment of 25 per cent in industry.
2. Imports of goods and service are not 5 but 10 units, because 5 units are paid for by dividends on foreign investment.
3. The concomitant 20 per cent rise in productivity in the service industries has increased the productive capacity of the existing workforce from 50 to 60. This is just enough to handle the increase in domestic industrial output and imports. *There is thus no increase in service sector employment.*
4. The effect of shifting a part of manufacturing capacity abroad is that the share of employment in industry falls sharply, but the slack is not taken up by the service sector. As a result, a part of the previously fully employed workforce becomes permanently unemployed.
5. The share of industry in GDP also declines from 40 per cent to 39.1 per cent.

Case 3 therefore conforms to the model of negative or pathological de-industrialisation developed by Rowthorn and Wells. It is worth noting that while the GDP has risen to 140 in both Cases 1 and 2, it has risen to only 115 in Case 3. The transfer of some of the manufacturing capacity abroad therefore slows down the rate of growth of the economy, *even when there is no decline in the growth of productivity in industry* This is the explanation of the paradox noted by Robert Z. Lawrence, which was referred to earlier and is discussed more fully below.

Stages of Industrialisation—The OECD Experience

Charting the share of manufacturing in the gross national product and in employment over a period of time makes it possible to identify the point when the industrialised economies move from one phase of industrialisation to the next. In the first phase of industrialisation both rise. The workers needed by the two sectors (manufacturing and services) are drawn from agriculture and later, from within the service sector, from domestic service. In the second phase, the share of employment begins to fall but that of manufactured output continues to rise. This is the 'mature' stage, in which de-industrialisation has set in but is positive, and there is no non-cyclical unemployment. In the third phase, the share of manufacturing in both output and employment decline, and unemployment starts to rise. This is negative or pathological de-industrialisation. Employing the above yard-stick, Table 4.2 gives the years when various OECD countries made the transition from Phase 1 to Phase 2 and from Phase 2 to Phase 3.

Table 4.2
Phases of Industrialisation: Year of Transition from Phase 1 to Phase 2, and Phase 2 to Phase 3, for Selected OECD Countries

Country	1st Transition	2nd Transition	Country	1st Transition	2nd Transition
USA	1968	1974	UK	1958**	1974
Japan	1974	1992*	Canada	1960	1974
Germany	1974	1974	Belgium	1974	1991
France	1974	1978	Netherlands	1958**	1985
Italy	1974	1990	Spain	1977	1981

* This must be taken with some caution. It could have been a little earlier.
** Or earlier.
Source: OECD, *Historical Statistics* (Paris, OECD, 1996), and UN, *Yearbook of National Accounts Statistics* (New York, UN, various years).

The above dates are approximate, as no attempt has been made to adjust the data on employment and manufactured product for cyclical changes in the economy. They do, however, permit us to draw an important con-clusion. Five out of the ten OECD countries experienced the transition from positive to negative de-industrialisation in the middle to late 1970s and two more did so in the early 1980s. The former group included the USA, UK, France and Germany, four of the five largest industrialised econ-omies of the world. This was the decisive beginning of the 'crisis decades', and the change was undeniably caused by the shift of manufacturing capa-city to low-wage Asian and Latin American countries.

The experience of the European and East Asian countries after the Second World War conforms closely to the model described above. The period 1950 to 1973 saw the OECD countries attain a GDP growth rate of 4.9 per cent, the highest of the entire capitalist epoch since 1820.[32] The high rates of growth were accompanied, not surprisingly, by very low rates of unemployment. Till 1973 the average for the G-7 countries was only 3.1 per cent. It rose during the oil shock and recession years of the 1970s to 5.0 per cent, but then went higher to 6.8 and 6.4 per cent in the next 14 years despite the drop in oil prices.[33]

The post-war years also saw a decline in the share of employment in manufacturing, and a rise in that of services. But significantly, for the G-7 countries, despite their being mature economies, the share of manufacturing actually rose marginally between 1960 and 1974. The rise in demand for labour in the service sector was met by agriculture, by inducting more women into the workforce, and by immigration. This phase of industrialisation ended quite abruptly in the 1970s for most of the G-7 countries. From 1974 to 1986 there was a sharp decline in employment in the manufacturing sector from 27.6 to 22.3 per cent. This was when positive de-industrialisation gave way to negative de-industrialisation in all the G-7 countries except Italy and Japan.

The shortage of labour in Western Europe during the post-war years not only stopped the outflow of migrants from Europe to North America that had been a dominant feature of the 1870–1914 period but also led to a sizeable inflow of immigrants into Europe. European immigration went from an annual outflow of 2.6 per cent between 1870 and 1914 to an outflow of 0.8 per cent in the 1950s. This dropped to nil in the 1960s and to a net inflow of 0.5 per cent in the 1970s. These data underestimate the true hunger for labour that developed in Europe in the 1960s and 1970s, because they do not take into account the high rate of temporary immigration (on time-bound work permits) from the less industrialised to the more industrialised countries within Europe; notably from Spain, Italy, Yugoslavia, Greece and Turkey to Germany, France Switzerland and the UK. However, after the European economies entered the stage of negative de-industrialisation in the mid- to late 1970s, immigration dropped to 0.1 per cent in 1980–85.[34] All these countries began to impose curbs on immigration in the late 1970s and 1980s when it became clear that the rise in unemployment was not cyclical but structural.

Table 4.3
Immigration into Europe and North America, 1870–1985

Region	1870–1914	1950–60	1960–70	1970–80	1980–85
USA & Canada	5.4	2.7	2.3	4.0	2.8
Europe	–2.6	–0.8	Negligible	0.5	0.1

Source: Dean Baker, Gerald Epstein and Robert Pollin (eds.), *Globalization and Progressive Economic Policy* (Cambridge, Mass.: Cambridge University Press, 1998), p. 12. Constructed from A.M. Taylor and J.G. Williamson, 'Convergence in the Age of Mass Migration', NBER Working Paper No. 4711; and OECD, *The Changing Course of International Migration*.

Clinching proof of the displacement of manufacturing abroad to serve the home markets of the industrialised countries is to be found in the rapid change in the pattern of export from Asia. Between 1913 and 1953, the share of manufactures in Asia's exports (excluding China and North Korea) rose very slowly from 21.2 to 25.3 per cent. Most of these exports were accounted for by Japan. But between 1970 and 1994 the share rose from 22.4 to 73.4 per cent. Indeed the change was even more dramatic because the real rise took place over just 14 years from 1980 to 1994.

Table 4.4
Share of Manufactures in Exports of Selected Regions

Country/Region	1913	1953	1970	1980	1994
USA & Canada	25.8	60.7	–	–	–
UK	70.0	73.3	–	–	–
Asia (excluding China & North Korea)	21.2	25.3	–	–	–
World	–	–	60.9	64.2	74.7
Industrialised countries	–	–	72.0	78.0	79.2
Developing countries	–	–	18.5	17.7	66.1
Of which Asia	–	–	22.4	23.5	73.4
Of which Latin America	–	–	10.6	14.7	48.7

Source: Dean Baker et al. (eds.), *Globalization and Progressive Economic Policy* (p. 7; Tables 3a and 3b)
Note: Comparable data is not available for blank cells.

The Slow Growth Mystery Resolved

The displacement of manufacturing to the developing countries also helps to resolve the slow growth mystery that pre-occupied American and European economists for almost a decade. As pointed out above, all attempts to explain the slowdown of GDP growth as a product of a decline in the rate of growth of labour productivity suffer from the weakness that they can explain the slower growth of per capita income and partly explain growing income inequalities,[35] but they cannot explain why the slowdown in growth should have been accompanied by a rise in unemployment. Robert Z. Lawrence has, however, identified an even more fundamental weakness in these explanations. The common starting point for the Krugman and Schumpeterian explanations is a decline in the growth of labour productivity in industry and more specifically in manufacturing. But in the US there has been no decline in the rate of growth of manufacturing productivity. On the contrary this rose between 1979 and 1989 at exactly the same rate—2.7 per cent per annum—as it did between 1955 and 1973.[36] There was thus no significant let-up in the application of new technologies to production during this period. In fact, 'the performance in manufacturing was the major reason (why) economy-wide productivity grew at all.' Outside the manufacturing sector, productivity growth slumped to 0.3 per cent per annum. This, however, makes the rise in unemployment in the 1980s even harder to explain. If productivity grew at about the same pace in manufacturing during the decade as it did till 1973, then why did the unemployment rate in the US climb from 3.5 per cent in 1968 and 1969 to over 6 per cent in the 1980s?

Lawrence himself supplies a clue to the answer: 'While economy-wide growth of productivity and real wage growth in Europe has been faster than in the United States, European employment growth has been much weaker.'[57] Could it be that a higher rate of growth of productivity in manufacturing actually worsens the unemployment problem?

The model of negative de-industrialisation presented above helps to explain this anomalous relationship. High non-cyclical unemployment and high labour productivity in manufacturing can co-exist when the rise in manufacturing *productivity* fails to get translated into a rise in manufacturing *output*. The mechanism that ensures that this will happen is collective bargaining. Collective bargaining ensures that the increases in productivity in the more dynamic industries are in large part translated into increases in real wages. This wage increase changes the standard for other industries where productivity is not growing equally fast. The stronger the trade unions in those industries, and the more they are organised on a craft basis spanning several industries, the more will the real wage rate in the economy as a whole rise in response to increases in productivity in the most dynamic manufacturing industries.

As that happens, the older or less dynamic industries find themselves saddled with rises in costs of production that they cannot absorb. They therefore become progressively more vulnerable to competition from imports. While some of the firms in these industries close down, others survive by finding ways to reduce their costs—more specifically, their labour costs. One of the ways they do this is to move their plants to areas of the country where labour or other costs are low. When the scope for doing that is exhausted, and if transport costs are not too high and communication is sufficiently easy, they move some or all of their production to countries where labour and other costs are low. In sum, therefore, rising productivity puts pressure on profits in the less technologically dynamic industries and lowers the rate of return on capital. To shore this up, capital moves—both within and, with increasing unification of world product markets, out of the country. Thus with strong unions, the more rapid the rise of productivity in manufacturing, the greater the displacement of manufacturing output to other countries. This leads to a fall in the share of manufacturing output in the GDP at constant prices and the emergence of chronic unemployment.

Notes

1. Paul Krugman, *Peddling Prosperity: Economic Sense and Nonsense in the Age of Diminished Expectations* (New York, W.W. Norton, 1994).
2. Steven A. Marglin and Juliet Schor, *The Golden Age of Capitalism: Reinterpreting the Post War Experience* (Oxford, Clarendon Press, 1991).
3. OECD: *Historical Statistics* (1996), Table 11.5, p. 114. Data are not available for the US and France.
4. Paul Krugman, *Peddling Prosperity*, pp. 40–47.
5. Paul Krugman, *The Age of Diminished Expectations*, 3rd edition (Cambridge, Mass., MIT Press), Chapters 1–3.
6. See for instance Robert Z. Lawrence, 'The Slow Growth Mystery' [review of *The End of Affluence* by Jeffrey Madrick], *Foreign Affairs*, Jan/Feb 1996, p. 146; and Paul Krugman, *Peddling Prosperity*, p. 270.
7. There is one circumstance in which this does not hold true. It is when a rise in industrial productivity is accompanied by a simultaneous transfer of manufacturing capacity to another country. This is discussed in detail in the latter half of this chapter.
8. Other than that caused by trade cycles.
9. The internet is steadily reducing the number of services that are non-tradable. For instance, two decades ago no one could have conceived of a firm doing all its accounting or an airline doing its ticketing out of a remote centre in another country. But despite that, it still remains broadly true that most products of the service industries are not tradable.
10. OECD, *Historical Statistics* (1995), p. 47.
11. Dean Baker, Gerald Epstein and Robert Pollin (eds.), *Globalization and Progressive Economic Policy*, Introduction, p. 12.
12. Ibid.
13. In his book, *Capitalism, Socialism and Democracy*, Schumpeter took issue with the classical definition of competition as something that took place between many buyers and sellers at a point in time. Competition, indeed the more important variety, took place between producers over a period of time, and came from the harnessing of new technology to the production process. Only large companies with sizeable surpluses were capable of regularly doing that. Thus Schumpeter turned the idea that the emergence of monopoly stifled competition on its head. Monopolies were necessary to generate the surpluses that could be ploughed into innovation. The emergence of monopolies in the last quarter of the nineteenth century therefore promoted—instead of stifling—competition, because it permitted the institutionalisation of innovation.
14. For a discussion of the distinction between invention and innovation as the words have been used here, see Joel Mokyr, *The Lever Of Riches: Technological Creativity and Economic Progress* (Oxford, Oxford University Press, 1990), p. 10.
15. *The Economist*, 'Survey of the World Economy', 28 September 1996, Survey, p. 10.
16. Ibid., p. 8, chart.
17. Ibid.
18. IDC Research. Accessed on 13 August 1999.

19. Click-Z statistics at http://www.clickz.com/stats/big_picture/traffic_patterns/article.php/3369221

20. The following table, compiled from Bureau of Labour Statistics data, gives the acceleration of productivity growth in the US:

	1994	1995	1996	1997	1998	1999	2000	2001	2002	2003
Labour productivity growth (%)	3.3	3.9	3.4	3.5	4.7	3.8	4.7	2.2	7.2	5.1

21. Peter F. Drucker, *Post-Capitalist Society* (Harper Collins Publishers, 1994), Introduction.

22. Anthony F. Giddens, *Beyond Left and Right* (Stanford University Press, 1994).

23. Robert Z. Lawrence, 'The Slow Growth Mystery', *Foreign Affairs*, Vol. 75. No. 1, January/February 1996, p. 149. Lawrence also points out that total factor productivity in manufacturing grew in the US during this period by 1.4 per cent a year, which was only marginally below the 1.7 per cent recorded between 1955 and 1973.

24. R.E. Rowthorn and J.R. Wells, *De-industrialisation and Foreign Trade* (Cambridge University Press, 1987), p. 7 and Chapters 5–12.

25. Michael Smith and Jane Renton, 'The UK Industry in Crisis', *The Observer*, London, 27 September 1992. The authors quote Department of Employment statistics.

26. Rowthorn and Wells, *De-industrialisation and Foreign Trade*, p. 223.

27. Smith and Renton, 'The UK Industry in Crisis'. The authors quote Department of Employment statistics.

28. Rowthorn and Wells, *De-industrialisation and Foreign Trade*, Chapters 9 and 12.

29. Angus Maddison, *Dynamic Forces in Capitalist Development* (Oxford University Press, 1991). Maddison's data till 1987 show that services sector productivity has, if anything, declined more sharply than productivity in industry. As for the years after 1987, OECD data on labour productivity in the two sectors shows no change in the trend—while productivity in industry grew by 2.5 per cent in the US, 2.6 per cent in Japan and 2.3 per cent in France, productivity in the service sector grew by 0.8, 1.1 and 0.7 per cent respectively (see Maddison, *Dynamic Forces in Capitalist Development*, Tables 5.13 and 5.14, pp. 150–151).

30. It is only the composition of this sector that has changed dramatically over time. As industrialisation has progressed, the share of domestic services has declined, while that of 'modern' industry and market-oriented services has increased.

31. Maddison, *Dynamic Forces in Capitalist Development*, pp. 15–19, Figures 1.2a and 1.2b. The constant price shares are obtained from a cross-section study of 100 countries in the UN International Comparisons Project, Phase III, and the more limited time series study by I.B. Kravis, A.W. Heston, and R. Summers, 'The Share of Services in Economic Growth', in Adams and Hickman (eds.) *Global Econometrics* (MIT Press, 1983).

32. Maddison, *Dynamic Forces in Capitalist Development*, p. 51.

33. Standardised rates of unemployment, taken from OECD, *Historical Statistics* (various years).

34. Baker et al. (eds.), *Globalization and Progressive Economic Policy*, p. 12.

35. Slower growth can intensify the struggle for a larger share of the existing cake. In this struggle the better-organised segments of the population will be more successful than the less well-organised. Usually the mechanism by which such transfers of income and wealth take place is inflation. Slower growth can intensify cost-push inflation,

which transfers income and wealth from fixed income groups and less well-organised groups to the property-owning and managerial classes, the self-employed, and the strong trade unions.

36. Robert Z. Lawrence, 'The Slow Growth Mystery', p. 149. Lawrence also points out that total factor productivity in manufacturing grew in the US during this period by 1.4 per cent a year, which was only marginally below the 1.7 per cent recorded between 1955 and 1973.

37. Ibid., p. 151.

5

THE RISE OF GLOBAL CAPITALISM

The previous chapter exposed a curious anomaly: nation state capitalism took root in England in the second half of the eighteenth century and in continental Europe and the USA in the second and third quarters of the nineteenth century. The first stage of their industrialisation therefore lasted for somewhere between 100 and 200 years. But in the ten mature industrialised countries depicted in Table 4.2 (see Chapter 4), the period of 'positive de-industrialisation' (when the share of industry in the labour force was falling but that of its product in the GDP was rising) was relatively short, with an average of just over 11 years. In the extreme case of Germany, it was less than a year. Why was the transition from positive to negative de-industrialisation so swift? Why did the transfer of manufacturing activity from high-wage to low-wage economies—which was responsible for the onset of negative de-industrialisation—take place within the same decade in nearly all the mature industrialised countries?

To the best of our knowledge, liberal economists have so far not even posed this question to themselves. Indeed, Rowthorn and Wells' distinction between positive and negative de-industrialisation has found little echo in the theoretical literature that has followed. But were the question to be posed to them, they would in all probability say that the answer lies in the speeding-up of technological change (particularly in transport and communications) that lies at the centre of 'globalisation'. This has brought down the cost and increased the speed of both to the point where it is possible to talk meaningfully of the world not only as a single market but also, increasingly, as a single manufacturing system. This explanation would not merely be unsatisfactory but positively misleading, for it would only explain why the world is being integrated into a single market and not provide a satisfactory explanation as to why capital feels obliged to move *out* of its home country to exploit it.

Globalisation is not a product only of the 'compression of space and time', but of a second crucial development in the twentieth century: the simultaneous blocking of the trans-border movement of labour. As is described in greater detail below, hard national boundaries, with severe restrictions on trans-border movement of people, came into being in the last quarter of the nineteenth century and were the most distinctive feature of the nation state. This was therefore the first point at which the forces of globalising capitalism came into direct conflict with the entrenched social and political institutions of the nation state. Global capitalism is resolving that conflict by bursting the container of the nation state and knitting the low-wage countries into a new, much larger 'container'. The nation state—and all the economic institutions that have been built around it—has therefore become its first casualty.

The Unification of the Product Market

The term 'market' has a very precise meaning. It is the geographical area in which economic agents, be they manufacturers, financiers, consumers or workers, can earn income/profit/satisfaction on a sustainable basis, i.e., without facing natural or man-made barriers that put them at a disadvantage in relation to their competitors. These barriers can be natural, such as distance, which raises transport costs and gives local producers an edge over those further away; or a lack of information, which inhibits the coordination of production and marketing, and restricts consumer choice. Or they can be man-made, and consist of tariffs, high local taxes, import restrictions, and other discriminatory laws. Advances in technology have been eliminating natural barriers to the spread of the market since the invention of clinker-built hulls, 'round-bottomed' ships, lateen sails and the compass, to name only a few. The deliberate elimination of man-made barriers to trade began in earnest only with the Kennedy round of GATT negotiations in 1968, and is being completed with a large measure of coercion even as we write, under the aegis of the World Trade Organisation.

The most necessary, and therefore most assiduously propagated, of the myths that serve to legitimise the wholesale destruction of the institutions of nation state-based capitalism that is accompanying globalisation is that this process is nothing new. The myth goes that it began at least as far back as the nineteenth century, if not centuries earlier. It yielded a hundred years of peace before the folly and short-sightedness of man disrupted the institutional base of that peace in 1914. The 31 years of war, crisis and genocide that followed was an aberration. Now that the course has been corrected and we are back on track once again, the march towards world peace has been resumed.

The plausibility of this myth rests entirely upon the incremental nature of technological change. Capitalism was always international, in as much as the vehicle for financial accumulation was inter-city or inter-state trade. With improvements in the technology of production and transport, the areas of the globe that it linked within its network of exchange grew steadily larger. The nineteenth century saw a dramatic acceleration in the speed of technological change. Consequently the spread of capitalism also gained momentum. The decline in transport costs and an even more dramatic decline in the cost of communications were the most important causes of the acceleration. The development of the railways had reduced land transport costs by as much as 85–95 per cent between 1840 and 1910.[1] The introduction of steamships halved ocean freight charges between 1868 and 1884.[2] By all physical indices, economic integration continued to gather momentum throughout the nineteenth century, right till the beginning of the First World War. Transport costs continued to be brought down by the rapid spread of railways across Europe and America, and steamships opened up the Western European and specifically the British market to grain, timber, cotton and other produce from North America, Argentina, India, China, Australia, Russia, Romania and Hungary.

An idea of the impact this had on prices may be obtained from the cost of shipping grain from Chicago to Liverpool. Between 1874 and 1881, the cost of transport from Chicago to New York fell from 33 cents to 14 cents per bushel. During roughly the same period, the cost of shipping it from New York to Liverpool fell from 20 cents to 2 cents per bushel. Thus the overall cost of shipping grain from Chicago to Liverpool fell from 53 cents to 16 cents a bushel, a fall of 72 per cent.[3] Similarly, the cost of shipping a tonne of goods from Marseille to Hong Kong was 200 French francs in 1875, but only 70 francs in 1906. This represented a fall from 7 months of a skilled artisan's wages to 2 months. In the 1880s refrigerated ships made it possible to ship meat from Argentina to Europe.

Not surprisingly, throughout the period from 1820 to 1913, the external trade of the 16 most industrialised countries grew faster than their GDP. While GDP grew by an average of just under 2.5 per cent per annum,[4] in no decade after 1820 did world trade grow by less than 2.3 per cent, and the peak rate of growth between 1840 and 1870 was about 5 per cent.[5] These developments together enabled international trade to grow 18-fold in real terms between 1800 and 1913.[6]

Through much of the nineteenth century, foreign direct investment as a proportion of GDP was also three to four times as large as it was in the 1960s, 1970s and 1980s. Between 1873 and 1914, Britain invested

5 per cent of its GDP abroad every year. Australia, Argentina and Canada obtained a third to half their total capital formation from British savings. By contrast, at the peak of its direct investment overseas, and during the recycling of petrodollars by American banks, total foreign investment out-flows barely reached 1 per cent of American GDP. At the height of its over-seas investment in 1987, Japan lent less than 1 per cent of its GDP abroad.[7]

Why Globalisation Does Not Mean 'Going Back to the Future'

But the 'internationalisation' of capitalism in the nineteenth century should not be confused with the globalisation that is taking place today. First, in 1913 most of the world was outside the modern system of exchange. Thus the actual integration of global economic activity was much more limited than the trade-to-GDP ratio would suggest. By contrast, in 1995 the World Bank estimated that less than 10 per cent of the workers of the world would remain outside the (global) economic mainstream by 2000.[8]

Second, differences of degree do eventually add up to a difference in kind. Satellite communications are not only faster than underground or undersea telephone lines, but have made transmission costs independent of distance. In the same way, air freight may be cheaper for a wide range of commodities than shipment by sea, but the main change it has made is in the speed of transport. No matter how much ocean freight rates declined, it would still have been impossible to ship freshly cut flowers from Kenya or India to Europe by sea.

No conceivable reduction in telephone charges could have unified the world's commodity, foreign exchange, money and stock markets into a single global market in which there was round-the-clock trading in real time. One needed permanent computer hook-ups on the internet to make that possible. It is the change in both the speed of communication and in the sheer volume of information that can be processed and transmitted in seconds, more than simply the decline in costs, which makes the present knitting together of global economy qualitatively different in kind from what occurred between 1850 and 1913. In 1913 while trade was inter-national, manufacturing remained wholly (or, in the case of Japan, largely) national. The difference is captured by the composition of foreign direct investment. In the nineteenth century three-fifths of foreign direct invest-ment went into the development of infrastructure that was designed to facilitate trade. By contrast, more than three-fifths of today's foreign direct investment is going into the establishment of manufacturing facilities abroad.[9]

The third and by far the most important difference is one that almost none of the legitimisers of systemic chaos ever mention. This is that in the nineteenth century it was not just capital but also labour that was free to move across national barriers. By contrast, today the movement of labour across national boundaries is at best marginal and mostly illegal. That is the reason why capital was forced to burst the bounds of the nation state.

The Blocking of Immigration

Till the 1880s there were no controls of any kind on the movement of people in and out of countries. This was not only true of the Americas but also of Europe. In the 1880s, a wave of racism combined with a growing concern for wage and job security, and led governments to place the first restrictions on immigration. These were placed mainly on Asian labour in the US and Canada, and on the immigration of Jews into Great Britain after 1905.[10] But the US placed no restrictions on the immigration of Europeans till 1920. In sharp contrast to the nineteenth century, developed countries not only continued to restrict immigration after the First World War, but made the restrictions even more stringent after the Second.[11]

If one looks back at the rise and spread of capitalism, it becomes apparent that without unhindered immigration in the nineteenth and early twentieth centuries, the highly industrialised metropolitan economies of today would not have come into being. It is possible to identify four phases of labour migration in the service of capitalism. The first was when there was an absolute shortage of labour in relation to the other factors of production, land and capital. Labour imports were needed to 'expand the capitalist mode of production into less or undeveloped areas'.[12] The transfer of slave labour to the American South, to central America and Brazil; the imposition of various systems of bonded labour on vanquished indigenous peoples of Latin America, such as *Mita*, *Peonage* and *encomienda*, and the recruitment of indentured plantation labour in India to work in sugar and other plantations in East and South-east Africa, Fiji, Mauritius, the Caribbean and Sri Lanka—and from China to work in Dutch British plantations in Southeast Asia and in North America—fall into this category.[13] These forms of labour organisation became necessary because ensuring a steady supply of raw materials was as great a preoccupation of early capitalism as ensuring the availability of labour for the mills. Trade with indigenous peoples could not, by itself, be relied upon to increase the supply of specific raw materials, as it dealt, by definition, in the surpluses generated out of the existing organisation of production. To feed the voraciously growing appetite of the mill sector for coal, ores, cotton, tobacco, sugarcane and tea, the traditional production systems had to be forcibly disrupted and surpluses created, not to meet limited local needs but to meet the huge demand of the emerging international market. Labour, often embodying specific skills (such as growing tea or sugarcane) had therefore to be physically enslaved or bonded and, if necessary, moved because it was not available in the areas where the materials were available. The use of low-paid labour in these peripheral areas was essential to sustain capital accumulation and rising employment and productivity in the metropolis.

Together these systems forcibly created a huge supply of 'free' labour, i.e., labour not occupied in meeting the subsistence needs of the family, either by tearing it away from its earlier subsistence activities or by forced or semiforced migration. Between 1701 and 1860, no less than 4.25 million slaves from Africa arrived alive in Latin America.[14] If one adds the numbers that went to Brazil and the US, the figure rises to 15 million.[15] Between 1834, when slavery was abolished in Britain, and 1941, when indenture was finally abolished in the Dutch colonies, up to 37 million indentured workers were used in 40 countries.[16]

The second type of labour migration took place directly into the emerging centres of capitalism to meet an absolute scarcity of labour in all sectors of the economy. The huge migration of Europeans to North and South America till 1920, totalling 45 millions, falls into this category. Thirty million of these migrants came to the US between 1861 and 1920.[17] This migration occurred because labour was a scarce factor of production from the start. In the US, people were needed not only by industry and the service industries, but also to settle the lands in the west.

The third type of migration was a response to the hectic growth of manufacturing industry, spurred by 'Schumpeterian' bursts of technological progress or intense managerial innovation. The migration of Irish labourers to the UK after the repeal of the Corn Laws to provide a pool of low-cost labour was perhaps the earliest example of this type of labour movement. By 1851 there were already over 700,000 Irish workers in Britain. Another 120,000 Jews entered the UK between 1875 and 1914.[18]

A similar migration also took place within continental Europe during the last quarter of the nineteenth century and the first part of the twentieth, from the then-underdeveloped countries to the then-developed ones: 6.8 million, or nearly half, the 15 million Italians who emigrated from Italy between 1876 and 1920 went to other countries of Europe, especially Germany, France and Switzerland. By 1907, as Lenin noted, Germany already had 1.3 million immigrant workers.[19] There were 1.2 million foreign-born workers in France in 1911.[20] In all, more than 100 million people crossed international frontiers to work in other countries.

The vital role that free or largely free immigration played in the development of capitalism may be judged from the fact that in 1913 the total population of the capitalist world and its colonial 'factories' and enclaves was only 332 million.[21] Nearly all of the more than fifty million Europeans who migrated to other countries were either from the poorer European countries and regions, like Poland, Hungary, Russia and the Balkans, or were escaping proletarianisation in the new industrial centres of Britain, France and Germany. Much the same urge impelled millions of Americans to leave the industrialised east and travel west across the continent. Judging from detailed figures for Italy, more than 80 per cent were young males, and practically all were active workers.[22] Not surprisingly, in 1920 in the US, foreign-born people made up 13.2 per cent of the population and a far higher proportion of the active workforce. In France foreign workers made up 10–15 per cent of the workforce.[23]

But the First World War brought the era of more or less free movement of labour to an end. There was a similar burst of immigration of 'guest workers' under one or other label into Western Europe after the Second World War, as the new technologies that had been developed in America just before or during the War were incorporated into the production process. But the numbers who were allowed to enter Europe then were a small fraction, both in absolute and relative terms, of the numbers who migrated every year in search of employment before 1914.[24]

Curbs on immigration ensured that the immense increase in productivity during the 'Golden Age' led to prolonged full employment in the industrialised countries, a rapid convergence of wage rates there and, most important of all, a rapid divergence of their wage rates from those of the newly industrialising countries of Asia and Latin America. With labour prevented from moving into the industrialised countries, capital began to move to the low-wage countries instead.

What Made the American Century So Short?

The effect that blocking immigration has had upon the development of capitalism can be better understood by posing the counterfactual question, 'What would the world have looked like today if there had been no barriers to the movement of labour?' The answer is simple: labour would have moved to wherever the wages were highest; wage rates would have converged all over the world, and there would have been relatively little capital movement to foreign countries. In practice, even in the absence of legal barriers to immigration, the movement of labour would have been less free than that of capital. This is apparent from the fact that capital has regularly moved to low-wage locations even within a country. Labour movement across international boundaries, especially from poor Asian and African countries, would have been constrained by the high cost of travel, the lack of language and other skills, and the reluctance of people to move from their homes. Substantial wage differentials would therefore have remained. Consequently there would have been some movement of capital to low-wage areas of the world.

The world would therefore have looked somewhat like it does today, but with far smaller differences of income, far smaller movements of capital, and a slower industrialisation of the nations of the periphery. Most important of all, the shift from positive to negative de-industrialisation of the industrial metropolises—i.e., from Phase 2 to Phase 3—would have been postponed by several decades, while the industrialisation of sections of the periphery that we have witnessed in the past 30 years would have been a good deal less hectic. *In sum, the blocking of labour movement is the main cause of the shortness of the 'American Century'.*

Intensifying Competition and the Search for Profits

The migration of capital to low-wage areas is not by any means new. Because labour is intrinsically far less mobile than capital, long before capital went abroad it was moving in search of profit to low-wage areas within the boundaries of the nation state. In all the industrialised countries the rapid decline in transport costs has enabled manufacturing industries to move from their original homes near raw material sources, ports and metropolises to the more industrially backward areas, where wages are low, trade unions are weak and local governments are willing to levy fewer taxes. Manufacturing enterprises began to shift within the US from the so-called 'frost belt' to the 'sun belt' as far back as the late 1950s.[25]

A much-discussed example was the decision of the United Aircraft Corporation to move the Chance-Vought division from Bridgeport, Connecticut, to Dallas, Texas. This was the beginning of a huge relocation of American industry out of the northern 'frost belt' states into the southern and western 'sun belt' states. In the 1970s, between 450,000 and 650,000 jobs were involved in such plant relocations. However, relocation was the only one of many, and by no means the most important, ways in which jobs went from the highly industrialised north to the south and west. The more common form of displacement was for old companies to close down in the frost belt states and new ones to start up in the sun belt. Data compiled by Dun and Bradstreet for manufacturing, offices, stores, bus companies, insurance and brokerage houses and other service industries throughout the US showed that between 1969 and 1976, 25 million new jobs were created but 22 million were destroyed. Of the former, only 25 per cent were in the frost belt, while 75 per cent were in the sun belt states. The reason industry went south was that wage rates were lower and there was a 'good business climate'.[26]

In Europe, capital has moved from the north of France to the south, from northern to southern Italy, and from England to Wales and Scotland. When the EEC was formed, it moved from the high-wage countries to low-wage ones such as Austria, Spain, Portugal, Ireland and, most recently, Greece. The migration of capital to even more distant countries in search of cheap labour was a logical extension of the same search for profit and competitiveness. The Dun and Bradsteet survey showed that migration abroad in search of cheap labour was already a main feature of industrial strategy in 1969. For instance, GE built a plant to produce steam irons in Singapore, and closed its plant outside Los Angeles. Ford and Pratt and Whitney also began to subcontract the production of components abroad. When the US tyre industry, which was the last to shift to radial tyres, was unable to compete with the radial tyres being sold by Michelin of France and Bridgestone of Japan, the industry closed 24 plants and retrenched 20,000 workers. However, Goodyear and Uniroyal, the tyre makers who closed the plants in the US, opened new plants in Brazil, Turkey, Spain and Austria. As wages were pushed up by new investment in the American South and West, manufacturers began to look further afield for cheap labour. As a result, 34 per cent of the plant closures in the South during this period took place because of the relocation of old industries abroad, mainly textiles, apparel, electronics assembly plants, and other labour-intensive industries.[27] From the 1950s onwards, there was an ever-growing flow of private investment abroad. Direct foreign investment rose from $12 billion (out of a gross private investment of $54 billion) in 1950 to $192 billion (out of 400 billion) in 1980. Most of it went to Canada and Western Europe, but as real wages rose in both, especially with the end of post-war reconstruction and the return of full employment, an increasing proportion began to be channelled to East Asia and Latin America. It is this shift of manufacturing to faraway countries with vastly different cultures that turned the search for profit from a tool of industrialisation into a tool for de-industrialisation in its pathological form.

Table 5.1, which gives the cost of labour to employers in 1960, 1970 and 1988–92 in some OECD countries, explains why, from the early 1980s in particular, the shift of manufacturing investment to the developing countries accelerated so rapidly. As the table shows, the reason was a rapid convergence of wage rates, expressed in dollars or (as here) in Euros within the OECD.

Table 5.1 helps to explain the pattern of displacement of manufacturing activity that the OECD countries have experienced in the past 35 years.

Table 5.1
Hourly Cost of Labour in Euros and Factors
Influencing it in Selected OECD Countries

Country	ULC*–1960	ULC–1970	ULC–88–92**
USA	2.96	4.68	14.8
Germany	1.80	4.34	23.4
France	1.09	4.49	14.0
Italy	1.09	2.97	13.0
UK	N.A.	3.49	12.0
Spain	N.A.	2.51	12.5
Japan	0.54	2.06	15.2

* ULC = Unit labour cost (per hour) in Euros
** For various years: 1988 for France and Italy, 1991 for USA and Japan, and 1992 for Germany and the UK.
Sources: 1. *Exchange rates*: IMF, *International Financial Yearbook* (1995).
　　　2. *Changes in unit labour costs in each country in its national currency in the business sector*: OECD, 'Economic Outlook', December 1995, Annex Table 1 3, and OECD, 'Economic Outlook 1960–1986', Table 3.10.
　　　3. Change between 1960 and 1970 has been calculated from hourly earnings in manufacture, as unit labour costs in the business sector were not available for 1960–68. Hourly labour cost: Eurostat, *Europe in Figures* (Bruxelles, Eurostat, 1995), p. 196.

In the 1950s and 1960s, wage rates in the EEC countries were far below those of the US. As a result, when US firms began to face competition from renascent European industries, they began to invest heavily in Europe. As wages in Europe rose, this investment went progressively to the countries with lower wage rates within Europe. An important spur for this investment was the existence of high tariff barriers in Europe and the consequent desire to get inside them. Although by 1960 these had already been reduced considerably from the 1950 level of 40 per cent, they were still nowhere near the level of 5 per cent achieved after the implementation of the Tokyo round of GATT agreements.[28]

By 1970, wage rates in Germany and France had caught up with those in the US. Their attraction as destinations for American investment had therefore waned, but investment in other less developed countries in Europe retained its appeal. What is more, by 1970, Germany, France, Belgium, Holland, Sweden and Denmark had also emerged as high-wage countries in Europe. As a result foreign direct investment from these countries also began to rise sharply in the 1970s. Lastly, as Europe as a whole began to lose its wage cost advantage over the US, American manufacturers and manufacturers from the high-wage countries of Europe began to invest more and more heavily in the low-wage countries of Asia and Latin America.

Industrialisation of the Periphery

Episodic evidence of these shifts has been available for more than three decades. As mentioned above, General Electric built a steam iron plant in Singapore, shutting one down outside Los Angeles.[29] When the US government closed down the 'Bracero' programme for importing Mexican labour for US agriculture in 1964, Mexico promptly announced a Border Industrialisation Programme. It declared a 12.5-mile strip of Mexico immediately south of the US border to be virtually tax and tariff free. The justification given for the programme by the Mexican minister for commerce to the Wall Street journal was itself significant: 'Our idea is to offer an alternative to Hong Kong, Japan and Puerto Rico for free enterprise.'[30] The programme was initiated in 1969. US garment, toys and electronics firms were the first to respond. By 1971 there were 72 American plants in the border belt. By 1974 the number had grown to 655. These employed 13 per cent of the border region's total labour force. By 1978, the automobile industry had woken up to the possibilities of cost reduction opened by Mexico next door. Seven General Motors and three Chrysler plants moved to Cuidad Juarez. In 1979, General Electric shut down its home appliances cordset manufacturing plant in Rhode Island, and moved to Nogales. The reason for the shift was apparent: the cost of labour was $2.00 per hour against $5.84 in Rhode Island.[31] Exactly the same considerations were impelling European capital overseas.

These trends are apparent in the estimates of foreign direct investment compiled by various authors for the 1960s, 1970s and 1980s. The rate of growth of foreign direct investment from developed to developing countries rose slowly during the Golden Age, from an average of 7 per cent between 1960 and 1968 to 9.2 per cent between 1968 and 1973. Then, as the Golden Age petered out and recessionary trends appeared in the industrialised countries, it rose sharply to 19.4 per cent between 1973 and 1980.[32] Foreign direct investment by American companies followed the same pattern. While investment in other developed countries continued to grow at a fairly constant pace—11.7 per cent between 1950 and 1966, 10.7 per cent from 1966 to 1973, and 11.8 per cent from 1973 to 1980—investment in the developing countries grew from 6.2 to 9.7 to 14.2 per cent in the respective periods.[33] In contrast to the American investment in Europe and European investment in the low-wage countries of the European Community, which was aimed mainly at gaining a permanent foothold in markets still protected by relatively high tariff barriers, investment in the developing countries was concentrated in the export-oriented industries from the very beginning.[34]

Two other developments during the 1970s underlined the importance of capitalising on low wage rates in a steadily more integrated global market. Between 1967 and 1975 American transnationals withdrew 30 per cent of their investments in the original six common market countries in order to invest in the low-wage developing countries.[35] The displacement of American capital, which first took place from the frost belt to the sun belt within the US and then from the US to Europe and the developing countries, thus also took place laterally from European affiliates to the developing countries.

The second was the explosive growth of German and Japanese FDI in the 1970s. Between 1970 and 1976, while the foreign direct investment of other OECD countries rose by 40 to 100 per cent, German FDI rose by 307 per cent, and Japanese by 408 per cent. This was exactly the period when German labour cost in dollars/ECUs shot ahead of those of all other OECD countries. It is also the period when Germany made its abrupt transition from Phase 1 of industrialisation, in which the share of manufacturing in GDP (at constant prices) and in employment was rising, to Phase 3, when both were falling. The German experience thus strongly supports the view that the emergence of a unified world market—and the consequent rise in the intensity of competition and the urgent need to exploit labour cost differentials—was the main cause of the displacement of manufacturing activity from the parent country via foreign direct investment flows.

The reasons why Japan also increased its foreign direct investment were offensive rather than defensive. When Japan decided to reduce costs by farming out the manufacture of components and later the assembly of its consumer goods to low-wage countries in its neighbourhood, its unit labour costs were less than half of labour costs in the US, France and Germany. Its reasons for doing so are partly buried in its colonial history, but are to be found mainly in its perception that it was taking on the established industrial powers with a number of initial disadvantages and could not afford to overlook any stratagem to reduce costs. Unlike the European powers, Japan located a large part of its heavy industry in its colonies from the very beginning. Thus steel, chemicals and, for a time, automobiles were located in Korea, Manchuria and Taiwan. The result was a substantial industrialisation of all three regions by 1940. Factory employment stood at 213,000 in Korea in 1940 and at 181,000 in Taiwan in 1941. Manufacturing output grew by 8 per cent per annum in Taiwan in the 1930s and by 10.2 per cent in Korea between 1929 and 1941.[36] Thus when the Vietnam war wound down and Japan began to feel the need to lower its costs, it turned naturally to doing what it had already done before.[37]

Notes

1. W.S. Woytinski and E.S. Woytinski, *World Commerce and Governments: Trends and Outlook* (New York, Twentieth Century Fund, 1955). Cited in Ronald Rogowski, *Commerce and Coalitions. How Trade Affects Domestic Political Alignments* (Princeton, Princeton University Press, 1989), p. 21.
2. Michael G. Mulhall, *The Dictionary of Statistics* (London, George Routledge and Sons, 1892); cited in Rogowski, *Commerce and Coalitions*, pp. 22–23fn.
3. Norman Stone, *Europe Transformed, 1878–1919 (The Fontata History of Europe)* (Fontana Paperbacks, 1983), p. 23. Another estimate by Mulhall in 1892 however put the decline in shipping costs from New York to Liverpool as being from 23 shillings a tonne in 1868 to 12 shillings in 1884.
4. Angus Maddison, *Dynamic Forces in Capitalist Development* (Oxford University Press, 1991), p. 50.
5. Rogowski, *Commerce and Coalitions. How Trade Affects Domestic Political Alignments* (Princeton, Princeton University Press, 1989) pp. 21–22.
6. Rogowski, *Commerce and Coalitions*, p. 20. Calculated from sources in notes 1 to 5 above, and W.W. Rostow, *The World Economy: History and Prospect* (Austin, Texas, University of Texas Press, 1978). The impact of the telegraph, developed by Samuel Morse in 1846, was even more dramatic because it not only gave access to information about demand and supply conditions in remote markets but also made it possible to make offers and transmit contract terms in a matter of minutes. The laying of the first transatlantic cable in 1866, and in the next two decades to Australia and most other parts of the world, lowered the time taken in sending a message and receiving an answer from as much as six months to a few minutes. This led directly to the development of international banking and *haute finance*, the unique network of family owned international banking institutions that coordinated, through its links with national banks and financial markets, the entire business of long-term capital lending in foreign countries. Statistics cited by Lenin in 1916 showed that capital invested abroad by Britain, France and Germany rose from 3.6 billion francs in 1862 (entirely British), to over 200 billion francs in 1914 (of which only between 75 and 100 billion francs came from Britain). More recent calculations confirm Lenin's estimates. According to a study published by the Brookings Institution, British banks and investors had invested $38.3 billion in the rest of the world by 1913 (Cleona Lewis, *Debtor and Creditor Countries* [Washington D.C., Brookings Institution, 1945], cited by Albert Fishlow, 'Lessons From the Past', *International Organisations*, Vol. 39 [1985], No. 3, p. 394).
7. Herman M. Schwartz, *States versus Markets* (New York, St Martin's Press, 1994), p. 153.
8. Ibid., p. 50.
9. Ibid.
10. Stephen Castles and Mark J. Miller, *The Age of Migration* (New York, The Guildford Press, 1993), Chapter 3.
11. Immigration into the USA, the most liberal of the industrialised countries, averaged 250,000 a year from 1951 to 1960 and 330,000 a year from 1961 to 1970, against 880,000 a year between 1901 and 1910 (Castles and Miller, *The Age of Migration*, p. 73).
12. Saskia Sassen, *The Mobility of Labour and Capital. A Study in International Investment and Labour Flow* (Cambridge University Press, 1988), p. 29.
13. Ibid., p. 32, and footnotes to Chapter 2.
14. Ibid.

15. Castles and Miller, *The Age of Migration*, p. 48, quoting R.T. Appleyard in *International Migration: The Challenge of the Nineties* (1991).
16. Ibid., p. 49, quoting L. Potts, *The World Labour Market: A History of Migration* (Zed Books, 1990).
17. Ibid., p. 51, quoting G.J. Borjas, *Friends or Strangers: The Impact of Immigration on the US Economy* (Basic Books, 1990).
18. Ibid.
19. Sassen, *The Mobility of Labour and Capital*, p. 189, n. 2. A more recent estimate by K. Dohse (1981) places the number at 950,000 workers. According to Castles and Miller (*The Age of Migration*, p. 57), 500,000 were in industry, 300,000 in agriculture and 86,000 in trade.
20. Castles and Miller, *The Age of Migration*, p. 57.
21. Maddison, *Dynamic Forces in Capitalist Development*, pp. 229, 231.
22. Luigi de Comite, 'Aspects of Italian Migration', in Ira A. Glazier and, Luigi De Rosa (eds.), *Migration Across Time and Nations* (New York, Holmes and Meir, 1986), Table 7.5, p. 154.
23. Castles and Miller, *The Age of Migration*, pp. 51, 58.
24. In 1975 the median proportion of migrants in the population of the seven countries of the Common Market was 7.8 per cent. Their share of the active workforce was probably twice as high (Castle and Miller, *The Age of Migration*, p. 71, Table 4.1). The import of Mexican labour into the American south and west in the 1950s and 1960s, under programmes like the 'Bracero' programme, also falls into this category.
25. Barry Bluestone and Bennett Harrison, *The Deindustrialisation of America: Plant Closings, Community Abandonment, and the Dismantling of Basic Industry* (New York, Basic Books, 1982).
26. Ibid., pp. 30–31, and Table 2.1.
27. Ibid. This loss was however offset by new jobs in energy (oil) and chemicals.
28. Lester H. Brown et al. (eds.), *Vital Signs 1993: The Trends that are Shaping Our Future* (Washington D.C., Worldwatch Institute), pp. 742–75.
29. Bluestone and Harrison, *The Deindustrialisation of America*, p. 26.
30. Ibid., p. 171.
31. Ibid., p. 172.
32. UN Centre for Transnational Corporations (UNCTC), *Transnational Corporations in World Development* (New York, United Nations, 1978), quoted in Sassen, *The Mobility of Labour and Capital*, pp. 100–101.
33. Sassen, *The Mobility of Labour and Capital*.
34. OECD, *International Subcontracting: A New Form of Investment* (Paris, OECD, 1980); Sassen, *The Mobility of Labour and Capital*, p. 103.
35. Sassen, *The Mobility of Labour and Capital*, p. 101.
36. Bruce Cumings, 'The Origins and Development of the Northeast Asian Political Economy: Industrial Sectors, Product Cycles and Political Consequences', in F.C. Deyo (ed.), *The Political Economy of New Asian Industrialism* (Ithaca, NY, Cornell University Press, 1987), pp. 55–56.
37. Arrighi, Giovanni: *The Long Twentieth Century. Money, Power and the Origins of our T Times* (London and New York, Verso, 1994), p. 342. The pressure to lower costs did not come from its wage rate in absolute terms, but from the USA. All through the Vietnam war the US had been happy to use Japan as a cheap offshore platform for producing many of the goods it needed to wage war. But when the war substantially ended in 1973, Washington began to put pressure on Tokyo to revalue the yen and open up the Japanese economy to trade and foreign investment. Japan responded to

the pressure by extending the multi-layered subcontracting system, which had been pioneered by Toyota as part of the system of flexible production and copied by other industries, to the low wage countries around it. In the end, it was the US dollar that had to be devalued. Between 1970 and 1978, in terms of the IMF's Special Drawing rights, its value fell from $1 per SDR to $1.3028 per SDR. With the breakdown of the Bretton Woods system of fixed exchange rates, the Japanese yen too appreciated, from 360 per SDR to 253. But this reflected Japan's growing economic power, born of its success in keeping down its costs and developing and capturing new markets, rather than any concession to US demands. As Arrighi remarks, 'The US government turned to close the stable door, but the horse had already bolted. Or, rather, the geese were flying.'

6

The End of Organised (National) Capitalism

The 'crisis decades' have seen almost every institution and every cosy belief of the golden age of capitalism turned on its head. In the industrialised countries, the once all-powerful trade union movement has been crippled; wages, working hours and conditions of work have been deregulated to the disadvantage of the worker; income differentials have widened; and social security benefits have been steadily cut down or privatised. Maxims of economics that had almost become truisms, such as that there could be no permanent (i.e., non-cyclical) unemployment in the industrialised countries; that international trade necessarily benefited all participants; and that factor prices tended to converge between trading partners in the long run, have all been brought into question by actual developments. All this has taken place within a short span of less than three decades, and has been collectively referred to as the end of organised capitalism.[1] But the phrase describes rather than explains what has happened. The common cause of all these near simultaneous changes is the onset of systemic chaos. As happened in previous cycles of its expansion, when capitalism broke out of the container of the nation state in the last third of the twentieth century and started to create a single global market, it began to destroy not merely the institution of the national market but also the framework of laws, conventions and organisations, built over two centuries, that had sustained and humanised it.

That framework, the modern welfare state, was a product of 'a 200-year developmental process that began with the revolutionary birth of modern nation states'.[2] In a profoundly perceptive essay, Jurgen Habermas has pointed out that the conflicts, tensions, contradictions and ambiguities that we collectively refer to when we seek to describe a society turn into political challenges only when the individuals who make up that society cease to believe that these are natural and immutable, and start to believe that they can change them through collective action. 'Society' then develops a normative meaning, as an organisation of human beings governed according to the principles of natural law. But such a society can be built only by all members working together within a clearly defined space in which they have the capacity to act. That requirement was fulfilled by the democratic nation state, with its sharply defined frontiers, and the option it gave to all of its members to participate in the framing of law and its implementation.[3] Globalisation has critically weakened the welfare state, not merely by softening the economic boundaries of the nation state but, more insidiously, by eroding the belief that the tensions globalisation is creating can be tackled by concerted democratic action. 'Since 1989,' observes Habermas, 'more and more politicians seem to be saying: if we can't solve any of these conflicts, let us at least dim the critical insights that turn conflicts into challenges.'[4]

The assault on the nation state has begun in the realm of the economy. The nation state is the political container of the national market. By creating a market and a manufacturing network that transcends the national market, globalisation is eroding the economic foundations of the nation state.

Competition and Regulation: The Origins of the National Market

To those who accept uncritically (and out of context) Adam Smith's definition of the market as a product of man's innate propensity to 'barter, truck and exchange one thing for another', the proposition that the 'global' and 'national' markets are two different institutions locked in a contradiction, such that the birth of one necessarily means the death of the other, may not be easy to grasp. Classical economic theory regarded (and neo-classical theory by and large still regards) markets as a natural development born in the barter system of the village and exchanges in the local market town, and steadily extended by the development of money as a medium of exchange, the improvement of water-borne and then overland transport and, finally, by the development of manufacturing to cover region, nation and the world. The theory goes that the increase in demand made possible a finer and finer division of labour, and therefore progressively raised labour productivity. Neo-classical economists therefore regard the present phase of development of capitalism as a *globalisation of the market economy* and not as *the birth of a global market economy*. This makes it difficult to identify any discontinuity and therefore any qualitative change in the nature of the market of a kind that would explain the changes that have taken place in the OECD countries in the last quarter century.

The idea that the global market economy is of a different logical order from the national market economy and is locked in conflict with it is easier to grasp when viewed from the perspectives of economic history and anthropology. Anthropologists hold a very different view of the origins of the market from economists. To them, the market is not natural, but a man-made creation that originated in long-distance trade and not in barter at the local level.[5] What is more, *it originated at least as much in an attempt to regulate and prescribe limits to competition as to foster it.*

Long-distance trade between communities developed as an alternative to war and plunder for obtaining what one did not have. The motive force behind the replacement of plunder with trade was the need to limit the ravages of war, which was the most extreme and destructive form of competition between societies. Trade therefore originated in the effort not to promote but to impose order upon, and thereby limit, the competitive instinct in man. Between primitive tribes this regulation was done by developing elaborate rituals and taboos, all of which cumulatively bestowed an aura of sanctity and magic on trade. This was extended to all forms of exchange, including those that took place in local markets.

Till well into the nineteenth century, the instinct for plunder survived in the form of piracy and the slave trade, but side by side there also grew the desire to curb this and other excesses of competition through regulation. In medieval Europe, as the mode of transport improved, long-distance trade between its semi-independent, walled cities flourished and increased the capital in the hands of the traders. The more this happened, the more did the Burgesses of the cities seek to segregate inter-city trade, which they could not regulate, from trade between each city and its hinterland, which they could. The purpose of segregation was to prevent the long-distance traders from commercialising some of the necessities that the village supplied to the towns and unleashing inflation and possibly famine. Either would gravely reduce the well-being of the majority of the townsmen, and increase inequalities in the distribution of income and wealth.[6]

The regulation of trade was an intrinsic part of nation building in Europe. The Crown made common cause with the long distance domestic traders to destroy the autonomy of the medieval towns, and create a national market that it could tax to assure itself of a secure base of power. At the same time it banned the export of a wide range of commodities that were deemed to be the keys to national power, notably foodgrains, coal, skilled artisans and, in England after the industrial revolution, machinery.[7] The long, gradual rise of free trade in Europe in the nineteenth century is a chronicle of economic forces overwhelming human endeavours to limit the impact of competition on society. The German *Zollverein* (customs union) was formed as a defence against the invasion of the markets of the

German states by British manufactured goods. Its purpose was not only to expand the internal market, but also to protect it and the nascent German industry. Even free trade was often advocated only to curb competition! In England, the repeal of the corn laws was advocated by the political economists of the Board of Trade—Bowring, Jacob and MacGregor—as a way of channelling German investment into agriculture and slowing down the growth of manufacturing industries that could compete with British industry.[8] What is more, as is described in greater detail below, both France and the US also deliberately used protection to foster the growth of their own manufacturing bases. The second half of the nineteenth century therefore saw trends both towards freer trade and towards greater protection, as the need arose.[9] Markets therefore developed over a period of time, in fits and starts, with both forward and backward movements. They were not the product of the individual's innate desire to trade, but of a compromise between two conflicting social forces—competition, born of the desire to acquire, and regulation, born of the need to protect society from the worst consequences of competition.

The balance between competition and regulation was abruptly disrupted, within the space of half a century, by the industrial revolution. Prior to this, national and international markets had traded in the products of human beings and the land. Trade therefore served the needs of both, but human beings and land remained outside the system of exchange. This changed abruptly with the industrial revolution. The tremendous increase in productivity unleashed by the spate of inventions and innovations disrupted the system of direct production in response to specific orders that had prevailed earlier, and replaced it with 'roundabout production', in which the producers lost contact with the buyers and had to estimate in advance how much of the product they were likely to sell. This led to periodic over- and under-estimation of demand and consequently of production. That gave birth to the trade cycle.

From National to Self-Regulating Market

The early decades of the industrial revolution saw immense fluctuations in foreign trade, which triggered large domestic trade cycles.[10] In England, the decade after the Seven Years War (1763) saw an enormous boom in trade, but the subsequent two decades were described by Burke as 'a bad cycle of twenty years'.[11] Inevitably the workers, who had by then lost their link with the land, found no dearth of work in good times but were thrown out unceremoniously in bad ones. Some sank into destitution, prostitution and crime in the cities. Large numbers went back to their villages and threw themselves on the mercy of their parishes, which were obliged to support them under the Poor Laws. By degrees, therefore, the industrial revolution converted human beings into 'Labour', a commodity like any other—to be bought and sold, or hired and fired.

The second factor of production to be turned into a commodity was gold. In mercantilist days, gold was a source of political and military power, acquired and hoarded to extend the power of the Crown. The state did this internally by using it to pay the civil servants who collected its taxes, and externally by maintaining a standing army or hiring mercenaries to fight foreign wars. But the new mills, with their vastly expanded scale of production and much longer production cycles, needed finance to organise production and await sales. Thus with the arrival of 'roundabout' production, gold became another commodity, whose 'price' was the rate of interest.

Finally, land too went the way of labour and capital, albeit more slowly. In Britain, it was not until the Great Depression of 1872–1896 (a period that should have been called the Great Deflation) that collapsing prices of agricultural produce finally forced land on to the market in large quantities and turned it into a commodity. The deflation was caused partly by the development of the railways and steamships, which led to large scale imports of cheap wheat and other grain from Eastern Europe, the USA and Australia, and partly by a sheer scarcity of gold in relation to the rise in the value of monetised transactions.[12]

The self-regulating market thus differs profoundly from the 'national' market of the pre-industrial epoch. In the self-regulating market, products and factors of production are bound together by a single inexorable, mechanical (and therefore non-human) law—the law of supply and demand. When the demand for products rises, the demand for factors of production also rises. When one falls, the other falls too. The self-regulating market therefore turned what was previously a one-way relationship into a two-way relationship—instead of commodities having value because they served human needs, humans found their own value tied to the needs of commodity production.

The rise of the self-regulating market in the late eighteenth and early nineteenth centuries represented the most complete victory of the forces of competition over those of regulation that humanity had ever known. Had it not been challenged by human beings, who banded themselves together to fight what they could not fight alone, it would have yielded 'a stark utopia' that could not have existed for any length of time without 'annihilating the human and natural substance of society'.[13]

Society's response took the form of protectionism in international economic relations, and the emergence of political economy in domestic relations. The origins of political economy lay in the debates on pauperism, which resumed in the second half of the eighteenth century after a hiatus of almost a century and a half. In England, the economic expansion after 1763 did not immediately improve the condition of the poor, either in the towns or villages, because it coincided with the second enclosure movement in agriculture. Instead, society found itself confronting an entirely new phenomenon—the emergence of a class of able-bodied destitutes, people who wanted to work but for whom there were no jobs. The response of the Crown was immediate but paternalistic. It took the form of the Speenhamland Act of 1795, which was designed to reinforce the Elizabethan Poor Laws. However, it was not long before those hurt by the emergence of the self-regulating market began to organise themselves. The Luddites in 1812, the Chartists in the 1830s, and the Owenite socialists a little later made early attempts to frontally oppose, or accommodate to, the self-regulating market. The opposition strengthened dramatically during the 'Great Depression' in the 1870s, 1880s, and 1890s. These decades gave birth to radicalism, mass politics, trade unionism and theories of class war, and in continental Europe and the USA a return to protection in order to foster industrialisation.[14]

The end product of the conflict was social democracy—democracy allied to the welfare state. Social democracy was an attempt to reconcile individual freedom with the primacy of society over the individual; in short, to reconcile the Liberalism of the Social Contract and the Manchester School with the Conservatism of Edmund Burke. The compromise it represented was a triumph of enlightened conservatism, in as much as it accepted the need to limit individual freedom in order to maintain social cohesion. This is the balance that the rise of global capitalism has set out to destroy.

Late National versus Early Global Capitalism

The contradiction between national and global capitalism becomes easier to understand when we relate it to the principal features of early and mature (or late) capitalism. Early or competitive capitalism has the following features:

1. There are many buyers and sellers of each product. Markets are therefore highly competitive.
2. The typical firm is small in size.
3. The main mode of competition is through price undercutting. Prices are therefore flexible, and change frequently.

4. Firms are keen to maximise profits, but the preoccupation is with immediate or short-term profit. The typical response to surges in demand is to raise prices.
5. Labour is not unionised. Wage contracts are therefore made with individual workers.
6. The market for labour is highly competitive. As a result, low wages, long working hours, and poor and unsafe working conditions are normal. Workers are fully commodified and enjoy no social security.
7. Trade cycles are huge and uncontrolled, because there is no automatic mechanism for sustaining consumer demand during a recession, such as would be provided by a social insurance system.
8. Cycles of employment followed by unemployment prevent the poor from building up any permanent assets. As a result, poverty, homelessness and crime are endemic.

By contrast, the principal features of mature capitalism can be listed as follows:

1. While there may still be many buyers, there are only a small number of sellers. Most markets for products and services cease to be competitive and become oligopolistic.
2. The typical firm is large in size and dominates its market. Competition continues to exist, but it takes a form different from that of early capitalism, for it is between giant firms that are capable of exploiting breakthroughs in technology to enter almost any market at will. Competition therefore takes the form of a threat of entry. It is not between many producers producing the same product at a point in time. Small enterprises also continue to exist, but they do so in a symbiotic relationship with the oligopolistic firms, as specialised suppliers of parts or materials. They seldom survive in direct competition with oligopolistic firms.
3. There is a substantial degree of price stability, born of unwillingness among the oligopolistic firms to enter into price competition with each other.
4. Short-term profit maximisation through price changes gives way to long-term profit 'normalisation' through price stability. Firms strive to increase their total profits by enlarging their share of the market.
5. Labour is highly unionised. Wages are set by collective bargaining, at least at the factory level, but in full-blown mature capitalism (such as during the 'Golden Age') at the industry-wide or national level as well. Blue-collar workers form the core of the trade union movement, and set the terms of wage bargaining for the country.

6. There is a fully developed welfare state.
7. The amplitude of the trade cycle is damped by the social insurance provisions of the welfare state. Unemployment benefits, child support and other family allowances, and old age pensions create a segment of income that is immune to the effects of the trade cycle. The larger this segment, the smaller the share of income that rises and falls with the trade cycle.

Comparing the trends being witnessed in the industrialised countries with the models of early and mature capitalism sketched out above shows how the rise of global capitalism is dragging the industrialised countries back towards a new variant of early capitalism:

1. There has been a sharp intensification of competition. This has been caused by the disappearance of natural and man-made barriers to the unification of the global market.
2. Within the national economies of the industrialised countries, there has been a 'deconcentration' of capital.[15] First, firms have grown 'leaner', by selling off subsidiaries and unrelated businesses, and concentrating on their areas of core competence. In most cases this has reduced their overall share of the home market. Second, these firms have at the same time entered into mergers and amalgamations with businesses in their own and in other countries that can add to their core competence. There has thus been a 'concentration' of capital in the global market, as fewer and fewer firms are left in each core area of production. Third, global concentration has increased further when firms have shifted manufacturing and service operations to low-wage countries. The second and third developments are reproducing on a global scale the process of transition from competitive to oligopolistic economies that the national market economies experienced during the middle stages of their own capitalist development.
3. There has been a wholesale dismantling of price and marketing regulations. This has resulted in the return of price flexibility and an intensification of price competition between firms.
4. The concept of profit normalisation is once more in retreat. Profit maximisation has increasingly become the corporate goal. This is not expressed directly but indirectly, as the need to keep share prices rising.
5. Trade unionism is in retreat. National-level collective bargaining has given place increasingly to firm or factory level bargaining and individual wage contracts.

6. The welfare state is also in retreat. Welfare payment are being reduced, privatised, or made more strictly conditional.

7. A class of working poor has been reborn. These are full-time or part-time workers who do not earn a subsistence wage. At the lower fringe of this class are the permanently unemployed. In an echo of the debates preceding the reform of the Poor Law in England in 1834, there is an increasing reluctance among law makers to acknowledge the existence of the able-bodied unemployed. This is reflected in terms like 'welfare scroungers'[16] and the imposition of time limits for the receipt of welfare.

8. Poverty, homelessness, crime and social disintegration are once again on the rise.

9. The amplitude of the trade cycle has once more expanded. This may look at first sight like a counter-intuitive conclusion, for it is patently not so within the industrialised countries. In them the up-and-down swings have been smoothed out to the point where towards the end of the great upswing of the 1990s in the USA, liberal economists had begun to talk of a 'new economy' in which the trade cycle had finally been tamed. The picture however alters sharply if one begins to think of the world as a single economy without borders. Within this economy, the freedom of capital movement, and the high level of integration of manufacturing has created conditions not dissimilar to those that existed in England at the time of Burke. For instance, a recession in consumer demand in the US or Europe gets translated into a decline in orders to firms in South Korea, Mexico and China. By the same token, when the central bank of an industrialised country raises interest rates to curb inflation during the last stages of an economic upswing, it causes investors to bring some of their money back from foreign markets. The resulting outflow of foreign exchange can trigger a balance of payments crisis, a sharp increase in interest rates, devaluation and recession in the developing countries to which the parent multinationals have outsourced their manufacture. The succession of economic crashes along the periphery of the global economy—in Mexico (1994), Southeast Asia (1997), Russia (1998), Turkey (2000) and Argentina (2002)—are the amplified reflection of impulses generated in the core of the global economy, amplified by mistakes in domestic policy and the herd behaviour of international investors. There are at present no contra-cyclical 'global' policies for controlling the spread of recession or boom across frontiers.

These changes are discussed in greater detail below:

Deregulation

The rise of trade unions, collective bargaining and the welfare state in the last quarter of the nineteenth century 'organised' the 'labour' side of the capitalist equation. There was a parallel organisation of capital. The key elements of this were the rise of monopolistic firms, the separation of ownership from management, and the rise of a 'service class' of salary-earning managers and administrators located between labour and capital. Together these developments humanised capitalism and enabled society to move away from the 'stark utopia' of its early days. These developments profoundly altered the goals of the firm. Where the owner manager had been primarily interested in maximising short-term profit, large professionally managed firms began to take a much longer-term view of the notion of profit. More specifically, they brought in the notion of sustainability. In an increasingly oligopolistic world, heavy profit taking by one company attracted new producers into the industry. This could easily trigger a price war that would leave all of them much worse off than they had been before. Long-term profit maximisation therefore required restraint in the short term.

In practice this meant that firms tried to take advantage of buoyant market conditions more by trying to increase their share of the total market than by raising their prices. The fact that professional managers earned salaries and only benefited indirectly from an increase in the company's profits reinforced the tendency to avoid frequent price changes. The market structure that emerged from this was designed to regulate competition, limiting and channelling it to minimise its adverse side effects. Tacit (though also sometimes explicit) codes of conduct came into being that spelt out which types of competition were acceptable and which were to be discouraged. These covered everything from pricing conventions to distribution margins, hours of work, shop opening and closing times, holidays, sales dates, and discount margins. Since organised labour had an interest in many of these issues, it cooperated with management in framing these regulations and conventions. Cooperation between employers and workers made it easy to enshrine the more important of these agreements in law. Cooperation begot more cooperation: the realisation that there were substantial areas in which the interests of labour and capital converged led to a further enlargement of the areas of cooperation.

This 'civilising' process has gone into reverse gear. On the capital side of the equation, the most striking change is 'deregulation'—a systematic dismantling of the rules governing the avoidance of price competition and other forms of competition. Beginning with an attack on resale price maintenance (and consequently on retail distribution margins) in the 1970s, deregulation has spread to every corner of the market for goods and services. It has invaded the service industries, such as stores, restaurants, hotels, airlines, bus and truck transport, and, most striking of all, has spread to the public utilities such as electricity, gas and telecommunication. The common feature of all deregulation is the withdrawal of state sanction to economic regulations that tend to limit competition. Its justification is that this is needed to promote competition, and that competition is necessarily beneficial to consumers and to the economy.

Deregulation has undoubtedly fostered competition. But it is competition among giants. In industry after industry, contrary to the expectations of the economists and policymakers, deregulation has led to a spate of takeovers and mergers. For instance, before the deregulation of the US telecom industry, there were seven large local telecom companies. A year later there were only five left.[17] Three years later there were only three. According to the UN's World Investment report, cross-border investments in mergers and acquisitions (M&As) among developed countries skyrocketed from $195 billion in 1996 to $233 billion in 1997 and to a record $468 billion in 1998, as deregulation and corporate restructuring gathered momentum in Europe. The number of M&As increased from 163 to 236 to 411 in the respective periods.[18] In 1999 the pace of M&As quickened further. Europe recorded $1.2 trillion dollars worth of deals, an increase of 50 per cent over 1998. The proportion of stock market activity generated by M&As in Europe exceeded that in America for the first time.[19] Equally significant is the number of changes in the regulatory regime that countries have enacted in the 1990s. Between 1991 and 1998, a total of 839 such changes were made. Of these, 789 were designed to facilitate foreign direct investment, while only 50 went the other way. The number of changes made every year increased from 80 in 1991 to 136 in 1998.[20]

But in contrast to what happened as capitalism matured within nations in the last quarter of the nineteenth century, the reduction in the number of firms in the global market and the increase in their size have not gone hand in hand with an increase in price and tariff stability, or better working conditions for the employees. On the contrary, the single-minded purpose of mergers has been to bolster profits by concentrating on areas of core competence, downsizing the labour force and beating down wages.[21]

For instance, Britain's British Telecom shed half its workforce after deregulation in 1984. Telecom Finland shed 40 per cent of its workforce after 1989.[22] All these were responses to the cut-throat competition into which computerisation, miniaturisation, and the 'digital' revolution had thrust firms that had once enjoyed a secure, oligopolistic existence. But they echoed the cut-throat practices in business and industry that existed in the late eighteenth century and most of the nineteenth century within national economies.

How Deregulation Works: The US Road Transport Industry

The US truck transport industry provides an excellent example of the way in which deregulation has triggered a 'race to the bottom' in workers' wages. Prior to 1935 the trucking industry was unregulated and suffered from most of the problems that have resurfaced today. It had extremes of price competition, very low rates of return, and consequently a very high rate of failure among trucking companies. All these tendencies were severely accentuated by the depression of the 1930s, and led to a succession of local strikes in 1934. As a result the Roosevelt administration passed a Motor Carrier Act in 1935 to regulate competition in the industry with the express purpose of preventing it from destroying itself. The act delegated the task of preventing 'destructive competition' to the US Interstate Commerce Commission (ICC). The ICC did this by regulating entry into the industry; setting up rate bureaus in which the carriers met to fix rates, and preventing a variety of discriminatory trade practices such as offering discounts to large shippers and refusing business from small ones. These regulations stabilised the industry by addressing the problems of the truckers, the shippers and the public, and provided a basis for resolving labour-management disputes. The Act did not immediately result in higher wages for truckers, but provided the foundation for future improvements. The task of wage bargaining was taken over by the Teamsters' Union, which became the most powerful union in the country.[23] Truckers' wages rose under the spur of collective bargaining during and after the war. Till 1958 their wages were comparable to those earned by the average blue-collar worker, but in the decade that followed, their earnings rose to match those of the autoworkers, then the highest-paid workers in manufacturing industry.[24]

The stage was set for deregulation when the Teamsters' Union over-reached itself in the early 1970s. In the battle of succession that followed after the Teamster leader James Hoffa was sent to jail in 1967, rival teamster leaders pushed up the wage rates by 20 per cent in real terms over the next six years. This coincided with the oil price shock, recession and the birth of an all-pervasive fear of inflation. By 1977 the ICC had begun to ease the regulations governing the industry in order to increase competition and hold down wages and trucking rates. In 1980 the US Congress passed another Motor Carrier Act that formally lifted all restrictions on entry into the industry, sharply limited collective rate fixation, and permitted the truck companies to indulge in price discrimination.[25] The effect on truckers' earnings was dramatic. Between 1977 and 1987 their average wages per truck mile fell by 44 per cent in real terms. Truckers compensated for the drop by working longer and driving faster. But despite that, by 1995 their average annual earnings in real terms had dropped by 30 per cent. This was four times the drop in real earnings suffered by blue-collar workers.[26] By 1996, membership of the Teamsters' Union had dropped to 25 per cent of trucking industry workers, as against 60 per cent in 1968. The average unionised road driver worked 65.7 hours a week against the legal work-week limit of 60 hours.[27] A survey by the US Department of Transportation showed that 15 per cent of all truck-related accidents were caused by fatigue.[28]

The airlines industry in the US, which was also deregulated in the late 1970s, has experienced both the trends described above—a rapid consolidation into a few giant carriers after an initial period of competition, followed by a segmentation of fares and a dispersion of wages. At the same time, consolidation has led to the downsizing of the workforce, especially the nonflying staff, and to successive rounds of wage agreements that have created a two-tier system of wages in which new entrants are hired at much lower salaries than existing staff.[29]

What is true of truck transport and airlines is true of the entire retail distribution sector. Deregulation has led to the displacement of hundreds of thousands of small neighbourhood stores by giant retail chains like K-Mart and Walmart in the US, or Safeways in Britain. Most of these are open 20–24 hours a day, seven days a week. They work on slim distribution margins that were unheard of in the 1960s and are a boon to budget-minded consumers. But the store staff work erratic hours, earn barely more than the minimum wage and strive to keep up a minimum standard of living by working overtime.

Deregulation of Financial Markets

Globalisation is most advanced in the financial sector. International banking had developed rapidly in the 1960s under the impact of the transnationalisation (then mainly across the Atlantic) of manufacturing, a boom in mergers in the 1960s and the rapid growth of international trade. But the pace of globalisation took a quantum leap with the formation of the Euromoney market. The origins of the Euromoney market lay in the role assigned to the dollar under the Bretton Woods system of management of the international payments system. Under this system, exchange rates were fixed, the price of gold was pegged at $35 to the troy ounce, and the dollar was the currency of accounting for international payments. The strength of the dollar lay in its fixed value and the readiness of the US government to exchange all dollars brought to the Federal Reserve for gold. Gold thus backed the dollar, and the dollar under-wrote international trade and investment. In these circumstances, as American companies increased their international business, they began borrowing from European banks. With the dollar being as good as gold, these banks began to denominate their loans in dollars instead of their national currencies. What is more, much of this banking began to take place outside the framework of national regulations. Since American companies could repay these loans in their own currency, they did not feel any need to earn foreign exchange to do so. Over time therefore they borrowed more abroad than they generated by way of foreign exchange earnings. This American deficit became a pool of Eurodollar deposits. As it was backed by the promise of conversion into gold, it became a part of the banks' assets, on whose basis they made further loans. Thus was the Euromoney market born.

When rising direct investment abroad, the shift of manufacture to offshore locations and the Vietnam war all turned the US' trade and payments surplus into a deficit in the late 1960s, the US began to pile up international debt. The more this grew, the more nervous the US government became about its capacity to honour its commitment to convert dollars into gold. To limit its exposure, it created a two-tier system for exchanging dollars into gold in 1968, and devalued the dollar in 1970. But each innovation further reduced the confidence of Eurodollar holders in the stability of the currency and increased the possibility of a future run on gold. As a result, on 15 August 1971 the US ended the convertibility of dollars into gold. Two years later, after another run on the dollar, the US gave up fixed exchange rates. That marked the demise of the Bretton Woods system.

The Eurodollar market was thus set adrift. The value of the dollar was thenceforth determined by demand and supply, by relative interest rates, and waxing and waning confidence in its stability. International borrowers and depositors now felt free to shop around for the best currencies in which to hold their deposits, so other offshore currency markets blossomed. As US deficits continued to pile up, the Eurocurrency market grew at a ferocious pace. The value of external claims on the international banks rose from $44 billion in 1969 to $800 billion by 1980.[30]

However, for want of an alternative to gold and in the presence of a wholly inadequate supply of the IMF's Special Drawing Rights, the US dollar remained the unit in which most countries held their foreign exchange reserves. This meant that while all other countries had to balance their external accounts, the US did not. For the US, the Euromoney market was like a goldmine at the bottom of the garden.[31] Throughout most of the 1980s, all of the 1990s and the first decade of the new millennium, the US was able to run up balance of payments deficits of between $200 billion and $500 billion a year,[32] without having to ever make good the amount. What was therefore to the rest of the world an international economic transaction became a domestic transaction for the US. The world, in short, became a part of the US domestic market. This is the reason why the US boom of the 1990s could be so prolonged. Faced with external payments deficits of $300 to $400 billion a year, any other country would have been forced to straightaway raise interest rates, in order to create a countervailing inflow of foreign investment on the capital account. The US last did that in 1979. After 1982 it kept its interest rates low and allowed the balance of payments deficit to grow.

The growth of regulation-free offshore finance was bound to generate pressure for deregulation in the domestic sector as well. That deregulation began in the 1980s in the UK, US and Sweden, and in a tentative way in 1993 in Japan. The UK lifted all restrictions on financial institutions with a 'Big Bang' in 1986. Japan carried out its Big Bang in 1998. In the rest of Europe deregulation gained momentum after the creation of the Euro. Deregulation involved giving free entry into the financial sector; breaking down the walls between international and domestic banking; allowing foreign banks to compete freely with domestic banks; and removing the walls that separated various types of financial activities, such as commercial and investment banking, management of pension funds and investment trusts, hire purchase, insurance, brokerage, and 'convenience' banking (like establishing ATMs in stores).[33]

Pressure to Maximise Profits

Deregulation has also put pressure on firms to adopt profit maximisation strategies as distinct from profit 'normalisation' ones. This is a consequence of the return of wage and price flexibility. Regulations governing these were mutually reinforcing elements of 'organised capitalism'. When these were knocked away, the behaviour of firms also changed radically. 'Deregulation of vital sectors such as Telecommunications and electricity is sharpening price competition and improving consumer choice,' wrote *The Financial Times* in a recent survey of Europe.[34]

But more specifically, the return of profit maximisation is a sequel to the deregulation of the financial markets. Both in the UK and the US, financial deregulation has caused an explosion in both the number and variety of financial instruments offered to shareholders. It has also brought large numbers of new players into the stock market, who were previously constrained from entering it or could only do so within strictly laid down limits. These new players include financial giants like pension and mutual funds, insurance companies, and hedge funds, whose decision to invest a portion of their capital in the share market, as against bonds and preference shares, has boosted share prices to unheard of peaks. As share prices have risen, the returns they offer, which are linked to the original face value of the share, have dwindled into insignificance. As a result, more than they ever did before, investors in the share market look to an appreciation in the price of their shares, rather than to the dividends offered by the company, to reward their investment. Dividends are, almost by definition, long-term returns. Investors who look to these as a source of income tend to be stable shareholders, whose shares come only infrequently on the market. By contrast, investments in shares, which are intended to obtain a return mainly through capital gains, tend to be short-term and, on the margin, entirely speculative. The linking of share and financial markets around the world, the advent of 24-hour trading, and the employment of computers programmed to buy and sell automatically on specified signals from the market has immensely increased speculation and enhanced the volatility of share markets.

The increasing preoccupation with capital gains has altered the way in which corporate performance is judged. Traditional measures of soundness, such as the return on capital employed, the size of corporate reserves, the ratio of assets to liabilities, the rate of growth of turnover, expansion and modernisation plans, and market share have given place to the singular concept of 'shareholder value', i.e., market capitalisation.

Shareholder value is driven mainly, although not entirely, by predictions of corporate profitability or revenue made by professional analysts attached to major banks, mutual funds and consultancy companies. The speculative nature of the stock market ensures that these forecasts drive share prices up or down by large amounts. Failure to fulfil the analysts' predictions causes even sharper dips in price, while over-fulfilment causes equally sharp up-surges. Typical of these swings was the performance of two blue-chip companies, Morgan Stanley Dean Witter, the US' second largest securities firm, and 'a darling of the stock market', and Intel Corporation, the world's largest micro-processor manufacturer. Morgan Stanley's net income rose by 28 per cent in the third quarter of 2000 over the same period of 1999, and earnings per share increased by 31 per cent. But these earnings fell 6.8 per cent short of what analysts had predicted. As a result, the price of Morgan Stanley's shares fell by 6.8 per cent. In the same quarter, Intel's shares fell in value by 20 per cent when the company announced that its sales revenue would increase by 3–5 per cent, against the analysts' predictions of 12–15 per cent. This fall occurred despite a forecast of a gross profit in the third quarter of 2000, to the tune of 62 per cent on capital employed! Nor did the share market take into account the possibility that the third quarter revenues had not risen as fast as expected because the rise in the second quarter had set a record.[35] Thirty years earlier, such marginal failures to meet expectations would have been shrugged away.

It would have been surprising indeed if the growing global preoccupation with quick returns on investment had not affected corporate strategy. The need to augment shareholder value has put immense pressure on the corporate managers of enterprises. Compelled to show improvements every quarter, they have reacted in ways that are both positive and negative. The positive response has been an immense increase in efficiency. For instance, it has immensely speeded up the implementation of new projects and the modernisation of existing plants and factories. It has also predisposed managers to analyse the causes of failure to meet analysts' expectations far more quickly than they would have done a half-century ago, and to adopt remedial measures more promptly. The negative responses include raising prices where this is feasible, downsizing the staff strength and beating down wages to reduce labour costs, and cutting down R&D expenses or postponing investment in upgrading technology, in order to boost distributed dividends and thus prop up or artificially inflate share prices. As the Enron bankruptcy case has shown, at its worst the response does not stop short of falsifying accounts and bribing the auditors.[36]

While these changes are most noticeable in the US and Britain, corporate behaviour has changed in important ways in Europe and Japan too. Under the spur of growing competition in saturated markets, and high wage and exchange rates that reduce their competitiveness, European concerns are forsaking long-term relationships with investment banks and going into the open market to raise capital on the most favourable terms. The banks on their part are less committed to long-term relationships with companies in which they 'nurse' the latter through rough patches, and share with them the risks involved in commercialising new technologies. Instead they are following the lead given by British and American banks, and treating their investments in companies purely as profit-making exercises, to be terminated when returns fall below a threshold level.

Some of the most significant changes are taking place in Germany, the bastion of neo-corporatist 'Rhenish' capitalism. In Germany, as in much of Western Europe, the post-war reconstruction was financed by commercial banks, as alternate sources of finance had virtually ceased to exist. This intensified an alliance of that had come into being in the late nineteenth century and had been responsible for much of Germany's hectic, technology-intensive growth in the inter-war years. In this 'Rhine-Alpine' pattern, banks took shareholdings in industrial enterprises, sat on their supervisory boards, and identified themselves with the companies' aspirations. This resulted in long-term commitments that were reflected in more stable shareholdings, small share markets, and lower returns for the banks for their shares than were to be found in the US or Britain. Since the banks, insurance companies and other financial institutions invested in many concerns, this also yielded a complex pattern of cross-holdings which meshed German industry together in synergistic relationships during the period of reconstruction and growth. Add to this strong trade unions, centralised bargaining, and worker representation both on the supervisory boards and works councils (and consequently the lowest strike rate in the industrialised world), and the result was the uniquely successful 'German model' of the Golden Age.

This structure showed the first signs of coming apart in the mid-1990s. A number of large conglomerates, like Hoechst and Daimler Benz, began to sell off peripheral businesses in order to concentrate on areas of core competence. In both these cases, this was a prelude to trans-border mergers, such as Hoechst with the French pharmaceuticals company Rhone-Poulenc, and Daimler Benz with Chrysler. The sale of thriving subsidiary businesses by the pioneers galvanised the stock market and sent prices zooming. Banks realised that this was an excellent way of simultaneously strengthening their companies and making a large return on their long and patient investments. In 1998 Deutsche Bank, which owned $30 billion worth of shares in German industry, reorganised its management structure and created a special unit that would treat its shareholding as a separate profit division, much as any portfolio manager would. Allianz, an insurance company with even larger stakes in industry, lured away a Goldman Sachs executive to do the same thing.[37] In 1999 Siemens unveiled a plan to sell off, on the stock market, businesses that employed a third of its workforce. By then venture capital businesses were booming, and a *Neuer Markt* (New Market, or small company stock market) had come into being. Not surprisingly, equity holdings of German families, which had made up 10 per cent of gross disposable income in 1990–94, shot up to 22 per cent in the beginning of 1999.[38]

German industry crossed a watershed at the end of 1999 when, in the first-ever hostile takeover of a major German concern, Vodaphone Airtouch of Britain bought Mannesman to create a huge $350 billion telecom giant. The open bid was made possible by the fact that Mannesman is one of the 20 per cent of German firms that is widely held. But the $150 billion

Vodaphone paid to shareholders demonstrated the benefits of 'shareholder value' to Germans as few other developments could have. The deal also made the German government clarify the legal and regulatory environment for hostile takeovers. As a result more such takeovers are bound to follow. These will integrate much of German industry with that of the rest of the industrialised countries, and dilute the German model further.

The Return of Price Flexibility

As the competitive ethos has taken hold, enterprises have also gradually lost their aversion to making frequent price changes. This is a not wholly unwelcome development. When costs are falling because of rapid technological change, competition ensures that the benefits are passed on to the consumer in the shortest possible time. This has happened in a vast range of products, notably home appliances, electronic goods and, above all, in computer hardware and software. In others, such as automobiles, while prices may not have fallen, the quality of the product has improved beyond recognition. However, where technological change has been slow, as in the development of commercial airlines, price deregulation has ushered in the practice of charging whatever the market will bear. Since the pace of technological change has been much slower in the service industries, it is not surprising that this is far more pervasive in industries that produce services than in those that produce goods.

The deregulation of the trucking industry led to a rapid segmentation of fares, and the disintegration of fare structures through the offer of discounts—a form of barter. Exactly the same change has taken pace in airline fares, hotel tariffs, and telecom charges. On high-density sectors, such as across the Atlantic, fares and tariffs can vary by as much as four times depending on when one chooses to fly, and how early one buys one's ticket. Airline fares were deregulated first in the USA but deregulation has now spread to all major international and many domestic airlines, and charging what the market will bear has become a near-universal practice. The hotel industry goes one step further than the airlines and discriminates not only between seasons, which is an old practice, but also between individuals, which is relatively new. Here price fixation has regressed to a form of barter, in which large corporate buyers are able to negotiate 'corporate' and 'conference' rates that depend on their strength and the amount of business the hotel chain expects them to put in its way. Barter has crept into the airline industry as well, as travel agents make block bookings at advantageous rates and then resell the seats to individuals.

The Retreat of Social Democracy

Social democracy was the towering achievement of organised capitalism. It was underpinned by an immensely complex system of laws and conventions, collectively designed to protect the losers in competition against having to pay the extreme penalty of social deprivation, pauperisation, and possibly death. Unlike communism and fascist corporatism, it did not try to derail capitalism or replace it with an alternative system in order to limit competition. It accepted that competition would remain the organising principle of a society that would be capitalist, individualistic and based on the free market. The principal tools with which it sought to soften the rigours of competition were the protection, by law, of trade unionism and the right of collective bargaining; the safety of consumers of manufactured products; the safety of workers in the workplace; and the protection of those whom old age, sickness or unemployment had temporarily or permanently ejected from the market system. Social democracy reached its peak at the same time as national capitalism, in the 'Golden Age' of national capitalism from 1945 to 1975. So it is not surprising that it has become the first casualty of global capitalism.

If the rise of capitalism is reflected in the proletarianisation of entire populations that had previously owned their means of production,[39] then the rise of social democracy is reflected in the proportion of the population of a country whose income was protected by income security programmes organised by the state, and the extent of replenishment of their incomes. The seeds of social democracy and the welfare state can be traced back to the provision of social insurance for the sick, the victims of industrial accidents and the elderly by Bismarck in the 1880s in Germany, and of similar legislation by Liberal Prime Minister Herbert Asquith in 1908 and 1911 in Britain.[40] By 1950, half of West Germans and two-thirds of Britons were covered by public pension schemes, to the extent of 41 and 28 per cent respectively of their pre-retirement earnings. The corresponding figures for coverage were 31 per cent for Italy, 40 per cent for the United States, 49 per cent for the Netherlands, and 100 per cent for Sweden; these schemes paid the beneficiaries 18 per cent, 39 per cent, 50 per cent and 27 per cent respectively of their pre-retirement incomes.[41] All these countries also had extensive systems of unemployment compensation. By 1950, moreover, eight out of the 17 larger member-countries of the OECD had consolidated all the five types of social security—old age and disability pensions, sickness and maternity benefits, compensation for industrial accidents, unemployment insurance, and family allowances—into a single over-arching system of social insurance. Another four countries had four out of the five types of social security programmes in place.[42]

Both coverage and income replacement increased sharply during the Golden Age. By 1980, the coverage of the pension schemes had risen to 69 per cent for the US and 92 per cent for the Netherlands, while Sweden remained at 100 per cent. The ratio of pensions to pre-retirement income rose from 28 to 50 per cent in the UK, and from 39 to 67 per cent in the USA. It rose from 41 to 61 per cent in Germany, 18 to 75 per cent in Italy, 50 to 68 per cent in the Netherlands, and 27 to 89 per cent in Sweden. There was a similar sharp increase in coverage and replenishment under the unemployment insurance schemes.[43] By 1980, 16 out of the 17 larger OECD countries had fully consolidated social insurance systems, and social insurance programmes met 13 per cent (Australia) to 39 per cent (Sweden) of the income requirements of the people.[44] The lone exception to full consolidation was the United States.

Trade unions were the driving force behind the rapid consolidation and extension of social insurance. If union density is taken as a proximate measure of the strength of trade unionism, then a comparison of the average union density of the 17 larger OECD member-countries between 1919 and 1950 with the year when full social insurance consolidation was achieved shows a startling correlation. With two exceptions, the higher the average union density, the sooner did social insurance get fully consolidated.[45]

As national capitalism matured, unions rose in status and importance from being defensive associations of workers trying, often in desperation, to gain a modicum of control over their lives, into essential props of the social democratic state, with responsibilities that far transcended simply bargaining for better wages. These included cooperation in maintaining full employment; moderating both upward and downward pressures on wages, keeping these broadly in line with productivity growth; and limiting the disruption of work through strikes by enforcing discipline on enterprise-level unions. This incorporation into the 'social compact' occurred at different paces and to differing extents in the various industrialised countries, but in all of them it led to the formation of industry-wide and sector-wide unions that pursued wage bargaining at the industry level, as opposed to the plant or enterprise level. It also resulted in a greater involvement of the unions in framing policies to safeguard and enlarge the scope of the welfare state. This was embedded in a public discourse that espoused universal ideals such as the need to redistribute income, wealth and authority, and to extend the concept of citizenship to include economic rights and obligations.

The incorporation of the trade unions into the system of governance reached its peak during the Golden Age of national capitalism after the Second World War. In these three decades, unions consolidated themselves into giant national federations and associations—and employers did the same. In some countries the 'organisation of the bottom' preceded the 'organisation of the top', while in others it followed.[46] But during the Golden Age, all industrialised countries developed to varying degrees models of collective bargaining, in which wages, work conditions, and a growing amount of associated legislation were decided by employer association–union negotiations at the national level, with the government acting as referee or participant. Organisation at the national level enabled unions to participate in the political process and to gain concessions from the parties and governments they supported. This facilitated the passing of laws that gave legal underpinning to collective bargaining, by regularising subjects like the right to form unions, the recognition of unions, the right of unions to strike and picket and to regulate the hiring policies of the employer.

There was, inevitably, a latent tension between the industry- and nation-wide goals of the trade unions and their primordial function, to obtain a better wage from the employer. The latter required a maximal approach to wage bargaining: the job of the union was to get as much as it could. How the employer survived the wage shock was his business. The former required the adoption of a normative approach to wage bargaining that took into account the problems of employers, and in particular the great differences in their capacity to pay. During the Golden Age, a unique conjunction of circumstances prevented the conflict from coming into the open. The spread of Fordist mass production to all branches of industry, and the simultaneous incorporation of the many technological advances of the war and depression years in a new generation of equipment, led to the highest and most sustained growth rates the industrialised world had known. For almost two decades these economies hovered close to full employment, and the labour market remained tight. The unions therefore increasingly followed the policy of letting the strongest in each branch or industry set the wage increase in negotiations with the strongest employer. To accommodate weaker employers, they did negotiate a degree of flexibility in its application. But few such compromises were needed at the height of the Golden Age. The high growth of productivity allowed the majority of the employers to pay the higher wages. Those who could not pay, despite the flexibility allowed by the wage agreements, became insolvent and sold out. This led to a concentration of industrial ownership that reinforced the monolithic character of collective bargaining.

Assault on Collective Bargaining

Given the pivotal role they played in the formation of the welfare state, it is not surprising that trade unions became the first casualties of the collision between national and global capitalism. When the Golden Age ended abruptly, the governments of the industrialised countries initially reacted to the onset of 'recession' by adopting Keynesian policies to restore full employment. The stagflation this unleashed increased the insecurity of the workers. They reacted by turning to the unions for protection. As a result the national unions found themselves see-sawing between co-operating with the employers and the government and fighting them. Union membership grew throughout the late 1960s and 1970s, but so did the number of strikes.

The pattern was most noticeable in Britain, where huge strikes in 1974 and again in 1978–79 played a crucial role in unseating the Conservative government of Edward Heath and the Labour government of Jim Callaghan. The failure of these strikes and the anger they aroused in the public did the groundwork for the Thatcher revolution of the 1980s: it rang the death knell of nationwide collective bargaining and began the retreat from social democracy and the welfare state.

Employers, who found their profit margins under pressure from growing international competition and domestic depression, responded by opting out of industry-level wage bargaining and pressing for single-employer wage agreements. As a result, while more than half of British workers were covered by industry-wide agreements in the 1970s, the figure had fallen to just over a third (36 per cent) by 1992. The agreements that were still being struck were more fragile. Between 1986 and 1997, at least 14 agreements, covering 1.2 million workers, collapsed. New firms, and particularly foreign firms, very seldom joined the industry-wide agreements, and insisted upon single-employer bargaining. In the new industry agreements that were still being struck, the employers insisted on greater flexibility regarding work practices, pay flexibility and the right to employ part-time workers.

Employers also derecognised at least 400 unions, covering an estimated 150,000 workers. But this is only explicit derecognition and covers a small fraction of the unions that have been derecognised in practice. Most of the withdrawal of recognition occurred because the older firms that recognised the trade unions had closed down. New firms overwhelmingly preferred to dispense with union representation altogether, or reduce the number of unions they recognised, most often to just one.

More important than the change that had already taken place was the change in employers' attitudes. In 1994 the British Institute of Directors called for the almost complete individualisation of industrial relations, with individual pay contracts and merit pay arrangements, individualised training and employee shareholding. It wanted unions to be eliminated altogether or to be confined to providing services for their employees.[47]

In Germany too, employers began opting out of collective bargaining or, alternatively, striving to introduce flexibility in their wage agreements. In *Gesamtmetall* (General Association of Metal-Industry Employers' Associations), the most important employers' association in Germany, membership fell from 54 per cent of all employers, employing 73 per cent of the workforce in 1980, to 43 per cent, employing 65 per cent of the workforce in 1995.[48] The smaller decline in terms of the workforce shows that it was the smaller employers who were unable to bear the strain imposed upon them by the national-level wage agreements being hammered out on their behalf.

The same trend appeared even in highly corporatised Sweden. High levels of collective bargaining combined with a high exchange rate (a product of the preponderance of raw materials in its exports) to make Swedish labour among the most expensive in the world. As a result, the 1980s saw an 800 per cent increase in foreign direct investment abroad by Swedish companies. Engineering companies in search of cheaper labour and more flexible contracts made nearly all this investment. High wage costs combined with the need to devote more funds to research, design and development to force Swedish employers to find ways to escape from the collective bargaining system enshrined in the 'Swedish model'. By 1993 the leading engineering firms had almost completely opted out of the centralised wage bargaining system.[49]

Japan: The End of Lifetime Employment

The most telling example of the profound change that is taking place is the gradual abandonment of the principle of lifetime employment in Japan. Despite the enormous benefits that Japan garnered from in effect co-opting the working class in the project of making Japan a major economic power, Japanese firms have become more and more chary of making such a large commitment to their employees under the growing strain of a slowdown of growth in the 1980s and nine years of recession that have made unemployment creep up from an insignificant 1 per cent in the late 1980s to 4.5 per cent in 2000. This is reflected in a steep rise in contract (as against lifetime) employees, from 7.9 per cent of the workforce in 1987 to 24.1 per cent in 1997.[50]

In addition, many firms have begun to downsize their workforce. The preferred method is to offer early retirement with generous separation benefits. Early retirement offers began to be made as far back as 1970. They were initially a response to the rapid aging of the workforce and reflected the desire to bring in more young workers, especially from the post-war baby boomers. But when Japanese growth slackened in the 1980s, the practice spread rapidly. As a result the proportion of companies with such schemes grew from 3.2 per cent in 1980 to 7 per cent in 1997. This average figure is misleading, however, because it includes large numbers of small enterprises, which are mainly family run and operated. Among larger firms that work with hired labour, the practice is now general. In 1997, 56 per cent of companies employing more than 5,000 workers, and 41 per cent of those employing more than 1,000 workers, offered early retirement. In roughly half the companies the schemes begin when the workers are in their forties.[51]

The Peace of Defeat

While there are considerable differences in the extent to which the unions have been weakened, especially between the US and Great Britain on the one hand and continental Europe on the other, the trend has been in the same direction throughout the industrialised world. In all countries the membership of trade unions has declined, the proportion of the workers enrolled in unions has fallen, and they have lost most of their bargaining power. Britain has seen the sharpest decline in the unions. Their membership fell for 19 straight years from a peak of 13.3 million[52] in 1979 to 7.3 million in 1999.[53] The 'density' of the unions, i.e., proportion of employees who were members of unions, also fell sharply from 55.4[54] per cent in 1979 to 30 per cent in 1997.[55]

There were similar declines in every industrialised country. In West Germany, trade union membership began declining in the 1980s, after having reached a peak of 9.7 million in 1981. In the 1990s, it swelled briefly after the unification of Germany, but then fell precipitously by a third between 1991 and 2000. The decline was particularly sharp in East Germany, where it fell by more than half.[56] As in Britain, the proportion of the workforce enrolled in unions fell steadily through the 1980s and 1990s, from 35.2 per cent in 1981 to 29 per cent in 1997.[57] French trade unions have suffered the same fate: between 1975 and 1993 their membership fell 42 per cent from 3.668 million to 2.121 million. Union density, which was always much lower in France than in other European countries, fell from 14 to 9 per cent.[58] Union density for salaried workers fell in West Germany from 39 per cent in 1991 to 29.1 per cent in 1995. Italy and Sweden experienced similar declines.[59] In the US, union density declined from 31 per cent in

1970 to 12 per cent in 1989. Even in blue-collar professions, union member-ship fell to 25 per cent of all workers. By the early 1990s, all that was left was 'pockets of organised workers in declining industries', highly remini-scent of the ghetto unionism of the 1920s. The wheel had thus turned almost full circle.[60]

The decline in membership and union density do not tell the whole story. The workers who remain in the unions are the older ones. Among young workers the proportion enrolled in unions is very much lower.[61] In Germany the number of young union members fell by more than half be-tween 1991 and 1996.[62] French unions fared even worse. In the late 1990s, the unionisation rate among workers under 24 was 1 per cent against the national average of 9 per cent.[63]

As the unions have weakened, there has been a sharp decline in their capacity to confront the employers. This is reflected in a dramatic decline in the number of workdays lost because of strikes. The decline has been sharpest in previously strife-torn Britain, from an average of 13 million working days in the 1970s and 11.964 million in 1980 to a mere 278,000 in 1994 and 282,000 in 1998.[64] The average annual loss in the 1980s was one-third the loss in the 1970s. The loss in the 1990s was one-seventh of that in the 1980s.[65] There was a similar decline in labour unrest in the rest of Europe. In France, workdays lost because of strikes fell from 1.523 mil-lion in 1980 to 521,000 in 1994; in Italy from 16.457 million in 1980 to 909,000 in 1995; in Sweden from 4.429 million in 1980 to an average of 184,000 a year in 1991–95. Only in Germany was there no clear declining trend. But this was because, except in two years after unification (1992 and 1993), the loss of workdays remained low throughout.[66]

Understanding the Decline of Collective Bargaining

The emergence of chronic high unemployment is held responsible for the decline in the trade unions' bargaining power, and the consequent fall in their membership. But this is practically a tautology, and therefore tells us very little. Two other explanations have been put forward for the debilita-tion of the trade unions. The first is a so-called 'double shift'—a simul-taneous shift of the locus of decision making, 'upward' from firms and employer associations operating at the national level to those operating at the transnational level, and 'downward to the local', i.e., individual factory, level. Both these shifts weakened the bargaining power of the federations of trade unions that had come into being during the Golden Age, because these were most effective at the national level. The second explanation is the abandonment of full employment as the prime goal of economic policy and its replacement with price stability.

Both these 'explanations' mistake the symptoms of the malady for its cause. The root cause of both these phenomena is the emergence of the global market and the resulting intensification of competition. As competition from low-wage production centres intensified, employers were forced not only to trim costs but also to seek greater flexibility of response in order to cope with new and unexpected threats. They adopted a variety of strategies to cope with the new situation. One was to merge with their peers in other industrialised countries in order to lessen competition and reap economies of scale. Another was to shift investment to low-wage locations abroad in search of cost advantages. Both resulted in increased transnationalisation, and were the cause of the 'upward shift'.

Globalisation also forced employers, who continued to work solely in the now increasingly exposed national market, to respond to the increasing specificity and unpredictability of the threats they were facing. This forced them to opt out of cumbersome industry-wide wage arrangements that could not be changed quickly, and to break the mould of collective national bargaining in all sorts of ways in their bid to survive. Localised wage bargaining was one of them. Other methods included hiring illegal workers and entering into agreements with the unions to show them in their books as earning legal minimum wages.[67] That was the cause of the 'downward shift'.

Piece Rates

Breaking the power of the unions facilitated other changes in the structure of the labour force that weakened them further. All these were propelled by the employers' search for greater wage flexibility. After the end of the Golden Age, employers became more and more reluctant to create full-time jobs in their enterprises. Instead, a rising proportion of the jobs they offered were part-time, temporary or contractual in nature. There was also a rapid increase in the employment of women, often at lower rates of pay than those obtained by men. By 1997, 38 per cent of British workers were in non-permanent or atypical employment.[68] In France, eight out of nine jobs created in 1988 were limited-term, part-time or temporary.[69] A decade later, at the height of Europe's longest and strongest boom, the proportion had remained virtually unchanged: four-fifths of the jobs created in 1998 were in the form of short-term contracts.[70] In West Germany such atypical employment expanded between 1980 and 1997 from 7 to 15.9 per cent of all jobs in the labour market.[71] In the US, the non-standard workforce, i.e., those not in full-time jobs rose steadily to 26.4 per cent of the workforce in 1995, before declining marginally to 24.8 per cent as a result of the boom of the late 1990s.[72]

Similarly, the employment of women has risen rapidly in all countries. In Britain, for instance, women's participation in the labour force rose from 63 per cent in 1979 to 71 per cent in 1991, while the participation rate for men fell from 91 to 88 per cent.[73] Had this happened only during the 'Golden Age' of capitalism, it could have been ascribed to the tight labour market conditions that prevailed during those decades, and a consequent need to draw previously excluded sections of the population into the workforce. But female participation continued to rise even more rapidly during the 1980s and 1990s. In the European Union as a whole, while the number of men employed fell by 4 per cent between 1975 and 1985, the number of women employed rose by 10 per cent. The bulk of the increase was in the service sector. The increase in the female labour force slowed down in the 1980s, but picked up once again in the 1990s. The reason was partly their lower rates of remuneration, but mainly their greater readiness to take up part-time and other atypical forms of employment. This fitted in better with employers' desire to lower wage costs and maintain flexible wage bills.[74]

Increased competition is not, however, the only reason for the rise of part-time and female employment. Behind both one discerns a change in the social values of employers, and indeed of society as a whole. The change is towards an increasing preoccupation with profit, especially short-term profit, and a dwindling concern for social harmony. In the 1930s the celebrated British economist J.M. Keynes, a conservative, had described the rise of collective bargaining as the long-term salvation of capitalism, because it reconciled the stark clash of interests between the workers and employers. Fifty years later, Mrs. Thatcher's government in Britain launched a sustained attack on collective bargaining that spread rapidly to the US, and is still gaining momentum in Europe.

Retreat from the Welfare State

The weakening of trade unionism is reflected in the gradual retreat of the welfare state and social democracy in the late 1980s and 1990s. Using the mean welfare effort put in by the larger OECD countries, spending on social insurance increased steadily as a proportion of the GDP till about 1984 and then levelled off, with a small but distinct decline after 1986.[75] This trend has continued in the 1990s, especially after 1993, but has been gradual and only noticeable when the effects on the rate of growth of

GDP of the economic recession from 1990 to 1993 and the recovery that followed have been allowed for.

The true magnitude of the crisis of the welfare state is revealed only when the irresistible pressures of an aging population and a secular increase in unemployment are 'netted' out, so that one is left with the more discretionary forms of social support: health, family allowances and workers' compensation for accidents. Expenditure on these as a proportion of GDP levelled off as early as 1975 and declined steeply after 1986. The decline is especially sharp for the less corporatist states, i.e., the US, France, Switzerland, Britain, Canada and Australia, than for Scandinavia and northern Europe.[76]

In the US, which does not have a consolidated system of social insurance but a number of separate programmes with different criteria for eligibility, the attack on welfare assumed an omnibus nature with the passage of a welfare reform bill by the Clinton administration in 1996. Under this act, the federal government replaced separate grants for each programme with a single block grant to the state governments to divide among the various programmes in whatever manner they saw fit. This introduced a welcome degree of flexibility in the administration of welfare programmes, but behind this veil also made a profound shift in the rationale of welfare itself. Till then the criteria of eligibility were laid down first and the total amount of spending determined by the number of eligible recipients. Under the new devolution plan the total amount was fixed, and the states were given the freedom to alter the criteria for eligibility to stay within their budgets. 'Welfare' payments—the package of entitlements on various criteria—were inevitably curtailed. Unemployment benefits were made conditional on the recipient having shown that a serious attempt had been made to get a job and failed. Another innovation was 'workfare': an obligation laid upon the state and municipal authorities to find work for as many welfare recipients as possible. The 1996 bill made it mandatory to reduce the number of persons on welfare in this way by 25 per cent in the first two years and by 50 per cent in four.

Britain too introduced two pilot 'workfare' programmes during the Conservative government of John Major, whose express purpose was to weed out the 'welfare scroungers'. Welfare recipients were given 13 weeks to look for a job. If they failed, they were given a job by the government for 13 weeks, which they had to take up. If they refused, they forfeited their unemployment benefits. Many stopped seeking benefits and others refused to appear for the job-seekers' allowance test. That was taken as confirmation that there had indeed been many welfare scroungers.[77] But this conclusion deliberately ignored the possibility that many welfare recipients had wives or husbands who were working, and were not therefore in such dire straits that they would accept jobs that were demeaning, onerous and poorly paid.

Since these people had been paying their social security contributions while they had jobs and were entitled to receive unemployment benefits, this amounted to 'privatising' their insurance by making their spouses bear the burden of their upkeep. When the Labour government came to power, it made only minor modifications to the scheme. One of these was to give the unemployed the option of going back to vocational or higher education as an alternative to 'workfare'. The second was to offer tax credits to unemployed persons with families to support when they took up jobs.[78]

The philosophy behind workfare has begun to take root in continental Europe as well. In 1999, advisers in the French socialist government of Lionel Jospin began talking of the 'Poverty Trap', claiming that high social benefits discourage people from looking for work. The government began to work out tax incentives and other benefit changes to 'steer' the jobless into work.[79]

Homelessness

Subsidised housing for low-income families has been one of the main casualties of the retreat from welfare. Section 8, a programme begun in the US during the Nixon years, which provided housing assistance to 3.6 million families by 1996, had its budget cut between 1992 and 1996 from $25.2 billion to $19.2 billion.[80] In New York city, one of the worst affected, the supply of apartments renting at $450 per month or less fell by 40 per cent between 1981 and 1993. As a result, in October 1996 there was a shortage of 300,000 low-income dwelling units, and 336,000 applicants were on the waiting list for housing assistance—the longest in the city's history. Even this figure understated the true number of those in need, for a year earlier, in 1995, the city's housing authority had closed its doors to fresh applicants for Section 8 rent subsidies, when it calculated that it would take six years to interview those who had already applied for assisted housing. In the summer of 1995, out of sheer desperation it declared that families that were living with other families would no longer be eligible for beds in city shelters. By then privatisation had become all the rage in 'urban renewal'. Not only had the city virtually stopped fore-closing on properties that were in arrears on their tax payments (the way in which it acquired the buildings that it later rented to the poor), but it was also doing all it could to return these to the private sector.[81]

The reason was that the federal assistance for Section 8 housing had fallen way below the cost of maintenance. In 1996 the city estimated that the shelter allowance for welfare had remained static at $286 per apartment for nearly a decade, but the cost of operating a rent-stabilised apartment had risen to about $386 a month.[82] To save on expenses, New York city was also doing its best to reduce its inventory of run-down buildings. It was doing this by encouraging private investors to buy the buildings and turn them into middle-class condominiums. The result was a rapid decline in the number of apartments available for subsidised rentals. To cite a single example, 11,000 apartments were removed in the 1980s from the stock of moderate- and low-income housing in Nassau County, New York, alone.[83]

The long boom in the 1990s accelerated the gentrification of what were previously slum dwellings. As rents rose in urban centres, even slum landlords who previously relied upon Section 8 applicants to fill their apartments began to find regular tenants prepared to pay higher rents. In Louisville, Ohio, a landlord who advertised two apartments in July 1996 received 143 calls, of which 100 were from people who did not need to use Section 8 certificates to pay their rent. As a result, he simply ignored the remaining 43 callers.[84]

In their desperate bid to find housing and to make ends meet, tenants and landlords are breaking existing housing and zoning laws with increasing frequency. Landlords are turning single-family units into tenements. Tenants, especially immigrants, are pooling their incomes and subdividing apartments into communal hostels, with common kitchens and bathrooms. A surprise inspection of an office building in Hicksville, Long Island, in Nassau County of New York State, revealed that the large open rooms had been subdivided into apartments and bedrooms that housed nearly a hundred immigrants. While illegal ghettos have always existed among immigrant communities, a detailed report in the *New York Times* outlined the structural nature of the problem. The bulk of the service sector and many of the blue-collar jobs in the county fetched not more than $250 a week. But there were almost no apartments available for under $900 a month, and very few even for under $1,000. As a result, not just immigrants but a growing proportion of the working class had no option but to subdivide these apartments, often into tiny cubicles, in order to make up the rent.[85] Another report in the same paper pointed out that while more jobs were created than were destroyed in Long Island in 1995, while the average salary in the fastest-shrinking industries on Long Island was $49,730 a year, it was $18,000 a year in the jobs that were being created.[86]

There has been a similar retreat from the welfare state in the UK. Between 1981 and 1994, the stock of public housing available to the poor fell from 6.5 million units to 5 million units, as local housing authorities sold off 1.45 million units to tenants. City authorities increasingly privatised the available housing, and encouraged prospective owners to form local housing associations to replace the local municipal authorities as providers of housing. However, as revenues dried up, government grants to local housing associations were also cut sharply. As recently as 1988, grants accounted for 90 per cent of their investment in housing. By 1994 their share had fallen to 62 per cent. This forced the associations to rely more on loans, and charge a higher rent from their tenants. In 1994 rents had risen to an average of 30 per cent of the tenants' incomes. The decline in social housing stock also led to homelessness. In 1994, in Britain, the original home of the welfare state, 200,000 persons were homeless, two-thirds with children.[87]

The assault on welfare has not spared even the core programmes of old age pensions and unemployment benefits. Both the UK and the US have seen sustained efforts to privatise public pensions. In the US, where under the state-run social security system, pensions are funded from the subscriptions to social security by current income earners, attempts to privatise pensions have been fuelled by mounting concern that when the post-war 'baby boom' generation retires and the number of pensioners skyrockets, the contributions of current workers will not suffice to meet the rising pension bill. The fear is well-founded, because the ratio of current workers to pensioners has declined from 5.1 in 1960 to 3.2 in 2000, and is expected to fall to 2 in 2030. The Clinton administration therefore appointed a Commission on Social Security in 1996 to suggest ways of increasing the pension fund. The commission suggested three possible ways: to invest 40 per cent of the pension fund in the share market, where the average long-term return was 7 per cent against 3.5 per cent in government bonds; to put 1.6 per cent of the income earner's income (about a fifth of the current social security contribution) into a personal retirement account, to be invested in the share market; and to cut the present guaranteed pension by half, while putting 5 per cent of the income of the income earner into a personal retirement account. All three proposals involved 'marketising' the pension. The second and third proposals also involved partial privatisation.[88]

There has been a similar effort to privatise the pension system in order to lower state expenditures in the UK. By 1994, two million people had been persuaded to forego the option of state-guaranteed pensions under the State Earnings Related Pension Scheme in favour of private pension schemes. Of these 450,000 had actually pulled out of the SERPS.[89] Their futures too were now firmly linked to the prices of shares in the stock market. In France and Germany, the government has tried to cope with the mounting pension bill without resorting to privatisation by raising the age of retirement. This has met with stiff resistance, especially in France, where in 1995 and 1996 the government faced a spate of strikes, mainly in the transport sector, and eventually had to back down when these threatened to bring the economy to a halt.

Growing Inequality and the Return of Sweated Labour

The rapid growth of income inequality in the UK and USA, where the dismantling of corporatist capitalism has gone farthest, has already been described in Chapter 2. In the US, the 'picket fence' growth of real incomes, in which the incomes of all quintiles grew by approximately the same amount every year, was replaced in the 1970s by a 'step ladder' pattern of income growth in which the incomes of the bottom quintile declined precipitously, while that of the top quintile rose dramatically with the middle three quintiles faring better as one progressed up the ladder.[90] The result was that while the median income of the top 5 per cent of the population declined from 14 to 11.3 times the median income of the bottom 20 per cent in the first period, it rose once more to 18.2 times by 1995.[91]

But what about the period after 1995, when America entered its longest boom in history, and when unemployment not only dropped below 5 per cent in 1997 but stayed there? Did the return of prosperity start closing the income gap once more? The most recent studies by Bernstein and Mishel show that it did not. While the boom raised the real income of the bottom quintile in real terms, and closed the gap marginally between it and the middle quintiles, the income of the top quintile continued to grow disproportionately. Wages of both low-paid men and women grew considerably faster (at 1.7 and 2.0 per cent) than did the wages of middle-wage earners, and at almost the same rate as wages for high-wage earners (1.8 and 1.9 per cent). But within the high-wage earners, the gap in earnings widened rapidly as wages at the top pulled further away from wages a little further down the ladder. At the very top, corporate CEOs salaries grew by 62.7 per cent over the period 1989–99 against 12.6 per cent for wage earners in the 90th percentile. Family incomes showed the same pattern. The median family income, which had dropped by $1438 (in 1995 dollars) between 1989 and 1995, grew by $3078 between 1995 and 1999. But while the median family income grew 3.6 per cent during this decade, that of families in the 95th percentile grew by 11.6 per cent.[92]

The Miracle of the 1990s: Miracle for Whom?

The celebratory tone of much that was written about the spurt in American economic growth during the 1990s obscured important differences between it and earlier surges of prosperity, notably in the 1950s and 1960s. The most important related to the behaviour of incomes and profits. In the surge of the 1950s and 1960s, family income grew at 2.8 per cent per annum, or seven times the rate of growth achieved in 1989–98. The growth between 1947 and 1970 was 0.4 per cent faster than even family income growth during the boom years from 1995 to 1998. What is more, even the boom after 1995, and the sharpest rise in labour productivity America has known (2.5 per cent per annum), did not push the rate of growth of family incomes any higher than it had been in the 1970s. The median family income grew at 0.4 per cent per annum between 1979 and 1989, when the disruption caused by globalisation was at its peak; and at 0.41 per cent per annum between 1989 and 1998, when America, if not the rest of the world, had completed the restructuring of its economy to take advantage of the change.[93]

The rate of profit also shows marked differences between the surge of the Golden Age and that of the late 1990s. Towards the end of the former, profits were sharply compressed by a slowdown in the growth of labour productivity, full employment and strong unions. Between 1995 and 1999, by contrast, they continued to grow despite the US economy coming as close to full employment as it had been in 30 years.[94] While the wage rate rose between 1995 and 1998 by 2.5 per cent per year, health benefits paid by American employers continued to decline despite the widening of coverage. As a result, labour costs to employers rose at 1.9 per cent per annum.[95] The difference of 0.6 per cent between the growth of labour productivity and labour costs went into a disproportionate rise in profit. The obvious difference between the 1960s and the 1990s was that in the latter period American capital, like capital in the rest of the industrialised countries, was able to tap into the cheap labour pool of the developing world. This defeated the full-employment constraint on profits that had operated when capitalism was still basically national. The change was a direct result of the unification of the global market and the globalisation of manufacture.

Profits have been further swelled by the freedom of investors to shop around for the lowest corporate taxes available. A study of 200 US corporations in the late 1990s showed that 'the average multinational firm with subsidiaries in more than five regions was able to use income shifting to reduce its tax burden by 51.6 per cent.'[96]

The global economy is thus reproducing the conditions of early capitalism with an uncanny precision. With the virtual abolition of distance, capital has all but lost its nationality and now has the same near-inexhaustible supply of low-cost labour that the second enclosure movement in agriculture created for capital in Britain. The ready availability of cheap labour in the global market has turned the high-income labour forces of developed country national markets into besieged, high-wage islands. The fall in the real wages of the working class, especially in comparison to managerial remuneration and profits, reflects this change.

Poverty and the Return of the Sweatshop

In the US, the boom years of 1995 to 1999 saw a perceptible decline in poverty as measured by several indicators. The proportion of the workforce working part-time fell involuntarily from 3.7 per cent to 2.6 per cent. The numbers who wanted work but had stopped looking also dropped by 400,000; and the proportion of jobs in which employers provided health insurance rose.[97] But it took an unprecedented spurt of growth at the end of a long period of economic recovery to make this difference. When the economy went into a recession in 2000, these trends were reversed. The experience of the period 1995 to 2003 only strengthened the conclusion that poverty had become endemic in the industrialised countries. But that is only half the story. The other half is a terrifying growth of insecurity.

The return of wage and price flexibility, the destruction of trade union power and the retreat of the welfare state have combined with the growing insecurity of jobs to individualise risk on a scale unknown since the early decades of the industrial revolution. As the protective cover of the social democratic state grows thin, people are being left more and more to fend for themselves or rely on private charity when they grow old, when they are out of a job, or when they fall ill. The failure of all safety nets is reflected by the return of pauperism (long-term unemployment of the able-bodied) and homelessness, by rising levels of crime, and by the break-up of community and family life as the out-of-work travel to distant places to take up new jobs or withdraw from church and community life when they lose their jobs.[98]

The vast majority of the jobs now being created pay only poverty-level or even below poverty-level wages. Only families with more than one income earner and people who are prepared to work long overtime hours beyond the stipulated 40-hour working week are able to rise above the resulting poverty trap. How difficult it has become to stay out of this trap was demonstrated by the case of Anna Welker, reported in the *Denver Post*. Ms. Welker, who with her two pre-school children had earlier been on welfare, found a job as a full-time accounting clerk. She had a monthly take home pay of $1,300. Out of this she paid $462 as rent, and another $75 for health care through her employer. The balance was sufficient for all three to live on, but only so long as she was part of a transitional programme designed to wean people off welfare. This programme looked after her medical aid and childcare expenses while she was away at work. When the programme ended, Ms. Welker would have to spend $800 on childcare alone. Even if she spent an absolute minimum of $200 a month on food, she would still be around $250 in the red. This estimate did not take into account transport, heating, clothes and medical expenses on her children, not to mention unforeseen expenses. When she was interviewed, Ms. Welker had been trying unsuccessfully for months to find a better-paid job, but time had almost run out, and she was resigning herself to going back on welfare to retain her child support.[99]

The reason why Ms. Welker and millions like her could not find better-paying jobs was highlighted by a report of the Chicago Urban League and the University of Wisconsin published in 1995. The report quoted a study by Kathleen Shankman of Northern Illinois University, which showed that the minimum annual income required by a mother of two pre-school children was $27,424 a year in Chicago (in 1993 prices) and $24,423 elsewhere in Illinois. The study found that the ratio of job seekers to available jobs that paid this much was 222 to 1![100]

Poverty is reflected in the way people live. In September and October 1996 the *New York Times* published a series of articles titled 'Barely Four Walls', which documented 'case after case of children growing up in rat-infested buildings that violate every applicable housing code'. Commenting editorially on its own findings, the *New York Times* wrote, 'Conditions rival those uncovered in the 1890s by the crusading photographer, Jacob Riis, whose book, *How the Other Half Lives*, awakened the country to the grim realities of tenement life.' But even the *New York Times'* editorial could not help giving away the fact that in 1996 America was going down the back of the slope into a new version of early capitalism. For far from calling for an awakening of conscience, it asked for a stricter enforcement of the law: 'Meanwhile the city's housing authorities stand helplessly by, hamstrung by a shortage of inspectors *and a housing law that exempts even the worst landlords from serious punishment.*'[101]

Deregulation, the debilitation of the trade unions, and the recurrence of permanent unemployment have combined, perhaps inevitably, to cause the rebirth of sweated labour. The three general characteristics of sweated labour, described in the extensive literature on the subject concerning the nineteenth and early twentieth centuries, were below poverty-level wages, overwork and unsanitary conditions of work. Two, and often all three, have reappeared at the fag end of the twentieth century. The race to the bottom that ensued after the deregulation of the trucking industry has already been described. What working conditions have become in the industry has been described as follows:

Imagine a world in which most people work more than 60 hours per week not to get 'ahead' but just to make ends meet.

Imagine a world in which most of us compete to offer our services at the lowest possible price but which is so competitive that we get what we want—but end up working longer hours just to earn enough to subsist.

Imagine a world in which people work like this but with no regular schedule—irregular days and irregular hours, switching from day to night and back again with little predictability.

Imagine a world in which production workers' wages stop abruptly with every hiccup in the assembly line.

Imagine a world in which employers decide which work to pay you for and which you have to perform free—and that work comprises 25 per cent of your work day!

Imagine no further because that is the life of the truck driver today.[102]

It is also the life of the janitor, the shop attendant, the waiter, the dustman, the delivery boy, the security guard and a host of other occupations.

Sweated Labour in the Garment Industry

The American garment industry has been the single biggest victim of globalisation. Factory after factory in New England and elsewhere has closed down because of its inability to compete with garments made by workers who earn less than 50 US cents an hour. The few factories that survive do so almost entirely because of the availability of illegal immigrants anxious to get any kind of work. Without paper these workers are unable to get jobs for more than $2.75 to $3.00 per hour (against the legal wage of $7.00 to $8.00 an hour). New York's 6,000 factories, which employ over 40,000 workers, stay in business almost entirely because of the availability of this cheap labour.[103] Typically such workers work 12-hour shifts, six days a week, to bring home $220 a week.[104] Felipe Garcia, a highly prized cutter who was an illegal immigrant from Mexico, explained the race to the bottom, saying that American workers wanted sick days and health benefits. 'For this work there is a lot of competition. No boss is going to pay.'[105]

The return of sweatshop conditions does not stop at the boundaries of the rich nations. On the contrary, it is even more in evidence in the export enclaves of the developing countries, to which capital from the rich nations has migrated in search of cost advantages. Even in that paradigm of successful economic transition, China, there is now an increasing 'job security panic'.[106]

Among the millions of Chinese workers who have launched themselves upon the free market, the number of losers is growing steadily and perhaps more rapidly than anyone had anticipated. As a result the bargaining power of those who go out in search of work on their own is very small. Migrant workers therefore typically earn only 70–80 per cent of what residents of the booming towns can expect, and can extract almost no social security benefits, such as their counterparts have, because their bargaining power is almost non-existent.[107] This has given birth to a new type of exploitation, dubbed 'sweatshop capitalism'. Sweatshop conditions are to be found mostly in the foreign and joint ventures, especially those located in the Special Economic Zones, but it is now spreading in Chinese SOEs too, as they struggle to survive. In the former a kind of wild-west *laissez faire* prevails. There are no rules, except those the employers dream up; no minimum wages, no right of collective bargaining, and no social security except that which the more enlightened employers provide to their workers. The relationship of dominance and dependence between capital and labour described by Marx is most fully realised in the SEZs; and the state, as the essential regulator and humaniser of the free market, is simply absent.[108] In the factories of Thailand, Malaysia, Vietnam, the Philippines, Indonesia and China, it is common to see workers, mostly women, locked into the factory dormitories after work, and penalised with pay cuts for supposed infringements of conduct norms to the point where they often do not know what their next pay packet will be. The practice of incarceration in dormitories has led to scores of tragedies, in which dozens, sometimes hundreds, of workers have perished in fires because they could not get out.[109]

The cheap labour to be found in the developing countries forms a single continuum with the cheap illegal immigrant labour and the sweatshop conditions of work that exist in the dying industrial centres of the industrialised world. Together they form the reservoir of unemployed or barely employed labour of the new global market and early global capitalism. The reservoir of industrial labour in the developing countries did not come into being spontaneously. Had the traditional economies never tried to industrialise and remained content to trade their agricultural products and their handicrafts with the products of the industrialised countries, there would have been no disruption of their economies, and consequently no surplus labour for the industrialised nations to tap. But the spread of mines and plantations and the invasion of their markets by cheap manufactured goods disrupted the integrated traditional economies that had existed previously, and created a surplus of labour, while the attempts by the developing countries to industrialise converted the labour into an industrial proletariat. Education made it possible for this proletariat to adapt to modern technology. It also facilitated its migration to and subsequent integration into the economies of the industrialised countries.[110]

The smallness of the developing countries' domestic market, and the fact that one or two factories or mills were sufficient to meet the whole of domestic demand, gave birth to a distorted parody of the experience of the early starters in industrialisation. The only way to correct the distortion was to break the boundaries of the national market. Thus globalisation was as much an imperative for the newly industrialising countries as for the highly industrialised ones. Having disrupted their domestic markets through attempts to industrialise (or having had them disrupted for them by colonising powers), developing countries were left with no option but to hook up with the world market. They did this by attracting investment and otherwise gearing themselves to produce for the global market, or by exporting their workers to the centres of global production. That is why, as Saskia Sassen has noted, the very same countries that have attracted the most foreign capital are also the main exporters of cheap labour to the industrialised countries.[111]

The Return of Manchester Liberalism

What completes the picture of a return to early capitalism is the change in social values that has accompanied the retreat from social democracy. The crippling of the trade union movement, the return to extremely short-term objectives as determinants of corporate behaviour, and the slow strangulation of the welfare state are not deemed to be unavoidable evils, forced on the industrialised countries by the ageing of the population and the rise of unemployment on the one hand, and the drying up of tax revenues because of a slowdown in growth and the increasing difficulty in taxing transnational capital on the other. All these changes are *good* and were overdue, because the previous state of affairs was *bad*. Trade unions had grown *too strong*, were *pushing up costs*, *reducing the competitiveness of exports*, and therefore *hurting the country*. Their power needed, therefore, to be broken. Deregulation is not the return of price discrimination, sweated labour and a 'race to the bottom', but an increase in the sovereignty of the consumers, because it gives them more options than they had before. Privatisation, such as of housing and pension funds, is *good* because it increases *efficiency*. The fact that it also increases risk is carefully discounted.

Wage flexibility is good because it prevents unemployment. The fact that the new jobs are as a rule available only at a fraction of what the old ones paid, and are far less secure, is again carefully glossed over. Growing income disparities are glossed over, usually by being ignored. But they are privately welcomed as a product of lower taxation and the adoption of supply-side economics. Criticism of the widening income gap is therefore met indirectly by citing other virtues that have a strong early capitalist flavour, such as the will to save and invest more, the rebirth of the spirit of enterprise and risk taking, the speeding up of technological innovation as reflected in the rapid growth in the number of venture capital financed enterprises, and, as was mentioned in Chapter 3, by citing the high income mobility of those in the lowest quintiles of incomes.

The erosion of the welfare state is not only regarded as a necessity forced upon governments by their growing fiscal burdens and the rising wage cost of manufacture, but as a long overdue reform with strong moral overtones. The welfare state did not only over-extend the state, but also directly promoted the development of a permissive society and the disintegration of the family. As the prolonged debate over the US budget for 1995–96 (when a newly resurgent Republican party tried to foist its 'Contract with America' on the people) showed, the Republicans regard social welfare as the main cause of the decline of family values in America.[112] To the right wing of the party, supporting unwed mothers amounted to encouraging promiscuity and lack of responsibility in teenage girls. Paying child support for more than one child to an unwed mother was therefore doubly immoral. Medical care for terminating unwanted pregnancies was abetting a crime before the eyes of God, and encouraging promiscuity at the same time.

Another belief that has resurfaced quietly and been accepted by both the major parties in the US is that unemployment benefits encourage idleness and should therefore be curtailed. In his State of the Union message in 1997, President Clinton took credit not only for 'mov[ing] two and a quarter million people off the welfare rolls', but also for enacting 'landmark welfare reform, *demanding that able bodied recipients assume the responsibility of moving from welfare to work*'. Clinton went on to set another goal, that of moving another two million recipients into jobs by the year 2000, and announced tax credits for businesses that hired people off welfare. He did this oblivious of the fact that these welfare workers would undercut further the wages of street cleaners, janitors, road menders and garbage collectors, who were already among the most poorly paid workers in the country.[113]

There is a strong element of *deja vu* about the 1996 Welfare Reform Bill, for it bears more than a passing resemblance to the Poor Law Reform of 1834 in Britain. The avowed purpose of the 1834 act was to reduce the ever-growing burden of poor relief upon the parishes by insisting that only those who entered the poorhouses would be entitled to doles. It thus cut off payments to the able-bodied unemployed who did not want to undergo the humiliation of entering the poorhouse, and forced them to take whatever jobs were available. The reform of the Poor Law had become unavoidable because of the unintended consequences of the Speenhamland act of 1795. Designed hastily as a measure to cushion the impact of growing cyclical unemployment, the Speenhamland act enjoined the parishes to pay a supplement to the income of the poor sufficient for them to obtain a minimum standard of living. This was spelt out in terms of a minimum consumption of bread and other necessities. Speenhamland did avert starvation and thereby the possibility of uncontrollable social turmoil, but its long-term effects were the opposite of what the Poor Law commissioners had intended. Instead of raising the standard of living of the workforce, it enabled employers to lower wages still further and leave the parishes to make good the deficit. The Speenhamland act did however restrict the supply of labour to industry because it tied the workers to the parish where they were born. The Poor Law reform freed the supply of workers to industry by forcing the able-bodied who were too proud to enter the poor-house off the welfare rolls and adding to the supply of labour in the market. Inevitably this depressed real wages in industry.[114] It is hardly surprising that throughout the first three quarters of the nineteenth century, when British pre-eminence in industry was unchallenged, and its average income the highest in Europe if not the world, the population of the cities was increased only by immigration from the rural areas, and later from Ireland. In the cities, the death rate exceeded the birth rate, as disease and malnutrition ravaged the working classes.

One final similarity between the value system the one now taking hold of the industrialised world and that of the early nineteenth century will help to complete the picture of a return to early capitalism. This is the growing concern over crime. The second enclosure movement in the late seventeenth and eighteenth centuries led to the abandonment of open-field cultivation in favour of fenced enclosures devoted to a single crop. The resulting displacement of peasants flooded the cities and towns with people in search of work. Desperation forced these migrants into showing truly extraordinary inventiveness in finding ways to make a living. Inevitably crime too flourished along with prostitution, gambling, cockfights, peddling in the streets, making bears dance, juggling and playing the barrel organ. The response of the establishment in the face of a phenomenon that was seemingly without precedent was to crack down on crime and other undesirable activities with all the harshness it could muster. Public hanging became the commonest mode of punishment, and the favourite of the crowds. Children of 12 years began to be hanged for the crime of picking pockets or stealing a loaf of bread, till the judges themselves revolted.[115] Today, in the face of rising unemployment, declining real incomes for the poorest third of the population, a concentration of unemployment, social disintegration and crime among disadvantaged minorities, growing job insecurity, high divorce rates and climbing rates of childbearing out of wedlock, and the break-up of families and the development of immigrant ghettoes in the poorer areas of the large cities of the West—all developments triggered directly or indirectly by globalisation, and every bit as destabilising as the disruption of rural life and the massive influx of socially displaced workers into the cities in the early days of national capitalism—a confused and increasingly demoralised western society is retreating from the belief that crime is at least partly a product of the environment, and that society has a responsibility for not only punishing criminals but also alleviating the social conditions that breed crime. In its place the conviction is hardening that the one sure way to combat crime is by hiring more police, building more jails and, above all, meting out harsher punishments. These have been staple fare in the agenda of the far right for over two decades, but have now filtered into the mainstream of social opinion even in the most open of democracies, the USA.

In 1990 President George Bush declared a war on drugs, which involved sharply increasing police forces and doubling the capacity of the jails in the USA. In 1993, President Clinton introduced a crime bill that would treat children over the age of 13 as adults and make them liable to a mandatory death sentence on no less than 13 counts. The punitive provisions of the bill received broad bipartisan support in both houses of the US Congress but did not pass because it contained provisions for controlling the purchase and possession of weapons, a move that was stiffly resisted by the gun lobby. In his State of the Union message for 1997, Clinton urged Congress to pass the bill with provisions that banned 'violent teen criminals' from ever being able to buy handguns, and made the installation of child safety locks on all handguns compulsory. This was a substantial dilution of the original provisions, but significantly his message envisaged no dilution of penalties against teenage criminals.

Conclusion: Disorganisation, Systemic Chaos and the 'Great Disruption'

The description given in the preceding pages takes the analysis of what Lash and Urry called the 'disorganisation' of capitalism, and what Arrighi dubbed the growth of systemic chaos, a step further. It attempts to show that these phenomena are part of a larger process—the rebirth of capitalism on a global scale, a birth that is still in its early stages.

The first and essential requirement for the emergence of global capitalism is the destruction of the regulatory structures and institutions and legal frameworks of mature national capitalism. These laws, institutions, structures and relationships had come into being with the purpose of humanising capitalism by softening the hard edges of the 'stark utopia' that it had created during the earliest phase of its development within the nation state. They did so by limiting and channelling, i.e., regulating, competition.

What the 1980s and 1990s have seen is a systematic dismantling of these laws, institutions, structures and relationships, in order to bring back an era of unrestricted competition. The removal of these restraints has triggered two very different races in society: on the capital side of the equation it has set off a 'race to the top', while on the labour side it has set off a 'race to the bottom'. The race to the top is reflected in an increasing preoccupation with maximising profit. This has led to the return of price competition, price differentiation and market segmentation on the one hand and a thirst for capital gains, cloaked in the euphemism of 'shareholder value' on the other. These changes have dispelled the aversion to quick profits that was axiomatic in large firms only three decades ago. The hunger for quick returns has not been confined to enterprises producing goods and services but has infected banking, investment and fund managing companies as well. This has led to the dissolution of long-established links between finance and industry and a 'marketisation' of the relationship, as each has searched for immediate profits or reductions in cost.

Freed from the restraint of collective bargaining, labour has rapidly bid wages down to poverty or below poverty levels.[116] This has forced workers to work longer hours and under more onerous circumstances. To make matters worse, a growing proportion of the new jobs are part-time, piece-rated or contractual, with no health, unemployment or pension benefits. Not only has employment become markedly poorer and less secure, but in fewer and fewer jobs do employers take any direct responsibility for the welfare of their workers.

All the above trends are far advanced in the USA and the United Kingdom, and less so in continental Europe and Japan. They have been welcomed as portents of a new age in the former, but are viewed with something akin to dread in the latter. But all the industrialised countries are moving inexorably in the same direction. Overall, the dissolution of the bonds that restrained competition is creating an atomised society that is in many ways far more disturbing than the one that was to be found in the burgeoning cities of early national capitalism. At that time the rapacity of the capitalist was constrained by the Protestant ethic to which he subscribed and the feudal, paternalistic values of the aristocracy that he wished to become a part of. At the other end of the scale, the hordes of migrants and destitutes who flocked into the cities in search of work were unorganised, but retained links to their villages and forged links in town with others from their villages or regions. Today these traditional relationships no longer exist outside immigrant communities. Instead there is only the waning camaraderie of the Union and the beer hall. As Robert Putnam has pointed out in his poignant book, *Bowling Alone*, this too is rapidly fading away.

The strain this is putting on society has to surface somewhere, and it is doing so in the breakdown of family and community. Francis Fukuyama has called this the 'Great Disruption'.[117] Throughout the western world, all major indicators of social stability—the incidence of crime, the rate of divorce, the proportion of children born to single mothers and the fertility rate—have all shown the same trends. Crime, out-of-wedlock birth, and divorce had all grown slowly till the mid-1960s, and then begun a sharp ascent that did not show any signs of tapering off till the mid-1990s.[118] The divorce rate was either stable or fell till the early 1960s, but then climbed steadily till it reached a plateau in the 1980s. It fell slightly in the US after the mid-1980s, but remained on the plateau or continued to rise in the other countries.[119] Births to single mothers showed a rising trend throughout the second half of the twentieth century, but the rise accelerated substantially in the US after 1960, and much more sharply in the UK after 1980.[120]

The fertility rate, on the other hand, shows a rise in the US till 1956, a plateau till 1964, and then begins to fall steeply. The fall has tapered off to a new plateau in the 1990s. In the UK and Sweden, fertility rates rose till the mid to late 1960s, but have declined ever since. Even a determined effort by the Swedish government to reverse the fall at the end of the 1980s by giving hefty tax incentives failed to stop the decline.[121] Fukuyama explains these trends as a consequence of the decline of 'social capital', i.e., 'informal norms promoting cooperative behaviour'. The loss of social capital is underlined by the immense contrast between what has been happening in Europe and the USA, and in Japan and other East Asian countries, notably Singapore and Hong Kong, which have attained comparable levels of per capita income. In Japan the crime rate has remained almost static throughout the last half century, and the incidence of violent crimes has come sharply down at the end of the century to a fifth of what it was in the late 1950s. The divorce rate has moved up gradually from just over 1 per 1,000 couples in 1950 to 1.7 in 1996, but not only is the rise much more gradual than for Europe and the US, but the rate itself is a little over half of that for the UK and less than 40 per cent of the divorce rate of 4.3 in the USA. Most striking is the rate of illegitimate births. Not only was it miniscule in the 1950s, but it has almost disappeared since then.[122] By contrast, one-third of the births in the UK and US and over two-thirds of those in Sweden in 1996 took place out of wedlock.

Interpreting these data is complicated as there is more than one influence at work. For instance the reporting of crimes has varied over time and may, in general, have improved. That makes it necessary to complement the crime statistics with those for violent crimes, which seldom go unreported. A more serious problem arises from the baby boom, which dramatically changed the number of people in the age groups capable of having children and most likely to commit crimes, get divorced or have illegitimate children. But as Fukuyama points out, even after allowing for these factors the graph has moved relentlessly up for Europe and America. What is more, except for fertility, these graphs have moved relentlessly down for Japan despite the fact that it too had a baby boom in the late 1940s and early 1950s. The conclusion Fukuyama draws from this is unambiguous. Social trust has been severely damaged in the West, while it has not been impaired in Japan and the newly industrialised countries of Asia. This was confirmed by a survey of trust among high school senior year students in the US (age 18–19) between 1975 and 1992. The proportion affirming trust in their peers declined from 35 per cent in 1975 to 18 per cent in 1992, while those denying it rose from 40 per cent to 59 per cent.[123] 'Trust,' writes Fukuyama, 'is not in itself a virtue but rather a by-product of virtue; it arises when people share norms of honesty and reciprocity and hence are able to co-operate with one another. Trust is damaged by excessive selfishness and opportunism.'[124] Selfishness and opportunism are a by-product, in turn, of untrammelled competition, which is precisely the direction in which the world has been moving since the end of the 'Golden Age'.

In his much-awaited book, *Bowling Alone*, Robert Putnam of Harvard University has meticulously charted the atomisation of American society with data as diverse as voting figures, membership of Lions, Elks, Kiwanis, and other 'animal' clubs, and the number of times people had others over for dinner. The results complement the statistics of the great disruption to an uncanny degree. After rising steadily for half a century after the end of the First World War, with only a temporary dip during the depression of the 1930s, all indicators turned simultaneously downwards during a three-year period in the mid-1960s, and are still falling! The late 1960s is when the transport and information revolutions really began to have an impact on society, and the disorganisation of mature national capitalism began.[125]

Today, for perhaps the first time in history, human beings are truly, terrifyingly, alone. Liberals celebrate this as the triumph of individualism. But victories have meaning only when they are secured against powerful contrary forces. Individualism is no different. In the seventeenth and eighteenth centuries it was a rallying cry against the suffocating grip of feudal monarchies that held human beings in bondage as serfs and vassals. The celebration sounds hollow when the individual is being pushed into solitude by the remorseless forces of economics, and has no choice but to submit. This is not the triumph of individualism but the birth of anomie.

Notes

1. Perhaps the best-known and most exhaustive treatise on the subject is Scott Lash and John Urry, *The End of Organised Capitalism* (Cambridge, Polity Press, 1987).
2. Jurgen Habermas, The Postnational Constellation: Selected essays (Polity Press, 2001), p. 60.
3. Ibid., pp. 58–112.
4. Ibid., p. 59.
5. Karl Polanyi, *The Great Transformation* (Boston, Beacon Press, 1957), Chapter 5. The entire description of the rise of the national market is taken from this chapter.
6. Ibid.
7. Herman M. Schwartz, *States versus Markets. History, Geography and the Development of the International Political Economy* (New York, St. Martin's Press, 1994). Chapter 1 of Schwartz's book lays out in schematic form, backed by the study of nation building in three European countries, the relationship between the creation of a national market and the creation of the nation.

    See also Charles P. Kindelberger, 'The Rise of Free Trade in Western Europe', *The Journal of Economic History*, Vol. 35, No. 1, 1975; and Paul Bairoch, *Economics and World History. Myths and Paradoxes* (University of Chicago Press, 1993), Chapter 2.
8. Kindelberger, 'The Rise of Free Trade', reproduced in Jeffery A. Frieden and David A. Lake (eds.), *International Political Economy: Perspectives on Global Power and Wealth* (New York, St. Martin's Press, 1995), p. 79.
9. Bairoch, *Economics and World History*.
10. Polanyi, *The Great Transformation*, pp. 91–93.
11. Ibid.
12. Norman Stone, *Europe Transformed 1878–1919. The Fontana History of Europe* (Fontana Paperbacks, 1983), pp. 20–41.
13. Polanyi, *The Great Transformation*, p. 3.
14. Stone, *Europe Transformed*, pp. 42–73.
15. Lash and Urry, *The End of Organised Capitalism*, p. 5.
16. See for instance *The Economist*, 'Working for Your Welfare', 29 March to 4 April 1997, p. 61.
17. *The Economist*. 'Economist Survey of the Telecom Industry', 13–19 September 1997, pp. 5–6.
18. United Nations, *World Investment Report 1998* (New York and Geneva, United Nations, 1998), Executive Summary, p. xviii; and United Nations, *World Investment Report 1999* (New York and Geneva, United Nations, 1999), Executive Summary, and Table 5.
19. *The Economist*. 'Bidding for the Future' (Survey of Europe), 12–18 February 2000.
20. UN, *World Investment Report 1999*, Executive Summary, Table 4.
21. *The Economist*, 'Bidding for the Future' expressed this as follows: 'European restructuring is at an early stage, with cost-cutting a priority. Having already cut costs, American firms, such as America Online, and Time Warner are by contrast merging to expand revenues or bring together convergent industries.'
22. *Economist*, 'Survey of the Telecom Industry', pp. 5–6.
23. Michael H. Belzer, *Sweatshops on Wheels: Winners and Losers in Trucking Deregulation* (Oxford University Press, 2000), pp. 15, 25.
24. Ibid., pp. 21–22.
25. Ibid., p. 29.

26. Ibid., pp. 5, 21. In real terms, dollars earnings in 1997 were $11,793 lower than in 1977, against a fall of $2,881 for blue-collar workers. Over the 19 years from 1977 to 1996, truckers cumulatively 'lost' $140,658 worth of earnings in 1997 dollars.
27. Ibid., p. 46.
28. Ibid., p. 39.
29. Ibid., p. 14.
30. Lash and Urry, *The End of Organised Capitalism*, p. 205.
31. Ibid., p. 204, quoting T. Evans, 'Money makes the World go round', *Capital and Class*, Vol. 24, 1985, pp. 99–124.
32. US Government, Bureau of Economic Analysis, balance of payments tables. Available at: www.bea.gov.
33. Naoko Nakamae, 'Interlopers blow wind of change (FT Survey: Japan's Internet Tsunami)', *Financial Times*, 3 March 2000, p. 4.
34. Tony Barber, 'A Political Will to Reform (Financial Times Survey of the Euro-Zone)'. 10 September 1999, Survey, p. 2.
35. Kenneth N. Gilpin and Lawrence M. Fisher in *The New York Times*, 22 September 2000, p. C-2.
36. For a detailed account of the Enron case, see *Washington Post*, 'Time line of Enron's collapse', 27 January 2004, and five articles by April Witt and Peter Behr, 'The Fall of Enron', 28 July–1 August 2002.
37. *Economist*, 'Bidding for the Future'.
38. Ibid.
39. In Germany, the independent labour force, i.e., self-employed workers, farmers and tradesmen declined from 25.7 per cent of the workforce in 1850 to 14.8 per cent in 1950. The corresponding figures were 44.1 and 22.4 per cent for Italy; 32.4 and 19.3 per cent for Sweden; and 19.6 and 12.8 per cent for Britain. Subsistence farming was still the rule in Britain at the end of the eighteenth century (see Anthony Hicks, *Social Democracy and Welfare Capitalism: A Century of Income Security Politics* [Cornell University Press, 1999], p. 6).
40. Ibid., pp. 13, 19. Britain had compensation for victims of industrial accidents since 1897.
41. Ibid., p. 3. Table 1.1 compiled from various sources.
42. Ibid., Table 2.1, p. 51.
43. Ibid., p. 3.
44. Ibid., p. 10, Table 1.4. This measure, termed 'de-commodification', was developed by Esping–Andersen.
45. Ibid., p. 115.
46. Lash and Urry, *The End of Organized Capitalism*, Introduction and Chapters 1 & 2.
47. Chris Howell, 'British Trade Unionism in Crisis', in Andrew Martin and John Ross (eds.), *The Brave New World of European Labour: European Trade Unions at the Millennium* (New York, Oxford, Berghahn Books, 1999), pp. 37–38.
48. Stephen J. Silvia, 'German Industrial Relations since 1980', in Martin and Ross (eds.), *The Brave New World of European Labour*, p. 89.
49. Rianne Mahon, 'Yesterday's Modern Times are no longer Modern—Swedish Unions Confront the Double Shift', in Martin and Ross (eds.), *The Brave New World of European Labour*, pp. 130–131.
50. Akira Takanashi et al., *Japanese Employment Practices* (Japanese Economy and Labour Series, No. 4, Tokyo, The Japan Institute of Labour, 1999), p. 39.
51. Ibid., pp. 28–29.

52. Howell, 'British Trade Unionism in Crisis', in Martin and Ross (eds.), *The Brave New World of European Labour*, p. 28.
53. British Labour Force Survey, 2000. Quoted by Barrie Clement, 'Unions' influence surges as membership stages a comeback', *The Independent*, London, 11 September 2000, p. 8.
54. Howell, 'British Trade Unionism in Crisis', in Martin and Ross (eds.), *The Brave New World of European Labour*, p. 28.
55. Ibid., p. 29.
56. Silvia, 'German Industrial Relations since 1980', in Martin and Ross, *The Brave New World of European Labour*, pp. 76, 79–80. Also see *The Economist*, 'Is consensus under threat?' 3 June 2000 (US edition).
57. Silvia, 'German Industrial Relations since 1980', in Martin and Ross, *The Brave New World of European Labour*, pp. 76, 80.
58. Anthony Daley, 'The Hollowing out of the French Unions', in Martin and Ross, *The Brave New World of European Labour*, p. 72. See also John Ross and Andrew Martin, 'European Unions face the Millennium', in Martin and Ross, *The Brave New World of European Labour*, p. 17, Table 1.1
59. Ibid.
60. Richard Freeman, 'Is declining unionisation of the US good, bad or irrelevant', in Lawrence Mishel and Paula B. Voos (eds.), *Unions and Economic Competitiveness* (New York, Armonk, 1992), p. 143.
61. Howell, 'British Trade Unionism in Crisis', in Martin and Ross, *The Brave New World of European Labour*, p. 56.
62. Silvia, 'German Industrial Relations since 1980', in Martin and Ross, *The Brave New World of European Labour*, p. 80.
63. Daley, 'The Hollowing out of the French Unions', in Martin and Ross, *The Brave New World of European Labour*, p. 176.
64. Ross and Martin, 'European Unions face the Millennium', in Martin and Ross, *The Brave New World of European Labour*, p. 17; and Pelham Research, UK, 'Medium-Term Policy Outlook', 1 September 2000.
65. Howell, 'British Trade Unionism in Crisis', in Martin and Ross, *The Brave New World of European Labour*, p. 31.
66. Ross and Martin, 'European Unions face the Millennium', in Martin and Ross, *The Brave New World of European Labour*, p. 17, Table 1.1.
67. Peter Kwang, *Forbidden Workers: Chinese illegal immigrants in the USA* (New Press, New York, 1999).
68. Howell, 'British Trade Unionism in Crisis', in Martin and Ross, *The Brave New World of European Labour*, p. 32.
69. Daley, 'The Hollowing out of the French Unions', in Martin and Ross, *The Brave New World of European Labour*, p. 176.
70. *The Economist*, 'Free to Bloom' (Survey of Europe), 12 February 2000.
71. Silvia, 'German Industrial Relations since 1980', in Martin and Ross, *The Brave New World of European Labour*, p. 86
72. Lawrence Mishel, Jared Bernstein and John Schmitt, *The State of Working America 2000–01* (Washington DC, Economic Policy Institute, 2000), Introduction.
73. Howell, 'British Trade Unionism in Crisis', in Martin and Ross, *The Brave New World of European Labour*, p. 32.
74. Ross and Martin, 'European Unions face the Millennium', in Martin and Ross, *The Brave New World of European Labour*, p. 12.

75. Hicks, *Social Democracy and Welfare Capitalism*, Figure 6.2 top, p. 183.

76. Ibid., Figure 6.2 bottom.

77. *The Economist*, 'Working for your Welfare', 29 March to 4 April 1997, p. 61.

78. *The Economist*, 'Free to Bloom'.

79. Ibid.

80. Michael Winerip, 'Doors Shut to Poor Seeking Houses', *The New York Times*, 22 July 1996.

81. Deborah Sontag, 'For New York City's Poorest, Life trapped in a Cage' (part of the series 'An American Place'), *New York Times*, 6 October 1996.

82. Dan Barry, 'For Landlords, Hard Numbers and Obligations' (part of the series 'Barely Four Walls'), *New York Times*, 10 October 1996.

83. Bruce Lambert, 'Raid on Illegal Housing shows Plight of Suburbs' Working Poor', *New York Times*, 7 December 1996.

84. Winerip, 'Doors Shut to Poor seeking Houses'.

85. Lambert, 'Raid on Illegal Housing'.

86. Kirk Johnson and Thomas F. Lueck, 'The Region's Economy in Fundamental Shift', *New York Times*, 19 February 1996.

87. Will Hutton, *The State We Are In* (London, Vintage Books, 1996), p. 209.

88. *The Economist*, 'The pensions conspiracy', 14–20 December 1996, pp. 27–28.

89. Hutton, *The State We Are In*.

90. The most recent estimates, in Mishel et al., *State of Working America 2000–2001* (p. 56), show that the income of the bottom quintile actually grew fastest between 1947 and 1973, while that of the top quintile grew slowest. The growth rates of the five quintiles (from bottom to top) were 3 per cent, 2.6 per cent, 2.7 per cent, 2.7 per cent, and 2.4 per cent for the top quintile. By contrast, between 1973 and 1994, the growth rates were minus 0.6 per cent; minus 0.2 per cent, plus 0.2 per cent; 0.6 per cent and 1.3 per cent respectively.

91. Ibid., p. 54

92. Mishel et al., *State of Working America 2000–2001*, Executive Summary.

93. Calculated from Table 1.2 of Mishel et al., *State of Working America 1996–97* (p. 45) and Mishel et al., *State of Working America 2000–2001*, Executive Summary.

94. 4.2 per cent in 1998 to 3.9 per cent in some months of 2000.

95. Ibid.

96. William Grieder, *One World, Ready or Not: The Manic Logic of Global Capitalism* (New York, Simon and Schuster, 1997), pp. 337–346. Grieder was quoting David Harris, Randolph Morck, Joel Slemrod, and Bernard Yeung, 'Income Shifting in US Multinational Corporations', in Giovannini, Hubbard and Slemrod (eds.), *Studies in International Taxation* (Chicago University Press, 1993).

97. Ibid.

98. There are harrowing descriptions of this withdrawal in Louis Uchitelle and N.R. Kleinfeld, in *The Downsizing of America: A Special Report* (New York, Times Books, 1996).

99. *The Denver Post*, 12 January 1997.

100. Julie Kosterlitz, 'Hard Realities', *The National Journal*, Vol. 29, No. 1, 4 January 1997.

101. *New York Times*, 'Rats and Squalor at $800 a month', 14 October 1996 (emphasis in original).

102. Belzer, *Sweatshops on Wheels*, Preface.

103. Celia W. Dugger, 'Raid and Release: A Special Report—A tattered crackdown on illegal workers', *New York Times*, 3 June 1996, Section A, p. 1.

104. Andrew Jacobs, 'The War of Nerves Downtown', *New York Times*, 14 July 1996, Section 13, p. 1.
105. Dugger, 'Raid and Release'.
106. Anita Chan and Robert A. Senser, 'China's Troubled Workers', *Foreign Affairs*, March–April 1997. The authors quote Beijing's *Economic Daily*, which first reported this in May 1989. Epidemics of job security panic broke out among the workers in 1992, 1993 and 1994, particularly in the north-east 'rust belt', where the majority of the heavy industries in the state sector are located. Writing at the end of 1996, the authors claim, 'Today a state of near panic grips a large section of China's work force.'
107. Chan and Senser, 'China's Troubled Workers'. This is actually quoted with approval in World Bank, *China 2020, Development Challenges in the New Century* (Washington DC, 1997).
108. Ibid.
109. William Grieder, *One World, Ready or Not*, pp. 337–346; Chan and Senser, 'China's Troubled Workers'.
110. Saskia Sassen, *The Mobility of Labour and Capital. A Study in International Investment and Labour Flow* (Cambridge University Press, 1988), p. 29; Samir Amin, *Unequal Development: An Essay on the Social Formations of Peripheral Communities* (Monthly Review Press Paperback, 1989).
111. Sassen, *The Mobility of Labour and Capital*. See also Saskia Sassen, *The Global City: New York, London, Tokyo* (Princeton University Press, 1991), p. 32.
112. This argument has been discussed in detail by Francis Fukuyama, *The Great Disruption—Human Nature and the Reconstitution of Social Order* (The Free Press, 1999). Fukuyama finds it less than convincing.
113. In October 1996, days after President Clinton passed the Welfare Reform bill, trade unions in New York protested at the cut of 500 jobs by employers, and their handing over to 'workfare' recipients. The pointed out that in New York, which had been implementing workfare programmes from 1995, there were 14 per cent fewer jobs than job seekers. Workfare did not create jobs; it only displaced better-paid regular employees with poorer-paid workfare recipients. They feared that employers might shift jobs to workfare and when that ended, not hire regular workers back again. The acceleration of growth in 1996 has pushed these fears into the background, but they will undoubtedly surface when the economy slows and unemployment starts rising (*The Economist*, 5–11 October, 1996, p. 33, emphasis added).
114. Polanyi, *The Great Transformation*.
115. Arthur Koestler, *Reflections on Hanging* (London: Victor Gollancz, 1956).
116. The fact that wages of those with college degrees have risen has given birth to a widespread belief that this is only a transitional phase, as it reflects a decline in demand for unskilled or low-skilled workers and an increase in demand for highly skilled and educated workers. It will therefore end when workers' skills and education have been suitably upgraded. But there is little concrete evidence to support this view. The studies of Mishel et al. (*The State of Working America, 1996–97*, p. 79, and *The State of Working America, 2000–2001*) show conclusively that income differentials have been widening among college graduates too. While the proportion who earned less than half the media income rose from 3.9 per cent in 1969 to 4.8 per cent in 1995, the proportion who earned more than 200 per cent of the median income rose from 37.2 to 42.1 per cent.
117. Francis Fukuyama, *The Great Disruption*.
118. Ibid., pp. 32–33.
119. Ibid., p. 42.

120. Ibid., p. 44.
121. Ibid., p. 39.
122. Ibid. The out-of-wedlock birth rate has dropped from about 2 per cent in 1950 to 1 per cent in 1995.
123. Tom W. Smith, 'Factors Relating to Misanthropy in Contemporary American Society', *Social Science Research*, Vol. 26, 1997, pp. 170–196 (quoted by Fukuyama, *The Great Disruption*, p. 51).
124. Fukuyama, *The Great Disruption*.
125. Robert D. Putnam, *Bowling Alone: The Collapse and Revival of American Community* (New York, Simon and Schuster, 2000).

7

DISORGANISATION OF THE PERIPHERY

At the same time that global capitalism is sweeping away the imposing edifice of the welfare state in the mature industrialised countries, it is recreating in the global market the conditions that had existed within the national market in the early years of the industrial revolution. Four parallels can be discerned.

The first is a rapid widening of the income gap between the richest and poorest societies, which closely parallels a similar widening of income differentials between the rich and the poor within each society in each preceding cycle of capital accumulation. This had been noticed by economic historians in the Italian city states, and in the cities of Holland and Germany in the fifteenth to eighteenth centuries. In all cases historical records showed a rise in the Gini coefficient in large cities like Florence, Augsburg and Amsterdam. They also showed a significantly lower degree of inequality in smaller towns and in the countryside.[1] The widening income gap during nation state capitalism has been analysed in detail by Simon Kuznets for the industrialised nations of the nineteenth and twentieth centuries. Kuznets found that income inequalities widened in the second half of the nineteenth and, in most cases, in the early twentieth century, but that after 1900 or 1920 the trend reversed itself and income differentials continued to narrow till the 1970s. Based upon this, he had predicted that developing countries would follow the same curve when they industrialised.[2]

The second parallel is the rapid spread of exchange and its corollary, competition, as the organising principle of society. This is reflected in the sudden demise, within less than a decade, of communism and other less extreme forms of socialist economic systems in countries that covered more than half of the globe. In fact this was a belated completion of the replacement of older principles of economic organisation (such as redistribution and reciprocity) with the system of exchange, embodied in the market.[3]

The third parallel is the emergence of a new global underclass that is very similar to the underclass of criminals, prostitutes and pimps, which emerged in the centres of national capitalism in the early years of its growth. The fourth is the re-emergence of pauperism, but now on a global scale.

Growing Inter-country Disparities

The rapid growth of inequality within the mature industrialised countries has already been touched upon in Chapters 4 and 6. The gap between the rich and the poor has grown even more sharply in the newly industrialised countries, with South Korea and Taiwan as perhaps the only exceptions. The sharpest increases have taken place within formerly socialist countries like China and Russia. All this is now taken as a regrettable fact of life. What many liberal economists firmly reject is the contention that globalisation has also widened the income gap between countries. According to them precisely the opposite has happened. The proportion of third-world population that suffers from hunger has dropped from 37 per cent in 1971—roughly the end of the 'Golden Age'—to 18 per cent in 2001. Since 1960, life expectancy in the developing countries has risen from 46 to 65 years and infant mortality has fallen from 180 per 1,000 births to 60. These statistics, they point out, are better than for the developed countries a century ago.[4] These trends were not reversed when globalisation gained momentum in the 1990s. The proportion of the world's population that lived in extreme poverty declined from 29 per cent at the beginning of the decade to 24 per cent at its end. The champions of globalisation ascribe this entirely to the decision of a large number of countries, including China and India (which account for more than a third of the world's population), to follow East and Southeast Asia, and open up their economies to world trade and investment. By the same token they attribute Africa's decline to the attempt of its governments to adopt policies designed to promote self-sufficiency and to rely on government monopolies after they attained their independence. Zambia, they point out, used to be almost twice as rich as South Korea in the 1960s. At the end of the millennium South Korea's per capita GDP was 27 times that of Zambia.[5]

The above data are unimpeachable, but do not support the conclusions that the authors seek to draw from them. Absolute indices of poverty, income, nutrition and health can measure the effect of economic development, i.e., of advances in medicine and production technologies on peoples' lives. This must not be confused with the specific impact of globalisation, i.e., the merging of national markets and production systems into a single global market economy. These data therefore constitute a defence of industrialisation but not of globalisation.

Industrialisation has led to growth in nearly all countries. Globalisation has led to the widening of income differentials between countries and between people in each country. The data that reflects this widening is equally plentiful and equally conclusive. Thus between 1870 and 1989, the gap between the per capita income of the richest countries and poorest countries has increased six-fold.[6] This trend has accelerated sharply after 1973, the year of the first oil price increase, which is taken as a convenient benchmark for the onset of globalisation. A more comprehensive picture of the impact of globalisation on inter-state income differentials is provided by a table constructed by Manuel Castells, comparing the rates of convergence of per capita GDP for 55 countries with that of the USA. Castells makes the comparison for two periods, 1950 to 1973, i.e., the 'Golden Age', and 1973 to 1992, after the onset of globalisation.[7]

Castells' calculations showed that the incomes of 22 out of 34 developing countries in the sample had converged with that of the US in the first period, but those of only 12 countries continued to do so during the second. Among these were, of course, the Asian 'tigers', China, Taiwan, South Korea and Thailand, which recorded very high rates of convergence. This handful of countries (along with Malaysia, Singapore and Hong Kong) has been used to create the illusion that globalisation creates only winners and no losers. In actual fact, the income gap between 22 of the 34 developing countries and the US widened, in most cases quite sharply, after the onset of globalisation (see Table 7.1).[8]

Table 7.1
Convergence and Divergence of Incomes Before and During Globalisation

Year/countries	1950	1973	1992	1950–73	1973–92
USA	100	100	100	0	0
Japan	20	66	90	47	24
Western Europe(16)	50	68	74	19	6
Eastern Europe (7)	23	32	21	+9	–10
Latin America (7)	36	34	28	–3	–6
Asia (10)	8	10	18	2	8
Africa (10)	9	8	6	–1	–2

Source: Castells, *End of Millennium—The Information Age: Economy, Society, Culture, vol. III* (Basil Blackwell), pp. 76–78, Table 2.1. The original GDP estimates are taken from Angus Maddison, *Monitoring the World Economy, 1820–1992* (Paris, OECD Development Centre Studies, 1995). The GDP estimates are converted into dollars at market or official exchange rates.

The conclusion stated above, that globalisation has led to a widening of income gaps between the rich and poor countries, does not conflict with the finding mentioned earlier, that a smaller proportion of the world's population is absolutely poor now than was the case three decades ago.

Castells' data need to be interpreted with some care. The latter half of the period 1973–92 saw a wholesale dismantling of command economies in the developing countries. So it can be argued that the decline in income relative to the US reflects a disruption of their economies during the transition, and does not rule out the possibility that they will start catching up with the US (and other mature industrialised countries) when the transition has been completed. This possibility cannot be ruled out, at least for some of the countries in transition, but on balance the conclusion he has drawn remains valid. For, while Eastern Europe and Russia might have been suffering the pangs of a particularly wrenching transition in the late 1980s and early 1990s, Latin America was not. On the contrary, this was a region where by 1973 the transition to an open economy was far advanced in all but one of the countries included in the sample. In spite of this, the rate at which per capita incomes diverged from that of the US accelerated after 1973 in five out of seven countries in Castells' table. This was true also of Mexico, which was considered a showpiece of successful economic reform up to December 1994. In Mexico, per capita income converged with that of the US till 1973, but diverged after that date, despite massive inflows of American direct investment and of foreign exchange earnings from the export of oil.[9] The 'liberal' argument that sub-Saharan African economies have been marginalised because they adopted autarchic policies is also suspect. On the contrary, if the trade-to-GDP ratio measures openness, Africa's economies have always been open. In 1980 sub-Saharan Africa accounted for 3.7 per cent of the world's imports. Its fewer than 400 million people exported $80 billion worth of goods to the rest of the world. In per capita terms this was higher than China's exports in the mid-90s. But by 1995 its share had fallen to 1.4 per cent. To some extent this decline was caused by an anti-export bias in their policies—notably the practice of levying taxes on imported inputs and exports, and insisting that a part of the latter be carried in vessels flying the exporting nation's flag. This caused its share of copper exports to the OECD countries to decline from 32 per cent in 1962–64 to less than 10 per cent in 1992–93. There was a similar decline in its share of exports of palm oil, palm nuts, groundnuts, vegetable oil and other agricultural products.[10]

But the main reason was a decline in demand. While the OECD's imports of non-oil products grew at a compound rate of 11.8 per cent between 1960 and 1990, its import of the type of products exported by sub-Saharan Africa grew at only 7.3 per cent per annum.[11] The reason was that Africa's exports have consisted almost entirely of raw materials,[12] while the explosive growth of trade under the spur of globalisation has taken place in manufactures.[13]

The decline in Africa's share did not take place because Africans were working less hard, or producing and exporting less in physical terms. It was because there was a sharp deterioration in the terms of trade for primary products in the 1980s and 1990s,[14] and because, thanks to the shift of manufacture to low-wage countries, the vast bulk of the expansion of trade occurred in manufactures.

The true index of the marginalisation of Africa is therefore the decline in its export of manufactures. The share of manufactures in its exports declined from 7.8 per cent in 1965 to 5.9 per cent in 1985.[15] This did not happen because the sub-Saharan countries adopted autarchic economic policies but because the rapid growth of world trade in manufactures was mainly taking place between branches of transnational companies located in different countries, and between the TNCs and nominally independent partner companies that were actually little more than ancillaries and suppliers to them. Such trade now accounts for half or more of total world trade.[16] The space left open for independent exporters of manufactured products in the developing countries is therefore steadily declining. Sub-Saharan Africa's declining share of manufactured exports thus reflects its failure, despite being a prime source of raw materials, to become integrated into the emerging global manufacturing system.

Castells' data also shows that for developing countries' incomes to converge with those of the industrialised countries during the era of globalisation, simply raising the share of manufactured exports is not sufficient. These must rise at rates not dissimilar to those of Southeast and East Asia. The gap between Latin America's per capita income and that of the USA actually grew faster after 1973, despite that fact that the share of manufactures in its exports rose from 5.2 per cent in 1965 to 18.6 per cent in 1985. The developing countries will need to achieve an Asian explosion of manufactured exports—from 28.3 per cent in 1965 to 58.5 per cent in 1985—to start catching up with the industrialised countries.[17]

Economic and Political Marginalisation

Can all countries eventually achieve such high rates of growth of manufactured exports? Put another way, will all countries, large and small, eventually join East Asia's skein of flying geese?[18] Since we are attempting to peer into the future we cannot rule this out altogether, but the likelihood is small, for just as the political and economic forces that led to the assimilation of some countries into the global production system are mutually reinforcing, those that are leading to the exclusion of others also tend to be self-reinforcing.

The tendency to exclude countries arises from the same compulsion that drives economic inclusion—the need to lower costs and remain competitive in an increasingly unified global market. Transnational corporations are attracted to countries with low wages. But wages are not the only component of cost. Transport, storage, energy and administrative costs also need to be no higher, or at least not much higher, than they are in the industrialised countries. If this condition is not met, then the labour cost advantage is neutralised by higher energy, infrastructure and administrative costs. Transnational corporations need a stable economic and political environment in the countries where they invest or form partnerships with local firms. These three conditions have been met only in East and Southeast Asia, and to a small extent in a few parts of Latin America. In the former it was a product of a unique conjunction of historical circumstances—the rise of Japan as an industrial power in the first half of the twentieth century; its explosive transformation into a capital-surplus, high-wage economy under the impetus of the Vietnam war and US pressures to revalue the yen after it was over; the early industrialisation of Korea and Taiwan by Japanese industry and consequently a ready availability of industrial manpower and financial infrastructure in these countries despite their having been ravaged by war;[19] and the special status of Hong Kong and Singapore as outward-oriented island enclaves that inherited the legal and economic systems of the British government. In Latin America most of the transnational integration took place between the US and the northern belt of Mexico. This was driven by proximity, US political dominance, and after 1995 by the formation of the North American Free Trade Area (NAFTA).

It becomes far easier to understand the forces that drive economic exclusion once the effect of these specific historical and political circumstances is excluded. For instance, low wages may attract transnational corporations to the poorer developing countries, but these countries also invariably have poor infrastructure facilities. That raises the non-labour cost of manufacture, and makes them less attractive to investors. The host governments can improve the infrastructure, but to do so they either need huge amounts of capital, which is precisely what they do not have, or are compelled to attract very large amounts of private investment. Private investors can build the infrastructure. But they will need to earn a 'normal' rate of return on their investment. This will force them to set a minimum price or tariff for the infrastructure services. More often than not, that tariff is more than the majority of the inhabitants can afford. The resulting narrowness of the market increases the risk of the investment going sour. Raising user tariffs to compensate for the inadequacy of demand will only constrict demand further. However, if foreign investors baulk at making the investment, the infrastructure will remain poor and the cheapness of labour will not suffice to attract investment.

Transnational corporations also much prefer to integrate firms into their global manufacturing chain if they are located in countries where they can be reasonably sure that production will not be frequently disrupted. That requires a high degree of political stability and a low level of labour mobilisation. This combination of conditions is found spontaneously almost nowhere in the world. It needs to be created by force, and that means by a strong, even authoritarian, state. Outside Southeast and East Asia there are very, very few states that are both authoritarian and stable. As is discussed in Chapter 14, the transnationals' craving for security is what is driving much of the political restructuring of the world that is being attempted, above all others, by the USA.

The Economic Origins of the Failed State

In theory the three pre-conditions outlined above still do not altogether invalidate the 'flying geese' model of globalisation. One can argue that they extend the time required for integrating the whole world into the single global economy far beyond what had been foreseen during the early years of buoyant optimism after the Cold War. But this view ignores the political impact of economic exclusion, and the way that the two reinforce each other to make it progressively more difficult to integrate at a future date countries that have once been excluded from the global production system. This is the observation that prompted Manuel Castells to remark that the low-income countries that fall outside the charmed circle that capitalism has already drawn for itself are not falling behind; they are being made irrelevant.[20]

The world hears of a massacre in Rwanda, the sudden disintegration of Yugoslavia or the eruption of civil war in Sri Lanka only when it actually happens. Reporting on these immense tragedies, which kill hundreds of thousands of persons, tear apart the lives of tens of millions, and deprive women of their safety and children of their future, is done in exactly the same way as the reporting of a famine, a flood or some other natural disaster. When the tragedy occurs hundreds of journalists flock to the afflicted country, occupy the best hotels, set up their communications dishes on the roofs and beam gory images of bloody corpses and terrified children to a world safe in its drawing rooms, and thankful to God that this is happening 'somewhere else'.

But these are not natural calamities. The breakdown of states and the descent into naked oppression and eventually genocide does not take place all at once. It is preceded by a long period of increasing social stress, a progressive loss of faith in the prospect of a better future for all and a sharpening struggle to appropriate as large a share as possible of a stagnant national wealth. Instant journalism ensures that none of the factors responsible are ever analysed in advance, and that there is seldom any advance warning. As a result every calamity comes as a surprise, and sets off a furious search for plausible, instant explanations. The categorisation of some countries as 'rogue', 'atavistic' or 'failed' states is born out of this search, and is readily accepted because it reinforces what people want to believe: the innate superiority of western civilisation and the primitiveness or savagery of the rest of the world.

Sub-Saharan Africa is globalisation's principal victim. It entered the modern era with a backlog of disadvantages heaped upon it by its colonial past. The boundaries of its 45 countries were drawn artificially by its colonial masters, with little or no regard for natural features or ethnic identities. As a result many of the boundaries ran through ethnic entities, with an imperial disregard for the consequences. African nationalism has therefore tended therefore to be weak, although often intense. The rapid, indeed sometimes precipitate, decolonisation of much of the region after the Second World War did not give its leaders, who were mostly western-educated and imbued with modern ideas of nationhood, a chance to bind these disparate groups together on the basis of a prolonged struggle or shared goals. Instead, the overlay of tribal notions of leaders' rights on a modern state led to the emergence of rapacious elites to whom control of the state became the avenue for personal enrichment. Pre-modern notions of entitlement, rather than socialism or developmentalism, prompted African leaders to nationalise their natural resources, create state trading monopolies, and appropriate a large part of the revenues generated by mining, commercial agriculture and trade.

In most sub-Saharan states, therefore, political competition has become a struggle to control the state for personal gain. The struggle has been waged by forming shifting, often unstable alliances based upon ethnic loyalties and various forms of clientelism, in which networks of supporters are built by dispensing favours and sharing the spoils of office. Castells and others have aptly described this as a kleptocratic, or predator state.[21]

As a global market emerged during the 1980s, as the terms of trade for primary products deteriorated and the growth of GDP slowed down, the size of the pie, over which the rival elites battled, shrank. Political competition therefore became more violent, and political alliances more unstable. Retaining power has therefore become a matter of life and death. The resulting oppression, and sporadic outbursts of violence have created the opposite of the conditions that transnationals need to invest in a country. It has therefore driven most countries in sub-Saharan Africa further and further away from integration into the global economy and deeper into isolation.

Africa is not, however the only area susceptible to global exclusion. South Asia contains one country that has dropped out of the world economic system; another that has opted out of it and is only now trying to find its way back; and one that is on its way to exclusion. The first is Afghanistan, the second is Myanmar, and the last is Nepal. Only India and Sri Lanka, and just possibly Pakistan, have the potential for integrating themselves into the new global economy fully, and even their success is by no means assured. Despite being the strongest economy in the region, India too is being shunned by foreign investors as the list of its unresolved economic problems grows longer and the state takes on, more and more, the mien of a predator.[22]

The Triumph of Exchange and Collapse of Socialism

Global capitalism is reproducing, on a global scale, another feature of early national capitalism. This is the replacement of economic systems that were not based upon exchange with one that is based upon exchange. Barter, which is the most primitive form of exchange, has existed ever since human society came into being. But larger and more complex forms of exchange required the birth of a market, and markets, in contrast to barter, did not always exist. On the contrary, they had to be created, and their creation became the prime function of emerging modern state.[23]

In early societies, apart from barter, there were three other ways in which people organised the allocation of goods among themselves. These were reciprocity, redistribution, and the household system.[24] Reciprocity created vast and complex rings of interdependence outside the biological family. These rings helped to identify the society or community to which its members belonged. Redistribution, the most commonly used system other than exchange, involved the surrender of produce to a single authority that decided which member of society would receive what. The household system created the primal division of labour between husband, wife and children, or the members of an extended family, and was therefore the first system of interdependence within the biological family unit. Applied to larger social groups, redistribution and the household system reinforced each other to centralise authority and create societies that were patriarchal (but not necessarily despotic).[25] Exchange, by contrast, *transferred the responsibility for making production and distribution decisions from the central authority to the individual.* It is hardly surprising therefore that the market system, capitalism, and concepts of democracy and individualism all came into being more or less together and are mutually reinforcing.

The spread of capitalism saw exchange replace reciprocity and redistribution at every level of the market, from the local to the international. These were then knit together into a single overarching system of exchange by the emerging modern sovereign state. The state did this in order to meet its growing need for a reliable source of revenue to fight wars, either to protect or expand its domains.[26] But the resources so mobilised, and the professional armies raised for this purpose, were also used to break down the intermediary layers of authority that characterised feudalism—duchies and local lords, the church and the medieval township, that circumscribed the authority of the monarch and made his relationship with his subjects an indirect one.[27] That created the unitary modern state and the national market—the pre-conditions for the birth of nation state-based capitalism. It created Hobbes' Leviathan.

The catastrophic disruption of the formerly socialist economies of Eastern Europe and their rapid absorption into the capitalist world economy via the privatisation and extroversion of their economies is repeating this process on a global scale in our time. Many reasons have been given for the failure of socialism. The most commonly accepted is that in closed economies, producers did not have to face competition, and therefore did not consider it necessary to encourage technological innovation or incorporate its fruits into the manufacturing process. This made them less and less able to compete in the market for manufactured exports, and relegated them to ranks of the exporters of primary goods and basic manufactures like steel, chemicals and non-ferrous metals. The longer their economies remained closed, the less capable they became of paying for their imports with exports.

But at a deeper level, the socialist economies failed because all of them had been constructed around the principle of redistribution, with a conscious desire to shun exchange and, consequently, the market economy.[28] In a mammoth reproduction of the household-cum-redistribution system, production and distribution decisions were all centralised at the apex of the political hierarchy. All chains of information, and consequently of decision-making, therefore ran *vertically*, from the producer to the Central Planning Authority (in the USSR, it was the Gosplan) and from the consumer to the Central Distribution Authority (Gosnab). Individualised, lateral *exchange* relationships, which are the very essence of the market economy, were consciously shunned. This system could survive and even present an alternative to capitalism only so long as the socialist economies could remain basically national and linked only peripherally to world markets through trade. Like the welfare state, this system too became an anachronism when national capitalism was swept away by emergent global capitalism.

The Deepening of Underdevelopment

In the socialist countries, globalisation destroyed sophisticated industrial economies that had been built around the principle of redistribution and not exchange. By contrast, in traditional economies the penetration of exchange continued, and even accelerated, the 'development of under-development', by hastening the destruction of the internal balance between agricultural, pastoral and artisanal activity that began with the arrival of commercial capitalism.[29] Africa is once more the prime example. The agents of this fresh round of disarticulation have been the international aid organisations and well-meaning non-governmental organisations. The marginalisation of the trade in primary products that has been the most notable feature of globalisation led to a debt crisis in sub-Saharan Africa in the 80s. The World Bank and IMF responded by imposing structural adjustment programmes in exchange for foreign currency bale-outs. While deflation and devaluation were expected to lower domestic demand and turn industry and agriculture towards the world market, trade liberalisation, low import duties and programmes for introducing cash crops in place of subsistence crops were intended to attract foreign investment that would produce goods for the world market. Many of these have not only failed to attract the desired investment and increase exports, but also disrupted traditional economic balances, reduced the availability of food per person and accelerated the inflow of rural migrants to the towns to join the urban underclass.[30] The attempt to turn agriculture outwards has compounded the effect of adverse weather conditions to reduce the per capita production of food crops in sub-Saharan Africa by about 8 per cent in 1996 compared to what it was in 1961.[31]

Misguided attempts to commercialise agriculture for export and to cater to consumption in the (globally linked) urban centres abound. For instance, in West Africa foreign companies tried to replace the indigenous acacia trees with more valuable species only to have to abandon the effort and go back to acacia because it needed far less water and also because, being a leguminous plant, it provided much needed high-protein fodder for cattle and goats. At Lake Turkana in Kenya, Norwegian experts converted 20,000 Turkana tribesmen from raising cattle to growing fish—Nile perch and tilapia—for the market, only to find that the cost of processing, chilling and transport from such a remote location made the product prohibitively expensive.[32]

Overall, a study of Africa's structural adjustment experience during the 1980s by the United Nations Population Fund concluded:

> One does not find a strong association between structural adjustment policies and economic performance. There are strong indications that adjustment policies may not be able to guarantee that African countries pursuing (them) will overcome the effects of external shocks even in the long run, *unless there is a more favourable external environment*. In many African countries pursuing structural adjustment what progress there has been has been confined to nominal growth of the GDP without any transformation of the structure of the economy. … In most countries covered by this study, small and medium enterprises have been marginalised by the exchange rate and trade liberalisation measures and high domestic interest rates, resulting from restrictive monetary and credit policies …'[33]

A decade after the above report was prepared, the external environment had further deteriorated. The global economic system born out of the search for cheap labour in faraway countries had stabilised. New countries were no longer getting drawn into the new world market economy in the manner and at the speed at which they had been drawn into it in the 1980s. The same 10–12 countries that were host to the bulk of foreign direct investment in the early 1990s continued to remain so.[34] The exclusion of Africa from the global economy had become more pronounced. At the same time, the displacement of industrial employment that had been created earlier behind import bans and protective tariffs had spread to many other countries, including relatively successful ones like India.[35]

The Emergence of a Global Underclass

In their study of the conditions of the English working class during the industrial revolution, G.D.H. Cole and Raymond Postgate described the rise of an urban underclass of handymen, vagrants, pimps, prostitutes, petty criminals, who lived on the fringes of society on the one hand, and of the prevalence of child labour and sweated labour in the 'satanic mills' on the other.[36] This was the result of the wholesale destruction of artisanal industry, the commercialisation of agriculture during the second enclosure movement, the overloading of the system of poor relief set up under Elizabethan Poor Laws, their consequent 'reform' and the repeal of the Statute of Artificers. All these resulted in an unceasing inflow of the poor and the near-destitute into the cities. Vast, uncontrolled cycles of prosperity and depression made the availability of a permanent 'labour reserve' in the cities a distinctive, and indeed necessary, feature of the early capitalist system. This underclass has been reborn in the last quarter of a century, but on a global scale.

Several elements of the rise of this underclass, such as an absolute decline in real wages of two-fifths of Americans, the rebirth of permanent unemployment, growing homelessness in the industrialised countries, and the exploitation of immigrant (especially illegal immigrant) labour, have already been discussed. This section seeks to demonstrate that the forces that have created the new underclass are the same ones that have created the global market and production system.

Child Labour for the World Market

The most striking features of social disorganisation on a world scale are a particularly odious form of child labour in the developing countries and the re-emergence of sweated labour in the industrialised countries based almost entirely upon illegal immigration.

Data on child labour need to be interpreted with care, especially because many of the international and non-governmental agencies that collect them do so in order to propel their governments into restrictive legislation. Not all child labour is reprehensible or exploitative. Child labour within the family has always existed in the farms and homes of pre-industrial countries. Parents taught their children various artisanal trades at home, such as weaving, pottery, and carpet-making. As capitalism penetrated the subsistence economies of the developing countries, these products began to be sold in local markets. With the displacement of handmade consumer goods by manufactures, the bulk of the former artisans were forced back on to the land as agricultural labourers, and took their children to the fields with them. Over time, a 'putting-out' system also appeared in the artisanal industries that survived, notably in the spinning and weaving of cloth and the making of carpets. Many landless labourers farmed out their children to these new 'factories' not only to maximise their precarious incomes or reduce the number of mouths they had to feed, but also because working in a carpet-making shed was less gruelling than working under the hot sun in the fields. A 'softer' alternative was to send them into domestic service. Here too, by degrees, children began to work in homes far removed from their villages and parents. These practices have become so widespread that, according to an ILO report of November 1996, there were 250 million children between the ages of 5 and 14 working for pay in the developing countries.[37]

But by no means are all these 'put-out' children victims of globalisation. The vast majority are employed as servants in better-off households and in other service industries that by definition produce 'non-tradable' products. Others work in a variety of small and unregulated enterprises, which as a rule produce fairly crude consumer products for the lower end of the market in their own countries. These can hardly be considered part of the global economy. Most of the children are victims of the spread of capitalism and urbanisation within the developing countries.

However, an increasing number are now producing directly for the world market, with the full, if tacit, connivance of policymakers in the industrialised countries who profess to deplore the practice. The most highly publicised examples are the carpet-weaving factories of India, Pakistan, Iran and elsewhere in the Middle East, which cater mostly to Western markets; and the garment-making industry in developing countries ranging from Peru to China. Another major global employer of children is the tourism industry, which uses children in every capacity from bellboys, drinks-servers and housemaids to female and male child prostitutes.

The ILO's 1996 study exposed the manner in which child labour has become a structural part of the outsourcing of manufactured consumer goods by the large department stores and trading houses of the high-wage countries. It pointed out that while the actual saving in costs by employing child labour was as low as 5–10 per cent of the producer's price (and therefore as little as 1–3 per cent of the market price in the industrialised country markets), exporters in the developing countries were forced by competition among themselves to shave off even these minuscule costs in order to obtain orders from large, monopsonistic international buyers. The margins were further shaved because, in order to put together the volumes required by these buyers, the prime contractor would be forced to sub-contract the actual production to a large number of subcontractors who would compete with each other in turn.[38] Child labour in export industries thus validates the Singer-Prebisch model of international trade, in which the gains from trade go almost entirely to the buyers when competing producers face monopsonistic buyers.

Illegal Workers in the Industrialised Countries

The emergence of sweated labour in the industrialised countries is the other face of the export-oriented child labour described above. All production cannot be outsourced. This is especially true of services. No matter how expensive labour becomes, people will still have to employ plumbers, carpenters, gardeners, waiters, laundrymen and the like from within hailing distance of where they live. Even in manufacturing, there are a sizeable number of producers who do not outsource their product and instead struggle to keep manufacturing for insecure niche markets within the industrialised countries. These employers have a powerful need to deliberately hunt out the cheapest labour they can find. This is the illegal immigrant. As Saskia Sassen pointed out, when the industrialised countries encouraged immigration to meet the demand for labour during the Golden Age, and later outsourced the manufacture of consumer goods to the developing countries, they created precisely the skills in the labour force of the developing countries that were needed by the remaining, struggling manufacturers in the mature industrialised countries.[39] When their governments put up barriers to immigration after the advent of globalisation, immigration continued but became, for the most part, illegal. These illegal immigrants have become the new sweated labour of the industrialised countries.

As the blue-collar working class has shrunk, trade unions reduced to impotence, and wages and working conditions 'deregulated', employers in struggling firms have increasingly given preference to these immigrant workers, who expect less pay, work harder and cannot complain if they are exploited. The burden of rising unemployment has therefore fallen on the underprivileged among the existing citizens. In Europe the worst sufferers have been the communities of immigrant workers who came to Europe during the Golden Age, severed their ties to their own countries, and became the newly enfranchised 'black' citizens of the 'old world'. In the USA it is the African-Americans and some of the Hispanic communities of the West Coast. In both continents, poverty and rates of unemployment among these disadvantaged groups are far, far higher than in the general population.[40]

These developments have set the stage for the emergence of the permanent underclass in the most industrialised countries of the world. Homelessness is the most obvious product of the disappearance of stable, permanent work, and the attrition of the welfare state. Only three decades ago homelessness was called vagrancy, and society considered it a duty to put vagrants in jail till they could be sent home or institutionalised. But by the end of the 80s they had become a permanent feature of the outdoor landscape of Britain and the USA. There were between five and nine million homeless in the US alone—between two and three out of every hundred persons. Around 7 per cent of all Americans had been homeless at some point in their lives.[41] Homelessness had also become a regular feature of that other 'deregulated' society, the UK.

The disappearance of stable employment has reduced the ability of disadvantaged African Americans and Hispanics to marry and raise families. This has increased the number of children born out of wedlock and the number of single-parent families. The lack of employment has also made more members of these groups gravitate towards crime, and this has furthered the disintegration of the family and the rise in out-of-wedlock births. Prison is the final destination of much of this underclass. In the US, which is not only the richest country in the world but the most 'deregulated' at home and 'globalised' abroad, there were 1.6 million persons in prison on 1 January 1996. Another 3.8 million were on parole or probation. These 5.4 million people made up 2.8 per cent of the country's adults. This was three times the number of convicts and parolees in 1980! The incarceration rate for blacks was 6.44 times that for whites, and 70 per cent of the parolees were either black or Hispanic.[42]

The majority of crimes for which people are in prison in the US are petty or non-violent in nature. In 1990, 28 per cent of those sent to prison were incarcerated for parole violations, mostly of a very minor sort. Of the remainder, 70 per cent had been imprisoned for non-violent crimes.[43] The similarity with the prevalence of petty crime during the early days of British capitalism is striking, and springs from the same underlying cause—the inability of society to understand that the rise in petty crime is a symptom of systemic breakdown. When society does not have a solution to a problem, its reflexive response is to sweep it out of sight. In early nineteenth century England, apart from filling the jails, society would hang thieves for stealing a loaf of bread. In the US of the end of the twentieth century, prison has become a refuse bin to which the underclass is consigned to keep it out of sight.

One particularly disturbing feature of this wholesale imprisonment is that 74 per cent of the women and 68 per cent of the men in prison in 1991 had children under 18. These children, along with those from out-of-wedlock liaisons, are rapidly forming a feral sub-society of their own. Deprived of emotional stability and parental control, they take to crime with fatal ease. Drugs have become the route to easy money and riches. Guns have become status symbols as much as weapons for 'defence'.[44]

The emergence of feral gangs of slum children has been a feature of the large metropolises of South America for several decades.[45] More recently they have made their appearance in the slums of a number of African cities as well. What is relatively new is their appearance in the inner cities and *banlieus* of the most affluent industrialised countries of the world.

The Globalisation of Crime

If child labour and sweated labour are the dark face of global outsourcing, the emergence of transnational crime syndicates is the dark face of the rise of the transnational corporation. Conclusions from two reports cited by Castells sum up both the growth of these syndicates and the danger they pose to the stability of nations and regions:

During the last few years the international community has experienced an in-creasing number of political upheavals, geopolitical changes and technological restructuring. No doubt, organised transnational crime, a new dimension of more 'traditional' forms of organised crime, has emerged as one of the most alarming of these challenges. Organised transnational crime, with its capacity to expand its activities and to target the security and the economics of countries, in particular developing ones and those in transition, represents one of the major threats that governments have to deal with ...[46]

International criminal organisations have reached agreements and understand-ing to divide up geographical areas, develop new market strategies, work out forms of mutual assistance and the settlement of conflicts ... And this on a planetary scale. We are faced with a genuine criminal counterpower, capable of imposing its will on legitimate states, of undermining forces and institutions of law and order, of upsetting delicate economic and financial equilibrium and destroying democratic life.[47]

Among the organisations that Castells lists are the Sicilian *Cosa Nostra*, the American *Mafia*, the Mexican and Colombian drug cartels, various Nigerian criminal networks, the Japanese *Yakuza*, the various Russian *Mafiyas*, the Chinese *Triads*, and the Jamaican *posses*, but there are similar criminal networks in every country. Most of the trade between these syndi-cates is centred on drugs, but other lucrative lines are arms sales and smugg-ling, money laundering, illegal immigration and the white-slave traffic. These criminal syndicates use their earnings to buy protection from weak governments and in the process subvert them. The process is very far ad-vanced in countries like Afghanistan, Sudan, Colombia and Bolivia, but the politics of a large number of other countries, such as Russia, Mexico, Panama, Peru, Venezuela, Turkey, Myanmar, Thailand and even Taiwan and Hong Kong, cannot fully be understood without taking into account the power of these international crime cartels.[48]

Colombia illustrates not just how a global criminal syndicate can be born, take over large parts of a country and influence its policies, but also precisely how globalisation can act as a catalyst in facilitating this process in other countries in coming years. The drug connection between Colombia, Peru and Mexico and the United States was first forged in the 1960s with the export of marijuana. There is a widespread and possibly correct belief that Colombians became aware of the income-generating potential of marijuana because of the reactions to its availability from US Peace Corps volunteers sent to the country at the time. However when the US Drug Enforcement Agency tightened controls on its inflow, people began to grow it in the USA. California soon became the prime supplier to the nation.

The marijuana smuggling cartels survived, however, but needed a new product to supply to the American people. Their opportunity came when Colombian industrialisation began to fail. Medellin's textile industry went into a crisis because of competition from cheap synthetics; Boyaca, which was the centre of emerald mining, faced a crisis in the emerald market partly because of unrestrained smuggling, and Cali's sugar industry was fatally damaged by the imposition of quotas on sugar exports. Not surprisingly these three cities became the centres of the drug trade. The old networks were revived, but they now dealt in cocaine.

The success of these cartels in influencing, even dictating, Colombian politics arose out of another feature common to many newly independent countries—the narrowness of their political elites. This made it possible for the drug cartels to mobilise support on the basis of appeals to nationalism and promises to implement populist policies designed to help the poor, while the tradition of political violence made it possible for them to enforce their writ through a spate of threats and political assassinations. In 1993 the Colombian parliament defeated the extradition bill.[49] Since then large parts of Colombia remain outside government control.

All the three ingredients that went into the making of what is to all intents and purposes a criminalised state are present in a dozen or more other poor countries: failing industrialisation, a narrow base of political power, and a weak democratic tradition (where it exists at all) and a tradition of violence in politics. What is more, as trade barriers go down under the onslaught of the World Trade Organisation and imports replace the products of struggling national industry, and as economic deregulation deprives criminal organisations of their earlier purely national modes of earning a living (such as smuggling and black marketing), these criminal gangs will be on the lookout for new sources of income and will hook up with international crime cartels. Today for these very reasons, a large part of northern Mexico is out of the control of the Mexican government and is once more growing marijuana for shipment across the border to the US.

In India, gangs that used to smuggle gold from Dubai into India before 1991 (when such imports were strictly forbidden) rapidly shifted to guns, explosives drugs and a variety of electronic goods in the 1990s.[50] In Pakistan a network of international truck transporters collectively known as the Asian Transport Mafia smuggles in drugs from Afghanistan for transshipment to the West, and electronic goods for the Pakistani market from Central Asia.[51] All these previously national organisations are speedily being integrated into the emerging international criminal system.

The end of this road is disturbingly evident. As the widening income gaps and increasing uncertainty of employment witnessed in the industrialised countries reproduce themselves in the developing and least developed countries, and as local industries set up to cater to national markets disappear and unemployment becomes rife, democratic systems will weaken even where they have sunk deep roots in society. Such nations will become increasingly criminalised. Failed states and criminalised, authoritarian states will multiply, and the global criminal class will acquire a succession of territorial safe havens from where to challenge the emerging new world order. One beneficiary of this development is international terrorism.

The Re-emergence of Pauperism

A striking similarity between the present, early stage of global capitalism and the corresponding period of national capitalism in the second half of the eighteenth century is the coexistence of a prolonged secular rise in incomes and productivity with growing poverty. The half-century that preceded the 1780s saw a sustained increase in British exports, and a visible rise in the affluence of the country. But it also saw a steady rise in poverty and a sharp increase in the number of paupers on relief. This happened not only during an industrial downturn and shrinking exports but also when trade was growing and industry prospering. So constant was the association that one contemporary observer was moved to remark that 'the greatest number of poor was not to be found in the most barren countries amidst barbarous nations but in those which are the most fertile and the most civilised.'[52] What profoundly disturbed the people was that they could find no explanation for this. They expected periodic industrial contractions to create hardship. What they could not understand was why it was creating paupers not merely in the cities but also in the villages.

Only much later was the connection between progress in the cities and pauperisation in the villages fully understood. The half-century before McFarlane made the above observation had seen a hitherto unprecedented rise in the productivity of British industry. The rise of industry had transformed economic and social relations in Britain. The growing demand for foodstuffs as well as the insatiable demand of the factories for wool had commercialised agriculture to an unprecedented degree. Commons had therefore continued to be fenced in and peasants continued to be evicted from cottages that they had lived in for generations.

A rising demand for labour in the towns cushioned the shock of the displacement caused by the enclosure movement. But that happened only when times were good. It was in the recessionary phases of the trade cycle (though not only in them) that the bulk of the pauperisation occurred. The second half of the eighteenth century and the first quarter of the nineteenth saw a number of such cyclical expansions and contractions of the British economy. The end of the Seven Years' War in 1763 was followed by a decade-long surge in prosperity and exports. But that gave way to what Edmund Burke described to Pitt in 1795 as 'twenty bad years'. By the end of that period, British exports had shrunk almost to the level of half a century earlier.[53] The Napoleonic wars gave another huge fillip to industry but their end in 1812 was followed by another decade-long decline in production. In each downturn, industrialists simply threw out their now unwanted workers. The workers had no means of sustenance in the towns. Trade union action might have mitigated their hardship, but 'Anti-Combination' laws passed at the end of the eighteenth century had made unionisation illegal. As a result the unemployed had no alternative but to return to their rural parishes and go on the dole there.

Two centuries later, the experience of Britain in the eighteenth century was repeated, but now encompassing the entire new container that capitalism had built for itself. This occurred in East Asia, where a three decade-long surge of growth was followed by the collapse and wholesale impoverishment of entire nations in 1997 and 1998. There were important differences between the surges and contractions of the second half of the eighteenth century and the surge and contraction of the last three decades of the twentieth. The former occurred within the confines of a national market, while the latter occurred across nations, in the global market. The former were triggered by surges and contractions in Britain's overseas trade, i.e., by events that affected the current account. The latter was triggered by surges and withdrawals of money on the capital account. Perhaps most important of all, these contractions set off conventional trade cycles in eighteenth century Britain, whose causes are now well understood, while the causes of the prolonged expansion followed by a still incomplete contraction, which first afflicted Japan and then Southeast Asia, are still obscure.

Yet the similarities remain: the surge of prosperity that began in East Asia, and in parts of Latin America in the 1960s caused profound alterations in the social and economic structures of those countries. Workers deserted the countryside for the towns in millions; agriculture got commercialised and mechanised; and the urban labour markets were essentially unregulated, with labour unions being weak. As a result when the sudden contraction in output began in the late 1970s in Latin America and in East Asia in 1997, new paupers flooded the countryside. The rural areas and not the cities became the resting-places of the destitute.

The East Asian Meltdown

The East Asian crisis began with the collapse of the Thai baht on 2 July 1997. The crash devaluation of that currency caused panic to spread like a contagion among investors in the East and Southeast Asian money markets. There was a rush of short-term capital out of these markets. One by one, the currencies of Korea, Malaysia, Indonesia and the Philippines collapsed. The Hong Kong and Singapore dollars came under severe pressure and lost a part of their value. The crash devaluation made companies that had borrowed abroad to finance investment within their own boundaries and therefore earned their returns in the local currency incapable of repaying their debts. This caused a round of bankruptcies that too spread like a plague through the East Asian economies. Like ninepins, each bankruptcy led to others, till the entire economy of the region was in crisis. This was how a currency crisis in a single country turned into a deep structural economic crisis in an entire region from which, as of 2004, it has still not fully recovered.

The East Asian crisis triggered an immediate spate of recrimination upon the heads of the rulers and governments of the affected countries. Their governments were riddled with cronyism. Money was loaned and projects assigned to favourites. Unsound projects were routinely sanctioned. The market was not, in short, allowed to exert its discipline. The lead in this criticism was taken by the IMF. But as economists like Jagdish Bhagwati, J. Sachs, and Joseph Stiglitz pointed out,[54] the problem originated in the very policies of excessive openness of money markets that the IMF had relentlessly pressed upon these countries. These policies included moving to full convertibility of their currencies, and striving to maintain stability of exchange rates. Thailand made the mistake of virtually guaranteeing exchange rate stability, while simultaneously following high-interest-rate policies at home to curb inflation. This made it fatally attractive for private borrowers to go abroad for low-interest loans and amass a huge debt in foreign exchange, of which the government had no clear estimate. Eventually various financial investors, like the notorious, completely unregulated hedge funds that had sprung up in the deregulated capital markets, spotted the growing weakness of the Thai baht and began to attack it. On 2 July 1997, upon the fourth such attack in six months, the Thai central bank ran out of dollars with which to sustain the currency and allowed the baht to collapse.

How little the crisis was understood, especially in its earlier phases, may be judged from the continuous reduction of growth forecasts, notably those of the IMF, as the crisis progressed. In August 1997, the IMF predicted that Thailand's growth in 1998 would be 3.5 per cent. In November it lowered this to between 0 and 1 per cent. In February 1998, it revised the forecast down further to between –3 and –3.5 per cent. In May it was –4 to –5.5 per cent.[55] As the year ended it became apparent that GDP would decline by 8 per cent. The Indonesian estimates of the contraction had to be revised upwards from –12.3 per cent of GDP in June 1998 to – 16 per cent in December. Estimates of the shrinkage of Malaysia's GDP in the first quarter of 1998 rose from 1.8 per cent in March to 2.8 per cent in June. In the second quarter of 1998 GDP growth was –6.7 per cent and in the third, against the expectations of the Malaysian National Bank, –8.6 per cent.[56]

Even these gloomy figures seriously underestimated the contraction of these economies. They were based on a 'robust' assumption that there would be some growth in the services sector of the economy despite the steep decline in industry and construction (in Indonesia in agriculture as well). But the health of most service industries is dependent upon the health of agriculture and industry. A better idea of the depth of the crisis can therefore be had from the fact that by November 1998 it had reduced the output of chemical and metallurgical industries in Indonesia by 57 per cent over pre-crisis levels, and of other industries by 38 per cent.[57] In Thailand the Governor of the Bank of Thailand, Mr Chathumongol Sonakul, told this writer that the manufacturing index was down to 52 per cent of the previous year, and the investment index was down to 9. 'In my 32 years in the Ministry of Finance, I have never known it [the former] to come down below 72,' he remarked. A World Bank report estimated the decline in investment in Indonesia at between 50 and 60 per cent.[58]

The crisis devastated the poor of Asia. But except in Indonesia, where the government made some effort to keep track, few governments had any precise notion of how many had been thrown out of work. In Indonesia, by the government's own estimate, the numbers thrown out of work touched 14.3 million at the end of 1998.[59] But other countries counted only those who were actively looking for work. This did not include the millions who had simply gone 'home' to their villages. Even then, in Thailand unemployment, defined as those looking for or willing to work, jumped from 2.1 per cent to 4.6 per cent within 6 months. Another 1.7 per cent of the labour force lost their regular jobs and took up part-time jobs working less than 20 hours a week.[60] In Malaysia the proportion of the workforce that was out of work doubled between the end of the first quarter of 1998 and the second, from 2.5 to 5.1 per cent of the workforce. But this left out not only those who had returned to their villages, but also the large number of Indonesians and Bangladeshis who were sent home as their work contracts expired.[61] The Indonesian government estimated that about 700,000 Indonesian workers had been sent home from various Asian countries by October 1998.

The sharp contrast with mature industrialised countries, and the similarity with eighteenth century England, was writ large over what was happening. In the current-day western economies, where fewer than 5 per cent of the population lives in the villages and the working classes have long since lost their connection with the land, economic dislocation on this scale would have led to riots, a breakdown of law and order, and the targeting of foreign workers by right-wing hoodlums. Except for a pale reflection in Indonesia, nothing even remotely comparable happened anywhere in Asia. There was no violence and no picketing. As the shutters came down and the cranes and bulldozers went silent, millions of workers left the cities to return to their villages to seek shelter and help from their extended families. In Thailand these returning workers found shelter readily, because the country had had an exceptional harvest. But in Indonesia, where drought had brought down the agricultural output to 72 per cent of normal in 1998, it spread poverty from the cities into the countryside. As a result, according to the Central Bureau of Statistics, by early July the number of people below the poverty line had risen to 79.4 million, from a bare 22 million before the crisis. This was 40 per cent of the population.

Even after the diaspora to the villages, the World Bank estimated in 1998 that Indonesia had about six million people who had lost all support systems and were in dire need of state-organised relief. There were no estimates of the proportion of the urban population who left the cities to go back to their villages or otherwise sank into sheer destitution, but a significant index of dislocation was the decline in school enrolment, which fell from 78 per cent of all children in the school-going age group in 1997 to 54 per cent in 1998.[62] By this yardstick, almost a third of the population lost its livelihood as a result of the crisis and had to take the children out of school. A major portion of the withdrawals must have taken place because the families had to leave their place of residence.

In England those who became paupers during the contractionary phases of the huge business cycles that racked the country before and after the Napoleonic wars were at least able to return to the parishes and seek the protection of the Elizabethan poor laws. This was because the state existed and could intervene to mitigate their suffering. But there is no corresponding global authority to which those pauperised by globalisation can turn.

Notes

1. J.L. Van Zanden, 'Tracing the Beginning of the Kuznets curve: Western Europe during the Early Modern Period', *Economic History Review*, Vol. XLVIII (4), 1995, pp. 643–664. The Gini coefficient is derived from a graph that relates the share of national income to the share of the population it accrues to. If income is perfectly equally distributed, then the graph makes a diagonal straight line. If income is unequally distributed, then the graph bulges downwards. The Gini coefficient is the ratio of the space inside the bulge (i.e., between it and the diagonal straight line) to the total area under

the straight line between the X and Y axes. The coefficient therefore ranges between 0, which is perfect equality, to 1, which is perfect inequality (when a single individual owns all the income of the society).

2. Simon Kuznets, *Economic Growth and Structure (Selected Essays)'* (Heinemann, 1966).

3. See Karl Polanyi, *The Great Transformation* (Boston, Beacon Press, 1957), Chapter 4, for a comparison of these alternative methods of organising economic activity in a society.

4. Johan Norberg and Roger Bate, 'Demonstrations of Misconception', *Business Standard*, New Delhi, 4 June 2001, p. 11. Norberg is a fellow of the Timbro Institute in Sweden and is writing a book on the benefits of globalisation. Bate is Director of the International Policy Network in London. These and other data cited are also to be found in World Bank, *World Development Report 2000*.

5. Ibid. The choice of Zambia reflects a desire to come to a predetermined conclusion. Zambia has suffered from an especially predatory government and a fall in the price of copper, its main export. As is shown later in this chapter, the two factors, predatory governance and declining commodity prices, are not unconnected.

6. L. Pritchett, 'Divergence, Big Time' (World Bank Policy Research working paper no. 1522, Background paper for World Bank, *World Development Report 1995*, October 1995).

7. Manuel Castells, *End of Millennium—The Information Age: Economy, Society, Culture*, Vol. *III* (Basil Blackwell), Table 2.1, pp. 76–78.

8. Ibid.

9. Ibid., p. 77.

10. Alexander J. Yeats, Azita Amjadi, Ulricke Reincke and Francis Ng, 'What Caused Sub-Saharan Africa's marginalisation in World Trade', *Finance and Development*, December 1996.

11. Ibid.

12. 92 per cent in 1995 (see Castells, *End of Millennium Vol. III*, p. 83).

13. See Dean Baker, Gerald Epstein and Robert Pollin (eds.), *Globalization and Progressive Economic Policy* (Cambridge University Press, 1998), p. 7, Table 3. Between 1970 and 1994, while the share of manufactures in the exports of the industrialised countries rose gradually from 72 to 79 per cent of the total exports, it rose from 22.4 to 73.4 per cent for the developing Asian countries and from 10.6 to 48.7 per cent for the developing Latin American countries.

14. World Bank, *World Development Report 1996. From Plan to Market*, Table 3, p. 192. This table shows a dramatic worsening of terms of trade in 18 out of 23 selected African countries between 1985 and 1994.

15. Ibid., p. 85.

16. UNCTAD, *World Investment Report 1993* (New York, Geneva: United Nations, 1993), Chapter VII, pp. 164–165.

17. Baker et al., *Globalization and Progressive Economic Policy*, Chapter 1.

18. The simile refers to the manner in which Japan took advantage of the US' need for a low-wage production platform in Asia for the Vietnam war to transform its economy and become a capital exporter and in turn transform the East Asian region. More generally one can theorise that as low-wage countries industrialise rapidly through integration into the world market, their wage rates begin to converge with those of the industrialised countries and they in turn become capital exporters to other low-wage countries, where the process gets repeated.

19. Terutomo Ozawa, *Multinationalism Japanese style: The Political Economy of Outward Dependency* (Princeton University Press, 1979); Terutomo Ozawa, *Foreign Direct*

Investment and Structural Transformation: Japan as a recycler of Market and Industry. Business and the Contemporary World, Vol. 5.2, pp. 129–150, quoted by Giovanni Arrighi, *The Long Twentieth Century. Money, Power and the Origins of our Times* (London and New York, Verso, 1994), Epilogue.

20. Castells, *End of Millennium, Vol. III*, pp. 82–128
21. Ibid.
22. See Prem Shankar Jha, *India: A Political Economy of Stagnation* (New Delhi: Oxford University Press, 1980) for a detailed description of the origins of the predator state. Also see Prem Shankar Jha, *The Perilous Road to the Market: The Political Economy of Reform in Russia, China and India* (London, Pluto Press, forthcoming), Chapters 4 and 5 in the India section, for the incompleteness of Indian reforms and its failure to integrate itself to any significant extent into the global economy outside the realm of information technology.
23. This proposition is not accepted by most liberal economists, who believe that markets are a natural extension of human nature and have always existed, and that they spring from what Adam Smith called 'man's propensity to barter, truck and exchange one thing for another'. From this Smith deduced that exchange is the most natural way in which human beings relate to each other in the realm of the economy. Its scope is restricted only by external constraints such as the amount a family can produce and the distance goods can be transported safely. As the division of labour and improvements in technology increase productivity and improve modes of transport, the area over which goods can be exchanged grows larger. Markets therefore grow naturally till they encompass the world. In this progression local markets come first. These mesh together gradually to form regional and national markets. International trade comes last. Anthropologists hold a different view. See Polanyi, *The Great Transformation*, Chapter 4.
24. Polanyi, *The Great Transformation*, Chapter 4.
25. Polanyi, *The Great Transformation*, Chapter 5 (titled 'The evolution of the market pattern').
26. Herman M. Schwartz, *States versus Markets* (New York, St Martin's Press, 1994), Chapter 1.
27. For a detailed analysis of this relationship, see Michael Mann, *States, War and Capitalism: Studies in Political Sociology'* (Oxford, Basil Blackwell), Chapter 3, pp. 87–120.
28. Soviet economists believed that competition was wasteful. Armed with a fanatical belief in the economies of scale, they provided Stalin and the Communist Party the intellectual justification they needed for consolidating existing factories, large and small, into huge monopolies, and doing the same with trading establishments. As a result, in 1991, out of 7664 products manufactured in the machine building, metallurgical, chemical, timber and construction sectors, 5,884, or 77 per cent, were produced by monopolies. Whereas only 26 per cent of all industrial enterprises in the USA employed more than a thousand workers, the proportion in the USSR was 73 per cent. In 1988 large- and medium-sized enterprises with more than 200 employees accounted for 95 per cent of production and employees.
29. Samir Amin, *Accumulation on a World Scale. Critique of the Theory of Underdevelopment* (New York, Monthly Review Press, 1974).
30. Castells, *End of Millennium, Vol. III*, pp. 115–117, cites the following authors and studies: Aderanti Adepoju (ed.), *The Impact of Structural Adjustment on the Population of Africa: The Implications for Health, Education and Employment* (Heinemann, 1993); Eboe Hutchful, 'Why Regimes Adjust: The World Bank ponders its star pupil', *Canadian Journal of African Studies*, Vol. 29, No. 2; and others.

31. Castells, *End of Millennium, Vol. III*, pp. 116–117.
32. Ibid.
33. Castells, *End of Millennium, Vol. III*, citing Adepoju, *The Impact of Structural Adjustment.*
34. The lone addition is the bulk transfer of software writing and business process out-sourcing services to India, but this is a new form of globalisation—the outsourcing of services—and not an extension of the previous form, which was the outsourcing of manufacture.
35. In 1998–99 there were approximately 18 million workers in the registered small-scale industries in India. These exported approximately 10 per cent of their output, which accounted for 44 per cent of the total exports of the country. In 2000 and 2001 the government removed import restrictions on more than 1400 items. The resulting inflow of cheap consumer goods, mainly from China, is threatening the livelihood of a substantial proportion of these workers, as Indian marketing houses switch the procurement of a variety of cheap consumer goods and intermediates such as domestic electric appliances, clocks and truck tyres from Indian to Chinese and Southeast Asian manufacturers. See Prem Shankar Jha, *A Jobless Future – Political Causes of Economic Crisis* (New Delhi, Rupa Books, 2002).
36. G.D.H. Cole and Raymond Postgate, *Common People* (London, Methuen, 1962).
37. Castells, *End of Millennium, Vol. III*, p. 149.
38. Ibid., p. 153.
39. Saskia Sassen, *Globalisation and Its Discontents* (New York, The New Press, 1998), Chapter 3.
40. In the US, against an average poverty rate of 14.1 per cent in 1989–95, the poverty rate among African Americans was 29.3 per cent. Among children, while one in five was poor, the figure for African Americans was 41.9 per cent nationally and for Hispanics 40.0 per cent (Lawrence Mishel, Jared Bernstein and John Schmitt, *The State of Working America 1996-97* [Washington DC, Economic Policy Institute], p. 11).
41. The Clinton Administration's 1994 report, ' Priority Home' gave these figures (Castells, *End of Millennium, Vol. III*, p. 136).
42. Castells, *End of Millennium, Vol. III*, pp. 145–147. In California in the 1990s, in absolute terms 1951 out of every 100,000 adult blacks were in jail against 215 per 100,000 whites. Overall the incarceration rate in California was twice as high as in Russia or South Africa.
43. Ibid., p. 148. Castells quotes a study by John Irwin and James Austin, *It's About Time: America's Imprisonment Binge* (Belmont (CA), 1994).
44. William J. Wilson, *When Work Disappears. The World of the New Urban Poor* (New York, Alfred Knopf, 1996). Quoted by Castells, *End of Millennium, Vol. III*, pp. 138–145.
45. For some details, see Castells, *End of Millennium, Vol. III*, p. 151
46. *Report of the United Nations Economic and Social Council, 1994*, p. 3.
47. Anti-Mafia Commission of the Italian Parliament, 20 March 1990.
48. Castells, *End of Millennium, Vol. III*, p. 187.
49. Ibid., pp. 196–201. Under the influence and with the support of the US, Colombian governments of the early 1990s fought a bitter war against the drug cartels, and tried to enact a law permitting the drug lords' extradition to the US to face trial. The cartels were decimated, but they won the political battle.
50. A consignment of RDX explosive, used by Islamic fundamentalists to set off a spate of bombs in Mumbai, India's commercial hub, in March 1993, was traced to a former gold smuggler named Dawood Ibrahim, who lives in Dubai. According to Indian intelligence sources, Ibrahim was provided the explosives by a member of Pakistan's Inter Services Intelligence Directorate (various newspaper reports, March–April 1993).

51. For a description of its activities, see Ahmed Rashid, *Taliban: Militant Islam, Oil and Fundamentalism in Central Asia* (New Haven, Conn., Yale University Press, 2000), p. 22.

52. John McFarlane, *Enquiries Concerning the Poor*, 1782, quoted by Polanyi, *The Great Transformation*, p. 103.

53. Polanyi, *The Great Transformation*, pp. 89–93.

54. Jagdish Bhagwati, 'The Capital Myth: The Difference between Trade in Widgets and Dollars', *Foreign Affairs*, May–June 1998; J. Sachs, 'Wrong Medicine for Asia', *The New York Times*, 3 November 1997; Joseph Stiglitz, *Globalization and its Discontents* (New York, W.W. Norton and Co., 2002), Chapter 4.

55. Ammar Siamwalla and Orphin Sopchokchai: 'Responding to the Thai crisis', Paper presented at UNDP 'High Level Consultative Meeting on Policy Response to the Economic Crisis and Social Impact in Thailand', Bangkok, Thailand, 22 May 1998.

56. Bank Negara Malaysia, quarterly bulletins for the first, second and third quarters of 1998.

57. Figures cited by Ms. Ibuhana Suharto, of the Indonesian Ministry of Trade and Industry, at a conference on Financing Infrastructure Development in Jakarta, 27 November 1998.

58. World Bank, 'Indonesia in Crisis. A Macro-Economic Update', July 1998, p. 213, Table 2.3.

59. Prepared speech of Secretary-General of Ministry of Trade and Industry given at the seminar on 'Infrastructure investment and development and the revitalisation of the Indonesian economy', Jakarta, 28 November 1998.

60. Siamwalla and Sopchokchai, 'Responding to the Thai crisis'.

61. At the peak of its growth cycle, 25 per cent of Malaysia's workforce was foreign.

62. World Bank: 'Indonesia in Crisis. A Macro-Economic Update', 16 July 1998, p. ix.

8

UNDERMINING ECONOMIC SOVEREIGNTY

In previous cycles of capitalism's rebirth, the lead in destroying existing institutions and creating new ones was taken by one hegemonic city or nation state. In capitalism's current rebirth, that task has fallen upon the United States. The striking feature of the US' response is a decisive shift from seeking order through consensus *between* nation states to imposing order through coercion *upon* nation states. The shift became apparent first in the economic relations between the industrialised and developing countries, in the late 1970s and early 1980s. It surfaced in the realm of international relations only in the 1990s, after the end of the Cold War.

Breaking the Economic Walls of the Nation State

One day in 1982, two middle- to senior-level officials from the US Department of Commerce arrived in New Delhi and began doing the rounds of the ministries and think-tanks. Their goal was to persuade the Indian government to agree to a new round of trade negotiations under the General Agreement on Tariffs and Trade (GATT). But they had a message that few of us, locked in our 'dirigiste' economy and struggling to balance the external account in the face of the second oil price shock of the previous year, had heard before. The world, they said had changed in a fundamental way. Trade was not the only link between nations; transnational investment was emerging as a far more important one. A sizeable part of international trade now consisted of intra-corporate transfers. Investment and not trade was therefore going to determine future economic relations. This raised a host of new issues, such as patent protection and equal treatment for foreign investors with domestic suppliers. Financial institutions had also gone global, and were seeking entry in emerging markets, and this was only the most important of a growing number of service industries, ranging from transport to corporate security, that had 'gone global'. Trade in services was therefore rapidly becoming as important as trade in commodities. GATT had not envisioned any of these developments and was therefore confined to regulating the trade in commodities. This ran the danger of making it more and more irrelevant and leaving larger and larger emerging areas of international interaction in a state of anarchy. The time had therefore come to rewrite the rules of the game. GATT's mandate had to be drastically revised to include the protection of intellectual property and trade in services. The time had also come, they said, to establish an 'International Trade Organisation' that would oversee international trade and investment on a permanent basis. This had not got off the ground at the founding conference in Havana in 1948 that set up GATT, but it could no longer be deferred.

To Indian intellectuals all this was new enough, but the tone of their discourse was newer still. The days when developing countries could sign up to GATT and claim exemption under various clauses were over. Henceforth, and especially in the proposed new areas, all agreements would have to be strictly reciprocal. With capital flooding into the developing countries and industrialising them at a hectic pace, the distinctions on which earlier GATT exemptions had been based had become irrelevant, except perhaps for a very few of the least developed countries. India did not fall into that category.

And then came the bombshell: the US Trade representative was drawing up a 'watch-list' of countries that, in Washington's assessment, had unduly restrictive trade or lax intellectual property laws. These countries would be 'persuaded' to change them and agree to a new round of negotiations, through selective denial of trade privileges agreed to under earlier rounds of GATT using two new domestic US laws labelled 'Super' and 'Special' 301. This was the genesis of the Uruguay round of trade negotiations and the World Trade Organisation.

In the Golden Age: Trade Negotiations through Consensus

Although the change of tactics by the US from negotiation through consensus to negotiations through coercion took the Indian government (and most other developing country governments) by surprise, it was not as sudden as it appeared to them. This had begun in a very small way as far back as the Kennedy round of trade negotiations in the mid-1960s. It gathered momentum in the Tokyo round that ended in 1979, and emerged full-blown in the Uruguay round in the late 1980s.

The move to restore free trade after the Second World War had been rooted in a relatively modest goal: avoiding the chaos in international economic relations of the 1930s. The uncoordinated resort to competitive devaluation, capital controls and protection of domestic markets, which had followed the collapse of the Gold Standard, had done immense harm to the economies of the world and was at least partly responsible for the Second World War. The goal of the Bretton Woods conference was to restore an orderly international trade and payments system. As a result it concentrated on creating a stable system of exchange rates, and an institutional mechanism for coordinating financial and monetary policy. Bretton Woods did not deal directly with the issue of a post-war trade regime.

It was understood that once again creating a non-discriminatory, rule-based trading system was the essential third element in the restoration of economic order. However, rule-based and non-discriminatory trade did not have to be free trade.[1] Accordingly, the goals of the General Agreement on Tariffs and Trade (GATT), which was signed by 23 'contracting parties' in Geneva in October 1947, were to prohibit all internal measures that could restrict trade or lead to discrimination between domestic and foreign goods or between goods from different countries; to eliminate as far as possible quantitative restrictions on imports; and to limit all restraints on trade to a single instrument, the tariff, to be applied absolutely without discrimination to all countries, whether members of GATT or not. The lowering of tariffs was to be done by negotiation between the members of GATT at a later stage.

The guiding principle of GATT was not so much free trade as reciprocity. The key to achieving this objective—the lynchpin of the post-war trading system that evolved under the agreement—was the MFN, the 'Most Favoured Nation' treatment clause of the agreement. This obliged the contracting parties to offer the trade concessions that it negotiated with any one country to all its trading partners, whether members of GATT or not.

Because the principle of national sovereignty was not challenged till the late 1970s, the journey towards free trade was fairly slow but harmonious. Both the developed and the developing countries lowered trade barriers in fits and starts and accepted the principle of reciprocity in a piecemeal and grudging way. Developing countries used quantitative restrictions on imports and freed themselves from the obligation to lower tariffs by taking advantage of clauses of the GATT that permitted them to do so when they faced foreign exchange difficulties, and to protect infant industries (the former was so easy to invoke that the latter was seldom used). Several countries also used a clause that permitted restrictions designed to protect morals in order to keep out various kinds of films and other information-related materials.

Initially most industrialised countries also dragged their feet over trade liberalisation. But they did so under clauses of the GATT that permitted bans on agricultural imports, subsidies to domestic products and exports, and the protection of local industry from 'serious' injury. They too used clauses permitting them to restrict exports to safeguard health, morals and national security.

The overall effect of these numerous exceptions was to limit liberalisation to trade in manufactures between the industrialised countries.[2] But even among this handful of countries, there were significant differences in the degree of commitment to trade liberalisation. The European approach was essentially defensive. Throughout the 1950s these governments lowered tariffs but relied on quantitative restrictions (QRs) to regulate imports. As a result the Annecy, Geneva, Torquay and Dillon rounds of trade negotiations under GATT, which focused on reducing tariffs, had little impact on their trading practices.[3] Each left the US, which had taken the lead in promoting the negotiations, feeling cheated.[4]

By contrast, the US concentrated from the very start on using GATT as the main instrument for securing the lowering of tariffs and the elimination of QRs. The US' reasons for promoting freer trade were precisely the same as those of Britain in the mid-nineteenth century. So long as it enjoyed a surplus in the trade in manufactures, lowering tariffs and eliminating trade barriers on a reciprocal basis benefited it more than it benefited it competitors. When continuing protectionism and the deployment of new technologies in Europe began to threaten its competitive edge, American firms invested their profits in Europe. When its high relative wages did the same, it outsourced labour-intensive manufacture to Latin America and Asia. Throughout the post-war period therefore, the US had the strongest of motives for enlarging the market for manufactures and then in keeping them open.

The Period of Transition

The US began to flex its muscles to push the free trade agenda seriously only when it lost its commanding position in the world economy. Although its trade account remained in surplus till 1971, and broadly in balance till 1976, its balance of payments had turned negative in the 1960s, mainly because of its heavy military expenditures abroad. In the 1960s, therefore, the US stepped up its pressure on the European Community to speed up the opening up of its markets. This pressure was applied on the industrialised nations during the Kennedy round of negotiations, which was concluded in 1967.[5] The most important change sought by the Kennedy round was to replace the request-offer system by a linear cut in tariffs. In this system, an across-the-board cut of tariffs was first agreed on in principle, and exceptions negotiated afterwards. This change did not alter the consensual basis of trade liberalisation, but put the onus of explaining why trade in particular commodities could not be liberalised to the agreed extent on the country seeking the exception. In the Kennedy round the *a priori* linear cut agreed to had been 50 per cent. After the effect of the numerous exceptions had been taken into account, the average reduction in tariffs amounted to 35 per cent. This was a great deal more than the 10 per cent achieved in the Dillon round that had preceded it.

Trade Liberalisation through Coercion

The change from a consensual strategy for trade liberalisation to a coercive one can be traced to the reports of two commissions set up in 1967 and 1971. By the end of the 1960s, the US' lead in trade, especially in manufactures, had all but vanished. Cheap consumer goods from Japan and East Asia had begun to displace domestic output at the low-wage end of the spectrum of manufactured products, while European and Japanese cars, engineering and chemical products had whittled away the American lead at the high-wage, high-technology end of the spectrum. A wave of protectionism had swept the USA in the late 1960s, but had been resisted by the US administration, which remained by and large wedded to liberalising international trade still further.[6] The US therefore found itself facing exactly the same dilemma that Britain had faced almost a hundred years earlier. In the 1880s, the Fair Trade League had campaigned vigorously for a measure of protection for British manufactures to offset the growing protection that the US, and France and Germany in particular, were giving to their industries. The arguments the Fair Trade League was making were unanswerable, but at that time Britain's export of manufactures were five times greater than her imports. Thus she stood to lose more from any round of tariff increases than she stood to gain. A century later, America was in the same position, so long as America's trade surplus in manufactures persisted.

The only way to reconcile the demand for protection at home with the compelling need to liberalise trade still further—in short, to reconcile the conflicting needs of labour and capital—was to redouble the effort to make other countries open their markets to American products. The two commissions set up by Presidents Johnson and Nixon provided the intellectual rationale for this effort. The first was the Public Advisory Committee on Trade Policy set up by President Johnson soon after the conclusion of the

Kennedy round, and the second was the Williams Commission, under Albert R. Williams of IBM, set up by President Nixon. The purpose of the PAC on trade policy, according to President Johnson, was 'to ensure that the Kennedy round did not mark the end of the drive towards trade liberalisation'.[7] But given the pressures that had led to their establishment, it is not surprising that while both reports urged the US to adhere to its liberal trading policies, they noted that America's exports were being restricted by the trade policies of other nations. The PAC devoted a good deal of space to describing the non-tariff measures that other countries, notably the Europeans and Japan, employed to restrict imports, and recommended that these be consolidated into a set of codes which would specify the conditions under which they could be used. The Williams commission went so far as to say that the rise in cheap manufactured imports had created a growing crisis of confidence in the United States. It concluded, 'the core of the present difficulty is that *government policies and practices and international arrangements for collective decision making* have not kept abreast of the high degree of economic interaction which has been achieved since World War II.'[8]

Both committees recommended another determined round of trade negotiations to drastically reduce if not end the restrictive practices of other countries. But by putting the blame for the deterioration in America's trade balance in manufactures on the restrictive policies of other countries, they paved the way intellectually for the assault on sovereignty in the name of global interdependence, which the US launched in the 1980s after the Tokyo round of negotiations was concluded.

The Tokyo round saw the most protracted negotiations of any of the trade rounds, but met with a great deal of success. Apart from negotiating a further cut in tariffs, it resolved the problems caused by the American Sales Price[9] and brought a measure of order to the application of the anti-dumping code. Only the Common Agricultural Policy of the EC remained largely impervious to change. The Tokyo round also failed to arrive at an agreement on the use of the safeguards clause of the GATT agreement. But since this was being invoked mainly against the developing countries, it did not create much friction between the EC and the US. Despite its success, however, the Tokyo round marked the end of the era of consensual reductions in trade barriers. Till then, despite many disagreements and disputes over details, the mode of trade negotiation had remained broadly unchanged. It was to make an offer to other countries and invite them to match it. Even the linear tariff cut principle adopted in the Kennedy round had only reversed the end from which the negotiations began but not changed their nature. After the Tokyo round the mode of negotiations became overtly coercive. Countries that did not agree to reduce their trade barriers faced bilateral trade sanctions. As with the attack on tariffs and later on non-tariff measures, the lead in this new phase too was taken by the US.

The reason was the continuing deterioration of the American economy. By the beginning of the 1980s, the built-in contradictions of the Reaganite policy of 'supply-side monetarism', with its lower taxes, higher defence expenditures and therefore escalating budget deficits on the one hand, and stringent controls on the growth of money supply on the other, had led to high real interest rates and a steep appreciation of the dollar (26 per cent by the end of 1982 and 40 per cent by the beginning of 1985). By 1981–82 American industry was in the same plight as British industry had found itself in about four years earlier, when the pound appreciated under the impact of the discovery of North Sea oil. Demands for protection from cheap imports became deafening, especially from the powerful automobile industry. The mode of reconciliation that the government once more chose was to maintain as far as possible a liberal trade regime, but push the cost of adjustment to the new economic conditions on to the exporters.

The change from consensus to coercion was marked by four changes in negotiating strategy that together eroded the foundations of GATT. These were:

  (i) direct protectionism, which took the form of a multiplication of Voluntary Export Restraints (VERs), and a misuse of anti-dumping and countervailing duties;
 (ii) a conditional extension of the MFN to selected countries;
(iii) a retreat from multilateral GATT negotiations, and even bilateral side agreements, to an aggressive unilateralism in trade negotiations backed by the threat of sanctions; and
 (iv) the abandonment of the principle of reciprocity, the lynchpin of the GATT, in favour of the 'National Treatment'.

The erosion of MFN, the retreat from the principle of reciprocity and the growing insistence on 'National Treatment' can all be traced directly to the structural change in international trade brought about by globalisation. The decline in transport costs and the rapid elimination of trade barriers between the US and the EC led to an international specialisation of production. One consequence was that more and more of the exports of the industrialised countries consisted of services, while more and more of their imports consisted of manufactures. Services were not part of the GATT; as a result this became an area in which reciprocity and MFN considerations did not apply. Trade in services, in contrast to trade in goods, required investment in the importing country. For instance, selling banking and insurance services to buyers in another country required setting up branches in that country. If they were to compete, these foreign branches needed the same freedom to operate as was enjoyed by the indigenous banks and insurance companies. The demand for 'National Treatment' was bound to arise.

As companies in the industrialised countries established branches and affiliates abroad, and as a growing proportion were located in developing countries, the nature of trade in commodities also changed. More and more of it became shipments of materials, components and finished products between branches of the same company. By 1992 fully one-third of international trade was accounted for by such intra-company shipments. As the investments involved were often large, rules were needed to give investors a measure of security against what they considered arbitrary action. This required at a minimum that foreign investors, once allowed in, should enjoy the same protection and privileges as domestic investors, and at a maximum that they be indemnified against various types of risk emanating from changes in national policy.

On the surface national treatment would seem to play a supportive role to the MFN. But in reality, it threatens its very survival, for it blurs the distinction between non-discrimination between foreigners and non-discrimination between foreign and domestic actors. Since the latter is an infringement of a nation's sovereignty, it has to be extracted through threats, i.e., a resort to aggressive unilateralism. In this the US is far better placed than the EC for extracting concessions, and the developing countries have no levers of power whatever. Thus national treatment has become a cloak for the extraction of concessions under duress by the US, with others getting whatever they can by invoking the MFN clause. It thus promotes bilateralism at the expense of multilateralism. Worse still, national treatment has become the excuse for demanding changes in domestic laws under threat of sanctions. The US, in particular, has taken advantage of such bargaining from strength to force industrialised developing countries like Brazil, Korea, Thailand, China, India and Indonesia among others to provide protection to intellectual property in accordance with developed country protocols, and is pressing them to adopt environmental regulations and humane wage standards and working conditions.[10]

Lastly, foreign direct investment and the sub-contracting of production to firms in the developing countries has raised concerns about the protection of intellectual property to a new height. This is especially so in products like designer garments and accessories, where what is being sold above all is the brand name; in electronic software products, such as computer software, video films and music, where piracy is easy; and in industries like pharmaceuticals, where discovering a new product is extremely expensive, but replicating it is easy.

These new areas of concern were all brought within the multilateral negotiation system in the Uruguay Round of trade negotiations (1986–93), and the method of negotiating the round was through blatant coercion. In the 1980s the US used the threat of applying sanctions under its domestic laws—the 'Super' 301 and 'Special' 301—to force countries to give national treatment to service industries making investments in the newly industrialised countries, and to change their domestic patent and copyright laws to give protection to brands and products instead of to processes alone. The Uruguay round was itself a product of threats of sanctions. The most important one was applied to the larger developing countries that initially resisted the inclusion of Trade in Services, Trade-Related Investment Measures (TRIMS) and Trade-Related Intellectual Property Rights (TRIPS) in the round, and insisted that GATT should be confined, as before, to trade in commodities. They were bluntly told that they would be 'left out' of the world trading system. Those that did not agree to the inclusion of these areas within the GATT protocols would cease to benefit from the MFN clause of GATT, which required concessions negotiated with some parties to be given to all, whether they were signatories of GATT or not. They also faced the withdrawal of specific concessions, such as the Generalised System of Trade Preferences (GSTP) that had been negotiated in earlier rounds to exempt developing countries from the full rigours of reciprocity.

In effect, therefore, bilateralism in negotiations, preceded by the threat of unilateral action under domestic laws to restrict imports in contravention of GATT, had reached a scale where the developed countries were prepared to destroy the consensual trading system altogether if their demands were not met. So great was the pressure put on the developing, newly industrialised countries that in the end most of them came to regard falling in line with the Dunkel draft of the Uruguay round agreement as the lesser of the two evils,[11] because any form of multilateral trading system was better than none. This was, in fact, the message that GATT officials kept giving to the delegates from the developing countries in Geneva throughout the round. The Dunkel draft secured for the developing countries two of their long-standing demands, the discontinuation of quotas on textiles and garments, albeit only after 2003 AD, and a limited opening of the European and Japanese markets to agricultural exports like cereals. It also strengthened the dispute settlement mechanism for determining whether safeguards and anti-dumping measures were being unfairly used to keep out specific manufactured exports. However, in exchange the developing countries had to fall in line and agree to protect intellectual property rights in products as distinct from processes, to strengthen their copyright laws on the basis of an agreed code, and to agree in principle to open their markets for trade in services, without getting any concession on their demand that trade in services should include the easing of restrictions on the transnational use of labour. They also agreed to move closer to giving national treatment to trade-related investment. The Uruguay round also legitimised the principle of cross-retaliation, in which default by a contracting party on one of its obligations would not lead to the withdrawal of concessions offered by the others only in that area of trade but could be punished by sanctions and withdrawal of concessions in others.

Lastly, the Uruguay round saw at long last the creation of the World Trade Organisation, and ended the anomalous position that GATT had occupied since the failure to set up the ITO in 1948. 125 countries signed the agreement in Marrakech in April 1994 to set up the WTO. The WTO formally came into being on 1 January 1995. In April 2004 its membership had expanded to 147 and included the trading giant China. The WTO's dispute settlement powers were considerably greater than those of GATT, and could therefore help to shore up the multilateral trading system against further erosions from bilateralism and the proliferation and strengthening of regional trade blocs. But the circumstances in which it was set up were vastly different from those in which the ITO had been envisaged half a century ago. By 1995 the consensual mode of trade negotiations had largely been replaced by aggressive strength testing and bilateral concessions. The practice of allowing developing countries to benefit from the most favoured nation clauses in trade relations without having to reciprocate had been whittled down till it survived only for the least developed countries. What is more, the US Congress was no more prepared to surrender any shred of its sovereignty than it had been in the 1970s, when it first asserted itself to pass domestic trade legislation and insist that it should have precedence over the country's international obligations.[12]

The Clinton administration not only endorsed the superiority of domestic law but made aggressive bilateralism its principal tool for prising open the markets of other countries.[13] In his State of the Union message to Congress in February 1997, Clinton said, 'America must prosper in the global economy. We have worked hard to tear down trade barriers abroad so that we can create good jobs at home.'[14] From the perspective of the developing countries, therefore, the formation of the WTO proved a mixed blessing. While it gave them a stronger forum to which they could appeal against arbitrary action, it put them permanently on the defensive, because in the WTO the introduction of new trade and trade-related issues no longer required prior agreement on starting a new round of trade negotiations. The pressure from the developed countries to make new concessions, backed by the threat of sanctions and withdrawal of trade preferences, therefore became continuous instead of episodic.

The Exercise of Hegemony

A crucial feature of hegemony is the ability of the hegemonic power to convince dependent countries that policies that serve its interest also, to a greater or lesser extent, serve theirs. In the realm of international economics, the hegemonic discourse was summarised in the rationale for the creation of the WTO, whose official website spells out the benefits from more open trade, stating:

> Evidence from studies shows that economies embracing open trade and investment policies have done better on average than more closed economies ...
>
> This greater interdependence allows countries to specialize in areas where they are competitive, providing opportunities for their working population to put their skills and talents to the best use, and providing their consumers with the widest choice of goods and services at the best possible prices.
>
> In some aspects, however, openness and interdependence can bring a sense of discomfort. Competition from foreign imports, and changes in export markets, demand an extra effort of adjustment, even beyond the constant and sometimes painful adjustments needed to meet domestic competition, technological advances and changing consumer tastes. Economic difficulties in one part of the world can affect exports and jobs in other countries.
>
> But the difficulties are far outweighed by the gains from trade, and the evidence is strong that countries, developed and developing, that are most open to trade also benefit the most.
>
> The gains from exporting are obvious enough: better jobs and higher earnings, and bigger markets that allow greater efficiency, spread costs and achieve greater profitability. No wonder everyone wants other countries to lower their trade barriers.
>
> But in fact, economists agree that the greatest gains go to the country that slashes its own barriers. Readiness to open up to foreign suppliers of consumer goods and of inputs to production improves choice as well as competition in price and services offered. Protection that gives special favours to one sector or another of the economy distorts the way a country uses its productive resources. Removal or reduction of distortions allows resources to be used more efficiently.
>
> And the payments made for imports are not lost: directly or indirectly, they come back. The additional purchasing power put in foreign pockets is used to buy other countries' goods and services, to meet debt obligations, to invest abroad, or to save.[15]

From the start of the Uruguay round, the US sought to persuade the developing countries that trade liberalisation, even when achieved through coercion, would accelerate their growth, create more jobs and increase their exports. Developing countries were persuaded to sign on to the wide-ranging commitments of the Uruguay round by meticulously crafted studies that showed that the resulting freer trade would increase world GDP by $213 to $510 billion a year. The rise in the developing countries would be $86 to 122 billion. They therefore agreed to bind, i.e., put a ceiling on, future tariffs on 61 per cent of their imports against 13 per cent till then. They also committed themselves to lowering their trade-weighted average duties on imports by 28 per cent.

But nine years later, studies carried out by research institutes in several developing countries and by UNCTAD showed that while the developing countries had exceeded the targets for liberalisation that they had accepted, the gains from the resulting trade had gone almost entirely to the developed countries. Not only had GDP growth in the developing countries slowed down but, if one excluded China, their share of global exports too had gone down from 34.06 per cent in 1980 to 32.50 per cent in 2002. In sum, trade liberalisation even under the Tokyo round of negotiations had not yielded the promised spurt in growth either of GDP or exports.

These studies also show that the rich countries have manipulated the commitments they made in the Uruguay round to suit their own narrowly conceived objectives. While they have brought down their average level of tariffs, they have done nothing to reduce, much less eliminate, the discrimination that exists in their tariff structure against simple manufactures from developing countries. The US, for instance, has brought down its average rate of tariff to under 2 per cent, but within this the trade-weighted tariff on simple manufactures is 10.5 per cent, while that on all other goods is just 0.8 per cent. Shoes and clothing are the worst hit. These make up just 7 per cent of its imports but fetch fully half its revenues from import duties. As a result of this anomaly, Nepal's $200 million worth of exports to the US pay $25 million in duties while Ireland's $18.6 billion pay $29 million. The duty imposed upon $2 billion of imports from Bangladesh exceeds the duties garnered from $30 billion of imports from France. All the countries of the Quad—the US, Canada, the EU and Japan—have similar duty structures.[16]

Market access for their products, particularly textiles, was another area in which the industrialised countries made commitments that they have fulfilled only in letter. By the beginning of 2003 they were supposed to have removed quotas on 51 per cent of all textiles and garments covered by the Multi-Fibre Agreement. In practice the products have been so chosen that in value terms the EU has lifted quotas on only 20 per cent of the textiles exports so far. The Quad are now demanding further access for their textiles beyond what was envisaged in the Uruguay round, in exchange for fulfilling their commitments under it.

These are only the tips of the iceberg of trade and investment discrimination by the rich countries against the poor. Other forms are proliferating non-tariff barriers, exclusions that make nonsense of the Quad's demand for free competition, and huge subsidies given to transnationals for investing in their countries. They wish to keep these out of discussions about freeing investment in the developing countries. They are masked as contributions towards research and development or in aid of employment generation. Until declared illegal by the WTO, the US was giving $4 billion a year in subsidies to large American exporters under the Foreign Sales Corporation Program. An indicative list of subsidies given for job creation showed that this ranged from $30,000 per job to Samsung in the UK in 1994 to a whopping $3.4 million per job to Dow in Germany in 1996. The total subsidy Germany gave to Dow for this project amounted to $6.8 billion. Southern US states gave $50,000 to $200,000 per job.[17]

The most severe discrimination, however, remains against agricultural imports from the developing countries. Typically, tariffs on agricultural products remain at anything from 14 to 900 per cent, and are as a rule higher on processed agricultural produce than on raw products. The RIS report cited above concluded that since 1994 the industrialised countries had actually increased their subsidies to their own farm sectors while dragging their feet on the reduction of import duties and increasing market access to the developing countries. The US, for instance, announced a sharp increase in farm subsidies, the most generous in its history, in 2002.[18] At Cancun it was the reluctance of the Quad countries to discuss reductions in these tariffs and non-tariff barriers, while insisting that the developing countries increase access to their home markets for the heavily subsidised agricultural exports of the industrialised countries, that broke up the conference.

Notes

1. Gilbert R. Winham, *International Trade and the Tokyo Round Negotiation* (Princeton, Princeton University Press, 1986), Chapter 2, pp. 79–80. As recently as 1973, the EC's overall approach to the Tokyo Round negotiations ruled out the elimination of tariffs.
2. The tariffs agreed to in the Tokyo round, although at a low 4.5 per cent on the average, discriminated systematically against simple manufactures, and therefore against manufactured imports from the developing countries. The highest duty of about 15 per cent was imposed on garments and textiles, followed by leather products. On the other hand, machinery and electronics goods attracted the lowest duties, because these were then manufactured almost exclusively in the OECD countries.

3. Winham, *International Trade and the Tokyo Round Negotiation*, esp. pp. 79–84. The EC had moved rapidly to reduce tariffs between its members, but was reluctant to place its entire trust in tariffs for protection on a worldwide basis, because countries could easily evade them by changing their exchange rate. This objection was made explicit in the run-up to the Tokyo round, but had informed the trade policies of the EC throughout the 50s and 60s.

4. In 1958, European governments took advantage of yet another exception to the MFN permitted by GATT—one that allowed contracting parties to set up regional preferential or free-trade organisations—to set up the European Common Market. The Common Market lowered tariffs and harmonised agricultural policies internally at a rapid pace, but adopted a defensive attitude towards the rest of the world, especially the US and Japan. In 1962 the EC adopted two pieces of restrictive legislation that made nonsense of MFN and trade liberalisation in general. The first was a Long-Term Agreement (LTA) on Cotton Textiles, which set quotas for imports. The second was to adopt a Common Agricultural Policy that fixed the minimum price at which any agricultural imports could be sold within the EEC and charged variable tariffs to equate the import price with the designated import sale price. In the 1960s the EEC also negotiated the admission of four new members, including the UK, Norway and Denmark, and extended preferential trade arrangements to include a large number of African countries under the Lome agreements. These regional trade agreements further undermined the MFN provisions of GATT.

5. Prior to the Kennedy round, countries had followed the request-and-offer method of negotiating tariff cuts. Each country submitted a list of the tariffs it was prepared to cut and the concessions it sought from others. These were then negotiated and, in consonance with the MFN principle, the final agreed cuts were applied to all trade. By the early 1960s it had become apparent that there was a growing gap between the progress being made on reducing tariffs and the lack of progress in eliminating other forms of trade barriers. Thus, while tariff reduction remained the central focus of the Kennedy round, a determined effort was made by the negotiators, spurred on by the GATT Secretary-General, Sir Eric Wyndham-White, to tackle the most glaring non-tariff barriers to trade.

6. While Europe spearheaded the LTA in cotton textiles, which was justified on the grounds of market disruption, the US placed its reliance on Voluntary Export Restraints (VERs) by the exporters, backed by threats of retaliation under domestic law if the exporting country refused to comply. In the early 1970s, the US had in place VERs on meat, steel, and woollen and synthetic textiles.

7. Winham, *International Trade and the Tokyo Round Negotiation*, p. 73. This was the instruction President Johnson gave to the US Special Representative for Trade Negotiations, William R. Roth, when asking him to work with the committee in order to make a study of future trade policy.

8. Ibid., p. 74 (emphasis added).

9. Till then the US fixed its duties not on the c.i.f. (cost including insurance and freight) price of imports but on the American Sale Price. This was the price at which an American company sold the product in the market. It in effect gave much higher actual levels of protection to American industry than the nominal tariff implied.

10. Charles K. Rowley, Willem Thorbecke and Richard E. Wagner, *Trade Protection in the United States* (UK: Edward Elgar Publishing Co., 1995), pp. 296–298, 312; see also Chapter 12.

11. This was presented by the secretary-general, Arthur Dunkel, to the conference in 1992, as the best possible compromise between the positions of the various countries

and groups engaged in the negotiation process. It was eventually accepted with relatively minor changes and became the agreement.

12. Rowley et al., *Trade Protection in the United States.*
13. Jeffrey A. Garten, 'Is America Abandoning Multilateral Trade?', *Foreign Affairs*, Vol. 6, November–December 1996, pp. 50–62. Garten, who was undersecretary of commerce till October 1995, rebuts criticisms of the US' determination to continue to use threats of sanctions under Section 301 of the Trade Act, to force other countries to negotiate what are in effect surrenders of sovereignty, by saying, 'The issue is not whether the Clinton administration fully supports multilateralism, because it certainly does. The more relevant question is what kind of multilateralism' (p. 51). Garten then rolls out the current mythology on US attitudes to trade liberalisation. 'Earlier, America was so wealthy that it could subordinate economic and commercial policies to the goal of strengthening its political alliances ... Today the US supports multi-lateralism because it is in its commercial interest.'

Garten goes on to say that 'the most ubiquitous multinational companies are American and most of them are globalising their products in ways that require trade liberalisation across many countries simultaneously.' The US' trade-to-GDP ratio, he points out, has more than doubled from 11 per cent in 1970 to 23 per cent in 1995. In 1985 exports supported 7 million jobs. By 2000, they will, according to US Commerce Department projections, support 16 million jobs. These jobs pay 15 per cent more per worker than the average manufacturing wage, 30 per cent higher benefits, and are less affected by cyclical slumps. Garten's explanation about why the US is more interested in trade issues than it was before is convincing, but his reasons for wanting trade liberalisation simultaneously across many countries are not. Had this been a prerequisite, there would have been little or no American investment in China. If a country does not open up its markets to foreign investment or protect IPRs, American multinationals have the option of going (and do go) elsewhere. The fact is that they chose to go to places like China first and afterwards asked their government to secure for them concessions like national treatment. This is not very different from what the foreign factories that went to China to trade did in the nineteenth century. Garten's article also blurs the distinction between non-discrimination between all foreign companies—a demand, as he points out, that America is making on the issue of corruption in the award of contracts for infrastructure projects—and securing national treatment for American investors in foreign countries, a demand that developing countries rejected at the first conference of the WTO in Singapore in December 1996.
14. *New York Times*, 5 February 1997.
15. www.wto.org/english/thewto_e/minist_e/min99_e/english/book_e/stak_e_3.htm
16. Research and Information System for the Non-Aligned and Other Developing Countries (RIS), *World Trade and Development Report, 2003 – Cancun and Beyond* (New Delhi, Academic Foundation, 2003), Executive Summary and Chapter 2.
17. Ibid., p. 29, Table 2.6.
18. Ibid., p. 3.

9

GROWING OBSOLESCENCE OF THE NATION STATE

In the realm of international relations, the shift from a world order based upon consensus among nation states to one based on coercion by a single superpower was signalled by President George W. Bush Jr., when he unveiled a new national security doctrine in June 2002. For most Americans the world had changed irrevocably on 9/11. Bush fed that belief when he said in his State of the Union address in February 2002 that, when faced with a stateless enemy, the USA could no longer rely upon the traditional tool of deterrence to prevent attacks upon its people and territory. It would therefore have to anticipate where such attacks *could be incubated* and take *pre-emptive* action to prevent them from materialising. But a closer examination of the way in which American foreign and military policy has evolved after the Cold War shows that the change from interventions designed to shore up the nation state system to interventions designed to undermine it began much earlier.

The trigger for this was the end of the Cold War in 1989. In the 15 years that followed, what began as a series of tentative military interventions into the domestic political affairs of other countries developed into a frontal assault on the institution of the nation state and the Westphalian order. The first military interventions of the post-Cold War era aimed at restructuring a nation state by decisively intervening in its internal political developments occurred in Bosnia, Somalia and Haiti between 1992 and 1994, and were small interventions involving from 3,000 to 25,000 US ground forces.[1] All these were carried out under the mandate of the United Nations Security Council. From there it took the US, supported by the UK, less than a decade to graduate to an unprovoked 200,000-strong[2] invasion of Iraq, carried out in the teeth of opposition from world opinion, without the sanction of the UN Security Council, and with the avowed messianic agenda of ousting the regime of Saddam Hussein, installing a government friendly to the

US, the West and Israel, turning Iraq into a model democracy and making it a beacon for the rest of the Arab world. It is therefore difficult not to conclude that something had changed irreversibly by the time the Cold War ended, which was exerting a remorseless pressure on the hegemonic power to intervene more and more frequently, and more and more obtrusively, in the internal affairs of member states of the UN. This pressure was making the preservation of the Westphalian state system, enshrined in the United Nations charter, progressively more difficult.

The Erosion of the Westphalian Order

That irrevocable change was the rise of global capitalism. In the 1970s it began to undermine the economic foundations of the nation state in order to create a single global marketing and manufacturing system. In the 1990s, it began to reshape the political and international system to suit its purposes. In an essay written in the early 1990s, Jurgen Habermas had pointed out that since democracy had been created to serve the purposes of the nation state, its survival was likely to be severely endangered by the latter's demise.[3] Habermas' fears proved well-founded. The first victim of the attack upon democracy was the state system born out of the Treaty of Westphalia and the Congress of Vienna, and enshrined, in its latest incarnation, in the UN charter. The Treaty of Westphalia was signed in 1648 by France and its allies with Spain's King Ferdinand the second, in order to end the Thirty Years' War that had devastated Europe. To achieve this aim, it conferred legitimacy on the existing rulers, settled their territorial disputes with each other and established ground rules for the future conduct of the states with each other. This stabilised frontiers and gave birth to the concept of national sovereignty, the two essential attributes of the modern European state. The principles governing inter-state relations that emerged from Westphalia were formalised by the Congress of Vienna.

Although the borders that these treaties defined were altered time and again by the rise of one European power or another with hegemonic ambitions, their underlying principles were invariably reaffirmed, and the Westphalian order restored, each time peace returned. These principles were respect for national sovereignty and national boundaries and a refusal to intervene in the internal affairs of another sovereign state, any such intervention being seen as a hostile act. The instruments through which the new order was maintained were diplomacy and military strategy. The aim of the former was to maintain a balance of power within the community of nations, while the purpose of the latter was to deter aggression.

In practice, the Westphalian system did not prevent war: in the seventeenth and eighteenth centuries the major nations of Europe fought 60–70 wars per century. But it did instil in all nations a profound aversion to disturbing the status quo, and a concomitant disapproval of unprovoked aggression by one country on another.

The Westphalian order attained the zenith of its efficacy during the 'Hundred Years' Peace' from 1815 to 1914. After the defeat of Germany in the Second World War, the Westphalian order was given a ringing and, as it has turned out, final endorsement by the Charter of the United Nations. Article 1 opened membership to sovereign states alone. Article 2(4) bound them 'to refrain in their international relations from the threat or use of force against the territorial integrity or political independence of any state, or in any other manner inconsistent with the purposes of the United Nations.' Article 2(7) forbade not just member states but the United Nations as a whole from intervening in the internal affairs of other states: 'Nothing contained in the present Charter shall authorize the United Nations to intervene in matters which are essentially within the domestic jurisdiction of any state.'

Reinforced by the threat of Mutually Assured Destruction, which came into being with the development of nuclear weapons, the UN system prevented the outbreak of any major war for the half-century of the Cold War. Only when the rise of global capitalism began to undermine the nation state itself did this system came under serious strain.

As the hegemonic power of the 'short' twentieth century, intent upon extending its hegemony into the age of global capitalism, the US led the attack upon the nation state system and the Westphalian international order. Liberal critics of US expansionism discount the idea of a sudden change and believe that the end of the Cold War brought to the surface an imperial strand in US foreign policy that can be traced back to the Monroe doctrine.[4] Chalmers Johnson traces the rise of American imperialism to the nineteenth century preoccupation with political and economic security, and the rush to acquire colonies and define spheres of influence that it triggered off in its last decades. This led to a militarisation of American society that grew more and more pronounced through 'The Age of Catastrophe'.[5] This changed the structure of American society and politics. The amassing of military power ceased to be a means to an end and became an end in itself. Thus, when one justification for maintaining a large military establishment evaporated, its place was quickly taken by another. Victory in the Cold War and the subsequent 'Revolution in Military Affairs' only removed the last remaining hurdle to the consolidation of an American empire.

The weakness of this hypothesis lies in its assumption of continuity. There can be no doubt that the creation of a network of military bases, and the acquisition of the territory on which to locate them, has been a continuous process. The first steps were taken in the decade after the Spanish-American war of 1898.[6] In its aftermath, and during the decade that followed, America planted bases in places as far apart as Guam, Hawaii, the Philippines, the Panama Canal Zone, Puerto Rico and Cuba. But it was the Second World War, and the Cold War that followed, which enabled the US to extend its network of bases to Western Europe, Okinawa, Japan, Korea, Thailand, Australia and New Zealand. The process continued after the Cold War ended. After the first Gulf War, American bases sprang up in Saudi Arabia, Kuwait, Qatar, Bahrain, Oman, Egypt and Djibouti. The break-up of Yugoslavia became the pretext for the creation of bases in Bosnia and Kosovo. The breakup of the Soviet Union led to the establishment of bases in Uzbekistan, Kazakhstan, Turkmenistan and Kyrgizhstan.[7] After 9/11 the US forced Pakistan, virtually at gunpoint, to join it in the newly launched global war on terrorism. Pakistan gave the US the use of three air force bases in Jacobabad, Pasni and Quetta. After the Afghan war the US acquired three more airbases in Afghanistan: at Bagram, outside Kabul, at Mazar-i-Sharif, north of the Hindu Kush range, and at Kandahar in the south.

But this continuity masks, and therefore fails to recognise, a very important difference in the way in which the bases were created. Some of them were created through coercion—the invasion of, or threat to invade—territory belonging to another sovereign state. *The rest, and these are still the majority, were created with the willing acquiescence of the concerned nations.*

Nor was the choice of method for extending American power and influence a random one. Coercion was used to acquire territory or bases in two distinct periods. The first was in the 1890s and the first decade of the twentieth century. The second was after the Cold War, and particularly after 9/11. During the intervening period, with rare exceptions, the extension of military power and influence by the US was acquiesced in, even welcomed, by the host nations.

The reason for the difference is to be found in the cyclical expansion of capitalism. The first resort to force coincided with onset of systemic chaos that marked the end of the third cycle of expansion and, consequently, of British hegemony. The second resort to force is a response to the systemic chaos that has been released by the end of the fourth cycle of capitalism's expansion and the onset of the fifth cycle, i.e., globalisation. It reflects America's attempt to shape the new global order and establish its hegemony over it. The vast, peaceful extension of the network of American bases in between these two epochs reflected the consolidation of American hegemony during the fourth cycle of capitalism's expansion. This was made easier by its assumption of the role of protector and friend during the Second World War and the Cold War, and by the fact that the expansion of capitalism that triggered America's rise took place within the framework of the Westphalian state system.

By contrast, the extension of American power after 9/11, especially in Afghanistan, Pakistan and Iraq, reflects an utter disregard for national sovereignty and reflects America's drive to replace the Westphalian state system with an American empire built upon military supremacy and the constant threat to use force in order to have its way. This has aroused world-wide alarm and forced countries that had earlier ceded bases and accepted American military hegemony to re-evaluate the desirability of continuing to play host to American bases. It has already made Saudi Arabia ask the US to close its bases in that country, and prompted France, Germany and Belgium to revive the proposal to create a European Defence Force outside the umbrella of NATO. It has alarmed American liberals not only because they find the notion of an American Empire repugnant, but also because it is destroying the hegemony created, for the most part peacefully, during the 'American century'.

Rationalising Empire—The Return of 'Manifest Destiny'

The imperialistic strand has never been wholly absent from American thinking. It can be traced back to the belief in America's 'Manifest Destiny', which was first articulated by John L. O'Sullivan in 1845. O'Sullivan encapsulated it in the following words:

> ... the right ... to spread over and to possess the whole of the continent which Providence has given us *for the development of the great experiment of liberty and federative development of self-government entrusted to us*. It is a right such as that of the tree to the space of air and the earth suitable for the full expansion of its principle and destiny of growth.[8]

Throughout the nineteenth century, 'Manifest Destiny' provided the metaphysical justification for unrestrained American expansion across the continent of North America at the expense of the native Americans, and for ousting Mexico from Florida, Texas and California. Inevitably, there-fore, it was a racist doctrine rooted first in notions of white racial supremacy and then in those of Anglo-Saxon dominance. It was not about grabbing pieces of land to settle but about creating space for the great experiment of federative democracy. That was an exclusively European, white man's, and to a large extent Anglo-Saxon concern. If the native Americans stood in its way, they simply had to be swept aside. So when British hegemony began to weaken during and after the Great Depression of 1872–96, it did not need much by way of intellectual gymnastics for American conservatives to convince themselves that they had a duty to liberate Cuba and other parts of Latin America from the clutches of corrupt, tyrannical and inefficient Spain.

After the First World War, Woodrow Wilson revived it as a tool for formalising American hegemony when he framed the 14 points for the management of the post-war international order. This set about systematically dismantling two out of the three empires that had existed before the War—the Austro-Hungarian and the Ottoman—and paring down the German and Russian empires. The justification was the spread of liberty and democracy. Wilson saw this as America's mission:

> [The United States is] destined to set a responsible example to all the world of what free government is and can do for the maintenance of right standards, both national and international, [to be] the light of the world [and] to lead the world in the assertion of the rights of peoples and the rights of free nations.[9]

It is not altogether surprising, therefore, that 'Manifest Destiny' has been reborn as systemic chaos, deepened after the end of the Cold War, and now permeates the thinking of the far-right in America. This is apparent from the writing of a number of conservative thinkers such as Robert Kaplan, Charles Krauthammer, Robert Kagan and Richard Perle. In an important article written in 1990, Charles Krauthammer gave the following justification for a new world order based upon the concept of Empire:

> ... thinking about post-Cold War American foreign policy has been framed by several conventionally accepted assumptions about the shape of the post-Cold War environment. First, it has been assumed that the old bipolar world would beget a multipolar world with power dispersed to new centers in Japan, Germany (and/or 'Europe'), China and a diminished Soviet Union/Russia. Second, that the domestic American consensus for an internationalist foreign policy, a consensus radically weakened by the experience in Vietnam, would substantially be restored now that policies and debates inspired by 'an inordinate fear of communism' could be safely retired. Third, that in the new post-Soviet strategic environment the threat of war would be dramatically diminished.
>
> All three of these assumptions are mistaken. The immediate post-Cold War world is not multipolar. It is unipolar. The center of world power is the unchallenged superpower, the United States, attended by its Western allies. Second, the internationalist consensus is under renewed assault. The assault this time comes not only from the usual pockets of post-Vietnam liberal isolationism

(e.g., the churches) but from a resurgence of 1930s-style conservative isolationism. And third, the emergence of a new strategic environment, marked by the rise of small aggressive states armed with weapons of mass destruction and possessing the means to deliver them (what might be called Weapon States), makes the coming decades a time of heightened, not diminished, threat of war.[10]

Krauthammer's essay was significant not just for its advocacy of unilateral action by the US to safeguard its national interest, but also for the clearly implied directive to act pre-emptively to prevent any future threat to the US from emerging. This is apparent from his disdain for the efficacy of deterrence. Not once did he concede even the bare possibility that a 'nuclear weapon State' with a few nukes or warheads filled with chemical or biological weapons could be deterred from using them by a threat of massive retaliation using similar weapons. This was despite the success of deterrence in the Cold War. Nor did its successful use by the US to dissuade Saddam Hussein from attempting to use chemical weapons lead to any subsequent change of mind.

Krauthammer also did not entertain the possibility that a weak state may want to acquire weapons of mass destruction only in order to prevent a strong state, such as the US, from threatening it with such weapons. The omission is of great significance because it unwittingly gives away the true purpose of so-called pre-emption, which is to retain the option of coercing any country at any time to fall in line with the US.

How should the US use its overwhelming power? Krauthammer's answer was brutally simple:

> What does hold the international system together? What keeps it from degenerating into total anarchy? Not the phony security of treaties, not the best of goodwill among the nicer nations. In the unipolar world we inhabit, what stability we do enjoy today is owed to the overwhelming power and deterrent threat of the United States ... In the unipolar world, the closest thing to a centralized authority, to an enforcer of norms, is America—American power. And ironically, American power is precisely what liberal internationalism wants to constrain and tie down and subsume in pursuit of some brave new Lockean world.[11]

In a widely acclaimed book, *Warrior Politics*, Robert Kaplan vividly described the chaos into which the world was slipping, and argued that only the US had the military strength and the moral ascendancy to impose order upon an increasingly ungovernable world:

> Historically ... every approach to a world society has been the product of the ascendancy of a single power. There is no sign that this has changed ... Greater individual freedom and more democracy may be the outcomes of a universal

society, but its creation cannot be wholly democratic. After all, two hundred-odd states, in addition to hundreds of influential non-state forces, mean a plethora of narrow interests that cannot advance any wider interest without the organizing mechanism of a great hegemon ... Our prize for winning the cold war is not merely the opportunity to expand NATO, or hold democratic elections in places that had never had them, but something far broader: *We and nobody else will write the terms for international society* ... there is no credible force on the horizon with both our power and our values ... A century of disastrous utopian hopes has brought us back to imperialism, that most ordinary and dependable form of protection for ethnic minorities and others under violent assault.[12]

In 1991, the advocates of imperialism were at the far-right fringe of American politics. But as the iron discipline imposed on much of the world by the Cold War broke down, and as globalisation began to create new winners and losers among the developing countries and widen the gap between them, systemic chaos deepened by leaps and bounds. This began to exert a steadily growing pressure upon the international community to intervene on one ground or another. As the most dominant nation of the world, the US had no option but to play the leading role in the intervention. The more it did so, the more did the doctrines of imperialism and manifest destiny move towards the centre of the political stage.

There was no grand design behind this. In 1991, the Cold War was over. The US and its western allies had won. The socialist system was coming apart at the seams. The industrialised democracies had no enemies left. There was a rush among the former socialist and autarchic states to join the global market economy, and the bonds they were forging with the IMF, the World Bank and transnational corporations were leading to a rapid growth of economic interdependence. As the Hundred Years' Peace had already shown, such interdependence was the best insurance against war. At that moment the US could, in theory at least, have withdrawn from the intense involvement in maintaining international balances that had characterised the Cold War years, delegated more of this task to the UN and to its allies in NATO, and devoted itself to repairing the damage that the stresses of the Cold War had done to the social fabric at home. Even President George Bush Sr. felt the power of the vision and responded to it by announcing large cuts in military spending:

Two years ago, I began planning cuts in military spending that reflected the changes of the new era. But now, this year, with imperial communism gone, that process can be accelerated. Tonight I can tell you of dramatic changes in our strategic nuclear force. These are actions we are taking on our own because they are the right thing to do. After completing 20 planes for which we have begun procurement, we will shut down further production of the B-2 bombers. We will cancel the small ICBM program. We will cease production of new warheads for our sea-based ballistic missiles. We will stop all new production of the Peacekeeper missile. And we will not purchase any more advanced cruise missiles.

This weekend I will meet at Camp David with Boris Yeltsin of the Russian Federation. I've informed President Yeltsin that if the Commonwealth, the former Soviet Union, will eliminate all land-based multiple-warhead ballistic missiles, I will do the following: We will eliminate all Peacekeeper missiles. We will reduce the number of warheads on Minuteman missiles to one and reduce the number of warheads on our sea-based missiles by about one-third. And we will convert a substantial portion of our strategic bombers to primarily conventional use...

I want you to know that *for half a century, American Presidents have longed to make such decisions and say such words*. But even in the midst of celebration, we must keep caution as a friend. For the world is still a dangerous place. Only the dead have seen the end of conflict. And though yesterday's challenges are behind us, tomorrow's are being born.[13]

The very next year, in his first State of the Union address, President Clinton went a long step further. In his entire State of the Union address of more than 4,000 words, he did not devote a single word to foreign policy, and did not identify a single new or potential threat to America's vital interests or security against which the country needed to remain vigilant. Defence got two small paragraphs adding up to 102 words. In these he promised to responsibly *reduce* America's defence budget.[14] But this moment was all too brief. Clinton was neither able to get his $30 billion job plan nor his health care reforms through Congress. On both he met combined opposition from both Republicans and Democrats that doomed his efforts. Instead he was driven willy-nilly into relying on budget cuts to lower interest rates and stimulate the economy. He was forced by the growing disorder in Eastern Europe and the Balkans into devoting more and more time to foreign policy. As for the defence budget, it remained stubbornly stuck at $290–300 billion throughout the Clinton presidency, only to rise to $401 billion by fiscal 2005.

As disorder became more pronounced, calls to the US administration to do something to restore order and prevent human rights abuses became more and more frequent and more and more insistent. The original Clintonian dream soon lost its shine. A return to isolationism, as it was speedily dubbed, was soon deemed impossible. The issue very rapidly became not whether the US would retain the right to intervene militarily in other countries, but when and how. Anthony Lake, Clinton's National

Security Adviser from 1992 to 1996, made a persuasive case against a return to isolationism:

'Imagine,' he told an audience at the National Press Club in Washington DC, on 27 April 1995,

> if Ukraine, Belarus and Kazakhstan joined the club of undeclared nuclear weapons states because we couldn't do deals to denuclearise them.
>
> If Russian missiles were still pointed at our cities because we couldn't de-target them.
>
> If thousands of immigrants were still trying to sail to our borders because we had not helped to restore democracy in Haiti. If nearly 1 million American jobs had not been created over the last three years alone—because we had not promoted US exports.
>
> If we had to fight a war on the Korean peninsula—the implication of what some critics urged—because we did not confront the threat of a North Korea with nuclear weapons.
>
> If another quarter of a million people had died in Rwanda because we had not deployed our military and they had not done such a fine job in the refugee camps.
>
> Or if we had paid tens of billions of dollars more and suffered more casualties because we insisted on fighting Operation Desert Storm against Iraq by ourselves.
>
> ...Each of these efforts cost money and the hard work of building international coalitions. But you and I are safer, better off and enjoy more freedom because America made these investments. If the back door isolationists have their way much of what we have worked for over two generations could be undone.[15]

Lake deliberately exaggerated the dangers of what he called back door isolationism, sometimes to the point of parody. But the dilemma that he believed the US faced after the Cold War was real. Two generations of Americans had sacrificed and struggled against fascism and then communism, had given money generously to rebuild Europe, to contain the Soviet Union, and to spread democracy and strengthen the chances of world peace. Any abrupt withdrawal from leadership in world affairs would gratuitously threaten the gains that had been made on all these fronts. Safeguarding them required the US to remain continuously engaged in international politics.

Lake candidly admitted, however, that the end of the Cold War had made it far more difficult to determine the primary focus of US foreign and military policy, for the country had no powerful enemies left, and therefore faced no immediate threat to its interests or way of life. What the world was experiencing was growing disorder. His assumption that

America had the responsibility to confront and limit this disorder was an unambiguous assertion of America's hegemonic position and the responsibilities that it entailed:

> During the Cold War policy makers could justify every act with one word: containment. We got the big things right ... and we won the Cold War. But even the best policy can become the worst straitjacket if it is pursued too rigidly and reflexively ... now we have the opportunity to think anew about the best ways to promote America's interests and ideals. Our tools of first resort remain diplomacy and the power of our example. But sometimes we have to rely on the example of our power. *We face no more important question than when and how to use it.*[16]

In speeches delivered at the Kennedy School of Government at Harvard University in October 1994 and George Washington University on 6 March 1996, he outlined seven circumstances in which the US would be prepared to use force:

1. To defend against direct attacks on the United States, its citizens and its allies.
2. To counter aggression.
3. To defend key economic interests, which is where most Americans see their most immediate stake in international engagement.
4. To preserve, promote and defend democracy, which enhances our security and the spread of our values.
5. To prevent the spread of weapons of mass destruction, terrorism, international crime and drug trafficking.
6. To maintain our reliability, because when our partnerships are strong and confidence in our leadership is high, it is easier to get others to work with us and to share the burden of leadership.
7. For humanitarian purposes, to combat famine, natural disasters and gross abuses of human rights with, occasionally, military force.

But Lake was not a hawk in dove's feathers, for he advocated the unilateral use of force only as a last resort:

> Not one of these interests by itself—with the obvious exception of an attack upon our nation, people and allies—should automatically lead to the use of force. But the greater the number and the weight of the interests at play, the greater the likelihood that we will use force—*once all peaceful means have been tried and failed,* and once we have measured a mission's benefits against its costs, in both human and financial terms.[17]

In sum, force should be used only as a last resort, and should be applied, whenever possible, multilaterally, with the backing of other governments, and preferably with the sanction of the United Nations.[18]

In what has turned out to be a prophetic remark, Lake also warned against an excessive reliance upon force to solve problems. 'We should never delude ourselves: deploying our military often will not solve underlying problems, and we must carefully limit the missions we choose. Force can defeat an aggressor but it will not conjure up democracy or flip the switch of prosperity.'[19]

Lake's was perhaps the most elegant formulation of a multilateralist foreign policy to come out of the Clinton administration. But Lake was aware that the role of hegemon rested, and had to remain with, the United States. 'When we do act, we will do so with others when we can, but alone when we must.' He also rejected the proposition that the US should limit the assertion of a sphere of influence in its own hemisphere and in limited areas further afield, and leave to others the task of maintaining stability and order in their own spheres:

> We recognise that all nations have greater concerns for their immediate surroundings than they do for distant regions. *But as a great nation whose interests and ideals are global in scope*, we cannot—and will not—cede to others a right to intervene as they wish in the affairs of their neighbours without regard to international norms.[20]

Lake's views summed up the Democratic Party's position on foreign relations. This was different from the somewhat vague 'unilateralism' that the Republicans professed. But in the early 1990s the difference between their positions was not great. Speaking to the UN Security Council at an unprecedented guest appearance on 20 January 2000, Senator Jesse Helms, Chairman of the Senate Foreign Relations Committee, and considered to belong to the rightward fringe of the Republican Party, made the following observations:

> The American people want the UN to serve the purpose for which it was designed: they want it to help sovereign states coordinate collective action by 'coalitions of the willing' (where the political will for such action exists); they want it to provide a forum where diplomats can meet and keep open channels of communication in times of crisis; they want it to provide to the peoples of the world important services, such as peacekeeping, weapons inspections and humanitarian relief.
>
> As matters now stand, many Americans sense that the UN has greater ambitions than simply being an efficient deliverer of humanitarian aid, a more effective peacekeeper, a better weapons inspector, and a more effective tool of

great power diplomacy. They see the UN aspiring to establish itself as the central authority of a new international order of global laws and global governance. *This is an international order the American people will not countenance …*

The sovereignty of nations must be respected. But nations derive their sovereignty—their legitimacy—from the consent of the governed. Thus, it follows that nations can lose their legitimacy when they rule without the consent of the governed; they deservedly discard their sovereignty by brutally oppressing their people … As we watch the UN struggle with this question at the turn of the millennium, many Americans are left exceedingly puzzled. Intervening in cases of widespread oppression and massive human rights abuses is not a new concept for the United States. The American people have a long history of coming to the aid of those struggling for freedom. In the United States, during the 1980s, we called this policy the 'Reagan Doctrine' …

The dramatic expansion of freedom in the last decade of the 20th century is a direct result of these policies. *In none of these cases, however, did the United States ask for, or receive, the approval of the United Nations to 'legitimize' its actions.*[21]

Where Lake saw unilateral intervention as a last resort, Helms saw the US' role in more messianic terms. The difference was small, but it widened rapidly as the disorder in the international state system increased and military intervention increased both in frequency and intensity.

The Changing Pattern of US Intervention

A close examination of the pattern of US military intervention of the 1980s and 1990s reveals three distinct trends: first, they became progressively more frequent; they became more prolonged and more intense; and more and more of them were carried out under the fig leaf provided by the protection of human rights. At the height of the Cold War, between 1949 and 1980, interventions were few and far between. This was true not only of US armed interventions but also of UN peacekeeping missions. Apart from Korea and Vietnam, the significant US military interventions occurred in 1958 in Lebanon, in 1961 in Cuba (the Bay of Pigs), in 1965 in the Dominican Republic, in 1971 in the India-Pakistan conflict,[22] and in 1975 to reclaim the cargo ship *Mayaguez* after it had been seized by the Cambodian navy. The common purpose behind all but the last of these interventions (as indeed behind the interventions in Korea and Vietnam) was to contain the Soviet Union and check or reverse the spread of communism. They were therefore, almost by definition, designed to maintain the status quo and thus reinforce the international state system. During approximately the same period (1948 to 1978), there were only 13 peacekeeping missions undertaken by the UN.[23]

Interventions by the US became more frequent in the 1980s as the Soviet Union began to weaken and the West to regain the upper hand. But these interventions remained limited in size and objective. Between 1980 and 1989, there were in all seven interventions: in Iran in 1980; in Lebanon again in 1982; in Grenada in 1983; in Libya in 1986; in the Persian Gulf in 1987; and in the Philippines and Panama in 1989. Only one of these—the invasion of Grenada—was intended to secure 'regime change', i.e., reverse a pro-communist *coup d'etat* that had brought to power a government friendly to Cuba and the Soviet Union. The remainder were prompted by a wide variety of concerns, but the need to protect human rights was not among them.[24]

Human Rights as Pretext for Invasion

As a pretext for intervention, human rights suddenly sprang into prominence only after the end of the Cold War. This has made sceptics, especially in the developing countries, believe that it is no more than a convenient excuse for assaulting their sovereignty. But the necessity for a concerted effort to tackle such abuses had been growing ever since the last quarter of the nineteenth century, when the territorial state metamorphosed into the nation state under the spur of industrial capitalism.

At the time of the Congress of Vienna, the nation state had not yet come into existence, except in Britain. The signatories of the Treaty of Westphalia, 170 years earlier, were territorial states of the old kind, with porous borders and considerable ethnic diversity. This porosity was both encouraged and safeguarded by the Dutch, not for moral reasons but out of expediency. The Dutch, who built the coalition against Spain, were traders above all else. Their overriding concern was that political relations between states and sovereigns should be insulated as far as possible from the normal commerce of individuals. This required an insulation of the affairs of individuals from the affairs of state. The Dutch merchants and bankers themselves capitalised on this by trading with, and acting as financiers to, all parties to the various disputes and wars that erupted regularly in Europe.

In such a state system, there were neither hard frontiers nor restrictions of movement across them. One belonged to a state because one happened to be living within its boundaries, and if one wanted to move to another state because of religious discrimination or in search of better economic prospects, one simply packed one's belongings and left. The concepts of inclusion and exclusion from the nation, which became central to the nation states of the nineteenth and twentieth centuries, had yet to be born. There was consequently no attempt on the part of the state to suppress local identities and cultures, and, above all, to force trans-border ethnic minorities into adopting the language, culture and loyalties of the majority, on pain of persecution, expulsion and even death.

In the nineteenth century, under the spur of industrial capitalism, the territorial state metamorphosed into the nation state. That led to a hardening of boundaries, and an application of the principles of exclusion and cultural homogenisation to define who belonged and did not belong to the nation state. Both involved the use of force against minorities. Systematic violation of human rights of their subjects by the state originated therefore in the transformation of the modern territorial state into the modern nation state. The prime goal of both the League of Nations after the First World War and the United Nations after the Second was to hasten the re-establishment of the Westphalian order. But it was now an order composed of nation states, and of new nations that were trying to follow the nation state model of state building. Most of the human rights violations that compelled the UN to insert clauses into its charter for their protection arose from the desire to somehow reconcile the sovereignty of the Westphalian state with the need to limit the license it gave to oppression in the quest for creating nation states.

Over the 10-year period that preceded the terrorist bombings of 11 September 2001, the US intervened militarily in other countries no fewer than nine times, and both the duration and intensity of the intervention increased dramatically. Only one of these interventions, the dispatch of two aircraft carrier-based task forces to signal US support for Taiwan in 1996, was designed to shore up the autonomy of a de facto independent state, and thus to reinforce the Westphalian State system. Two others, an airstrike on Iraq in 1993, and another on terrorist training camps in Afghanistan and an antibiotics plant in Sudan (mistaken by American intelligence to be a chemical weapons plant), were punitive attacks.[25]

No fewer than four of the remaining six interventions were justified as a defence of human rights. These were in Somalia in 1992, Bosnia in 1993, Haiti in 1994, and Kosovo in 1999. But in none of these did the goal of the intervention remain confined to the protection of human rights. In Somalia, where internecine civil war had caused the state itself to disintegrate, the intervention began as a purely humanitarian operation under UN auspices, designed to police the delivery of international food aid to the drought-affected parts of the country. But this expanded by degrees into an ambitious project to restore calm to the capital city of Mogadishu, disarm and arrest the warlords who were attacking the UN peacekeepers, and establish a credible local police force in the major population centres—in short, to recreate a legitimate modern state in the country.[26] Such an ambitious task required a very large contingent of UN forces, and went far beyond the realm of peacekeeping, into the dangerous ground of what Richard Haass has called peace-making and nation building.[27]

The defence of human rights was also cited as a prime, if not the only, reason for the remaining three interventions. In Bosnia, there were two almost simultaneous interventions. The first, by the United Nations Protection Forces (UNPROFOR) was to monitor agreed cease-fires between Croatia and Serbia, and then between the Bosnian Serbs and the Bosnian Muslims. It was by and large successful in Croatia because the peace was brokered between two states that wanted hostilities to end. The second was a miserable failure because a peacekeeping process that had been designed to monitor the cessation of hostilities between consenting states was extended to warring groups in a civil war, who had arrived at no such agreement.

The second intervention was a far more ambitious one spearheaded by NATO, whose aims ranged from ensuring uninterrupted supplies of food, medicine and essential supplies to Bosnian cities blockaded by Bosnian Serb forces[28] to defending Bosnia's territorial integrity, redrawing the internal map of the new state to create a quasi-federal state containing Serb- and Muslim-dominated enclaves, forcing a peace settlement between the Bosnian Serbs and the Bosnian Muslims, and preventing Serbian attacks upon the civilian population in Muslim-dominated cities like Sarajevo, Goradze and Srebenica. In this intervention the defence of human rights rapidly became secondary to a more ambitious programme of nation building.

Although it played an important role in both of them, the US did not take the lead in either of the above interventions because its vital interests were not involved. That was not so in the case of the intervention in Haiti. Although this too was born out of a UN Security Council mandate to countries to use 'all necessary means' to oust the military dictatorship, facilitate the return of Haiti's elected president, and create a secure and stable environment,[29] the US took the lead in the intervention from the very beginning. Its purpose was not so much to alleviate human suffering in Haiti, as to change the conditions within the country that were causing it, and as a consequence creating a problem for the US. More specifically it was to get economic sanctions, which had been imposed upon the country by the Organisation of American States in October 1991 after a military coup against the elected president Jean-Bertrand Aristide, lifted as soon as possible in order to check an illegal influx of poverty-stricken Haitians into the US by boat. This required not merely the restoration of democratic government, but also a prolonged attempt to rebuild Haiti's shattered economy. The defence of human rights was therefore a small and almost incidental part of another ambitious attempt at nation building.

NATO's military intervention in Kosovo has been widely touted by the US and the European members of NATO as a shining example of the defence of individuals' human rights against a misuse of sovereignty by nation states. But a close look at the way in which the intervention developed shows that this pretext was used by US, using the shield provided by NATO, to achieve a wholly different purpose. This was to prevent the kind of nation state formation that Europe and the US itself had gone through a century earlier, and pave the way for empire. From the American point of view, Slobodan Milosevic was a throwback to an earlier era, for he was deliberately using Serbian nationalism to arrest the dissolution of the Yugoslav state after the secession of Slovenia and Croatia. This attempt could no longer be tolerated because it ran counter to the grain of globalisation, which required the removal of economic frontiers and the elimination of the sentiment of nationalism on which the nation state was founded.

Kosovo thus represented a watershed in the US' response to the disorder in the post-Cold War world. Till then it had been willing to live in a multipolar world, and to deal with local disorder through the UN or with its retrospective sanction. In sharp contrast, Kosovo was the first conflict in which the US shed its inhibitions about involvement and committed itself to providing as much military power as was needed. It was also the first action in which the US, backed by NATO, decided to dispense with the legal cover of a UN Security Council resolution. Most important of all, it was the first unabashed attack on the Westphalian international order, for its purpose was to prevent the Serbian state from crushing a violent secessionist movement by force. Kosovo reflects the extent to which the ultraconservative doctrines based on the concept of America's 'Manifest Destiny' had infiltrated the multilateralist camp by the end of the 1990s. Since this is a very different interpretation of the events that occurred there, it is dealt with at length in the next chapter.[30]

Notes

1. In July 1993 the US sent 300 ground troops to join 700 Scandinavian troops in Macedonia. This was intended to prevent the war spreading from Bosnia to Macedonia. It sent 20,000 troops to Haiti and 25,000 to Somalia, but only kept them there till they could be replaced by other UN troops (see Richard N. Haass, *Intervention. The Use of American Military Force in the Post Cold War World*, (Washington DC, Brookings Institution Press, 1994), pp. 41, 45 and 159).
2. This figure includes the reserves and support facilities that were held in Kuwait and created in Qatar.

3. Jurgen Habermas, *The Postnational Constellation: Selected Essays* (Cambridge, UK, Polity Press, 2001), pp. 56–112.
4. See, for instance, Michael Mann, *Incoherent Empire* (London, Verso, 2003); and Chalmers Johnson, *The Sorrows of Empire: Militarism, Secrecy and the End of the Republic* (London, Verso, 2004).
5. The term is Eric Hobsbawm's, taken from *The Age of Extremes* (Michael Joseph, 1994).
6. See, for example, Johnson, *The Sorrows of Empire*, Chapter 2.
7. Ibid., p. 171 Map.
8. Excerpted from John L. O' Sullivan, 'The Great Nation of Futurity', *The United States Democratic Review*, Volume 6, Issue 23, pp. 426–430 (emphasis added). The complete article can be found in *The Making of America* series at Cornell University (http://cdl.library.cornell.edu/cgi-bin/moa/moa-cgi?notisid=AGD1642-0006-46).
9. For a clear-eyed view of how this concept originated and how it was applied, see 'From Manifest Destiny to Global Co-Hegemony: Presidential Ideologies in the Early Twentieth century', available at: www.geocities.com/florigkr/ForeignPolicyHistory. html#Manifest%20Destiny:%20Its%20Religious,%20Racial,%20and.
10. Charles Krauthammer, 'America and the World', *Foreign Affairs*, 1990–91, Vol. 70, No. 1.
11. Charles Krauthammer, 'Democratic Realism: An American Foreign Policy for a Unipolar World', The Irving Kristol Lecture, Washington, February 2004. Available at the American Enterprise Institute website: www.aei.org/news/newsID.19912/news_detail.asp.
12. Robert D. Kaplan, *Warrior Politics. Why Leadership Demands a Pagan Ethos* (New York, Vintage Books, 2003), pp. 146–47 (emphasis added).
13. George H.W. Bush, 'State of the Union Address', 1992 (emphasis added).
14. William J. Clinton, 'State of the Union Address', 1993.
15. Anthony Lake, Speech at the National Press Club, Washington DC, 27 April 1995.
16. Anthony Lake, Speech at Georgetown University, Washington DC, 6 March 1996 (emphasis added).
17. Ibid. (emphasis added).
18. Anthony Lake, Speech at the Kennedy School of Government, October 1994.
19. Ibid. (emphasis added).
20. Ibid. (emphasis added).
21. www.newsmax.com/articles/?a=2000/1/28/211810 (emphases added).
22. The US sent an aircraft carrier to the Bay of Bengal in December 1971 as symbolic support to its Cold War ally Pakistan and to signal to India that it would not stand by and allow any further dismemberment of that country beyond the creation of Bangladesh out of what had previously been East Pakistan. No military intervention actually took place because the war was over by the time the aircraft carrier arrived in the Bay of Bengal.
23. Haass, *Intervention*, p. 57.
24. Three of them, in Lebanon, the Philippines and Panama, involved an intervention in the domestic politics of the country and had very little to do with the maintenance of an international status quo. One of the three, in Panama, was explicitly designed to secure a regime change for reasons that had nothing to do with the Cold War, but everything to do with the emergence of international drug cartels, that new stepchild of globalisation.

   The failed intervention in Iran was for the limited purpose of freeing the American hostages trapped in the American Embassy in Teheran. The intervention in Lebanon was really two interventions. The first was as part of a multinational force invited by the Lebanese government to oversee the withdrawal of the forces of the Palestine Liberation Organisation (PLO) from Beirut, and was largely successful. The second, also as part of the same multinational force, occurred a month after the initial withdrawal, in the wake of the assassination of the Lebanese president, and was intended to restore order and shore up the authority of the badly shaken Lebanese government. This degenerated by degrees into an involvement in the Lebanese civil war, more or less on the side of the Christians, and ended when a suicide bomber rammed a truck full of explosives into a US marine barracks and killed 241 marines.

The April 1986 bombing of Libya was a punitive strike designed to punish the government of Moammer Gaddafi for its sponsorship of terrorism. It was triggered by the terrorist bombing of a discotheque in Berlin that killed one American soldier and wounded 60 others. It may have achieved its purpose because in the year that followed the attack, according to the US State Department, the number of terrorist attacks backed by Libya dropped to 7 from 19 in the previous year.

The US interventions in the Gulf and the Philippines were also very limited in nature and were designed to protect the vital interests and security of trusted allies. In the Gulf the US navy gave protection to Kuwaiti shipping from Iranian attacks, but significantly only after first re-flagging the ships as American carriers. In the Philippines it gave symbolic but powerful support to the government of Corazon Aquino, who was facing a rebellion by some of her generals, by simply sending two fighter aircraft to fly over the rebel bases. The coup collapsed the next day.

The largest and most ambitious military intervention occurred in 1989 in Panama. Its purpose was to oust the defence chief-turned-dictator, Manuel Noriega, who was heavily involved in trans-shipping narcotics from South America to the United States, and had sought to shore up his popularity by demanding that the Panama Canal be handed back to his country. 25,000 US troops and large number of aircraft took part in the action, which ended with the removal and imprisonment of Noriega and the restoration of an elected government to power.

25. The former was a reprisal for an Iraqi intelligence-backed conspiracy to assassinate former President George H.W. Bush while he was on a visit to Kuwait, and the latter was in response to the bombings of the US embassies in Nairobi and Dar -es Salaam in 1998.

26. Haass, *Intervention*, pp. 44–45.

27. Ibid., pp. 59–61. Peace-making, sometimes referred to in the mid-1990s as acting under chapter six-and-a-half of the UN Charter, requires UN peacekeepers to use force in order to create a situation in which traditional peacekeeping can take over. It becomes necessary when one of the parties to a dispute refuses to either accept the status quo or the presence of outsiders in the country, or both. Nation building is an extremely intrusive form of intervention that seeks to bring about a change in the political leadership of a country, and/or create political institutions that are very different from those that exist.

28. UN Security Council Resolution 770 authorised the member states to use 'all necessary measures' to ensure the delivery of humanitarian supplies.

29. UN Security Council Resolution 940 of 31 July 1994.

30. The three remaining interventions of the decade all occurred in Iraq and took place with scant regard for legality. In these the US acted with the backing of neither the UN nor NATO, and with only the UK as its ally. They are dealt with in Chapter 11.

10

REHEARSAL FOR EMPIRE

In the years that have passed since NATO's air war on Serbia, all but a handful of Western Europeans and Americans have come to view it as an eminently successful military intervention in defence of human rights, in this case the rights of the more than 1.5 million Kosovar Albanians who were fighting to secede from Serbia and were suffering appalling human rights abuses as a consequence.

The accepted version of the events that led to NATO's military intervention in Kosovo goes as follows: Kosovo's Albanians had always been a down-trodden lot. But human rights abuses, organised and carried out cold-bloodedly by the Serbian state, began in 1998, when, in a series of punitive forays into Kosovo, Serbian military and paramilitary forces killed about 2,000 Kosovar Albanians, and rendered many thousands more homeless. In the winter of 1998–99 Belgrade increased the military pressure on Kosovo's Albanians. The numbers who were forced to flee their homes and become internal or international refugees mounted rapidly. When the NATO powers received intelligence reports towards the end of 1998 that Belgrade was planning to push a large part of the Albanian population out of Kosovo, and when the last-ditch Rambouillet peace talks failed, they were left with no option but to take military action.

Speaking on the evening of 24 March, when the bombing began, President Clinton had this to say:

> President Milosevic, who over the past decade started the terrible wars against Croatia and Bosnia, has again chosen aggression over peace. He has violated the commitments that he, himself, made last fall to stop the brutal repression in Kosovo. He has rejected the balanced and fair peace accords that our allies and partners, including Russia, proposed last month, a peace agreement that Kosovo's ethnic Albanians courageously accepted. Instead, his forces have

intensified their attacks, burning down Kosovar Albanian villages and murdering civilians.

As I speak, more Serb forces are moving into Kosovo, and more people are fleeing their homes—60,000 in just the last five weeks, a quarter of a million altogether. Many have headed toward neighboring countries. Kosovo's crisis now is full-blown. And if we do not act, clearly it will get even worse. Only firmness now can prevent greater catastrophe later.

Speaking the same day, the British Prime Minister, Tony Blair, explained the decision as follows: 400,000 people in Kosovo had been displaced, 250,000 remained homeless. Milosevic had 'thrown aside' the ethnically balanced arrangements which held Yugoslavia together for 45 years, stripped Kosovo of its autonomy and had helped trigger the war in Bosnia in which some 250,000 Bosnians were killed. 'He gave to the world the hideous term "ethnic cleansing" as over 2 million people were driven from their homes, mainly by the Serbs. Nobody can say he wasn't warned.'

As little as a decade earlier, this cocktail of motives, based on dubious statistics, a blatantly one-sided recital of recent events, and the demonisation of a single individual, would have been treated as a fig leaf for naked aggression. But by 1999 the erosion of the Westphalian order had progressed so far that the air war was given a ringing endorsement by no less important a person than the Secretary-General of the United Nations, Kofi Annan. Speaking on 7 April at the opening session of the UN Commission for Human Rights, Annan unveiled a doctrine with profound implications for international relations in the new millennium. The air strikes against Yugoslavia, he said, showed that the world would no longer permit nations intent on committing genocide to 'hide' behind the UN Charter. 'The protection of human rights must take precedence over concerns of state sovereignty.'

'As long as I am secretary-general,' Annan concluded, the United Nations 'will always place human beings at the center of everything we do.' With these words, Annan put very stringent limits on the applicability of Article 2 of the UN Charter.

According to the official version of history NATO did not act a moment too soon, for within days of the commencement of air strikes, hundreds of thousands of Kosovar Albanians were driven by the Serbian army across the borders of Macedonia, Montenegro and Albania. The aerial bombing, however, had the desired effect. After two and a half months of bombing, Serbia's President, Slobodan Milosevic, caved in. The refugees were able to come back. Kosovo regained its autonomy from Serbia and came under UN administration, and gradually international aid began to turn it into a viable political entity.

This account of the intervention substantially distorts what actually happened in Kosovo. There is unimpeachable evidence that NATO's intervention did not prevent but accelerated, and may even have been the cause of, Serbian efforts at ethnic cleansing. In her first formal address to the UN Security Council on 8 May, the UN High Commissioner for Refugees stated that on 23 March, when her organisation had to leave Kosovo, it was looking after 89,500 refugees outside Kosovo. In the first week of May the number had risen to about 700,000. She also refused to call what the Serbs had done genocide—in sharp contrast to Democratic senators in the US senate, and countless NATO spokespersons.[1]

Nor was the human rights situation in Kosovo significantly improved by the ejection of the Serbian administration. In an article written in response to Robert Fisk, the renowned columnist of the London-based daily newspaper *The Independent*, George Robertson, a former British Defence Minister and then secretary-general of NATO, conceded that in June, immediately after 'liberation', Kosovo experienced 190 murders a month (in a population of less than two million). By December this had come down to 25 a month. By implication he also confirmed that all but a few of the initial victims were Serbs, for he said with some pride that fewer than half of the 25 killed in November were Serbs![2]

The 'establishment' view also glossed over the fact that, contrary to the claims made for the deadly efficacy of its precision bombing, NATO's air war did not dent Serbia's capacity to undertake military operations in Kosovo against the Kosovo Liberation Army. Assessments by NATO's analysts after the war revealed that the air strikes had not damaged or destroyed more than 20 per cent of Yugoslav guns and armour in Kosovo.[3] What brought Milosevic to his knees and made him accept the peace that was offered in June was the terrible damage that the bombardment, first of Kosovo and then Serbia, did to the Yugoslav economy. The entire burden of this fell upon civilians. In 50 days of bombing, NATO flew almost 6,000 bombing missions and dropped 20,000 bombs on Serbian targets. By its own estimates it knocked out half of Serbia and Montenegro's airports, all its oil refining capacity, 31 bridges (including all but two on the Danube), 70 per cent of its power supply, two railway systems that linked the rest of · Serbia to Kosovo, and most of its telecommunications system.[4] According to the Yugoslav prime minister, by early May these raids had taken 1,200 civilian lives and seriously injured another 5,000 Serbs. The bombardment also violated Convention IV of the 1949 Geneva Convention and Article 2 of the 1977 addendum to that convention. But there was no one to hold the perpetrators responsible.[5] NATO's relentless harping on Milosevic's human rights abuses was also intended to obtain legitimacy for a decision that was virtually without precedent. This was to declare war on a sovereign country without any provocation whatever. Even Hitler had sought to justify the invasion of Poland in 1939 by accusing the Poles of having attacked Germany first.[6]

In fact, NATO's intervention in Kosovo was of a qualitatively different order from the nine other US-led interventions in the decade after the first Gulf War. To begin with, it was by far the largest. By mid-April 1999, three weeks after the bombing of Kosovo and Serbia began, US General Wesley Clarke, the chief of the NATO forces, had committed 1,000 aircraft to a non-stop bombing of Kosovo and Serbia, and the Clinton administration had raised its estimate of what the war was likely to cost the American taxpayers from between $3 and $4 billion to $5.9 billion[7] and a week later to $8 billion.

Second, it was the first military engagement by the US that was open-ended. At a White House Press briefing about the fiftieth anniversary of the formation of NATO, held on 19 April 1999, Wolf Blitzer, CNN's correspondent for the White House, asked the US Secretary of Defence just where he thought the Kosovo intervention was going. When NATO took the decision to bomb targets in Serbia, Blitzer said, correspondents had been told in several informal briefings that the bombing would last for at most three or four weeks, and would be over well before NATO's fiftieth anniversary (which was celebrated on 20 April). Stone-faced, William Cohen, the Secretary for Defence, denied that there had been any such time limit in the policymakers' minds. 'We were going to bomb Serbia till as long as it took to make them accept the [Rambouillet] peace plan.'

Third, it was the first intervention in which bringing about a regime change within a country was a declared objective. During the same White House briefing, Samuel (Sandy) Berger, the National Security Adviser to President Clinton, spelt out three goals for NATO: to force Serb troops to withdraw from Kosovo, to bring in an international peacekeeping force, and to make it possible for the refugees to return. Secretary of State Madeleine Albright endorsed these goals and added a significant rider: 'We will not negotiate with him [Milosevic]. We believe that the Serb people will be better served by a democratically elected government.' In short, there was a fourth objective: to get rid of Milosevic.

Fourth and last, it was the first time since offensive war was outlawed by the UN Charter that a coalition of nations had committed an act of war against another country without the sanction of the United Nations. It was also the first time that any group of nations had arrogated to itself the right to redraw the boundaries of another sovereign state by force. There was some disagreement within the Clinton administration and within NATO on this. In an article written for the *Sunday Times*, President Bill Clinton wrote, 'I continue to believe that the best answer for Kosovo is autonomy, not independence. Kosovo lacks the resources and infrastructure to thrive on its own.' But a day later, his junior comrade-in-arms, Tony Blair, said in England that Kosovo must become free. He did not see, he said, how after all that had happened, the refugees could go back to a country that was a part of Yugoslavia.

The Fig Leaf of Human Rights

To create the moral justification for the attack on Serbia, the history of Milosevic's dealings with the Kosovar Albanians has been distorted almost beyond recognition. A close examination of what the Serbian state tried to do in Kosovo shows that its goal was to put down a violent secessionist movement and not to push Albanians out of Kosovo. The secessionist movement it was seeking to put down was not the non-violent, widely supported movement led by Ibrahim Rugova but the violent movement launched by the Kosovo Liberation Army.

In terms of history and religion, Kosovo lay at the very heart of Serbia. The identification was not so much geographical as emotional, for an important part of the Serb identity was bound up with Kosovo. While Serbs and Albanians both claimed to be the original inhabitants of Kosovo, by the twelfth century AD Kosovo was very much at the core of Serbia. Stefan Nemanja, the great Serb political and spiritual leader, who was a master builder of Orthodox churches and monasteries, built an especially beautiful church at Decani, which still stands with intact icons and paintings kept in almost pristine condition by a community of monks. The most powerful of the Serbian kings, Stefan Dusan, who reigned from 1331 to 1355, consolidated the Orthodox religion in Kosovo, and built ever-grander churches and monasteries in Pec, Prizren, Mitrovica and Pristina.[8] It was in the plains of Kosovo that the Serbs lost the crucial battle against the Ottoman Turks in 1389 AD that ushered in 500 years of Turkish rule. Most of the Albanian influx took place during the Turkish period, when both Serbia and Albania were part of the Ottoman empire and the present frontiers of Serbia did not exist. Conversions to Islam, by Serbs in Bosnia and Albanians in Albania and Kosovo, were a by-product of the natural desire for protection and preferment under Turkish rule.

During the Tito period, a much higher birth rate among the Kosovar Albanians did not create any great anxiety among the Yugoslav elite because the country was already a mish-mash of ethnicities. The ethnic question resurfaced only when the Yugoslav Federation began to fall apart. This changed the way Serbs began to view what was happening in Kosovo.

The Yugoslav Republic was an ethnic federation of very recent origin. It began to show signs of strain not long after the death of Tito. These strains were exacerbated by the economic downturn that occurred in the 1980s, partly because of the two oil price shocks of 1973 and 1979, but mainly because of the inability of a command economy to cope with competition in a technology-driven world.

Unlike India, another federation built up out of ethnic nations, the various nationalities in Yugoslavia did not have the depth of shared history, culture and experience that make it possible for the richer parts of India to share the fruits of their labour with the poorer parts. Nor did Yugoslavia have a democratic system that would enable disagreements to be resolved amicably on the basis of compromise. Slovenes and Croats began to complain that they were working themselves to the bone, but Belgrade was pouring their savings down a bottomless pit. Belgrade (and the Serbs) complained that resources were being wasted because the fractiousness of the republics made it impossible to plan investment rationally. As a result, as far back as 1983, when Belgrade hosted the sixth UN Conference on Trade and Development (UNCTAD), political observers in Belgrade were expressing the fear that the republic would not hold together.[9]

It was the prospect of imminent disintegration that gave birth to a virulent form of Serb nationalism. In 1986, a group of intellectuals belonging to the Serbian National Academy of Sciences published a document that became the manifesto of Serbian nationalism. It was seized upon by Milosevic, an un-intelligent practitioner of politics, who used Serbian nationalism to seize power and then did not have the finesse to bring it back under control.

One result of the growing insecurity of the Yugoslav Federation was a change in the way Serbs began to view what was happening in Kosovo. In the 15 years that Kosovo had enjoyed autonomy, there had been a sharp decline in the number of Serbs living in Kosovo. On a BBC programme aired during the war in Kosovo, a KLA spokesman ascribed this to a systematic neglect by Belgrade of the economic development of Kosovo Serbs, as a result, migrated to Serbia proper, where there were jobs to be had. Neglect, however, was only one side of the coin. The other was a systematic, if low-grade, ethnic cleansing of Serbs by Albanians in the Kosovo countryside. According to some estimates, Kosovo was 'cleansed', one way or another, of 200,000 to 300,000 Serbs in the late 1970s and early 1980s.

In the 80s, a non-violent movement for independence developed under the leadership of Ibrahim Rugova. Belgrade was able to ignore this movement so long as the Yugoslav Federation existed. But when in 1989 Rugova declared himself openly for independence, Milosevic responded by stripping Kosovo of its political autonomy and leaving it only a nebulous 'territorial autonomy'. Rugova's movement responded by 'withdrawing peacefully' from the Yugoslav Federation and setting up a de facto state within the Yugoslav state. The Kosovar Albanians withdrew their children from government schools, stopped paying taxes, set up their own administration and, to finance it, started col-lecting taxes from 600,000 ethnic Albanians living and working in Europe and America. Some of this money went into the purchase of arms. On 24 May 1992, the 'Kosovo Albanian Republic' elected Rugova its president.

Despite that, Kosovo remained by and large free from violence during the Bosnian civil war. This was in part because Belgrade was preoccupied with the war in Bosnia, but the main reason was the adoption of a non-violent strategy of 'civil disobedience' by Rugova, and the construction of a 'parallel civil society'.[10] The Kosovar Albanians under Rugova were sure that Kosovo would not be left out of any final peace settlement. But the Dayton accord, brokered by the US, did not mention Kosovo. In defer-ence to Milosevic, who would never have agreed to a change in the status of Kosovo in addition to with-drawing support from the Bosnian Serbs, the US excluded Kosovar Albanian delegates from the Dayton talks and avoided a discussion of the Kosovo prob-lem.[11] Rugova and his non-violent strategy were discredited and he began to lose ground to the KLA. After 1995 the Kosovo Liberation Army's strength began to grow by leaps and bounds and the inflow of arms swelled rapidly. More and more of the money collected abroad for the parallel Albanian administration in Kosovo was diverted to the KLA and went into the purchase of arms. Albania be-came the training ground for the KLA and also the main source of arms, but many of the weapons that the KLA showed foreign journalists in 1998, such as sophisticated sniper rifles, were obtained in the West. These weapons were used to create safe areas for the KLA within Kosovo.

Belgrade could not ignore what was happening in Kosovo forever. In Serbia's eyes, an independent Kosovo was preposterous. Immigration had admittedly changed its population composition drastically, but that did not justify, by any stretch of imagination, a movement for secession. Immi-gration, much of it illegal, has been altering the population composition in various countries ever since the birth of the nation state. An inflow of Mexicans and other Hispanics has drastically altered the population com-position of the southern states of the US. Chinese and Koreans have been streaming into the mineral-rich Russian Far East since the late 1980s and could soon form the majority there. A steady inflow of Bengali Muslims from Bangladesh into the adjoining Indian states of West Bengal and Assam had altered the religious balance in both states, and in 1977 this sparked a full-blown insurgency in Assam. But neither in the US nor in Russia and India would any government brook a demand for secession. From the

Serb nationalists' point of view, the Kosovar Albanian demand for independence was even graver. In American or Russian terms, it was as if the commonwealth of Virginia or the St. Petersburg oblast were trying to secede.

By the end of 1997 Serbian government officials, both Serb and Albanian, were able to move out of the towns only in convoys. In February 1998, Belgrade finally sent its security forces into the central Drenica region where the KLA had established a number of safe areas. Around 70 persons were killed in the fighting that ensued. A large number of them (the KLA claimed over half) were women and children. Thousands of villagers were displaced from their homes. The media reports on the fighting verged on hysteria. Allusions to Bosnia, and behind it to the holocaust, were freely aired. Even the objective and restrained *New York Times* reported, 'The Serbs, rather than hunt down armed groups, blasted villages into rubble with 20-millimeter cannon, grenade launchers and .50-caliber machine guns. Those trapped in the houses died and many of those who fled were gunned down, according to witnesses. Many bodies, laid out at mass funerals, bore signs of mutilation and summary execution.'[12]

This flood of condemnation drowned out a plaintive statement from Belgrade that several civilians had died because the KLA had prevented them from leaving their houses and executed those who had tried to run away. The Serbian explanation does not sound quite so lame to those who have had experience of other insurgencies. It should therefore have been investigated. Instead both the government and the media of the NATO countries ignored or dismissed it.[13]

The February offensive failed to curb the KLA. Instead its ranks swelled rapidly. Where guerrillas would roam the countryside in groups of four or five, there were now four times the number. The indigenous Albanians had been reinforced by what the *New York Times* called 'Foreign Mercenaries whose heavily accented Albanian as well as their appearance and martial demeanor suggests experience in other war zones'.[14]

By June the KLA controlled fully 40 per cent of Kosovo and was making daily hit-and-run attacks on the police and paramilitary forces.[15] The latter were on the defensive, keeping their heads down to stay alive. In the *New York Times*, Chris Hedges reported, 'The police remain in heavily fortified emplacements in the province, despite calls from abroad that they be withdrawn. In many villages, like Jablanica, about 30 miles northwest of Djakovica, women and children have been sent away to live with relatives *in anticipation of the looming combat* ... The guerrillas move within a few hundred yards of sandbagged police checkpoints and open fire frequently on passing police convoys.'[16]

By June it was also clear that Serbia had been unable to seal off the mountainous and desolate border with Albania. The KLA had established a number of safe areas all along the Albanian border, and weapons and guerrillas were flowing back and forth through these freely.[17] The KLA had grown from strength to strength, equipped with a seemingly inexhaustible supply of light armaments. In early May, it cut the road between the capital, Pristina, and the Serb-dominated town of Kijevo. Milosevic had to either let Kosovo go or send his troops in once more.

The purpose of the second offensive, which began in June, was therefore to seal the border with Albania. To do this the Serb forces cleared a *cordon sanitaire*, several kilometres deep along the border with Albania, in order to break the supply chain and give themselves the leeway to fight. This led to the eviction of between 60,000 and 80,000 persons from their homes, but it is difficult to see what else a state fighting against a guerrilla force could have done. Clearing the border belt was a more humane alternative than leaving the civilians there and then hunting down the KLA in their midst. But not a single international news report from Kosovo discussed either the purpose of the assault or the dismal choice that Milosevic faced.

The June offensive provoked another outburst of condemnation from the US and some other members of NATO. This was despite the fact that till the end of June not more than 250 people had been killed in the fighting. NATO reacted not by deploring the acquisition of arms by the KLA, not by forcing the KLA and Belgrade to sit down and negotiate,[18] *but by threatening military action against Serbia*. The message this conveyed to the Kosovar Albanians was thus unambiguous: Serbia's unity was dispensable. At the end of the month, its guerrillas seized hold of the coal-mining town of Belacevac, which provides much of the coal to two power plants that supply parts of Serbia and Macedonia. In the process they ejected more than 8,000 Serbs from Belacevac, who had to take to the woods.[19] Belgrade was left with no option but to escalate the level of military activity yet again.

It would be tedious to continue this month-by-month account of the escalation that followed. Suffice it to say that in October Belgrade bowed one last time to American pressure and agreed to a cease-fire, withdrawal of military and paramilitary units, the posting of international observers in Kosovo, and the resumption of talks with Rugova. The agreement was brokered by Richard Holbrooke, the US' chief negotiator at Dayton. But Holbrooke's October agreement once again contained no curbs on the KLA.[20] According to a later statement by President Clinton, Milosevic had agreed to hold democratic elections in Kosovo, to restore a great deal of autonomy and above all allow the Kosovars to have their own police. All this implied the preservation of the unity of Serbia. But neither Clinton nor Rugova were calling the shots any longer.

Milosevic was universally condemned for breaking this agreement, but the criticism was both harsh and uninformed. The agreement came unstuck because it did not take him long to realise that the cease-fire was being used by the KLA to build up its military strength. The inflow of arms continued, and the KLA quickly occupied the areas that the Serb troops were vacating in keeping with the terms of the agreement. He too therefore stopped moving his forces out.[21] In the next few months, the attacks by the KLA continued to grow in intensity. This set the stage for Belgrade's final assault in December.

The December offensive was preceded by 11 days of incessant attacks by the KLA, which started with the murder of six Serbian youths in a coffee shop and a government ambush in which 36 KLA members were killed while trying to smuggle in weapons from Albania. The KLA retaliated by killing a Serbian police officer and wounding three others. A few days later a Serbian government official was murdered. Finally a state security official was killed.[22]

The Serbs soon learned how much stronger the KLA had become. A column of 40 tanks and armoured cars that attacked a village, which the KLA had taken over and turned into one of its strongholds, was repulsed by guerrillas using anti-tank weapons with deadly effect. Belgrade realised that if it wanted to hold on to Kosovo, it was now or never. Correspondents in Belgrade reported that a huge counter-offensive was about to be launched.

The turning point came with two developments around January 16. German intelligence claimed that it had obtained information that Serbia was planning an operation to push hundreds of thousands of Albanians out of Kosovo, and 45 bodies of farmers and their children executed at close range were found in and around a village called Racak. The killing had been done by hooded men dressed in black, and wearing gloves. William S. Walker, an American diplomat who headed the Observers Group, accused Serb soldiers of the atrocity, but the Serbian government 'fiercely protested its innocence' and declared Walker *persona non grata*. Both these pieces of information were at least of debatable quality. Intelligence reports are often wrong, or capable of being interpreted in more than one way. As for the executions, given how close the KLA was to pulling NATO into the civil war on its side, could Walker have been absolutely certain that it was not the work of KLA agent provocateurs?

The US Secretary of State, who had been itching to bomb Serbia for eight months, entertained no such doubts. On 19 January, in the absence of a distraught Clinton, who was facing impeachment, Madeleine Albright unveiled plans to force a settlement upon the two sides. There was however a catch. If the Serbs did not find the plans to their liking, they would be bombed till they did.

How the US Stoked the Tragedy

From the very beginning of the Yugoslav tragedy, NATO leaders said one thing about Kosovo and did something completely different. They professed to understand the difference between Bosnia and Kosovo, and reiterated, times without number, that peace could only be restored by restoring Kosovo's autonomy within Serbia. 'No one in the West challenges Serbia's sovereignty over Kosovo or the right of the authorities to put down an armed insurrection there,' wrote Chris Hedges from Belgrade in the *New York Times* on 10 March 1998. 'At issue is the brutality with which Milosevic has moved to repress the Albanians, and the American conviction that unless he is checked, the kind of ethnic purging that changed the face of Bosnia will begin again.'[23]

Thirteen months later, President Clinton continued to reject the creation of an independent Kosovo even while his air force was bombing Belgrade and Serbian troops in Kosovo. In an article in the *Sunday Times* (of London) on 18 April, he wrote, 'I continue to believe that the best answer for Kosovo is autonomy, not independence. Kosovo lacks the resources and infrastructure to thrive on its own. Instead, its independence could actually spur more instability.'

But NATO's actions did not match its words. As far back as 29 December 1992, President George H.W. Bush warned Milosevic against taking any military action against the KLA in Kosovo, and told him that NATO would be forced to intervene if he did so. This was three years after Rugova had declared his intention of seceding from Yugoslavia, two years after he had formed a parallel government in Kosovo and ceased paying taxes to the Central government, and seven months after he had been elected 'President' of the 'Kosovar Albanian Republic'. Clinton repeated the warning a few months later in 1993.

From 1992 till the assault on 24 March 1999, the US and NATO continued to subscribe to the fiction that the Albanians would accept autonomy if only Milosevic were to make them a sincere offer. They did this despite abundant proof that Rugova wanted independence, not autonomy, and was not prepared to settle for less. They ignored the radicalisation of the secessionist movement that had taken place after 1995. And they chose not to notice that even if Rugova was prepared to accept autonomy, after 1995 he was in less and less of a position to make the agreement stick because of the rise of the KLA. Belgrade, which had to deal with Kosovo daily, of course had no such illusions. Milosevic knew that to get a solution based on autonomy after the break-up of Yugoslavia, the West would have to exert a great deal of pressure on both Rugova and the KLA. But not once in the seven years that it took the tragedy to unfold did the US or its NATO allies even think of mounting such pressure. Instead all the pressure, all the castigation and all the threats were reserved for the Serbs, and for Milosevic in particular.

Incredible as it may seem, no one in Washington seemed to realise that when it chastised one party in a conflict, it automatically emboldened the other. Washington and the European capitals should not therefore have been surprised when the Albanians redoubled their attempts to build a military force that could take on the Serbian police. Armed conflict was therefore inevitable and NATO's behaviour made it all the more so. It finally broke out in earnest in 1996.

All through 1997, the KLA followed the textbook methods of political mobilisation that all secessionist movements have followed since the beginning of history. Writing in the *New York Times*, its correspondent, Chris Hedges reported, 'It [the KLA] has carried out numerous attacks over the last year against Serbian police, senior Serbian officials *and ethnic Albanians accused of collaborating with the Serbian government.*'[24] These are precisely the tactics that insurgents used in Punjab and Kashmir in India, in Chechnya in Russia, and in Sri Lanka. Attacks on officials were intended to paralyse the police, administration and judicial system, and force the government to fall back on its weapon of last resort: the armed forces. That would alienate many people who were previously sitting on the fence. Slowly the middle ground of peace-loving, apolitical people would vanish. The ranks of the guerrillas would swell, and that in turn would force the government to use still more force.

The killing of collaborators, or those whom the KLA judged to be collaborators—a barbaric violation of human rights—was another classic guerrilla tactic. Its main purpose was to terrorise local people into not informing the government of the movements and whereabouts of the KLA terrorists. This would enable them to create safe areas among the ethnic Albanian population, from where they could attack Serbian and other government officials and convoys.

If any of this registered on policymakers in Washington, they chose to overlook it. Instead the US responded to the February offensive by sending a State Department official, Robert Gelbard, to talk to Milosevic in Belgrade. Gelbard, who was known for his short temper, castigated Milosevic in 'unusually blunt language'. 'You have done more than anyone to increase the membership of the KLA,' he told Milosevic. 'You are acting as if you were their secret membership chairman.'[25] Gelbard was right.

The February offensive did prove a turning point in KLA recruitment. But his hectoring tone pre-empted any possibility of getting the notoriously thin-skinned Milosevic to agree to a plan for defusing the confrontation in Kosovo.

Gelbard returned from Belgrade convinced that the only way to deal with Milosevic was to bomb him into submission.[26] His first convert was his boss, Secretary of State Madeleine Albright. By May 1998, Albright was vigorously advocating the bombing of Serbia, claiming that this was the only language Milosevic would understand. At this point there had been just one Serbian military incursion into Kosovo, and a total of 70 persons killed by KLA estimates. Yet Albright deemed that sufficient cause to stop negotiations and bomb Belgrade into submission. Fortunately, she was opposed by the head of the National Security Council, Samuel (Sandy) Berger.

However, Albright did not have to wait long to renew her advocacy. Belgrade's June offensive, and the scenes of burned-out and burning homes and homeless Kosovars that the international media presented on television, strengthened her hands. It did this despite the fact that in comparison with civil wars in other countries, the actual violence that took place was small beer. According to western newspaper reports, by the end of June the death toll had risen to around 250.

In March the US had debated whether to follow through on Clinton and Bush's promise of unilateral action against the Serbs, but had decided against unilateral action and opted instead to involve NATO. When the second Serb offensive began, NATO's defence ministers met on June 12, and commissioned contingency plans for air attacks on Serbia, involving 40 aircraft from six countries. A day later the foreign ministers of the G-8 countries, meeting in London, warned Milosevic to accept international monitors, allow the refugees who had fled from Kosovo to return, and resume talks with Rugova, who had in the meantime also met the foreign ministers in London.

The foreign ministers' group did tell Rugova to explicitly reject violence and acts of terrorism, and make the 'Kosovo Albanian Extremists' refrain from violent acts that the Serbs could use as a pretext for continuing their violence.[27] But the effect of the joint statement was more than nullified by the statements made by Madeleine Albright and the British Foreign Secretary, Robin Cooke. Albright made no secret of her belief that Milosevic, not Rugova, was at fault for the premature suspension of negotiations that had been arranged in May by US special envoy Richard Holbrooke. 'The violence escalated to such a point that the talks had to be suspended,' Albright said. The United States did not believe Rugova had any choice but to break them off.

Cooke went a step further, saying, 'President Milosevic will be making a grave mistake if he imagines the international community will be as slow to respond in Kosovo as it was in Bosnia.' This threat was issued despite the fact that Milosevic has already held two rounds of talks with Ibrahim Rugova, in May and again on 5 June. Cooke or Albright should at least have entertained the possibility that the talks broke down because Rugova remained unyielding in his demand for independence, and that this might have been so because, with the rise of the KLA threatening his leadership, Rugova was no longer in a position to strike any compromises with Milosevic.

Between his meetings with Milosevic, Rugova had also met Clinton in Washington on 27 May. At that meeting he had warned Clinton that a civil war was about to break out and that only a sharp increase in pressure by the Americans could prevent it. Clinton, one can only presume, expressed his opposition to secession. One has no idea what Rugova promised him, and whether he was prepared to tone down his demand for complete independence. But it soon became clear that he was not calling the shots any more in Kosovo. In October, the chief KLA spokesman in Europe, Barduhl Mahmuti, said bluntly that the KLA was prepared for a three-year cease-fire provided that there was a referendum at the end of that period on self determination.[28]

Thanks to Albright and Cooke, NATO's message to the Kosovar Albanians could not therefore have been less ambiguous: Serbian unity was expendable. The KLA got the message. At the end of the month, its guerrillas seized hold of the coal mining town of Belacevac, which provides much of the coal needed by two power plants that supply parts of Serbia and Macedonia, and closed the road from Pristina to Kijevo. In the process, its guerrillas ejected more than 8,000 Serbs from Belacevac, who had to take to the woods.[29] Incredible as it may seem, this little bit of ethnic cleansing did not unduly disturb the US government. On the contrary, Richard Holbrooke, who was in Serbia for four days trying to broker a cease-fire, warned Belgrade against trying to force open the road to Kijevo.[30] Shorn of even a whisper of support from the US and NATO, Belgrade was left with no option but to find a way to contain the KLA on its own. The June offensive was the direct outcome.

The US saw Belgrade's second offensive as a challenge to its own and NATO's authority. From August, its representative to NATO, Alexander Vershbow, began to press for the definition of an 'end game strategy for Kosovo'.[31] This was to turn Kosovo into an international protectorate, and police its frontiers with Serbia with 60,000 ground troops. Needless to say, Milosevic would have to be 'persuaded' to accept this 'peace plan' with the help of some aerial bombing. But in their arrogance, NATO's planners, bolstered by reports from their intelligence agencies, assumed that a few days of bombing would bring him to his senses. When some of the alliance members voiced reservations, US Defence Secretary William Cohen taunted them at a meeting in late September with their lack of cohesion and purpose. If NATO could not even muster a threat to Milosevic, he asked, what was the point of the alliance?[32]

In October 1998, in a letter to leading senators, President Clinton outlined a plan for air strikes on Serbia.[33] The only snag was that the plan required the deployment of ground troops only days before the mid-term congressional and gubernatorial elections in the US. So for purely domestic reasons, the Clinton administration backed off, and in the beginning of October the doves in Washington got one last chance to send Richard Holbrooke to reason with Milosevic.

Over nine days of negotiations, Holbrooke brokered terms that gave Yugoslavia the last glimmering of hope for peace. The crux of his accord with President Slobodan Milosevic of Yugoslavia was the stationing of 2,000 international observers in Kosovo, NATO reconnaissance flights to monitor Serbian troop and police withdrawals from Kosovo, and a resumption of talks between Milosevic and Rugova. The accord was not reached easily. It took nine days, because even then Milosevic refused point-blank to allow foreign troops to be stationed on his territory. As a result the monitors were to be unarmed. Holbrooke said that as part of the accord Milosevic had also committed himself to elections in Kosovo and amnesty for those accused of taking part in the fighting on behalf of the ethnic Albanians.

Contrary to what NATO spokesmen said later, there were indications that Milosevic wanted the agreement to work. Had he intended to break it all along, he would not have fought so hard to eliminate clauses that he could not live with, such as the posting of armed NATO observers (where he succeeded) and the lifting of the NATO order that gave authority to launch strikes immediately (where he failed). He told his nation on TV that the agreement had saved the nation's honour and safeguarded its vital interests. But it takes two to make peace. The KLA were now on the verge of committing NATO to attacking the Serbian army and softening it up for a KLA victory. There was still not a single word of censure from NATO of its activities. All they had to do was keep provoking the Serbs.

They did exactly that. No sooner did the Serb forces vacate an area, then the KLA would move in. And the inflow of arms continued unabated.[34] When, after weeks of mounting provocation, the Serbs opened their December offensive, the KLA had won. Crafted by Madeleine Albright on the back of the Racak Massacre, the US, with NATO in its obedient wake, gave Milosevic an ultimatum: take part in peace talks at Rambouillet, or face bombardment. Milosevic agreed to the peace talks. But his delegation soon realised that these were intended to foist a thinly disguised version of the Vershbow plan on them and turn Kosovo into a NATO protectorate. Belgrade had to pull back all of its military units and allow NATO military observers to take their place. There would be elections in Kosovo, and the new government would have its own police. After three years the Kosovars would decide their future through a referendum. What was particularly galling for the Serbian government was a clause that demanded free right of movement and monitoring for the NATO troops not only in Kosovo but the whole of Serbia. The KLA read the plan for what it actually was—a face-saving formula by which Milosevic could hand over Kosovo to them—and accepted it. Milosevic refused and precipitated the attack on Kosovo.

Notes

1. Judith Miller, 'Kosovo emptied brutally, Agency says', *International Herald Tribune* (from *New York Times*), 7 May 1999. This is the same journalist who four years later uncritically published a succession of stories in the *New York Times* endorsing the Bush administration's claim that Saddam Hussein's regime in Iraq was building weapons of mass destruction, and forced the newspaper's editors to apologise to their readers (see Chapter 13). One also needs to remember that while 89,500 is not a small number and might be seen as an adequate justification for NATO intervention (though not perhaps for air strikes) Clinton had actually written to US Congressmen informing them of the plan for air strikes six months earlier, when there were almost no refugees outside Kosovo.
2. George Robertson, 'Things are getting better in Kosovo so don't pick holes in its reconstruction', *The Independent*, 3 December 1999.
3. R. Jeffrey Smith and Diana Priest, 'Serbs met their goals in Kosovo, experts say', *Washington Post Service*, *International Herald Tribune*, 12 May 1999.
4. Various NATO briefings in early May, and *International Herald Tribune*, 'Russia backs NATO on Kosovo troops', 7 May 1999.
5. Leonora Foerstel and Brian Willson, The United States' War Crimes. Centre for Research on Globalisation. 26 January 2002. Available at: www.globalresearch.ca/articles/FOE201A.html.
6. Equally unprecedented was the reaction of many countries that did not belong to NATO. Not only did they express little outrage, but when Russia and China moved a resolution in the Security Council, co-sponsored by India, asking NATO to cease bombing Serbia, only Namibia voted for the resolution.
7. Steven Lee Myers, 'Pentagon plans a call-up of 30,000 reservists', *New York Times*, 17–18 April 1999.
8. Jane Perlez, *New York Times*, 6 May 1999.
9. One of them was Milan Misic, then on the staff of the weekly journal *Polityka*. Misic expressed his fears in a conversation with the author in June 1983.
10. James Hooper, 'Kosovo: America's Balkan Problem', *Current History*. April 1999, vol. 98, no. 627.

11. Ibid.
12. Chris Hedges, 'Ranks of Albanian rebels increase in Kosovo', *New York Times*, 6 April 1998.
13. In India, in Kashmir and earlier in Punjab, militants regularly holed up in peoples' houses and opened fire on police or army search parties, forcing the latter to use heavy weapons against the buildings. In Sri Lanka, the LTTE often used women and children as human shields. In Kashmir, during cordon-and-search operations the troops invariably warned civilians to leave when militants were suspected to be hiding in the houses. Just once in a while the militants would prevent them from leaving.
14. Hedges, 'Ranks of Albanian rebels increase in Kosovo'.
15. Chris Hedges, 'Milosevic moves to Wipe Out the Rebels', *New York Times*, 2 June 1998. Also see Elaine Sciolino and Ethan Bronner, 'The Road to War: A Special Report', *New York Times*, 18 April 1999.
16. Hedges, 'Ranks of Albanian rebels increase in Kosovo'.
17. Ibid.
18. This was what India did with the Sri Lankan government and various Tamil separatist movements in Thimpu, the capital of Bhutan, after a full-blown Tamil insurgency erupted in 1983.
19. Chris Hedges, 'Serbians unleash series of heavy attacks against Albanian separatists', *New York Times*, 30 June 1998. Other than his passing mention, that little bit of ethnic cleansing did not make waves in the international media.
20. Jane Perlez, 'Conflict in the Balkans: The overview – Milosevic Accepts Kosovo monitors, averting attack', *New York Times*, 14 October 1998.
21. Sciolino and Bronner, 'The Road to War'.
22. Mike O'Connor, 'Attack by Serbs shatters a two-month cease-fire in Kosovo', *New York Times*, 25 December 1998.
23. *New York Times*, 'U.S and Allies Threaten to Impose Sanctions on Yugoslavia', 10 March 1998.
24. Hedges, 'Ranks of Albanian Rebels Increase in Kosovo' (emphasis added).
25. Told by Gelbard to Elaine Sciolino, quoted in Sciolino and Bronner, 'The Road to War'.
26. Ibid.
27. Craig R. Whitney, '8 Nations Demand End to Serb Attacks in Kosovo', *New York Times*, 13 June 1998.
28. Barduhl Mahmuti, a KLA spokesman in Switzerland, reiterated the separatists' stance for independence, but added: 'We agree to a three-year transition period that would lead to self-determination. If Mr. Milosevic accepts that we are satisfied.'
29. Hedges, 'Serbians unleash series of heavy attacks against Albanian separatists'.
30. Ibid.
31. Sciolino and Bronner, 'The Road to War'.
32. Ibid.
33. Ibid.
34. Ibid.

11

THE END OF THE WESTPHALIAN ORDER

The aerial war on Serbia was the beginning of the attempt to replace the Westphalian order with one structured as an American empire. But the US had still not dispensed with multilateralism. It did this when it invaded Iraq. Iraq first invited military intervention when it invaded Kuwait in 1990. But President Bush Sr. organised the intervention that followed squarely under the banner of the United Nations, after invoking Chapter VII of the UN Charter. In the sharpest possible contrast, the invasion of Iraq in 2003 took place despite stiff opposition to military action from the majority of the members of the Security Council and therefore with no international sanction whatsoever.

In 1991 the US had not begun to question the Westphalian state system or the Charter of the United Nations in which it was enshrined. The Security Council's resolutions had explicitly asked only that Iraq be driven out of Kuwait and not that the government in Baghdad be overthrown. Consequently, when the allied troops drove Iraqi forces out of Kuwait in February 1991, President Bush Sr. resisted fervent appeals from the American right that US troops should continue to chase Iraqi soldiers all the way to Baghdad, capture the city and either kill or depose President Saddam Hussein. In the weeks that followed the defeat of the Iraqi army, the US stood by while Saddam Hussein's government crushed rebellions among the Kurds in northern Iraq and the Shias in the south-east. This restraint came back to haunt the Clinton administration, for it provided the emerging empire builders of the American right with precisely the ammunition they needed to keep the multilateralists permanently on the defensive and facilitate the shift toward Empire. The ensuing decade-long struggle between the multilateralists and the unilateralists on how to deal with Iraq's stubborn defiance of the US' writ turned Iraq into a catalyst for the destruction of the Westphalian order.

The way in which the US, backed by the UK, built a case for the invasion of Iraq in 2003 bears a disturbing similarity with the way in which the same two countries built their case for the aerial bombardment of Kosovo and Serbia. To justify the unprovoked use of force against Serbia in Kosovo, they demonised Milosevic. To justify it in Iraq, they demonised Saddam Hussein. Through 13 years of relentless propaganda, swallowed and regurgitated without demur by the international media, the US and the UK sought to put all the blame for Iraq's woes on its ruler, Saddam Hussein. According to them, he was a bloodthirsty, unpredictable dictator who had killed hundreds of thousands of his own people. He had invaded neighbouring countries not once but twice—Iran in 1980 and Kuwait in 1990. Despite the fact that Iraq had signed the chemical weapons convention in 1972, he had not only used poison gas against the Iranians, but also against his own people, the Kurds of Northern Iraq, and he had done so not once but at least 40 times.[1] After the first Gulf War, he had suppressed a Shia rebellion in southern Iraq in the most brutal way, slaughtering at least a hundred thousand Shias. And despite the fact that Iraq had signed the Nuclear Non-Proliferation Treaty, he had been developing nuclear weapons, and had come within months of success in 1991.

After losing the Kuwait war, Hussein accepted Resolution 687 of the UN Security Council, and promised to rid his country of all weapons of mass destruction within 15 days. The UN was prepared to lift the economic sanctions on Iraq once it had verified that he had done so. But Hussein did not adhere to his promise. Instead he continued to hide his weapons of mass destruction, research and manufacturing facilities and deceive the inspectors. When they finally came too close to the truth in 1998, *he threw them out of the country*. He used revenues earned under the UN's oil for food programme to build palaces for himself, and to pursue his dreams of power, while his people did not have the drugs they needed to save the lives of children and the aged. By playing cat and mouse with the weapons inspectors, Saddam made it impossible for the UN to lift its economic sanctions on Iraq. Therefore he, and not the US, was the architect of the Iraqi peoples' misery—or so the version of the UK and the US went.

After pushing out the UN weapons inspectors in December 1998, Saddam Hussein re-embarked upon the production of weapons of mass destruction. According to the British prime minister, the British Joint Intelligence Committee had come to the conclusion that some of these weapons could be deployed in as little as 45 minutes! Saddam had also built links with Osama bin Laden's Al Qaeda. After 9/11 the possibility of Iraq transferring its advanced chemical, biological and nuclear weapons technology to Al Qaeda had become very real. Saddam had therefore to be disarmed once and for all.

The invasion of Iraq was therefore a defensive action—a defence of Iraq's neighbours, a defence of the authority of the United Nations, and a defence, in the final analysis, of the Iraqi people's human rights. The US (and UK) was forced to do something that it would never in normal circumstances have contemplated. And Saddam Hussein was to blame. Jonathan Powell, British Prime Minister Tony Blair's chief of staff, said as much in an e-mail to the chief of the British Joint Intelligence Committee on 17 September 2002.[2] Condoleeza Rice, Bush Jr.'s National Security Adviser, explicitly put this on the record in October 2003. The US and UK had invaded Iraq, she said, to strengthen the United Nations, not to supplant it as a forum for the resolution of disputes. The US invaded Iraq to enforce the resolutions of the UN Security Council. If it had not done so, the effectiveness of the Security Council as an instrument for enforcing the will of the world and keeping peace, would have been greatly weakened.[3]

But unlike Kosovo, where the subsequent chaos has been hidden from view by a wall of media indifference, the self-serving dishonesty of the case for the invasion of Iraq has become the single most discussed subject in the world. This happened because the success of the invasion eliminated the possibility of further obfuscation.

All the justifications put forward for the war turned out to be false. No weapons of mass destruction were ever found in Iraq, even after the country had been conquered and Saddam's regime destroyed. By the end of 2003 it was apparent, beyond reasonable doubt, that the Iraqi government and UNSCOM (the UN weapons inspectors) had destroyed all the former's remaining stockpile of weapons of mass destruction and their fabrication plants by 1995, and possibly a good deal earlier.

The US' second pretext for invading Iraq, that it had formed links with Al Qaeda and was on the point of handing over weapons of mass destruction to it for use against the US, was also given a public and conclusive burial in August 2004 by the 9/11 commission set up by Bush himself.[4] In the two years that followed, a compelling volume of evidence emerged that the Pentagon, which was by then running US foreign policy, and the prime minister's office, which was doing the same in the UK, had deliberately selected titbits of rumour and gossip from the mountains that the CIA and MI6 regularly received and rejected, to fabricate a case for invading Iraq that would persuade their legislatures and the public that Saddam Hussein was an imminent threat to peace and had to be taken out. So when Iraq presented a 12,000 page report to the United Nations Security Council in November 2002 and claimed that it had no weapons of mass destruction, it was telling the truth. It was the US and UK, with their piles of alleged intelligence, who had lied.

The realisation that they were misled by their own governments is forcing a re-evaluation of the entire story of Saddam's perfidy, and a different story is emerging. Its outlines are that Saddam was not simply assisted by the US and UK in his war on Iran, but was very likely encouraged to launch it by the US in a secret agreement made two months before it started; that the US had at least a full week's warning from him that if Kuwait did not make some reparations for pumping oil laterally out of Iraq and did not help it to bear a part of the cost of the war (which, both it and the US agreed, had stopped Iranian Shia expansionism after the revolution in that country), then it would be left with no option but to invade and annex Kuwait. But the US did not take him seriously and did nothing.[5] Perhaps most important of all, there is incontrovertible evidence that it was mainly the Iranians who used poison gas—cyanide—in Halabja in March 1988, and not the Iraqis, who had only mustard gas.[6]

Could the invasion of Iraq have been a ghastly mistake? Was it born out of ignorance and paranoia following the exit of the UN weapons inspectors in December 1998? Or was it designed to serve a different purpose? A close examination of the events that led up to it shows the latter to be the answer. Iraq had been deliberately selected by the neo-conservative far right to be the guinea pig for their embryonic design to create an American empire, at least as far back as the early 1990s, and, possibly, the 1970s.

The roots of the enterprise went back to the last years of the Cold War. Iraq's potential as a 'troublemaker' in the Middle East had been highlighted by a small group set up in the Pentagon as early as 1977. In a secret assessment of threats to the US, the group highlighted Iraq's outsized armed forces and unresolved territorial disputes, and raised the possibility that it might one day attack Kuwait or Saudi Arabia. The group had been convened by Paul Wolfowitz, then a relatively new arrival at the Department of Defense.[7] When Iraq attacked, or was prevailed upon to attack, Iran instead, these fears were put aside as the US entered into its covert alliance with Iraq.

However, when Saddam occupied Kuwait in 1990 he revived all these dormant fears. The fear lay coiled at the root of the pressure that George Bush Sr. came under from members of his own administration to send the US army all the way to Baghdad in order to depose Saddam Hussein in 1991. In 1992 Wolfowitz presided over the writing of a 'Defense Planning Guidance' paper which not only foresaw another war against Iraq, but did so on the basis of a broader policy proposal that envisioned waging pre-emptive war on any country that was bent upon acquiring nuclear, biological or chemical weapons.[8] Wolfowitz was then the under-secretary for policy in the Department of Defense and Dick Cheney was the Secretary for Defense. This 46-page paper, which spelt out America's mission in the post-Cold War years, circulated among senior levels in the Bush (Sr.) administration for several weeks, till it was leaked to the *New York Times* and the *Washington Post*. The White House then instructed Cheney to rewrite it.

This may have had the opposite effect, because its key ideas became part of bipartisan thinking on foreign policy in the coming years. The paper was to prove of crucial importance because it did three things: replace the age-old international objective of maintaining peace with maintaining complete US dominance of the world; replace deterrence with a doctrine of pre-emption (strictly speaking, prevention) for doing so; and selecting Iraq and North Korea as the first places in which to implement this policy.[9] There was no mention in the draft document of taking collective action through the United Nations. Instead the document stated that coalitions 'hold considerable promise for promoting collective action', but the US 'should expect future coalitions to be ad hoc assemblies' formed to deal with a particular crisis and which may not outlive the resolution of the crisis. The document stated that what was most important was 'the sense that the world order is ultimately backed by the US', and that 'the United States should be postured to act independently when collective action cannot be orchestrated' or in a crisis that calls for quick response.

In 1993, when the Clinton administration continued Bush Sr.'s policy of non-intervention in Iraq, Wolfowitz, now no longer in the administration, launched a blistering attack on the policy in an article in the *Wall Street Journal*, entitled 'Clinton's Bay of Pigs'. In it he derided the US' policy of 'passive containment and inept covert operations' and clearly implied that the right course was to oust Saddam Hussein. By 1994 Wolfowitz was explicitly proposing a military invasion of Iraq.[10] It was this relentless pressure from the ultra-conservatives to reshape the world as an American Empire that, over a decade, emasculated multilateralism and pushed even the liberal Clinton administration into becoming a reluctant promoter of the empire project. This shift was reflected by the ambivalence of its policy towards Iraq.

The Clinton Years: Abuse of Sanctions

Once Saddam Hussein had survived Iraq's rout in the Gulf War, the US was faced with a dilemma that it could not resolve. The UN Security Council had determined that Iraq had to be disarmed, and its capacity to embark on yet another costly and dangerous misadventure eliminated. In its Resolution No. 687 of 3 April 1991, the Council laid down elaborate conditions for Iraq to comply with. It had to declare all its stocks of nuclear, chemical and biological weapons, materials, components, subsystems, R&D, manufacturing and support facilities within 15 days. It was given four months, till July, to destroy them. It then had to furnish proof of the destruction to the UN, and allow its weapons inspectors to verify that it had met its commitments. A UN Special Commission (UNSCOM) was to be set up to verify and supervise the destruction.

UNSCOM embarked upon a thorough destruction programme. President Clinton testified to its success in February 1998, on the eve of bombing Iraq, when speaking at the Pentagon. He confirmed, 'Despite Iraq's deceptions, UNSCOM has nevertheless done a remarkable job.'[11]

An account of Scud-type missiles purchased or manufactured by Iraq, presented by Prime Minister Tony Blair to the British parliament in September 2002 also confirmed UNSCOM's success, albeit for a different purpose.[12] UNSCOM also discovered and destroyed suspected bio-weapons production, or dual-use equipment, at two more biological products plants at Al Dawrah and Al Hakam, and dismantled production and research facilities at 13 Iraqi plants devoted to the production of missiles, guidance systems and propellants.[13]

Overall, UNSCOM's mission was a success. Scott Ritter, an American member of UNSCOM, entrusted with countering Iraq's concealment activities, concluded, in a book written before the invasion of Iraq, that by the time the UNSCOM inspectors left Iraq in December 1998 they had destroyed 90–95 per cent of all Iraqi weapons of mass destruction.[14] As it turned out, even this estimate proved far too conservative.

The US' Dilemma

When the work of UNSCOM began to wind down, the US found that it could no longer postpone facing the central dilemma of its policy towards Iraq. This was that even if UNSCOM succeeded in destroying every last WMD or missile, and every single associated component, production and research facility, as long as Iraq's universities, and professors continued to function, it could not destroy Iraq's *capability* to rebuild its weapons of mass destruction at some future date. Paragraph 22 of Resolution 687 committed the UN to lifting economic sanctions as soon as UNSCOM certified that Iraq was free of weapons of mass destruction. To prevent Iraq from 'going rogue' again, the US and the international community either had to bring it in from the cold and bind it to accepted norms of behaviour through a mixture of the stick and the carrot, or to invade it, remove Saddam Hussein from power, and hope that a successor regime would prove more amenable to US control. The first option would have respected the Westphalian order and the Charter of the UN; the second would begin its replacement by an American empire. The Clinton administration did not want the second option, but it came under intense and steadily growing pressure as the entire American establishment succumbed to visions of empire. These were cloaked in frequent invocations of President Woodrow Wilson's mission for America and reminders of its duty to spread and safeguard democracy. Saddam offended the Wilsonian vision in almost every respect.

The Clinton administration could not therefore bring itself to take the first option, so it temporised. Between 1991 and February 1998 the Central Intelligence Agency made four covert and spectacularly unsuccessful attempts to dislodge Saddam Hussein and was cobbling together a fifth when the *New York Times* broke the story in 1998.[15]

The Clinton administration took the first irrevocable step towards empire in April 1994, when Secretary of State Warren Christopher unilaterally withdrew the promise contained in paragraph 22 of UNSC Resolution 687 to lift sanctions when UNSCOM's work was over.[16] Three years later the new Secretary of State Madeleine Albright took the second step and paved the way for 'regime change' by stating bluntly that sanctions would not be lifted so long as Saddam remained in power.[17] From then till the invasion, the US refused to brook any discussion of a quid pro quo: the lifting of sanctions in exchange for Iraq's full cooperation in destroying its weapons of mass destruction.[18] The US was therefore the first to violate Resolution 687 of the Security Council. But the guilt had to be shared by the other permanent members of the Security Council. Despite their increasing differences with the US in later years, from 1994 onwards till the invasion of Iraq in 2003 not a single UN resolution reiterated the promise contained in paragraph 22 of Resolution 687.

The US' dilemma became acute when UNSCOM's departing chairman Rolf Ekeus presented his last report. In it he stated, 'The accumulated effect of the work that has been accomplished over six years since the ceasefire went into effect between Iraq and the coalition is such that *not much is unknown about Iraq's retained proscribed weapons capabilities*' (emphasis added). The report did underline discrepancies that remained in the accounting for the missiles and chemical and biological materials, but this could not hide the fact that UNSCOM now considered its work to be almost over. From 1997 support for the economic sanctions in the Security Council began to erode rapidly. Russia and France both began to insist that they should be lifted as soon as possible, as part of a coherent medium-term strategy that combined the lifting of sanctions with the installation of a long-term monitoring mechanism in Iraq.[19] To prevent this, the US resorted to more and more underhand ways of prolonging the sanctions. It did so by making sure that UNSCOM never proclaimed itself satisfied with Iraq's compliance with Resolution 687, and brought up fresh inspection demands whenever it seemed that the work was drawing to a close.

The Strange Role of Richard Butler

The Iraqi government soon realised that the US had no intention of ever lifting the sanctions upon it while Saddam remained in power. It therefore used the last weapon in its armoury. In a dangerous game of brinkmanship it began to withdraw cooperation from UNSCOM in the hope of forcing the US and UK to put a time limit on the sanctions in exchange for allowing the inspectors to resume work. Sharpening differences between the five permanent members of the Security Council emboldened Iraq to bar American inspectors from the inspection teams in October 1997 on the grounds that they were spying on Iraqi defence facilities and feeding the information to the US air force to enable more accurate targeting of Iraqi installations. It also threatened to shoot down U-2 planes assisting UNSCOM, accusing them of spying from the air.

In particular, Iraq accused Scott Ritter, a senior American weapons inspector entrusted with looking for concealed sites relating to weapons of mass destruction, of being an American intelligence agent, and insisted that he should be withdrawn. The US denied that Ritter was any such thing.[20] When Iraq expelled Ritter, the US responded by threatening to bomb Iraq. This was averted by a British compromise proposal, but that only emboldened Iraq to indulge in more brinkmanship.

In November 1997 Iraq declared a number of sites to be presidential palaces and put them out of bounds for the inspectors. The next crisis therefore erupted in February, when the head of UNSCOM demanded access to various presidential palaces that the Iraqis had declared off-limits. The US again assembled its forces for an attack and embarked upon an unprecedented public relations campaign to persuade the American public of the need to go to war. Following a last minute intervention by UN Secretary-General Kofi Annan, who went personally to Baghdad after ten days of discussions with the members of the Security Council, the Iraqis once more caved in and agreed to let the sites be inspected. The only condition Baghdad placed was that in deference to Iraq's sovereignty, the inspectors should be accompanied by members of the diplomatic corps. Annan agreed to the request.

The US made no secret of its lack of enthusiasm for Annan's mission. It insisted that his only job was to make Iraq agree to comply 'fully' with all UN resolutions. It expressly forbade him from making any deal that involved a quid pro quo for Iraq. In short, Annan was to offer Iraq no relief from sanctions, and no time frame for their removal in exchange for complying fully with the UN resolutions. Annan apparently did not agree to these terms, insisting that he was not prepared to go to Baghdad solely as a messenger.[21] The Clinton administration eventually relented. At a two-hour meeting with Annan on February 15, Secretary of State Madeleine Albright laid down a series of 'red lines' that Annan was not to cross. Chief among these was that UNSCOM, and not the Security Council, would be the judge of compliance. This became the gateway through which Washington sabotaged the last effort to bring Iraq in from the cold.

In a personal meeting with Saddam Hussein, hours before his departure from Baghdad, Annan offered some kind of assurance to Iraq—intended to clear roadblocks to the resumption of inspections—that the sanctions could be lifted by the end of the year if it complied fully with UNSCOM's inspection requests.[22] Then followed a honeymoon period of two months, the only honeymoon that Iraq and UNSCOM had known. On 14 March, on his return from Iraq, Richard Butler, an Australian who had succeeded Ekeus as chairman of UNSCOM, praised the Iraqi government for the new spirit of cooperation it was displaying. 'We were given access of a kind we've never had before, both in terms of places we got into and in terms of the number of inspectors and the way we got into those places,' he told the *New York Times*.[23] Three months later, during a visit to Baghdad from 11–13 June, Butler said that Iraqi cooperation on the new 'road map' of remaining disarmament steps would lead him to present an unprecedented favourable report to the UN Secretary-General in October. Butler said that only a small though not unimportant amount of work remained for UNSCOM to do.[24] The road map was designed to obtain confirmation that Iraq had indeed destroyed 45 chemical and biological missile warheads, and to obtain more information on Iraq's long-range ballistic missile and biological warfare programmes. While Butler expected corroboration of the first, he felt that UNSCOM needed more information on the second to complete its job. The UN Secretary-General's special representative, Prakash Shah, echoed Butler's optimism: 'The expectation is the next six-month report will be very important and a crucial one in the activities of UNSCOM. Both Butler and the Iraqis have expressed that they want to finish the work in the coming few months.'[25]

Annan's intervention seemed therefore to have broken the stalemate over weapons inspections and bridged the yawning gap between UNSCOM and the Iraqi government. But the terms he hammered out with the Iraqi president only made the American dilemma more acute. The weapon that it chose to sabotage the completion of weapons inspection was the UNSCOM chairman, Richard Butler.

On 24 June, six days after Butler and the Iraqi government set a time limit and established a detailed agenda for completing the weapons inspections, the *Washington Post* disclosed that a US army laboratory had found traces of the nerve gas VX on fragments of destroyed warheads recovered by UNSCOM inspectors from a destruction pit at Taji in March. This, US spokespersons claimed, was a very serious development, as Iraq had steadfastly claimed that while it had produced experimental quantities of VX gas, it had never succeeded in mating it to a warhead to create a usable weapon.[26] This deception meant that Iraq was still trying to hide some elements of its WMD programme and was therefore still violating its commitments to the UN Security Council.

Butler made a similar disclosure a few hours later in New York at a closed-door meeting of the UN Security Council. The analysis, he told the members, had been completed two weeks earlier on 10 June. Iraq reacted with an angry outburst that this was nothing more than an attempt by the US to prevent the lifting of sanctions, and demanded that the tests be carried out in more 'neutral' countries.[27] Fragments of the warheads were therefore sent to laboratories in France and Switzerland. However, far from waiting for a confirmation, immediately after the Security Council meeting Butler repeated his allegations to the press. He told the *Washington Post*: 'I explained to the Council that this was very serious because Iraq always insisted it never weaponised VX.' 'Facts are facts,' he added, 'Iraq has been deceiving the international community with weaponisation of nerve gas.' The US was very quick to respond. 'This is a very serious violation,' said the US Ambassador to the UN, Bill Richardson, and continued, 'It means *Iraq won't have the sanctions lifted.*'[28]

A number of features of this disclosure by Butler suggest that Iraq's accusation was not far from the truth. First, the *Washington Post*'s story was not based upon hearsay. It obtained a full copy of the findings of the Aberdeen Proving Ground of the US army in Maryland, from, of all sources, the Iraqi National Congress, an exile group based in Washington, with close ties to the US administration.[29] This made it virtually certain that the US had leaked the document deliberately.

More significantly, the leak to the *Washington Post* was timed to appear on the same day that Butler addressed the UN. The Aberdeen proving ground had concluded its tests on 10 June. So the US sat on the report for a full 14 days before leaking it. This synchronised disclosure was obviously meant to shock the world and create as much distrust of the Iraqi government as possible. Its only possible purpose was to hustle the Security Council and American public opinion into prolonging the sanctions on Iraq.

Butler's behaviour throughout this crisis, and his role in creating it, is hard to explain on any other grounds than his willing complicity in the US' plans. When he departed for Baghdad on the evening of 10 June, he already knew about the Aberdeen test results. But he did not once bring up Iraq's alleged duplicity during the two days of his meetings in Baghdad. On the contrary he described his talks with the Iraqi government as highly successful and went on to draw up the last portion of his 'road map' for the completion of weapons inspections and the lifting of economic sanctions. In view of the importance that he later ascribed to this 'concealment', how does one explain his silence in Baghdad?[30]

The only explanation is that the results of the test did not come as a surprise to him because *they confirmed what he already knew*. The Iraqis had already disclosed that they had been trying to make nerve gas warheads and had failed. What is more, UNSCOM had already obtained preliminary confirmation from its destruction pit excavations that a large number of warheads had been destroyed. What it was looking for, and what it duly reported a year later in the Amorim report, was confirmation that the special warheads were among those that had been destroyed.[31] Thus when the US informed him that traces of nerve gas had been found on the missile warhead shards, Butler, who had sent the shards to Aberdeen in March, no doubt took it as confirmation that the Iraqis had lived up to their promises and destroyed the special warheads too.

The US, however, saw in the results an opportunity to derail the completion of inspections, and it therefore decided to withhold the information till it could be released in such a manner that it would have the maximum impact. And in a crucial decision that sealed the fate of Iraq five years later, Butler fell in with the US' plan.[32] Not only did he never mention that UNSCOM had sent the shards for testing only to confirm that Iraq had kept its part of the bargain, but, having raised not even a murmur about the test results while he was in Baghdad, Butler made the first disclosure of the alleged seriousness of the finding at the place where he knew it would do the most damage. To maximise the impact, Butler went public and spoke extensively to the press the very same day, immediately after the Council meeting.[33] There have been few more fateful abuses of media power by an unscrupulous government in a democratic state, as this event proved to be the turning point at which Iraq was pushed off the track of rehabilitation on to the path to destruction.

In retrospect, the reason why the US, and the by now complaisant Butler, made such a fuss about Iraq not disclosing the nature of its tests fully was to heighten suspicion of Iraq's willingness to comply with the inspection regime, and thereby justify their raising the bar and demanding still higher standards of compliance and accounting from Iraq.

Two examples given by Ritter—in a book written four years after he resigned from UNSCOM in August 1998, accusing the US of not wanting to complete the inspection process—illustrate the lengths to which a by now thoroughly co-opted Butler was prepared to go to prevent the inspections from being completed. In 1998, the head of UNSCOM's biological inspection section was a former biological weapons officer with the US army named Richard Spertzel. Throughout 1998 Spertzel refused to allow the inspection of Iraq's presidential palaces—the very same palaces to gain entry into which the US had almost gone to war. When the Iraqis confronted him, demanding to know why he was not permitting their inspection, he said that he had never expected to find any biological weapons in them and hadn't wanted to give them the benefit of a negative reading.[34] Butler knew what Spertzel was up to, at the very least because of Ritter's vigorous protests, but did nothing.

The second episode occurred in September 1997. An UNSCOM biological weapons inspector, who did a surprise inspection of the Iraqi National Standards Laboratory, saw two gentlemen with a briefcase trying to sneak away. When, after a chase and several gunpoint confrontations, she managed to obtain the briefcase, it turned out to contain documentation from Iraq's Special Security Organisation, Saddam Hussein's personal security group. When a quick survey revealed words like '*botulinum* toxin reagent test kits' and '*clostridium perfingen* reagent test kits', UNSCOM was sure that it had made a major breakthrough—Saddam Hussein was using his personal bodyguard units to move sensitive documents around and away from the inspectors. However, when the documents were translated, they turned out to contain painstakingly detailed test reports on each and every thing that Saddam Hussein ate, wore and touched. What UNSCOM had stumbled onto was Saddam Hussein's elaborate precautions for keeping himself alive! Despite this Butler continued to cite this discovery on American national radio and television as proof of Iraq's continued work on biological weapons.[35]

Providentially for Butler and the US, UNSCOM found fresh grounds for scepticism in July when it discovered a letter at Air Headquarters, Baghdad, which suggested that Iraq had overstated the number of chemical weapon bombs that it had used in the war against Iran by 6,000. As pointed out earlier, these could have been part of another list, and might anyway have been discovered and destroyed by 1998. But it gave Butler another pretext for going back on his tacit commitment to complete UNSCOM's work by August and submitting a report that could pave the way for the lifting of sanctions, and instead demanding a fresh batch of inspections, this time with no restrictions and no time limit.

To this UNSCOM added a third ground for continuing the inspections: it claimed that it had reason to suspect that Iraq had built at least three implosion devices which only needed to be filled with enriched uranium to be converted into nuclear bombs. This charge was specifically refuted by the IAEA, which said that it had 'no indication of prohibited nuclear material or activity in Iraq'. David Kyd, IAEA's spokesman, specifically denied any knowledge or suspicion of Iraq's possession of implosion devices. But such is the power of disinformation that four years later this became one of the principal reasons cited by the US and UK for deciding to declare war on Iraq.[36]

When the two-month period agreed to by Butler and the Iraqi government came to an end in August, Butler again went to Baghdad and demanded a long list of fresh documents and site inspections. The by then thoroughly incensed Iraqis refused to give him either and accused him of simply playing out a part assigned to him in a US-scripted drama to prolong sanctions. The talks failed completely and Butler came back to the UN complaining that the Iraqis had withdrawn cooperation from UNSCOM.

Butler's complaint, broadcast worldwide through the press and putting all the blame on the Iraqis, gave the US precisely the pretext it was looking for. 'Saddam's decision to suspend co-operation with the ... UN special commission is a violation of the agreement he reached with UN Secretary-General Kofi Annan less than six months ago, and is a direct challenge to the authority of the Security Council,' wrote Madeleine Albright.

Albright once more spelt out the goals of the US: 'What Saddam really wants is to have sanctions lifted while retaining his residual weapons-of-mass-destruction capabilities. We will not allow it. ... If the Council fails to persuade Saddam to resume co-operation, then *we will have a free hand to use other means* to support UNSCOM's mandate.'[37]

Albright's threat differed only in her choice of words from the one that President George W. Bush was to brandish before the entire world at the UN in 2002. Albright's statement was the first hint given by the US that it was already contemplating unilateral military action against Iraq on the basis of a manufactured and patently false accusation of not cooperating with the UN. *It was made a full three years before the destruction of the World Trade Centre and five years before the invasion of Iraq.*

Iraq had no illusions about what the 26 October 'revelations' meant for the economic sanctions. So it went back to playing the only card that a weak and isolated country had left to play: on 31 October it banned even the monitoring of existing sites by UNSCOM. Tariq Aziz explained that his country was not gambling or seeking a confrontation, but had been left with no choice when it realised that cooperating with UNSCOM would not get the sanctions lifted. But it must also have hoped that by provoking another crisis it would be able to get the issue reopened and the friendlier Security Council members into the act again.

The Iraqi action did set off a crisis, but it did not go the way Iraq had wanted. The Security Council met on 5 November and condemned its action, demanding that it resume full cooperation immediately. When Iraq did not immediately comply, it walked neatly into the US' trap. The very next day US officials let the press know that the Clinton administration had lost faith in weapons inspection because Iraq would never allow the process to be completed, and that it was thinking of other ways to contain Iraq, including the continuation of economic sanctions and military action.[38] The state department's spokesperson, James P. Rubin, also insisted that the US did not need any additional authorisation (from the UN) to use force. This was a reference to the Security Council's resolution of 2 March, which had warned Iraq that it would face 'the severest consequences' if it failed to give unrestricted access to UNSCOM.[39] To underline the message, UNSCOM pulled 26 out of its 140 inspectors out of Baghdad on 6 November.[40]

After a week of trying to stick to its stand that it would allow the inspectors to resume work only if there was a clear response to its 'legitimate demand to lift the unjust embargo', Iraq caved in on 14 November, even as American bombers loaded with cruise missiles were in the air.[41] It agreed to open any and all sites targeted by UNSCOM and to hand over two documents that UNSCOM had demanded, without getting any reassurance from the Security Council on the lifting of sanctions in exchange for compliance.

Inspections were immediately resumed but Butler was by then working to a script that had already been written in Washington. Within days of Iraq's capitulation he sent a request for access that was virtually impossible to comply with. It contained not only a request for 12 specific documents, but also a general authorisation to inspect any defence and other ministerial archives that it chose to examine. Iraq had no objections to turning over two of the documents. These were the letter (or document) UNSCOM had found in the air headquarters in July on chemical bombs, and records of a brigade that was being equipped as a missile unit. But Butler also asked for the Iraqi government's report on the 1995 defection of Saddam's son-in-law, Hussein Kamel, additional documents on the attempts to create VX gas, documents to prove that Iraq had destroyed all its stock of Scud missile propellants, and two diaries of persons involved in the missiles programme. Iraq said that it could not comply because there had been no investigation of Kamel's defection (only a summary execution) and that the two diaries had been destroyed. Without refusing to turn over the files on propellants, it asked UNSCOM to be satisfied with its earlier verification that all, or nearly all, missiles and warheads had been destroyed.[42]

However, in addition to asking for these documents and for unrestricted access to archives, Butler made an even more provocative request. This was for the minutes of the meetings of the 'high-level concealment committee' that had been set up in 1991 to hide proscribed materials. The Iraqi Deputy Foreign Minister Riad-al-Qaysi responded that since instructions on concealment had been given orally, there were no records of the meetings.[43]

Iraq made a determined bid to live up to its promise. According to Richard Butler himself, between 15 November and 17 December, when Clinton finally unleashed American and British bombers on Iraq, UNSCOM carried out 400 site inspections, all but six of which were done with full Iraqi cooperation.

In the remaining six, Iraq allowed inspections but made some conditions. Butler's efforts to fulfil the Security Council's 5 November mandate lasted just three weeks. On 17 December, these six sites and Iraq's inability, or reluctance, to furnish all the documents Butler had asked for became the basis for a report by him to the UN Security Council that 'Iraq's conduct insured that no progress was able to be made in the fields of disarmament. In the light of this experience, and in the absence of full cooperation from Iraq, it must regrettably be recorded again that the commission is not able to conduct the substantive work mandated to it by the UN Security Council, with respect to Iraq's prohibited weapons programs.'[44]

Did Iraq's supposed transgressions justify such a huge step into the unknown? The contents of Butler's report showed, as Kofi Annan noted in his forwarding letter to the Council, that UNSCOM did not enjoy 'full cooperation' from Baghdad. But they do not come even close to suggesting that the scope for inspections was over, or that there was enough left out of them to justify the unprecedented step of bombing the country without any further authorisation from the UN. Clinton's justification for doing so was that

> In four of five categories set forth, Iraq has failed to cooperate. Indeed it has placed new restrictions on inspections. Here are some of the particulars:
>
> Iraq repeatedly blocked UNSCOM from inspecting suspect sites. For example it shut off access to the headquarters of its ruling party ... even though UN resolutions make no exception for them and *UNSCOM has inspected them in the past.*
>
> Iraq repeatedly restricted UNSCOM's ability to obtain necessary evidence. For example ... to photograph bombs related to the chemical weapons program. It tried to stop an UNSCOM biological team from videotaping a site and photocopying documents and prevented Iraqi personnel from answering UNSCOM's questions.
>
> Prior to the inspection of another site, Iraq actually emptied out the building, removing not just documents even the furniture and the equipment.
>
> Iraq has failed to turn over virtually all the documents requested by the inspectors. Indeed we know that Iraq ordered the destruction of weapons-related documents in anticipation of an UNSCOM inspection.[45]

If all this could have been taken at face value, it would have provided ample grounds for a further resolution by the Security Council, possibly authorising the use of force. But by then UNSCOM's objectivity was already being seriously questioned. To begin with, by far the most important document that Butler asked for was shown to the inspectors in the presence of Prakash Shah, Kofi Annan's special representative in Baghdad. This was the letter or document discovered by inspectors in the air headquarters in July. Its demand to view documents that related to the Iran-Iraq war of the 1980s was nothing more than a fishing expedition. While such scatter-gun investigative tactics may have been justified in the early phases of an investigation when the investigators were looking for leads, they made little sense after the investigation had been in progress for 90 months and at least 95 per cent of Iraq's WMD capability had already been destroyed.

As for access to the Baath party headquarters, an enterprising journalist disclosed that the Iraqis had not objected to the inspection but to the very large number of inspectors Butler was insisting upon. The Iraqi authorities pointed out that the number had been fixed by an agreement with UNSCOM in 1996. Butler responded that the numbers had been revised repeatedly since then. The journalist Roula Khalaf of the *Financial Times* found out from another senior western diplomat in Baghdad that the numbers and other modalities for site inspection had been revised for large military installations and not for the typical Baghdad house in which the Baath party headquarters was located.[46]

Finally, Butler himself noted in his report that Iraq had largely co-operated with monitoring teams that inspected dual-use facilities. What it had objected to was the photographing of the bombs, citing concern for its national security.[47]

Butler's report, and particularly its bleak conclusion, surprised the entire diplomatic community, which had been closely monitoring the inspections. 'We did not consider that the problems reported during the one month of inspections were major incidents,' said a diplomat. Such differences were unavoidable. 'UNSCOM's mandate says it should have full access but take into account Iraq's sovereignty, dignity and national security concerns. This leaves room for questions and will always give rise to problems.'[48]

Butler's Final Report

The doubts that Butler had raised among the members of the Security Council and in the diplomatic community in Baghdad were confirmed by the way in which he prepared and submitted his final report. At around 2 pm on 14 December, while Butler was still finalising the draft of his report to the Security Council, the White House Chief of Staff John Podesta was informing Congressional leaders that US forces would launch an attack on Iraq the next day. Butler did not submit his report to Annan till around 6 pm that evening, but by then, aboard Air Force One, Clinton had already ordered the attack on Iraq.[49] The conclusion was unavoidable: Butler had informed the US administration of his conclusions even before he had finalised his report, and long before Kofi Annan had had a chance to add his comments to it before sending it to the members of the Security Council. This led the Russian Ambassador, backed by China and some of Annan's senior advisers, to accuse Butler of drafting his stark conclusions to serve Washington's war aims.[50]

Other evidence, although still circumstantial, strengthened the suspicion. On 14 December, before drafting his report, Butler made four visits to the United States' permanent mission to the UN, across the plaza from the UN building.[51] Butler also ordered the UNSCOM inspectors to evacuate Baghdad on Tuesday night (probably Iraq time), when most members of the Security Council had still not seen the report. In short, Butler, like Clinton and John Podesta, knew that the US was going to attack Iraq when Annan and the Security Council were still in the dark about the contents of the report.

When taxed to explain these 'coincidences', US Administration officials admitted that they had advance knowledge of the language Butler would use in his report, and had influenced it, as one official said, 'at the margins'.[52]

To sum up then, Iraq placed some restrictions on access to sites, but these were minor ones that could be justified on the grounds of national sovereignty or security. In numerical terms it did not furnish most of the additional documents that Butler had asked for in August 1998. While some of these may have been destroyed earlier or did not exist, some were in any case of questionable value, being needed largely for accounting purposes. It is also possible that some had been destroyed on the government's orders specifically because Butler had asked for them. But in the final analysis, how important were the documents and the restricted sites?

So far as the Baath party's headquarters were concerned, they were housed in an ordinary house that *had been searched before*.[53] As for the documents that Iraq did not furnish, according to Scott Ritter they were of almost no value anyway, and had been asked for only to create a pretext for declaring that Iraq had failed to cooperate with UNSCOM.[54] One is therefore forced to the conclusion arrived at by Ritter, that the weapons inspections and documents asked for were intended mainly to provoke the Iraqis.

The close cooperation between Butler and the US administration achieved the desired end. Sanctions were not lifted. Instead, armed with this report, the US and UK began four days of intense bombing of Iraqi installations in an operation code-named 'Desert Fox', which left most of its painfully reconstructed infrastructure once more in ruins. Just how much this was the pre-ordained end of a pre-scripted charade was made clear by the fact that the bombing began two hours *before* the Security Council had even received Butler's report.

Iraq had been bombed frequently after 1991. It was bombed in 1993 as a punishment for planning the assassination of former President Bush Sr. in Kuwait, and again in 1994. Indeed minor reprisals for Iraq's transgression of the no-fly zones imposed upon it by the US and its allies occurred almost daily. But the bombing of Iraq in December 1998 was qualitatively different. Not only was it far more intense than anything it had suffered since the Gulf War, but it was done without the sanction of the United Nations Security Council.

The US and UK claimed that the sanction existed in the mere fact that Iraq was defying Chapter 7 resolutions of the Security Council. They specifically claimed authority from the 2 March Resolution no. 1154, which had warned Iraq that further violations of UN resolutions would entail 'the severest consequences for Iraq'. But one has only to compare the wording of Resolution no. 1154 with that of Resolution no. 679 of 29 November 1990, which did explicitly authorise the use of forces, to conclude that Resolution 1154 did no such thing. Resolution 679 authorised 'member states to use *all necessary means* to uphold and implement resolution 660'. It thus devolved the responsibility for further action upon member states acting individually or in concert, and it left the choice of means upon them. Resolution 1154, by contrast, warned Iraq of severe penalties, but did not even hint at anyone having the right to inflict them without another authorisation, perhaps similar to Resolution 679, from the Security Council.[55]

On 17 December, therefore, the US and UK thus crossed a meridian in the development of the international state system. For the first time since the end of the Second World War and the establishment of the United Nations, two countries, which by virtue of their power, pre-eminence and special status within the Security Council, had a special duty to uphold the Charter of the United Nations, knowingly violated its most important clause. This is the obligation of member states not to wage war upon one another except in pursuit of an explicit resolution of the Security Council authorising them to do so. The 17 December attack was thus not simply an attack on Iraq but on the United Nations itself. Nor is this all. Since the UN Charter enshrined the basic principles of the Westphalian state system, it was an attack upon that system too. What is more, as the events that followed were to show, this was not an aberration, but a giant first step into a new world.[56]

Clinton's unilateral and pre-emptive use of force only heightened the US' insecurity. With the exit of UNSCOM it had lost its eyes and ears in Iraq. During the next four years, it had only the vaguest idea of what Saddam Hussein was up to. Thus after the terrorist attacks on America on 11 September 2001, the fear that a resurgent Iraq might pass on its technological expertise to the likes of Al Qaeda came back to haunt the US again. All that the drama of 1998 achieved was to give its paranoia a hard new edge.

The Invasion of Iraq

Iraq's fate was sealed when George Bush Jr. won the most controversial presidential election America had ever experienced. Until the revelations of former treasury secretary Paul O'Neill and former head of counter-terrorism Richard Clarke,[57] no one had seriously doubted that the US administration was pushed into unveiling a new National Security Doctrine in 2002 by the terrorist attacks on the World Trade Towers and the Pentagon.[58] But neo-conservative pressure to invade Iraq and make it the showcase for the future American empire had been mounting throughout the late 1990s.

In January 1998, Wolfowitz, along with Donald Rumsfeld and William Kristol, the editor of the *Weekly Standard*, a highly influential periodical started in 1997, were among 18 co-signatories of a letter addressed to Clinton urging him to take all necessary diplomatic and military measures to depose Saddam Hussein:

> We are writing to you because we are convinced that current American policy toward Iraq is not succeeding, and that we may soon face a threat in the Middle East more serious than any we have known since the end of the Cold War ...
>
> It hardly needs to be added that if Saddam does acquire the *capability* to deliver weapons of mass destruction, as he is almost certain to do if we continue along the present course, the safety of American troops in the region, of our friends and allies like Israel and the moderate Arab states, and a significant portion of the world's supply of oil will all be put at hazard. The only acceptable strategy is one that eliminates the *possibility* that Iraq will be able to use or threaten to use weapons of mass destruction. In the near term, this means a willingness to undertake military action as diplomacy is clearly failing. *In the long term, it means removing Saddam Hussein and his regime from power.*[59]

The stress on words like 'capability' and 'possibility' showed that the authors no longer considered it necessary for the US to be actually threatened first, let alone attacked. The mere capacity of some state or government to pose a threat was sufficient cause for a 'pre-emptive' military attack.

The authors sent a similar letter to Senate majority leader Trent Lott and former speaker of the House of Representatives Newt Gingrich on 29 May.[60] When George Bush Jr. became president, this group moved from the fringes of foreign policy making to its dead centre. Eight out of the 18 signatories to the letter went on to occupy senior positions in the Department of Defense.[61]

The coming together of these eight was not a coincidence. In the Bush Sr. administration, Wolfowitz had been part of a tight-knit neo-conservative group that also included the then defence secretary, Dick Cheney, his wife Lynne Cheney, and Donald Rumsfeld. This group stayed together during the eight Clinton years and became members and scholars of the American Enterprise Institute (AEI), a conservative think-tank founded in 1943, which became the home base of the neo-conservative movement during the Clinton years. In 1998 they became part of a neo-conservative think-tank, the Project for the New American Century (PNAC), set up by William Kristol. It was, and is, housed in the same Washington, DC, office building as the American Enterprise Institute. The two share far more than an address: the PNAC was set up under the New Citizenship project, which is also headed by William Kristol and is also an offshoot of the AEI. This project received $1.9 million from a right-wing foundation, the Bradley Institute, which is also a substantial contributor to the John. M. Olin Institute for Strategic Studies at Harvard University, which was till 2000 headed by Samuel Huntington. A large number of the participants in the PNAC are fellows of the AEI. A similar overlap is found among all the neo-conservative think-tanks: Hudson Institute, Center for Security Policy, Washington Institute for Near East Policy, Middle East Forum, and Jewish Institute for National Security Affairs. The main organ of the neo-conservatives is Kristol's *Weekly Standard*, which has a circulation of 55,000, but commands an influence far greater than its circulation suggests. The *Weekly Standard* is funded by Rupert Murdoch, owner of the *Fox News* TV network in the USA, which scaled new heights of jingoism during the invasion of Iraq. These close interconnections gave the agenda of a relatively small clique of influential thinkers the appearance of widespread consensus.[62]

Since it was set up, the PNAC has argued vigorously for untrammelled unilateralism in foreign policy, for a sharp increase in defence spending, from the then 2.8 per cent of the GDP to 3.5 to 3.8 per cent, and for giving the American armed forces the capacity to fight multiple, simultaneous major theatre wars. The arguments used by the authors of the report were eerily similar to those of the Reaganite right-wing in the early 1980s, when it was arguing for a sharp increase in defence spending in order to confront a resurgent Soviet threat. Years of cuts in defence spending, the report

claimed, had 'eroded American military combat readiness, and put in jeo-
pardy the Pentagon's plans for maintaining military superiority in the years
ahead.'[63] There was a curious unreality about these arguments. The Cold
War was over. America already accounted for 37.5 per cent of the defence
spending of the entire world, more than the combined spending of the
next 15 countries, and had no discernible rivals. So what did it have to fear?
The sense of unreality, bordering on insanity, persists till one realises that
these prescriptions had nothing whatever to do with defence. Kristol's
think-tank was in fact laying out a blueprint for the total and unfettered
domination of the world by the US in the twenty-first century.

When George Bush Jr. came to power in 2000, and appointed Dick
Cheney his vice-president and Donald Rumsfeld his secretary for defense,
Kristol's think-tank finally acquired the power to shape American foreign
policy that it had craved for so long. 9/11 only enabled the empire builders
to bring Bush on board.

9/11: The Pretext for Empire

President Bush seized upon 9/11 to declare a 'war on terrorism'. But the very
nature of this war turned it into an unbridled attack upon the Westphalian
order. Although he used the term 'war' to describe what the United States
was embarking upon, it was apparent from the beginning that what he had
in mind was something very different. Throughout human history the
word had referred to armed conflicts between territorially defined states
or societies. The war that Bush declared on 15 September was not against
a state but against individuals who subscribed to a feeling—hostility to the
changes that the world was undergoing. If international terrorism was a
rebellion against the way the world was changing, then a war upon it was
no more than an unthinking defence of those changes. If terrorism was a
protest against the perceived injustice of the emerging international political and economic system, then the war against it was designed to stamp
out the protest instead of addressing its causes. And if the protest was
coming from people in many countries, then the war would have to be
fought in many countries. Since these were sovereign states, the US had
to seek their cooperation. When it was not forthcoming, or when the state
was too weak to offer effective cooperation, the war on terrorism required
the US to step in and do the job of crushing the terrorists directly. This
was the genesis of the US' new National Security Doctrine that Bush unveiled nine months later, and which laid the foundation stone for empire.

The concept of national sovereignty was the first casualty of 9/11. This
was to some extent unavoidable once states found themselves under attack
from non-state actors. But pre-emptive interventions on the territory of

other countries had to be a last resort, to be tried only when all attempts at curbing terrorism through cooperation had failed. In such a circumstance it was virtually inconceivable that a beleaguered state would not receive international sanction and possibly military support, especially from the five permanent members of the Security Council, all of whom have suffered grievously from terrorist assaults.

Had Bush been content with this definition of pre-emption, the Westphalian state system and international order would have remained essentially intact. But under the spur of the empire builders in his cabinet and defence department, Bush went a long step further and launched a wholesale attack on the very principle of multilateralism. The assault had three components: first, the rejection of the military doctrine of *deterrence* in favour of a doctrine of *'pre-emption'*; second, the subtle, stage-by-stage elimination of the difference between *'pre-emption'* and *'prevention'* as a justification of military action; and third, the abrupt overthrow of the UN as the emerging seat of international authority and legitimacy and its replacement by what Wolfowitz had described a decade earlier as 'ad hoc coalitions of the willing'.

9/11 therefore gave the neo-conservatives in the defence department the pretext they had needed to sell their vision of an American empire to the American public. But the proving ground they had chosen a decade earlier for their new global design was Iraq. That was why, as the 9/11 commission later heard, plans to attack Iraq were put forward within three days of that outrage.

The empire builders lost no time in institutionalising their control over policy making. Most of the eight found themselves in a newly established 'Office of Plans' in the Defence Department, whose main function was to prepare a case for the invasion of Iraq. Their infallible weapon was paranoia. Till 9/11, they argued, the US had one inveterate enemy in the Middle East: Saddam Hussein. Now it had a second in Osama bin Laden and Al Qaeda. Having seen what Al Qaeda could do and having found out, from documents captured in Afghanistan, how determined it was to acquire weapons of mass destruction, they posed the simple question, 'Can the US afford to take the chance that the two enemies will not unite their effort and capabilities one day?'

Paul Wolfowitz had harboured the notion that Iraq might be behind the increasingly frequent terrorist attacks on US citizens and assets for some time. He had read and endorsed a book by a journalist, Laurie Mylroie, sponsored and financed by the American Enterprise Institute, titled *A Study of Revenge*, which appeared in 2000 (republished as *The War Against America* in 2002). In 2001 he was openly sceptical of Al Qaeda's capabilities and in a meeting briefed by Richard Clarke leaned strongly towards the thesis that bin Laden had a state sponsor, i.e., Iraq. Clarke recorded the following remark by Wolfowitz: 'You give bin Laden too much credit. He could not do all these things, like the 1993 attack on New York, not without a state sponsor. Just because FBI and CIA have failed to find the linkages does not mean that they don't exist.'[64] Clarke was appalled because Wolfowitz was giving credence to a thesis that the CIA had investigated for years and found absolutely unfounded.

Since both the CIA and the State department were against military action in Iraq,[65] the neo-conservatives were not able to make an invasion of Iraq a part of the US' new war strategy. They therefore launched a relentless two-pronged campaign to tilt the balance in favour of a military invasion. The first consisted of essentially raiding the raw intelligence that the CIA and other agencies received in order to pull together bits that pointed to Iraq's involvement with Al Qaeda. The second was to leak some of this to William Kristol's *Weekly Standard*, in order to discredit the analysis of the CIA and offer a rationale for attacking Iraq.

Days after the destruction of the World Trade Center, Douglas Feith, one of the original neo-conservative signatories of the letter to Clinton, who had become undersecretary for defence policy, set up a two-man unit in the defence department, called the Counter-Terrorism Evaluation Group, to sift through all the raw intelligence they could get their hands upon to trace who was behind the attack. That two-man group sifted through tons of raw intelligence that the CIA analysts had rejected, often adopting underhand means to get it out of the latter's hands, and came to the conclusion that there was a strong possibility that Iraq had forged ties with Al Qaeda and could have been the state sponsor behind the 9/11 attacks. According to a report in the *New York Times*,

> Old ethnic, religious and political divides between terrorist groups were breaking down, the two men warned, posing an ominous new threat. They saw alliances among a wide range of Islamic terrorists, and theorized about a convergence of Sunni and Shiite extremist groups and secular Arab governments. Their conclusions, delivered to senior Bush administration officials, connected Iraq and Al Qaeda, Saddam Hussein and Osama bin Laden.[66]

Soon selected elements of this raw intelligence and the conclusions drawn from it began to appear in the *Weekly Standard*. In a special issue published after 9/11, Gary Schmitt, who was by then the executive director of the Project for the New American Century, laid out the case for invading Iraq in an article titled 'Why Iraq?'

> Shortly before getting on a plane to fly to New Jersey from Europe in June 2000, Mohammed Atta, the lead hijacker of the first jet to slam into the World

Trade Center and apparently lead conspirator in the attacks of September 11, met with a senior Iraqi intelligence official. This was no chance encounter. Rather than take a flight from Germany, where he had been living, Atta traveled to Prague almost certainly for the purpose of meeting there with the Iraqi Intelligence official, Ahmed Samir Ahani ... US officials have responded to reports of this meeting (and others between Atta and Iraqi intelligence operatives) by denying that they provide a 'smoking gun' tying Iraq to the attacks of September 11. That might be true by the standards of a court of law, but the United States is now engaged not in legal wrangling but in a deadly game of espionage and terrorism. In the world where we now operate the Prague meeting is about as clear and convincing as evidence gets—*especially since our intelligence service apparently has no agents in place of its own to tell us what was in fact going on.*

This much, however, is beyond dispute: Regardless of the differences between their visions for the middle east, Saddam Hussein and Osama bin Laden share an overriding objective—to expel the United States from the Middle East. *Alliances have been built on less.'*[67]

Schmitt went on to cite much more of what he considered evidence of the Iraq-Al Qaeda link. He claimed, for instance, that the anthrax that was sent in letters to members of the American media and Senator Tom Daschle in September 2001 came from Iraq; that Ramzi Youssef, the mastermind behind the bombing of the World Trade Center in 1993, was linked to Iraq via a passport and other details, and that Saddam's intelligence had set up a special terrorist training site in Iraq. He strongly implied that this was for the use of Al Qaeda. Lastly Schmitt repeated the bald assertion that Iraq was continuing to build weapons of mass destruction. He concluded by citing German intelligence, which he said believed that it was not only pursuing a nuclear weapons programme but was within three years of having its first bomb.

In retrospect it is apparent that Schmitt's article was little more than an outpouring of paranoia. His so-called evidence consisted of low-grade reports of the kind that intelligence agencies all over the world get everyday and routinely discard. That is how the CIA and the National Security Council had treated it. This was obviously the case with the crucial Prague meeting, on which he had built most of his case for invading Iraq. US intelligence sources said that the information had come from Czech officials. It later turned out that Atta had been in the US when the alleged Prague meeting took place. The 2003 summer congressional report on the 9/11 attacks stated that 'The CIA has been unable to establish that [Atta] left the United States or entered Europe in April under his true name or any known alias.'[68] But this allegation was used by Vice-President Dick Cheney in NBC's 'Meet the Press' programme in late 2001.

Several other allegations by Schmitt were proven to be false by subsequent investigations. For instance, the anthrax was shown to have originated in the US. Ramzi Youssef, the mastermind behind the World Trade Center attack in 1993, is a Baluch from Pakistan. The allegation that he is in reality an Iraqi agent who stole the identity of a deceased Pakistani boy was made by Laurie Mylroie. The Clinton administration had dismissed her as a 'nut case'.[69] Lastly the allegation that Iraq had a nuclear weapons programme in 2001 was conclusively disproved by the International Atomic Energy Agency's weapons inspectors in March 2003.[70]

But for those who were neither prepared to rehabilitate Saddam Hussein nor continue to depend upon Osama bin Laden's supposed animosity towards him, Schmitt's main argument remained irrefutable. The US simply could not gamble on Saddam not building links with Al Qaeda in the future, for too much was at stake. Schmitt summed up the threat as follows:

> There is no question that Iraq has been involved in terrorism in the past ... But the far more important justification for extending the war on terrorism to toppling Saddam's regime is the terrorist threat he will pose in the near future when his effort to acquire still deadlier weapons comes to fruition.[71]

Twenty-three days after this article appeared on 5 December 2001, Bush called for the review of plans to invade Iraq.[72]

Over the next twelve months the Bush administration launched a systematic campaign to familiarise the world with a new security doctrine. This consisted of two parts. The first was that in the face of international terrorism America could no longer rely upon deterrence alone to maintain the security of the United States, and would take recourse in the future to preventative military intervention (later renamed pre-emption) to do so. The second was that it no longer felt itself bound by the Charter of the UN and older concepts of international law not to attack sovereign states, if it suspected them to be sponsors of international terrorism. He left no one in any doubt that Iraq was at the top of that list.[73]

Undermining the United Nations

An unprovoked invasion of Iraq would however have been a direct violation of Article 2 of the UN Charter and therefore an open declaration of war on the UN. In 2001 the US, and particularly the State Department, was not prepared to go that far. Somehow the US needed to create a pretext for invasion that stayed within the UN resolutions on Iraq. This was the genesis of the elaborate web of deceit that the US and UK wove around Iraq's non-existent weapons of mass destruction.

Had Iraqis welcomed the American and British troops, instead of resisting them, mended the damage done by the invasion to its infrastructure, and held fair and democratic elections, one wonders whether the spate of enquiries that took place from 2003 to 2005, which exposed the depths of the Anglo-US conspiracy to invade, would ever have been fully exposed. The media had by and large carefully refrained from passing value judgements on Bush and Blair's war plans and repeated accusations against Saddam. They would probably have continued to do so. The failure to find any weapons raised the possibility that they had been lied to. The enquiries followed. But for those who were not willing to swallow the official barrage of accusations, there was abundant evidence of deceit from the very outset.

The US and UK left no stone unturned to persuade the world at large that Iraq had concealed weapons of mass destruction and created new facilities for manufacturing them; that it was still bent upon deceiving the weapons inspectors and retaining its destructive capability, and that it was therefore itself leaving the international community with no alternative but to disarm it by force.[74]

But the rest of the world was not so easily convinced. As the *Weekly Standard* had foreseen, the Achilles' heel of the Anglo-US strategy was that it gave those who opposed the invasion of Iraq a chance to propose an alternative. If Iraq agreed to take back the inspectors, cooperated wholeheartedly with them, answered all their questions, allowed them free and unfettered access to all sites, and permitted them to interview whomsoever they chose, and if the inspectors declared themselves satisfied with the cooperation they were receiving, then there would be no need for an invasion or for a change of regime. Therefore, in July and August 2002, when Iraq made a determined attempt to cooperate with the UN, this strategy backfired. In the months that followed, the more Iraq cooperated with the UN inspectors under Hans Blix and Mohammed al Baradei, the stronger became the case against military action and the more difficult did it become for the US to push through its invasion plans and still retain a cloak of legitimacy.

The US and UK were therefore compelled to strike a compromise with France, Russia and other members. This was reflected in Resolution 1441, passed on 8 November 2002. Paragraphs 1–10 incorporated the stiff conditions that the US and UK had demanded in their draft of the resolution, but paragraphs 4, 11 and 12 incorporated the insistence of the majority of the Security Council members that only the Security Council could decide that Iraq was in further material breach of its obligations.[75] No single member or group of members, acting on its own, could make this judgement. Even less could it, or they, take military action and claim to be acting under the umbrella of the Security Council. The phrase 'in that context' linked paragraph 13 firmly to paragraph 12. The four paragraphs together spelt out that it was for the Security Council to decide when Iraq would have to face 'serious consequences', a euphemism for military action, if it failed to meet its obligations.

According to the resolution, Iraq had 30 days to submit a full and detailed account of all of its weapons of mass destruction. UNMOVIC and the IAEA had a further 60 days to certify that Iraq had given a full account, that it was cooperating fully in the verification process, and that the WMDs that remained were being destroyed. But the weapons inspection began even before Iraq's 30 days were up. Weapons inspectors began moving into Baghdad on 18 November and the first inspections began on 27 November. By 3 December, inspectors in Baghdad were telling journalists that they were receiving 'full cooperation'.[76] These preliminary indications of Iraqi cooperation put the US in an increasingly difficult position. Iraq would be in 'further material breach' of its obligations only if it failed to get the inspectors' certification of full cooperation. Iraq seemed determined not to give it that opportunity.

No one was surprised, therefore, that when Iraq presented a 12,000 page document to UNMOVIC on 7 December, both the US and UK took only days to denounce it as incomplete. The document was in Arabic and had first to be translated before its contents could be examined to determine whether Iraq had lied, or was otherwise in material breach of its obligations. Despite that it took Colin Powell only ten days to denounce it as an attempt to inundate the inspectors with worthless material, in order to distract them from the issues on which it was silent. Powell refused to believe Iraq's categorical assertion, when presenting the report, that it was completely free of weapons of mass destruction. He pointed out that the document had not accounted for stocks of chemical and biological weapons and precursor compounds that had remained unaccounted for when UNSCOM pulled out of Iraq in December 1998. He thus seized upon precisely the same weakness in the evidence of Iraq's compliance with Resolution 687 that had been exploited by the Clinton administration and the complaisant Butler, four years earlier, to prolong the economic sanctions. This was that Iraq could not produce incontrovertible proof of the amounts of chemical and biological weapons it claimed to have destroyed unilaterally before the July 1991 deadline for unilateral destruction expired.

A day later, British Foreign Secretary Jack Straw cleverly turned Iraq's continuing failure to account for all the chemicals and precursors it had in 1991 into definite proof that Iraq was hiding them. He did not even dismiss the possibility that Iraq had failed to keep accurate records, for to do so he would have had to raise the possibility first. Instead he baldly accused Saddam Hussein of lying about his WMD programmes and insisted that

Iraq be declared in 'further material breach' of its obligations.[77] Even as he flung this accusation, the British government began to charter ships to move heavy armour and weapons to the Gulf. Exactly a day after Straw had set the ball rolling, the US also accused Iraq of being in further material breach of its obligations.

Unfortunately for the US and UK, events on the ground did not go the way they wanted them to. On 31 December, five weeks after the weapons inspectors began their work, they admitted finding 'zilch'. By this time they had visited the most important of the sites that the US and UK intelligence reports had submitted to them as the most likely places to find Saddam's weapons of mass destruction or production facilities. This was therefore a significant admission. But the inspectors also said that they had received very little guidance from Western intelligence sources. The two remarks cast a great deal of doubt upon the veracity and accuracy of the intelligence reports on the basis of which the US and UK had built their case for war.

The US' plans received a further setback when Hans Blix and Mohamed ElBaradei presented an interim report on 27 January. Baradei made it clear that his teams had not discovered any evidence of a nuclear weapons development programme and asked for more time to investigate a number of specific allegations, such as Iraq's purchase of aluminium tubes for gas centrifuges and its reported attempt to purchase uranium yellow cake from Niger. Blix reported that in over 400 site visits, including visits to all the suspect sites named and photographed by British and American intelligence, UNMOVIC and IAEA had not found a single new chemical or biological weapons-making facility or actual stockpile of proscribed weapons. On 27 January the only facility over which some doubt remained was a reconstructed plant at Al Fallujah, which the Iraqis claimed was intended to produce phenols and chlorine. UNMOVIC had not ruled this out but wanted more time to determine whether it could also be used to manufacture chemical weapons (it later gave that plant too a clean bill of health). The only infringement of the ban against the manufacture of proscribed weapons that UNMOVIC had discovered was a minor one: two missiles that Iraq had developed had actual ranges of 161 and 183 km, against the limit of 150 km prescribed by the Security Council.

But Blix inadvertently left a wormhole open in his report for the builders of empire to exploit. He said that while the Iraqi authorities had cooperated well in the *process* of weapons inspection, on the *substance* of inspection, which required it to come forward on its own with details of its programmes and explanations of what had happened to them, it had not been sufficiently forthcoming. He concluded that Iraq seemed not to have come to a genuine acceptance of the need to comply with the UN resolutions. Blix urged

Iraq to cooperate in substance with UNMOVIC and the Security Council to remove the doubts that remained.

Given what we know now, it is doubtful whether anything could have stopped the US from invading Iraq to depose or kill Saddam Hussein. But the distinction that Blix drew between process and substance helped to seal Iraq's fate. Nothing he or ElBaradei said at subsequent meetings erased the impression he succeeded in giving that Iraq had, at least to start with, wanted to drag its feet on inspections.

This was not what Blix had intended. 'While I had hoped that my frank speech would jolt our Iraqi counterparts to stop foot-dragging and further petty bargaining,' he later wrote, 'I had not foreseen that hawks in Washington and elsewhere would be delighted with the rather harsh balance they found in my update. I had not gone along with the US and UK assertions that there existed weapons of mass destruction in Iraq or suggested that there were glaring breaches in the November resolution, but I had confirmed that the unresolved disarmament issues remained and that there were troublesome limitations in Iraq's cooperation on substance.'[78]

Britain and the US immediately seized upon his caveats to accuse Iraq of being in further material breach of UN resolutions. But other members of the Security Council were not convinced. Iraq had insisted that it did not have any weapons of mass destruction. If this was true, then it could not declare weapons of mass destruction that it did not have. The fact that nothing had till then been found by UNMOVIC left the possibility open that Iraq was indeed telling the truth. Only further painstaking investigation by UNMOVIC, with the full cooperation of Iraq, could resolve this question. The Blix report therefore strengthened the hands of those who wanted weapons inspectors to be given more time to complete their work and Iraq another chance to cooperate fully with them.

Scepticism of the US case for war was deepened by an interview Blix gave to the *New York Times* on 31 January.[79] The newspaper reported:

Mr. Blix took issue with what he said were Secretary of State Colin L. Powell's claims that the inspectors had found that Iraqi officials were hiding and moving illicit materials within and outside of Iraq to prevent their discovery. He said that the inspectors had reported no such incidents.

Similarly, he said, he had not seen convincing evidence that Iraq was sending weapons scientists to Syria, Jordan or any other country to prevent them from being interviewed. Nor had he any reason to believe, as President Bush charged in his State of the Union 2003 speech, that Iraqi agents were posing as scientists.

He further disputed the Bush administration's allegations that his inspection agency might have been penetrated by Iraqi agents, and that sensitive information might have been leaked to Baghdad, compromising the inspections.

Finally, he said, he had seen no persuasive indications of Iraqi ties to Al Qaeda, which Mr. Bush also mentioned in his speech. 'There are other states where there appear to be stronger links,' such as Afghanistan, Mr. Blix said, noting that he had no intelligence reports on this issue.[80]

Faced by a rising tide of scepticism about the reliability of their intelligence reports, American and British spokesmen first refused to elaborate further on the information they possessed, other than to say that their information was based upon intelligence inputs, much of it from sources within Iraq who would be imperilled if more precise details were aired in public. But faced with a further weakening of the case for an invasion, the Bush administration took the unprecedented step of sending Secretary of State Colin Powell personally to present more detailed intelligence information to the Security Council. The new information in his 35-minute presentation on 5 February was:[81]

- Two monitored conversations showing that there was a determined effort to clean out or 'evacuate' sensitive materials on the eve of the IAEA inspectors' visit.
- 2,000 pages of sensitive documents relating to Iraq's nuclear weapons programme were discovered in the home of an Iraqi scientist. This was proof that the regime was hiding sensitive documents in the homes of Iraqi scientists and Baath party members.
- Two photos taken by satellite. The first showed munitions bunkers with two telltale facilities (one of them a decontamination vehicle), which were 'signature' items that betrayed the presence of chemical weapons. The second showed the same bunkers without the signature items. UN inspectors' vehicles could be seen entering the compound at the bottom of the picture. Powell concluded that the chemical weapons had been moved minutes before the inspectors arrived and hazarded the guess that the Iraqis had been 'tipped off'. He also asserted that the inspectors were under constant surveillance by Iraqi intelligence.
- One day before Powell was to speak, the British, again not coincidentally, distributed a paper prepared by their intelligence agencies that described 'in exquisite detail' Iraq's deception activities. Alluding to it Powell called it a 'fine paper'.
- Three more photographs of ballistic missile facilities showing large cargo trucks and a truck-mounted crane. Powell concluded that since these sites were known to UNMOVIC, the Iraqis were sanitising them before its visit.

- As evidence that Iraq was preventing access to its scientists, Powell claimed that on Saddam's orders Iraqi officials issued a false death certificate to one Iraqi scientist, who went into hiding. A dozen other experts had been placed in house arrest not in their own houses, to prevent their interrogation.
- The first-hand account of an engineer involved in the program, which proved that Iraq had mobile biological weapons laboratories mounted on trucks and railway wagons, which could within a matter of months replace all the biological agents that Iraq had produced before the Gulf War. Powell produced evidence from three other such human sources. On the basis of their evidence, the US had concluded that Iraq had at least seven mobile bio-weapon production facilities.
- A taped conversation between two officers of the Second Republican Guard, which strongly suggests that they were stocking 'these horrible nerve agents'.
- Covert attempts to purchase high-strength aluminium tubes of tolerance specifications far higher than those used by the US in its own rocket manufacture. The demand for higher and higher tolerance requirements in successive batches of tubes. The purchase, in its last batch, of tubes with an anodised coating on their inner and outer surfaces.
- Attempts to purchase a magnet production plant from Russia, India, Slovenia, and Romania, to produce magnets of 20 to 30 grams weight—the size required in a gas centrifuge plant.
- Attempt to buy machines that can balance gas centrifuge rotors.
- The purchase of 380 SA-2 rocket engines in violation of Resolution 687, as late as December 2002, after the passage of Resolution 1441.
- The construction of a rocket engine test stand capable of testing engines with a range of 1,200 km.
- The development of a UAV (unmanned aerial vehicle) capable of flying 500 km non-stop. This could be used to deliver chemical and biological weapons
- In all, Powell asserted that Iraq could have 25,000 litres of anthrax stored in a dry form that would last years, 550 tons of mustard gas, 30,000 empty munitions and 500 tons of chemical agents to fill them with, and 6,500 chemical bombs left unaccounted from the Iran-Iraq war. At a conservative estimate, he concluded, Iraq had between 100 and 500 tons of chemical weapons agents. This was enough to fill 16,000 battlefield rockets. It was not clear whether this included or was in addition to the amounts he had mentioned earlier.
- Powell also went to some lengths to establish that Saddam's regime had formed a link with Al Qaeda, and that the transfer of WMD to it

was therefore at best only weeks or months away. Noting that Al Qaeda had set up an armed camp under an organisation called the Ansar-ul-Islam in Kurdish territory not controlled by Iraq, Powell asserted that it had been invited to Iraq by an agent of Baghdad who was at the most senior levels of this organisation. In May 2002 its leader Abu Musab al Zarqawi had visited Baghdad for medical treatment. During his visit no fewer than two dozen extremists had converged on Baghdad to establish a base of operations there. Two Al Qaeda operatives arrested crossing from Iraq into Saudi Arabia were believed to be part of this new cell. Powell then went on to detail accusations that Iraq had reached an understanding with Osama bin Laden as far back as the early 1990s, when the latter was still in Sudan. Osama would spare Iraq in exchange for unspecified help from it. An Iraqi diplomat in Pakistan had been the liaison between Al Qaeda and Baghdad between the late 1990s and 2001.

Powell's speech had a powerful impact upon the listeners, the media and above all on American public opinion. It did not take long, however, for the shaky base of some at least of Powell's conclusions to surface. In his statement to the Security Council on 14 February, Mohamed ElBaradei stated that the 2,000 pages of documents found at the scientist's home referred to 'activities or sites already known to the IAEA and appear(ed) to be the personal files of the scientist in whose home they were found … Nothing contained in the document alters the conclusion previously drawn by the IAEA concerning the extent of Iraq's laser enrichment program.'

On the same day Blix also punctured another of Powell's assertions. Warning the Council about the limitations of intelligence and its susceptibility to misinterpretation, he said,

> The presentation of intelligence information by the US Secretary of State suggested that Iraq had prepared for inspections by cleaning up sites and removing evidence of proscribed weapons programmes. I would like to comment only on one case, which we are familiar with, namely, the trucks identified by analysts as being for chemical decontamination at a munitions depot. This was a declared site, and it was certainly one of the sites Iraq would have expected us to inspect. We have noted that the two satellite images of the site were taken several weeks apart. The reported movement of munitions at the site could just as easily have been a routine activity as a movement of proscribed munitions in anticipation of imminent inspection. Our reservation on this point does not detract from our appreciation of the briefing.[82]

Other holes appeared soon afterwards in the case against Iraq. Most of these related to the deliberate abuse of intelligence by the British and

American governments to hustle their own legislatures into approving of the war on Iraq. Within a day of Powell's speech, the British intelligence report that detailed Iraq's evasion of the inspectors, to which he had referred with so much admiration, turned out to be a crude fabrication out of published material and a student's Ph.D. thesis of the late 1990s.[83] In short, the detailed description of Iraq's deception activities that it contained related to the early 1990s, i.e., immediately after the first Gulf War. The brazen and conscious misrepresentation had been cobbled together in the communications department of the prime minister's office. It was thus anything but an intelligence report on current Iraqi evasion strategies.

A far worse scandal erupted over the British allegation, picked up by Washington, that Iraq had been trying to buy 500 tons of uranium yellow cake from Niger, enough to extract 100 bombs' worth of fissile uranium. It had been referred to tangentially in Blair's dossier against Saddam Hussein of 24 September. Although Powell had not referred to it at the UN, he had apparently used it in briefings of the Senate Foreign Relations Committee to still doubts about the need to launch an invasion of Iraq, and secure the passage of a joint congressional resolution authorising the president to declare war on Iraq.[84] Bush finally incorporated it into his state of the union speech for 2003.

This lie was exposed on 7 March, when Mohamed ElBaradei told the Security Council that the documents concerning the deal were fakes. One of the correspondents, the Niger minister for foreign affairs, Allele Habibou, had been out of office since 1989. This suggested that the disinformation had originally been prepared for use before the 1991 war. It had been transferred to 2002 with a callous disregard for truth. The uranium yellow cake produced by the Niger company was also so completely pre-sold to France, Japan and Spain that it was virtually impossible to siphon off such a large quantity.

In the three weeks that elapsed between 27 January and the second report of the inspectors under Resolution 1441 on 14 February, Iraq made increasingly desperate and, in retrospect, pitiable efforts to meet some of Blix's criticisms of its attitude to UNMOVIC. Sometime in January, facing criticism of its declaration, Iraq had invited a delegation from South Africa to learn from it how it had gone about its destruction of WMDs. During a visit to Baghdad on 8–9 February, Blix and ElBaradei ran into its members. During their meetings with Iraqi officials, Iraq agreed to remove all constraints on the use of surveillance aircraft for weapons inspection and monitoring. On 13 February, the day that Blix was to address the Security Council, Iraq announced domestic legislation banning research and manufacture of all proscribed weapons. Finally, Iraq began to actively persuade its scientists to agree to interviews by UNMOVIC inspectors, in the absence of tape recorders and Iraqi officials. These measures made Blix give a far more upbeat report to the Security Council on 14 February. But Colin Powell dismissed all these acts, saying, 'These are all tricks being played on us [the Council].' But by then the US and UK were beginning to look more and more isolated. Opinion both within the Security Council and around the world continued to harden against war and in favour of continuing the inspection regime.[85]

The case for war received one final round of buffeting when Blix and ElBaradei submitted their (as it turned out) final reports to the UN Security Council on 7 March.

ElBaradei's report categorically refuted the US assertion that the high-strength aluminium tubes that Iraq was importing were for uranium enrichment. The IAEA also concluded that all the magnets that Iraq had imported had been put to non-nuclear uses. These magnets were of varieties that could not be used in a gas centrifuge.

Blix's final report also greatly weakened the case for war by pointing out that Iraq's cooperation, while belated, had in recent weeks become 'proactive'. Blix therefore said that the completion of weapons inspections would not take years, or weeks, but months. He thus made as strong a case for the continuation of weapons inspections and therefore against a military invasion as it was possible for an 'apolitical' international civil servant to make.[86]

In the UN, the case for war was by this time in tatters. The US and UK stuck to the position they had taken after Blix first expressed his dissatisfaction with the Iraqi declaration of 7 December,[87] i.e., that Iraq was in further material breach of Resolution 1441 and therefore had to face 'serious consequences'. But each step that Iraq took to respond to Blix's criticism and cooperate more actively—allowing unfettered aerial surveillance and unmonitored interviews with its scientists, and destroying its Al Samoud-II missiles—reinforced the belief of the remaining members of the Council, including France, Russia, Germany and China, that since the threat of a military invasion had proved sufficient to make Iraq cooperate fully with UNMOVIC, it made absolutely no sense to abandon the inspection route and invade the country, so long as Blix and El Baradei felt sufficiently satisfied with Iraq's cooperation to urge the continuation of inspections.

The differences came out in the open immediately after Blix presented his 7 March report, when, in a move that had been carefully premeditated, to be made irrespective of what Blix had to say, British Foreign Minister Jack Straw announced a ten-day ultimatum to Saddam Hussein. Straw asked the Council to tell Iraq that it would face the threat of an invasion 'unless, on or before 17 March 2003, the council concludes that Iraq has demonstrated full, unconditional, immediate and active cooperation in accordance with its disarmament obligations.'[88] This was no more than an offer of a fig leaf to France, Germany, Russia and China, to hide a decision to defer to the US' demand, as a resolution on these lines would have required only one veto to fail and automatically trigger an attack on Iraq. The French Foreign Minister, Dominique de Villepin, however, saw through the ruse immediately and rejected the proposal. Chile then proposed a time-bound disarmament plan but this was rejected by the US. Straw persisted by presenting Iraq with a six-point charter of demands, but the French and Russian vetoed that too. As the ten days clicked away, France made one more effort, proposing a 30-day extension of the deadline for Iraq to comply fully with the UN resolutions, but that too was rejected by the US. The US announced that it would persist with introducing the second resolution and would 'override' a French or Russian veto, so long as it got nine positive votes. But in the end all it had for certain was the support of Bulgaria. The remaining members of the Security Council let the US know that they would either vote against such a resolution or abstain. In the end, the US, UK and Spain found that they did not have even the nine positive votes they needed to claim a moral victory at the UN.

Bush and Blair were able to maintain their high moral tone only by denigrating the capacities of the UN inspectors. Faced with the IAEA's categorical assertion that Iraq not only did not have a nuclear weapons programme but was not, as of March 2003, trying to establish one, Powell retorted that this was the same organisation that in 1991 had come within a hair's breadth of declaring that Iraq had no nuclear weapons programme, until a defector provided information that showed that Iraq had been as little as two years away from a nuclear device. So far as chemical and biological weapons were concerned, Powell, Straw and other spokespersons began to insist that if Iraq did not actively cooperate with UNMOVIC, the latter could burrow around in Iraq for years and find nothing. In saying this they conveniently forgot the achievements of UNSCOM, which had faced even more determined obstruction from the Iraqi government, but succeeded in eliminating, even by their own biased estimates of the time, at least 90 per cent of all of Iraq's WMDs, and all its WMD manufacturing facilities.[89]

The 7 March meeting of the Security Council therefore stripped the US and UK of all remaining legal cover for their proposed invasion of Iraq. But by that time the US had decided that it was facing a new adversary in its quest for world dominance—the United Nations. In the days that followed, Bush's references to the UN became more and more unfriendly. US spokespersons let it be known that they were prepared to ignore French, Russian and Chinese vetoes, and would consider any nine votes in favour of a second resolution declaring Iraq to be in further material breach as an endorsement by the UN of their invasion plans. Colin Powell went so far as to tell the press that he expected six more members to back the second resolution. In its desperation to get any kind of advance information on how the six supposedly undecided members would vote, the US administration asked the British government to bug the offices of these countries at the UN. The British dutifully obliged. But the six refused to be swayed.[90] In the end, the three sponsors of the resolution, Britain, Spain and the US, were unable to get anywhere close to the nine votes they needed in their favour. Thus was the struggle to legitimise the invasion of Iraq finally lost. When the UK and US invaded Iraq on 19 March, they did so in a straightforward exercise of power with no international sanction whatsoever. That violated Article 2 of the UN Charter. With no collective machinery for redress that could be brought to bear upon the lone superpower, this brought the 350 year-old Westphalian international order to an end.

Notes

1. US Department of State, International Information Programs, 'The Lessons of Halabja: An ominous warning' (Background note circulated by the US Department of State).
2. *The Guardian, The Hutton Inquiry and its Impact* (London, Politico's Guardian Books, 2004), p. 128.
3. Quoted in Hans Blix, *Disarming Iraq: The Search for Weapons of Mass Destruction* (Bloomsbury, 2004), p. 268.
4. The National Commission on Terrorist Attacks Upon the United States, *The 9/11 Report* (New York, St. Martin's Paperbacks, 2004), pp. 477–78. See also Hope Yen, '9/11 upholds Al Qaeda findings', Associated Press, 7 July 2004.
5. See the official transcript of Saddam Hussein's last interview with US Ambassador April Glaspie, on 25 July 1990, published in the *New York Times*, Sunday, 23 September 1990. One presumes that the *New York Times* checked the authenticity of the transcript with the State Department before publishing it. The implications of Saddam's statements and Glaspie's silences and concurrences have been drawn out in Prem Shankar Jha, *The End of Saddam Hussein: History Through the Eyes of the Victims* (New Delhi, Rupa Books, 2003).
6. Stephen C. Pelletiere, 'A War Crime or an Act of War?' *New York Times*, 31 January 2003.
7. Bill Keller, 'The Sunshine Warrior', *New York Times*, 22 September 2002.
8. Ibid.
9. Some key excerpts from the paper are:

> Our first objective is to prevent the re-emergence of a new rival. This ... requires that we endeavor to prevent any hostile power from dominating a region whose resources would, under consolidated control, be sufficient to generate global power. These regions include Western Europe, East Asia, the territory of the former Soviet Union, and Southwest Asia.
> There are three additional aspects to this objective: First the U.S. must show the leadership necessary to establish and protect *a new order that holds the promise of*

convincing potential competitors that they need not aspire to a greater role or pursue a more aggressive posture to protect their legitimate interests. Second, in the non-defense areas, we must account sufficiently for the interests of the advanced industrial nations to discourage them from challenging our leadership or seeking to overturn the established political and economic order. Finally, we must maintain the mechanisms for deterring potential competitors from even aspiring to a larger regional or global role (emphasis added).

10. In an article in the *Wall Street Journal*, Wolfowitz criticised Clinton bitterly for leaving the Kurds and Shias in the lurch and called it Clinton's Bay of Pigs. He unambiguously, albeit implicitly, advocated an invasion of Iraq (cited in Bill Keller, 'The Sunshine Warrior').

11. William Jefferson Clinton: Address to the Joint chiefs of Staff and the Pentagon staff 17 February 1998 (http://www.cnn.com/ALLPOLITICS/1998/02/17/transcripts/clinton.iraq/). 'Its inspectors', he said, 'have uncovered and destroyed more weapons of mass destruction capacity than was destroyed during the Gulf War. This includes nearly 40,000 chemical weapons, more than 100,000 gallons of chemical weapons agents, 48 operational missiles, 30 warheads specifically fitted for chemical and biological weapons and a massive biological weapons facility at Al Hakam equipped to produce Anthrax and other deadly germs.'

12. 'Iraq's weapons of mass Destruction: The assessment of the British Government', presented by Tony Blair to the British parliament in September 2002, pp. 15, 16. According to Blair's report, Iraq had purchased or built an unknown number of Scud and Scud-type missiles in 1980s. It had fired more than 500 out of them at Iran and 93 at Israel, Saudi Arabia and Bahrain during the Gulf War. Since the CIA's report on Iraq's WMDs placed the number of SCUD type missiles at 819, this meant that Iraq was left with 226 missiles or thereabouts in April 1991. UNSCOM, according to the same report, had destroyed 'very large quantities of chemical weapons and ballistic missiles and associated production facilities by 1998'. This looked on the surface like an attempt to give UNSCOM its due credit. But through his imprecision Blair succeeded in giving the British parliament the impression that Iraq still retained some missiles.

   In fact this was a genuine piece of 'misdirection', to put it mildly. UNSCOM's last report to the UN Security Council, dated 25 March 1999, carried the following table (Table 11.1 on page 262) on the acquisition and disposal of the Scud missiles.

   UNSCOM had thus accounted for just about *all* the SCUD type missiles Iraq had acquired. There were none left to convert into the 20 Al-Husayn rockets that British and American Intelligence claimed Iraq still possessed. It was no surprise therefore that after the occupation of Iraq no such missiles were found.

13. US Central Intelligence Agency, 'Iraq's Weapons of Mass Destruction Programs', October 2002.

14. William Rivers Pitt and Scott Ritter, *War on Iraq* (Context Books, 2002), p. 29. In a face-to-face session with the editors of the *Washington Post* sometime in October 1998, the UN Secretary-General Kofi Annan had admitted that it would probably not be possible to rid Iraq of all its WMD potential and that UNSCOM and the Security Council would have to settle for a determination that such weapons (as remained) in the hands of Baghdad did not pose a threat to its neighbours. This wise counsel went unheeded (see *The Hindu*, 'Iraq suspends co-operation', 2 November 1998. Also available on the FT intelligence wire).

Table 11.1
Summary of the Material Balance of the 819 Proscribed
Combat Missiles Imported by Iraq

Expenditure/Disposal Event	Declared	Accounting Status
Pre-1980 expenditures, such as in training	8	Accounting is based on documentation provided by Iraq.
Expenditure during the Iran-Iraq war (1980–88), including the War of the Cities in February–April 1988	516	Accounting is based on documentation provided by Iraq. Iraq's data on some of these missile firings, in particular during the War of the Cities, was corroborated by independent sources.
Testing activities for development of Iraq's modifications of imported missiles and other experimental activities (1985–90)	69	Accounting is based on documentation provided by Iraq. Iraq's data on a number of these test firings was corroborated by independent sources.
Expenditures during the Gulf War (January–March 1991)	93	Accounting is based on documentation provided by Iraq. Iraq's data on nearly all of these firings was corroborated by independent sources. A discrepancy in the accounting of a small number of fired missiles exists between Iraq's data and data provided by other sources.
Destruction pursuant to Security Council Resolution 687 (early July 1991)	48	UNSCOM verification during the destruction.
Unilateral destruction by Iraq (mid-July and October 1991)	85	Accounting is based on documentation provided by Iraq. The Commission carried out laboratory analysis of remnants of the unilaterally destroyed missiles excavated in 1996–97. The Commission identified remnants of engines from 83 out of the 85 missiles declared.

Source: Report of the First Panel established pursuant to the note by the President of the Security Council on 30 January 1999 (S/1999/100), concerning Disarmament and Current and Future Ongoing Monitoring and Verification Issues, S/1999/356, 27 March 1999.

15. Tim Weiner, 'The Deal on Iraq: The CIA; CIA drafts covert plans to topple Hussein', *New York Times*, 26 February 1998. A sixth attempt was being planned in October 2002, even as President George W. Bush prepared America to go to war against Iraq. See Julia Preston and Eric Schmitt, 'U.S. split with France deepens. But Bush team explores options short of war in Iraq', *New York Times*, 16 October 2002.
16. George Monbiot, 'Inspection as Invasion', *The Guardian*, London, 8 October 2002.
17. Ibid. This was reported at the time and later. See Philip Shenon, 'Rebuking ex-Arms Inspector, Albright defends US Role', *New York Times*, 10 September 1998.

18. Barbara Crossette, 'With New Inspection setup a New Annan-Iraq link', *New York Times*, 10 March 1998.

19. Steven Erlanger, 'Gulf war alliance: Six years later seams fray', *New York Times*, 5 November 1997.

20. The US did this despite the fact that Ritter, as he later himself confessed, was a member of American Marine Intelligence and had maintained a constant, close relationship with Israeli intelligence that UNSCOM knew about and encouraged. There was nothing intrinsically wrong in Ritter, or UNSCOM for that matter, obtaining help from the intelligence agencies of member nations of the United Nations. Once Iraq had decided to conceal as many of its weapons as possible, UNSCOM had no option but to rely upon help from member states' intelligence agencies.

21. Elaine Sciolino, 'Standoff with Iraq: For the UN chief, scarcely room for negotiating', *New York Times*, 18 February 1998.

22. Michael R. Gordon and Elaine Sciolino, 'Fingerprints on Iraqi accord belong to Albright', *New York Times*, 25 February 1998.

23. Christopher S. Wren, 'Chief UN Inspector says Iraq is granting much wider access', *New York Times*, 14 March 1998.

24. Roula Khalaf, 'Butler sees progress on Iraq', *Financial Times*, 12 June 1998.

25. Roula Khalaf, 'UN envoy warns on impact of Iraqi sanctions', *Financial Times*, 15 June 1998.

26. John M. Goshko, 'Iraqi nerve gas tests confirmed; UN Chief Inspector briefs Council', *Washington Post*, 25 June 1998.

27. Ibid. See also Associated Press story datelined 28 November 1998, 'Iraq responds to UN requests'. In November, Riad al Qaysi, Iraq's deputy foreign minister, went on record accusing the US of planting the nerve gas on the warhead fragments taken for testing. It insisted that it had never succeeded in producing stable VX gas, and that the question of being able to load warheads with it did not therefore arise. It accused the US of planting the nerve gas on the warhead fragments taken for testing (*The Star Tribune*, Minneapolis).

28. Ibid (emphasis added).

29. Ibid.

30. Letter from Executive Chairman of UNSCOM to the Security Council, 17 June 1998. The relevant paragraphs read as follows:

> The discussions were held in a cordial and professional manner, which reflected the new spirit of cooperation between both sides following the signature of the Memorandum of Understanding between the Secretary-General and the Government of Iraq on 23 February 1998 (see S/1998/208).
>
> As a result of the talks, the Deputy Prime Minister and I agreed on a schedule for work to be carried out by both sides during the next two months in order to try to resolve most of the priority disarmament issues.
>
> I believe that if the Government of Iraq provides the full cooperation it undertook to provide, in the Memorandum of Understanding between the United Nations and Iraq, it should be possible for the Commission to resolve remaining issues and begin to formulate reports on its work pursuant to paragraph 22 of resolution 687 (1991) [S/1998/529, 17 June 1998. Paragraph 22 referred to the lifting of sanctions].

31. Roula Khalaf, 'UN envoy warns on impact of Iraqi sanctions', *The Financial Times*, London, 15 June 1998. See also the Amorim report to UN Security Council, 25 March 1999. The key paragraph is reproduced below:

Table 11.2 provides a summary of the assessment of recovered warheads remnants relevant to the material balance.

Table 11.2
Summary of the Assessment of Recovered Warheads
Remnants Relevant to the Material Balance

Category of Warheads Destroyed	Declared Quantity	Recovered or Otherwise Accepted as Accounted for
Special warheads destroyed unilaterally (modified imported and indigenously produced)	45	43–45
Imported conventional warheads (Iraq's unilateral and UNSCOM-supervised destruction)	107	83
Indigenous warheads of all types (accounting method is by imported rings, as key elements in a warhead structure)	196–200	170–180

Issues related to remnants of warheads that have not been recovered, but which have been declared by Iraq as unilaterally destroyed (some 25 imported warheads and some 25 Iraqi manufactured warheads), remain outstanding in the accounting of proscribed warheads that Iraq claimed to have destroyed unilaterally. The full and verifiable accounting for proscribed missile conventional warheads remains essential for the verification of the premise that Iraq has not retained any proscribed missiles and that all proscribed missiles and their warheads indeed have been destroyed.

32. This may not have been the first time he did so, and it certainly was not the last. Diplomats in the Security Council remembered, when interviewed in June, that after praising Iraq's cooperation when he was in Baghdad, Butler had come back to New York and reported to the UN Security Council that 'no progress had been achieved in the previous six months' (Roula Khalaf, 'UN envoy warns on impact of Iraqi sanctions').

33. John M. Goshko, 'Iraqi nerve gas tests confirmed'. Goshko's precise words are, 'Butler spoke after giving a closed-door briefing to the 15-member council ... By speaking out immediately in public he defeated the entire purpose of closing the session to the public. Thus was Kofi Annan and the UN outmaneuvered.'

34. Scott Ritter, as told to William Pitt, *War on Iraq*, p. 43. Ritter claims in the book that he got into shouting matches with Spertzel on this issue in the morning staff meetings, but Butler did nothing (p. 44).

35. Ibid. pp. 45–46.

36. Roula Khalaf, 'Baghdad to cut deal on weapons inspections', *Financial Times*, London, 2 October 1998. The suspicion that Iraq already had the trigger device for a bomb also permeated the CIA and British Intelligence reports on Iraq's WMD, which were released in September and October 2002. It was not voiced explicitly but is implied by the concern with which both the US and Britain viewed Iraq's alleged attempts to obtain enriched uranium from Africa.

37. Madeleine K. Albright, 'Saddam rattling his cage, but he cannot break out of it', *Houston Chronicle*, 18 August 1998 (emphasis added).

38. Steven Erlanger, 'US set to give up arms inspection for curbing Iraq', *New York Times*, 8 November 1998.

39. Steven Lee Myers, 'US works to win allies' support for using force against Iraq', *New York Times*, 5 November 1998.
40. Roula Khalaf, 'Cohen berates Iraq on weapons checks', *Financial Times*, 7 November 1998.
41. R.W. Apple Jr., 'Crisis with Iraq (News Analysis): Who backed down?', *New York Times*, 16 November 1998.
42. Roula Khalaf, 'UN inspectors play for high stakes in Iraq paper chase', *Financial Times*, London, 23 November 1998.
43. Ibid.
44. Butler's 17 December report to the UN Security Council. Quoted by James Bone and Michael Binyon, 'UN arms inspector faces the bombing backlash', *The Times*, London, 22 December 1998.
45. Transcript of President Clinton's address to the nation, published by the *New York Times*, 17 December 1998 (emphasis added).
46. Roula Khalaf, 'UNSCOM report UN inspectors encountered serious problems but not fatal blow to their work', *Financial Times*, 17 December 1998.
47. Ibid.
48. Ibid. Diplomats were equally surprised. See David Usborne, 'How Iraq yet again broke its promises to the UN', *The Independent*, London, 17 December 1998.
49. Barton Gellman, 'Top inspector denies aiding US war aims', *Washington Post*, 18 December 1998.
50. Ibid.
51. Ibid.
52. Ibid.
53. Roula Khalaf, 'UNSCOM report UN inspectors encountered serious problems'. The modalities for entering this site were fixed in 1996, which is when it was first inspected.
54. Ritter told BBC's 'Radio 4 Today': 'I can guarantee you that every piece of information used to support this most recent inspection was of a dated nature.' 'Butler,' he said, had 'allowed the US to manipulate the work of UNSCOM in such a fashion as to justify an air strike' ('Attack Data Old, claims expert; Ex-Inspector criticises strikes', *The Herald*, Glasgow, 24 December 1998).
55. Four years and eight months later, the Security Council tacitly took this view in Resolution 1441, by explicitly requiring a second resolution to authorise military action.
56. The UN was bypassed again in the attack on Serbia to liberate Kosovo in 1999, and yet again in George Bush's war (or near-war) against Iraq in 2002.
57. Ron Suskind, *The Price of Loyalty: George W. Bush, The White House, and the Education of Paul O'Neill* (New York, Simon & Schuster, 2001); Richard A. Clarke, *Against All Enemies: Inside America's War on Terror* (New York, Free Press, 2004).
58. Bob Woodward, *Plan of Attack* (New York, Simon & Schuster, 2004), p. 3.
59. Jason Leopold, 'Rumsfeld and Wolfowitz's war on Iraq began before 1998—now it's official' (posted on the internet website *On Line Opinion*, February 25, 2003, available at: onlineopinion.com.au/view.asp?article=1499) (emphasis added). Leopold is a former bureau chief of the Dow Jones Wire Services.
60. Ibid.
61. Bruce Murphy, 'Neoconservative clout seen in US Iraq policy', *Milwaukee Journal Sentinel*, 5 April 2003.
62. Ibid.
63. Thomas Donnelly, Donald Kagan and Gary Schmitt, *Rebuilding America's defenses. Strategy, Forces and Resources for a New Century* (Washington DC, Project for the New American Century, September 2000), Introduction, p. i.

64. Clarke, *Against All Enemies*, pp. 231–232.
65. Ibid.
66. James Risen, 'How Pair's finding on terror led to clash on shaping intelligence', *New York Times*, 26 April 2004.
67. Gary Schmitt, 'Why Iraq?', *The Weekly Standard*, 19 October 2001 (emphasis added).
68. Dana Milbank and Claudia Deane, 'Hussein link to 9/11 lingers in many minds', *Washington Post*, 5 September 2003.
69. Keller, 'The Sunshine Warrior'.
70. See Mohammed El Baradei's report to the UN Security Council, 7 March 2003.
71. Gary Schmitt, 'Why Iraq?'.
72. Woodward, *Plan of Attack*, p. 55ff.
73. George W. Bush, 'State of the Union address', 29 January 2002. The full doctrine of prevention, now re-labelled 'pre-emption' to claim for it the shelter of international law, emerged in the document entitled 'The National Security Strategy of America', released by the White House on 17 September. This was the first comprehensive review of America's security policy after the terrorist attacks of 9/11. The salient points were:

- In the Cold War, especially following the Cuban missile crisis, we faced a generally status quo, risk-averse adversary. Deterrence was an effective defense. But deterrence based only upon the threat of retaliation is less likely to work against leaders of rogue states more willing to take risks, gambling with the lives of their people, and the wealth of their nations.
- In the Cold War, weapons of mass destruction were considered weapons of last resort whose use risked the destruction of those who used them. Today, our enemies see weapons of mass destruction as weapons of choice.
- Traditional concepts of deterrence will not work against a terrorist enemy whose avowed tactics are wanton destruction and the targeting of innocents; whose so-called soldiers seek martyrdom in death and whose most potent protection is statelessness. The overlap between states that sponsor terror and those that pursue WMD compels us to action.
- For centuries, international law recognized that nations need not suffer an attack before they can lawfully take action to defend themselves against forces that present an imminent danger of attack. Legal scholars and international jurists often conditioned the legitimacy of preemption on the existence of an imminent threat—most often a visible mobilization of armies, navies, and air forces preparing to attack. *We must adapt the concept of imminent threat to the capabilities and objectives of today's adversaries* [emphasis added].

74. The strategy they followed has been described in detail in the Chapter 12 in the section 'Manufacturing Consent'.
75. These paragraphs were:

4. Decides that false statements or omissions in the declarations submitted by Iraq pursuant to this resolution and failure by Iraq at any time to comply with, and co-operate fully in the implementation of, this resolution shall constitute a further material breach of Iraq's obligations and *will be reported to the council for assessment* in accordance with paragraph 11 and 12 below.
11. Directs the executive chairman of UNMOVIC and the director general of the IAEA to *report immediately to the council* any interference by Iraq with inspection

activities, as well as any failure by Iraq to comply with its disarmament obligations, including its obligations regarding inspections under this resolution;

12. Decides to convene immediately upon receipt of a report in accordance with paragraphs 4 or 11 above, *in order to consider the situation* and *the need for full compliance* with all of the relevant council resolutions in order to secure international peace and security (emphasis added).

The italicised portions show over and over again that the Security Council was bent upon retaining the right to take further action.

76. This and the following chronology is taken from the *Guardian*. The judgements they contain are also those of its correspondents.

77. Ibid.

78. Hans Blix, *Disarming Iraq: The Search for Weapons of Mass Destruction* (Bloomsbury, 2004), pp. 141–42.

79. The editorial opinion in *Guardian* on January 28 summed up the feelings of those who were opposed to war:

> John Negroponte, the US ambassador to the UN, claimed immediately after hearing the reports that Iraq was running an 'active programme of denial and deception'. He demanded that the council urgently consider its 'responsibilities' in the face of Iraq's 'clear violations'. But this sounded like canned condemnation, pre-emptively pre-scripted. It was echoed, shamefully, by Jack Straw; and by the White House which, putting a notably mendacious spin on the UN assessments, flatly asserted that Iraq had been proven to be in non-compliance with last autumn's resolution 1441 and that this constituted grounds for war.
>
> This will not be how most of the rest of the world views Mr Blix's and Mr El Baradei's scrupulously fair and balanced findings. Britain's UN envoy, Jeremy Greenstock, was much closer to the mark when he referred to 'a catalogue of unresolved questions' that the Iraqi government must answer.

80. Judith Miller and Julia Preston, 'Blix says he saw nothing to prompt a war', *New York Times*, 31 January 2003.

81. www.guardian.co.uk/Iraq/Story/0,,889531,00.html.

82. Blix speech available at: www.un.org/Depts/unmovic/blix14Febasdel.htm.

83. *Guardian*, 'Downing Street admits blunder on Iraq Dossier', *Guardian*, 7 February 2003).

84. Seymour Hersh, 'Who lied to whom? Why the administration endorsed a forgery about Iraq's nuclear program', *The New Yorker*, 31 March 2003.

85. Julian Borger and Ewen MacAskill, 'A case for war? Yes, say US and Britain. No, say the majority', *The Guardian*, Saturday, 15 February 2003. The article stated:

> The US and Britain's drive to gain international backing for a war with Iraq was in deep trouble last night in the face of unexpectedly upbeat reports by United Nations weapons inspectors.
>
> American and British diplomats had hoped to circulate draft language as early as today for a new UN resolution authorising an invasion. But after yesterday's heated security council showdown, in which the overwhelming majority made clear their opposition to war, that strategy is in jeopardy…

86. Timothy L. O'Brien, 'Bitter split deepens at UN. Arms inspectors give ammunition to both sides', *International Herald Tribune*, 8–9 March 2003. Contrary to the impression

created by many news reports of his address, Blix did not assume in his report that there were weapons of mass destruction in Iraq that were still to be found.

87. On 8 January, Blix said that the Iraqi declaration was 'incomplete', *The Guardian*, 9 January 2003.

88. Julian Borger, Gary Younge and Patrick Wintour, 'Showdown as Britain sets March 17 deadline on Iraq', *The Guardian*, Saturday, 8 March 2003.

89. In an interview given to BBC on April 22, Blix took strong objection to the way in which the US and UK had sought to denigrate the work of the inspectors (Sally Bolton and agencies, 'Blix attacks US war intelligence', *The Guardian*, Tuesday, 22 April 2003). According to this article, 'The chief UN weapons inspector, Hans Blix, has claimed that the US tried to discredit his team and used "shaky" intelligence to make the case for war in Iraq ...'

90. Ewen MacAskill, Richard Norton-Taylor and Julian Borger, 'How a US bugging operation was exposed by one lone whistleblower', *The Guardian*, 26 February 2004.

12

STRUGGLE FOR HEGEMONY

The invasion and subsequent occupation of Iraq threw into bold relief the extent to which the world had already moved from an international order based on the principles of the Peace of Westphalia towards one based upon the principle of American empire. Five key elements of the change were far advanced:

1. The US had begun to rely more and more on coercion, often called 'compellence', to have its way in international affairs. The corollary to this was a growing neglect of co-optation as a means for maintaining peace or securing compliance. Iraq furnished the most striking evidence of this change. In twelve years of tortured relations after 1991, the US never offered, and never allowed any other country to offer, inducements to Iraq to make it cooperate wholeheartedly with the UN weapons inspectors. On the contrary, by threatening to use its veto, it withdrew, unilaterally, the only inducement that Iraq had ever been offered—the lifting of sanctions in exchange for compliance. It even disapproved of Kofi Annan's insistence on reiterating this clause of Security Council Resolution 687 when he went to Baghdad to stave off war in February 1998. Nothing short of unconditional, grovelling submission to its will would satisfy the US.
2. A corollary to this was Washington's intense, unreasoning anger with the French and the Germans when they stood up to it and refused to fall in line with its plan to invade Iraq, without giving the UN inspectors more time.[1]
3. Iraq was not the only example of the US' growing preference for dealing with other nations through compellence rather than co-optation. By including Iran and North Korea, and later Syria, in 'the Axis of Evil', it signalled that this was the way it intended to

deal with 'rogue' states in the future. Even after members of the Bush administration began to admit that it might be caught in a quagmire in Iraq, it continued to deal with other 'rogue' nations in much the same way. In contrast to the Europeans, including its ally Britain, it continued to rely upon threats of sanctions to make Iran stop producing enriched uranium. It paid no heed to Iran's frequent signals that it was prepared to accept the IAEA's enhanced safeguards and even suspend the production of enriched uranium if its security concerns were accepted and addressed. It was equally unreceptive to North Korean hints that it would suspend its nuclear weapon programme in exchange for economic aid and a guarantee that it would not be subjected to pressure to change its domestic policies.

4. Even before 9/11 the US had begun to show a growing reluctance to rely on deterrence to maintain peace. This was reflected not so much in its own penchant for pre-emptive military intervention (which only became a part of its national security doctrine in 2002) as in its growing unwillingness to accept the right of other nations to deter attacks upon them by arming themselves, if necessary with weapons of mass destruction.[2] The growing disdain for deterrence was not confined to the Republicans. Liberal policymakers showed that they shared it when they criticised Bush for having entangled the US so deeply in Iraq that it no longer had the power to coerce Iran or North Korea, whom they regarded as the 'real threats to world peace'.[3]

5. While the US moved steadily towards regarding any attempt by other nations to acquire offensive weapons as a hostile act that justified pre-emptive intervention, it refused to recognise the right of any nation other than itself to make such a determination and take pre-emptive action. This too was not just the position of the neo-conservatives, but had been enunciated as a theoretical proposition by Anthony Lake, Clinton's National Security Adviser, in 1994.[4] The US put it into practice when it refused to recognise Milosevic's right to send the Yugoslav army into Kosovo to pre-empt a takeover of the region by the KLA and the continued inflow of arms and guerrillas across the Albanian border.

All these changes stemmed from the steady drift in the American mindset towards empire. A willingness to negotiate with and offer concessions to a hostile nation amounted to conceding sovereignty and juridical equality. Recognising that a country had the right to arm itself to deter attacks upon it did the same for it conceded to others *the same right that the US claimed for itself*. Both were the antithesis of empire. The claim that it had the exclusive right to step outside the bounds of Article 2 of the UN Charter and take unilateral or pre-emptive military action was an assertion of para-mountcy, another essential attribute of empire. The excoriation of the UN and the violent, unreasoning response to the French and German refusal to toe the American line on Iraq was the anger of an imperial power that sensed a challenge to its authority.

But while empires can be built by brute force, they can only be sustained by hegemony. Hegemony has been defined in a variety of ways but refers most often to the permeation *throughout* society of an entire system of values, attitudes, beliefs and morality that has the effect of supporting the status quo in power relations.[5] Giovanni Arrighi has defined international hegemony as follows:

> The concept of world hegemony ... refers specifically to the power of a state to exercise the functions of leadership and governance over a system of sovereign states. In principle this power may involve just the ordinary management of such a system as instituted at a given time. Historically, however, the government of a system of sovereign states has always involved some kind of trans-formative action, which changed the mode of operation of the system in a fundamental way.

Arrighi distinguishes sharply between 'hegemonic power', and 'dominance'. The former is

> something more and different from 'dominance' pure and simple. It is the power associated with dominance *expanded by the exercise of intellectual and moral leadership* ... Whereas dominance will be conceived of as resting primarily on coercion, hegemony will be understood as the *additional* power that accrues to a dominant group by virtue of its capacity to place all issues around which conflict rages on a 'universal' plane.
>
> The claim of a dominant group to represent the general interest is always more or less fraudulent. Nevertheless ... we shall speak of hegemony only when the claim is at least partly true and adds something to the power of the dominant group. *A situation in which the claim of the dominant group to represent the general interest is purely fraudulent will be defined as a situation not of hegemony but of the failure of hegemony.*[6]

From the moment when the invasion of Iraq became a real possibility, Bush and his neo-conservative advisers were aware that the US would be crossing a line that had last been crossed by Germany in 1939. Opinion polls carried out regularly across Europe had shown that the vast majority of the people were against the war. Even in the US, a CBS-*New York Times* poll conducted in October 2002 revealed that by a 2-to-1 margin Americans wanted to give UN weapons inspectors more time to do their work before endorsing military action. A majority, 56 per cent, said that one country should not be able to attack another country unless it was attacked first.[7] Within Western Europe, public opposition to an invasion of Iraq was even stronger in the countries whose governments had backed the US openly, notably Spain, Britain and Italy.[8] They showed their opposition to the war in mass rallies across the globe that had no precedent. In the first of them, on 16 February 2003, an estimated 30 million people demonstrated against the impending invasion, in over 60 cities.

Behind the mass protests was a nagging unease that no amount of American and British government propaganda was able to eradicate: that this would be an unjust war. The sentiment was summed up by Ignacio Ramonet, who wrote: 'Everyone expects the world's mightiest power to be an ethical power, a champion of respect for law and a model of submission to law. At the very least [one expects] it not to turn its back ostentatiously on the grand principles of political morality.'[9]

Two months earlier, on 15 January 2003, more than 500 eminent international jurists and judges sent an appeal to the UN Security Council not to countenance an invasion of Iraq, claiming that it would go against every principle of international law.[10] The US and UK were therefore aware from the start that they had to build a hegemonic justification for invading Iraq.[11] From the very early days of the preparations for invading Iraq, therefore, both governments launched a high-pressure campaign to 'manufacture consent'.[12]

In America, the need to 'manufacture consent' had first arisen before the First World War. This may not have been pure coincidence, for that was when the American 'short century' was just dawning and a similar, if not so vast, change in the international order needed to be signalled. Woodrow Wilson was elected president of the United States in 1916 on the platform of 'peace without victory' to keep America out of the European war, when in fact he was personally committed to entering it. This was in keeping with his grand vision of America as the defender and promoter of democracy in the world. Wilson's administration delegated the task of persuading Americans of the need for war to a specially appointed commission, the Creel Commission. By selectively planting stories of German atrocities and imperialistic designs in the media, in as little as six months the Creel Commission turned a pacifist American population into one that hungered for war.[13]

A similar propaganda campaign, on an incomparably larger scale, was unleashed by the US and UK before the Iraq War in 2003. Once again, the media was made to play a catalytic role in disseminating it. The elements of this campaign were not much different from similar campaigns run in the past. It consisted first of frightening the public with threats of imminent danger till it went into a war-mongering frenzy in which it would justify any military action. The second element was to present a statement, the veracity of which had still to be established, as a self-evident and well-established truth, and repeating it ad nauseam, without a single reservation or condition. The third was to persuade or if necessary coerce the media into carrying only its version of the story. The combined effect would be to persuade a punch-drunk public, which did not have access to an alternative stream of information, that it was the truth.

The fourth, based upon the successful completion of the first three, was to claim a moral, almost divine, sanction to take military action. What they contemplated doing had to be done. It was the duty of civilised people to do so. God was rather obviously on their side.

To build the base for a new hegemony, both countries embarked upon a highly *public* campaign to justify the invasion of Iraq, a campaign that used speeches by the president and the vice-president, calculated leaks to the press, and off-the-record briefings by spokespersons. From June 2002, if not earlier, both prepared, in effect, for war on two fronts. The first was the 'real' war, for which troops, armour, ships, aircraft, munitions and supplies were sent to Kuwait and Qatar. The second was the virtual war, for the hearts and minds of Americans, Europeans and then, as a bonus, the rest of the world. This duality persisted not only through the war, but for months afterwards, till the pretence of morality died an ignominious death at the hands of an international media infuriated at the way in which its trust had been abused.[14]

Manufacturing Consent

Bush and Blair used two choice morsels of disinformation to frighten the US Congress, the British parliament and the public in both countries into endorsing war. The first was the claim that Saddam had WMDs ready for use and that the Iraqi army could deploy them within 45 minutes. The second was that he had retained an active nuclear weapons programme—witness his attempt to purchase uranium yellow cake from Niger. The first proved the most potent argument in an otherwise colourless presentation to the British parliament, and proved pivotal in making the Conservatives decide to back the Labour government. The second helped Bush to convince the US Congress that Iraq was a real and imminent threat. Both these 'intelligence findings' turned out to be false, but only long after they had served their purpose.[15]

The moral case for invasion was built upon four separate accusations: Saddam's penchant for war and unpredictability; his past use of proscribed weapons of mass destruction, especially on his own people; his total disregard for the human rights of his subjects; and his links with Al Qaeda. Had the public not been bludgeoned into passive acceptance by incessant propaganda, it could easily have found out that three of these accusations were intentionally exaggerated. The fourth was subsequently proved false.

In highlighting Saddam's penchant for war, the US conveniently forgot that it had actively encouraged the attack on Iran by reopening relations with Iraq *in secret* two months before the Iran-Iraq war began and later supplying it with weapons, radar jamming support from AWACs, battlefield intelligence, cluster bombs and know-how for chemical and biological weapons.[16] It needed this convenient amnesia to turn Saddam into a special kind of head of state—one on whom deterrence would not work.

As for his human rights record, while it was appalling, it was not quite as bad as the US and UK were making it out to be. All the while that they were accusing Saddam of having gassed the Kurds at Halabja on 16 March 1988, the US was in possession of a report prepared by the Defense Intelligence Agency that had pointed out, as far back as 1991, that the bodies of the dead Kurds showed that they had been killed by a blood agent, in this case a cyanide-based gas. Cyanide gas was used by the Iranians and not by the Iraqis, who used only mustard gas. Based on this, the DIA had concluded that at Halabja the Kurds had been killed by the Iranian army. This was revealed in an article in the *New York Times*, written by Stephen Pelletiere, who was the senior CIA analyst on Iraq during the Iran-Iraq war and in 1991 headed an army investigation on how Iraq would fight a war against the US. Pelletiere pointed out that Halabja had seen a battle between the Iranians and the Iraqis, and had first been captured by the former. Both sides had used gas in the combat, but since the victims they examined had been killed by cyanide gas, it was virtually certain that they had died in the Iranian attack. He concluded:

> I am not trying to rehabilitate the character of Saddam Hussein. He has much to answer for in the area of human rights abuses. But accusing him of gassing his own people at Halabja as an act of genocide is not correct, because as far as the information we have goes, all of the cases where gas was used involved battles. These were tragedies of war. There may be justifications for invading Iraq, but Halabja is not one of them.[17]

Bush's third accusation—that Iraq was forming links with Al Qaeda, and could pass on its weapons of mass destruction to it at any moment—was even weaker. It was convincingly put to rest by the 9/11 Commission in August 2004.

Only the fourth accusation—that Iraq had played hide-and-seek with the UN weapons inspectors for 12 years; that several stockpiles of chemical weapons and chemical and biological weapons had not been accounted for when UNSCOM left Iraq in 1998, and that Saddam Hussein had enjoyed four unpoliced years in which to add to Iraq's weapons of mass destruction—contained enough ambiguity to 'add something to the power of the dominant group' and thereby sustain the US' claim to hegemony. That was why, as December turned into January and then into February without UNMOVIC discovering any weapons of mass destruction in Iraq, both governments began to look for an alternative hegemonic justification for the war that they had already decided to wage.

Blair was off the mark first. On 15 February 2003, as nearly a million Britons braved piercingly cold winds to register their protest against a war on Iraq in the largest peace-time rally the country had ever seen,[18] he told the Labour Party's spring conference in Glasgow, 'Ridding the world of Saddam would be an act of humanity. It is leaving him there that is in-humane.' Blair went on to build this 'moral' case for a war by detailing the privations, repression and torture endured by the Iraqi people ... 'But these victims will never be seen. They will never feature on our TV screens or inspire millions to take to the streets. But they will exist nonetheless.'[19]

Blair's justification for waging war disclosed the full extent to which the international law that had governed the Westphalian state system had already collapsed. On behalf of the 'civilised world', Blair had laid claim to prosecuting, judging and executing anyone, or any regime, that did not meet its standards of conduct, standards of which the US and UK were in-creasingly the prime custodians. If Bush was a modern-day conquistadore, then Blair had become his pet Jesuit priest.

In the five weeks that preceded the start of the war, it was Blair's justifi-cation that dominated the hegemonic discourse. Saddam Hussein had imprisoned, tortured and killed hundreds of thousand of Iraqis. It was Saddam and not the US that was to blame for the sufferings of the people during the 12 years of economic sanctions. Iraq was not, therefore, being invaded but 'liberated'. Tyranny would be replaced by freedom and dem-ocracy. The sanctions would end the moment he was ousted. The people would therefore welcome the American and British troops. The Iraqi army would not fight, but surrender in droves. British and American aircraft flew repeatedly over Iraqi lines not just exhorting the soldiers to surrender but advising them of how they should go about doing so.

When, to their consternation, British and American troops met deter-mined resistance and found no cheering crowds awaiting them, the Iraqi fighters became 'irregulars', 'Baath party fanatics', 'Saddam loyalists', 'Fedayeen' and, after Bush officially declared the war to be over, simply 'terrorists'. They were never 'resistance groups' or 'guerrillas', still less 'nationalists'. Indeed the one word that was never used during the entire Iraq drama was 'nationalism'. Instead it was implied that 'positive' nationalism, of the kind that had gone into the making of the modern nation state, was a preserve of the West. Nationalism in the 'third world', as earlier in Nazi Germany and Eastern Europe, was a destructive force built upon atavistic loyalties and needed to be rooted out.

When Saddam Hussein's government collapsed and the entire administration melted away and anarchy reigned, US and UK spokesmen hastened to claim that Iraqis were revelling in their newly restored freedoms. Rumsfeld dismissed the havoc in Baghdad with his now immortal phrase, 'stuff [i.e., shit] happens'. Richard Boucher, spokesman for the State Department, sought to give the looting and revenge killing a positive spin. 'The flowering of Iraqi politics on such a rather quick basis is really something to behold,' he told reporters at the daily State Department briefing on 23 April.[20]

The Media and the Manufacture of Consent

Both in Kosovo and Iraq, the US' claim to hegemony turned out to be largely fraudulent. But it could never have been built without the help of an immensely powerful but by and large complaisant international media. Some degree of partisanship is only to be expected from war correspondents who live and travel with troops and see them being killed. Indeed the institution of the war correspondent can be traced back at least to the Crimean War. But after the Cold War ended and the US began to chip away at the foundations of the Westphalian order in a proliferation of small wars, journalists were thrust into a new role, as the legitimisers of military intervention. The Anglo-Saxon media, especially in the US, willingly stepped into this new role. It did this by making a small, seemingly innocuous change in its reporting practices. This was to deny the 'opponent'—in this case the victims of coercive action—a voice that the world could hear.

The Media and the 1991 War
The transformation first became apparent in the coverage of Iraq before, during and after the first Gulf war. During the six months between Iraq's invasion of Kuwait and the start of the war, no western newspaper or TV channel gave space to any senior member of the Iraqi government to explain why *they* felt justified in invading Kuwait. When the Iraqis passed an official transcript of the records of April Glaspie's last meeting with Saddam Hussein to the *New York Times*, the *Times* published it, but without comment, especially without noting the strong suggestion it contained of

US-Iraqi collusion in the launching of the war on Iran.[21] When the Bush Sr. administration began to call Saddam Hussein the 'Butcher of Baghdad', and accused him of having gassed the Kurds in northern Iraq, specifically in Halabja, major TV networks in the Anglo-Saxon world and the wire services carried these accusations without once distancing themselves with phrases like 'according to the State Department spokesman' or by using tired but useful words like 'alleged'.[22] When Bush continued to demonise Saddam Hussein as 'another Adolf Hitler' and to invoke the biblical term 'evil' to describe his regime, TV channels and wire service reports made no disclaimers. Still less did they consider it necessary to get Baghdad's response to these epithets. This barrage convinced TV viewers, and the readers of all but a handful of newspapers, that Iraq was ruled by a tyrannical, bloodthirsty, irrational and power-hungry despot, who needed to be stopped from gobbling up other Middle Eastern countries at any cost. That this description of Saddam was not entirely wrong only made his demonisation easier.

When the war began, the media treated it 'like a video game all the family could play. There was a demon to fight; hi-tech weapons to fight him with; it was all over quickly and "we won". The bonus was the miraculously small number of casualties.'[23] Journalists hugged this belief to their breasts because it 'freed (them) from their humanitarian "dilemma"'.[24] The dilemma was none other than the obligation to report what the war was doing to the other side.

The spin masters in the allied military command were quick to seize upon this sudden liberation of the journalists' conscience. They nursed it with carefully edited video clips of bombs falling precisely upon bridges, factories and munitions dumps. Faith in the smartness of the new generation of weapons came close to becoming a religion. The military never told the journalists that only 7 per cent of the munitions they used in the war were 'smart'. And only long after the war was over did the US authorities reveal that 70 per cent of the 88,500 tonnes of bombs they dropped on Iraq missed their targets. Many of these fell on civilians. But that again was seldom reported. To this day nobody, at least in the western world, knows how many Iraqis died during operation Desert Storm.[25]

The first Gulf War also saw the start of the news management system that flowered into the 'embedding' of journalists with invading forces that was practised in 2003. The device used then was the 'Pool'. A British invention used in the Second World War, the pool allowed only selected journalists to visit the front, and then under military escort. They then shared their reports with their colleagues. Those who attempted to strike out on their own were often blackballed or denied military 'cooperation'. This meant being denied transport, a stratagem that effectively stopped them from seeing any more of the 'action'. The pool system ensured that journalists saw only what the military intended them to see. Thus when columns of retreating Iraqi soldiers were strafed and bombed from the rear as they were fleeing, in what carrier-based navy pilots later described as a 'turkey shoot', or when the US army used bulldozers and snow ploughs mounted upon tanks to bury Iraqis, dead or alive, in 70 miles of trenches, there were no journalists around to report the massacres.[26]

What was even more disturbing than the media's willingness to knowingly put itself in a position where it could report only one side of the story was its unwillingness to believe anything that might give the lie to the official version that they were uncritically feeding to their readers and viewers.

A revealing example of this profound bias was the treatment it gave to the US bombing of the Al Amiriya bunker, in which 300 to 400 women and children were burnt to death. When the Iraqis voiced an angry protest and aired TV footage showing that it was only an air raid shelter, US military spokesmen insisted that it was a military facility and that the bombs had zeroed in on communications that had been emanating from it. This was swallowed without a murmur, and the Iraqi protest dismissed as propaganda not only by the tabloid press in the UK but also by most of the respectable news media. *The Sun* reported, 'Saddam Hussein tried to trick the world yesterday by claiming that hundreds of women and children died in a bomb attack on an "air raid shelter". He [note the personalisation] cunningly arranged TV scenes designed to shock and appal.'

The major networks edited their tapes, allegedly to spare their viewers distress, but also left open the possibility that Saddam may indeed have been using the bunker as a command post. Only after the war was over and the unedited tapes of CNN and WTN became available to the *Columbia Journalism Review* was it finally established that this had indeed been an air raid shelter.[27]

The Media and Kosovo

The new legitimising role that was thrust upon the media was not immediately apparent because the Gulf War was a 'popular' war. It was fought to sustain the institution of the nation state. It had the full backing of the United Nations and conformed strictly to the provisions of the UN Charter. The allies who came to Kuwait's defence broke none of the rules governing the international order that the world was familiar with. Till the 'turkey shoots' of Iraqi soldiers trying to surrender at the end of the war, 'right' was very obviously on the side of the coalition.

In the military interventions that followed, the media continued to play the same role. The cause behind which it aligned itself was the defence of human rights, but since human rights was the pretext behind the majority of military interventions after the fall of the Soviet Union, this defence increasingly legitimised the erosion of the Westphalian order. The change in the role of the media became evident during the Kosovo crisis.

The method used by the US and its allies in NATO to build the hegemonic discourse was very similar to what had been followed during the Gulf War. Before the war, the opponent was, literally, robbed of his voice. During the war the opponent was demonised. After the war inconvenient facts were quietly buried or consigned to the pages of the 'serious' journals that only intellectuals read.

To cite a particularly telling example, for fifteen months before the NATO alliance began to bomb Serbia in March 1999, the *New York Times* carried outstanding reports on what was happening in that province, initially every week and then virtually every day. But during the entire period, even this highly esteemed newspaper did not consider it necessary to allow a Serbian to explain Belgrade's reasons for sending its troops repeatedly into Kosovo. Readers were therefore exposed to only the European and American assertions about Belgrade's motives, and the investigative reporting of its own journalists. These journalists too were inevitably influenced by what they had already been exposed to, and therefore found themselves swimming upstream when they tried to understand the war from Belgrade's point of view.

The *New York Times*' coverage was at least sufficiently objective and detailed to allow readers to draw their own conclusions. The television coverage was entirely one-sided. It left the impression on viewers that Slobodan Milosevic, a hypernationalist Serbian and one of the last of the old-time communist dictators, was determined to put down any attempt at self-determination by the Albanian population of Kosovo, without regard for human suffering. As a result hundreds, possibly thousands, of Kosovars had lost their lives and tens of thousands had lost their homes in what was beginning to look like a repeat of Bosnia. He therefore had to be stopped. There followed a systematic demonisation of Milosevic, which was uncannily similar to that of Saddam Hussein. That Milosevic was an autocrat and had deliberately played upon Serbian nationalism to come to power again only made the demonisation easier.

Since the Serbs were effectively denied a voice in the international media, the complexity of the situation in Kosovo—especially the way in which the rise of the KLA and the weakening of Ibrahim Rugova progressively reduced the options before Belgrade, and the vast differences between Kosovo and Bosnia, all of which have been described earlier—were completely obliterated.

Once the war began, the media once again tamely fell in line. 'Pool' journalists at NATO headquarters in Brussels, and their editors in the NATO countries, vied with each other to spread the fiction that the NATO attacks were intended to stop an ethnic cleansing that had already begun, and to overlook discrepancies in timing that suggested that the real cleansing began after the NATO attack had begun. The possibility that the NATO attack actually triggered the ethnic cleansing was thus simply not entertained.

Correspondents who covered the attack on Serbia displayed the same unwillingness to publish, or even believe anything that could tarnish the image of the attackers or cast doubt on their monopoly of virtue. Thus when NATO spokesman Jamie Shea blandly denied that the 'allies' had bombed a convoy of Albanian refugees, the centre of Kosovo's capital, Pristina, and a hospital at Surdulica, and gave grotesquely exaggerated estimates of the number of Serb tanks that had been destroyed, almost everyone chose to believe him. Not till journalists, taken to the site of the bombing of the convoy by the Serbs, were able to identify computer coding on the bomb parts at the scene did Shea finally admit that it was not a military convoy that the pilots had bombed.[28]

Virtually none of the pool journalists of the TV channels asked why and just how a bombing campaign that was to have lasted 'three or four weeks', and be confined to military barracks and Serbian armour in Kosovo, turned into a ruthless campaign to bomb the Serbian economy back into the stone age by destroying its infrastructure. The video footage that Shea was providing was simply too seductive—who would risk having their daily 'fix' cut off?

In much the same vein, none of the TV media, and pretty well none of the American print media, questioned the speculation emerging from Brussels that the Serb army was indulging in systematic murder. When a convoy of refugees that crossed the border into Albania contained only old men, women and children, virtually every TV newscaster speculated that the Serbs may have separated the young males for possible elimination. When the men turned up a few days later, the TV cameras were notably absent.

By the end of the first month of the bombing, the figure of 100,000 Kosovar Albanians killed in the Serbian 'ethnic cleansing' was being bandied about casually by the media. The source of this estimate was never given. But by May it was a part of the folklore of the allied 'humanitarian' action in Kosovo. On 16 May, when the bombing had been going on for seven weeks, William Cohen, the US defense secretary, refined it a shade further by claiming that according to US estimates the Yugoslav army had killed 100,000 Kosovar Albanian *males of military age*.[29]

The media also frequently sidelined the truth when it proved inconvenient. For example, by the onset of winter 1999, when the ground froze and further digging became impossible, the American-established (but retrospectively UN-sanctioned) International Criminal Tribunal for Yugoslavia (whose mandate was extended to cover Kosovo after the bombing stopped in June 1999) had inspected over 300 sites where massacres were supposed to have taken place, but found only 2,106 bodies bearing marks of a violent death.[30] But, unlike the figures of 100,000 liquidated and half a million rendered homeless, this figure hardly made it into the international print media and was ignored by the TV networks. The following excerpt from an article in *The Spectator*, London, tells the story of Serbia's demonisation. None of it would have been possible without the help of a complaisant media:

> On 16 May, the US defence secretary William Cohen said that Yugoslav army forces had killed up to 100,000 Albanian men of military age. This number was declared missing, the refugees having all claimed that their menfolk had been separated from them as they fled Kosovo. Tony Blair himself implied that the numbers might be even higher when he wrote in *The Times* on 5 June, 'We must be ready for what we know will be clear evidence of ... as yet unknown numbers of people missing, tortured and dead.' On 17 June, the then minister of state in the Foreign Office, Geoff Hoon, announced that some 10,000 people had been killed in more than 100 massacres but added, 'The final toll may be much worse.'
>
> As journalists followed NATO troops into the province, the newspapers were strewn with maps showing scores of mass graves. There was particular excitement when 'the biggest mass grave ever' was announced to have been discovered in Ljubenic. It was said to contain 350 bodies, a figure which was blazed across the world's media. Reporting was markedly less energetic, however, when the true figure turned out to be only seven. Billed as the 'biggest mass grave in Kosovo', Ljubenic was in fact not a mass grave at all. Similarly, on 11 October a spokesman for the International Criminal Tribunal in the Hague announced that no bodies or bones had been found in the mines at Trepca in northern Kosovo—rumours had been circulating in Kosovo that Serbian forces had dumped the bodies of as many as 700 Kosovars into its shafts. Various experts have confirmed that the more extravagant claims were fantasy. In August, Pdrez Pujol, a Spanish forensic expert, told *El Pais*, 'I have been reading the data from the UN. They began with 44,000 deaths. Then they lowered it to 22,000. And now they're going with 11,000. I look forward to seeing what the final count will really be.' The chief Spanish inspector, Juan Lopez Palafox, added, 'They told us that we should prepare ourselves to perform more than 2,000 autopsies. The result is very different. We only found 187 cadavers and now we are going to return [to Spain].' Later the same month, a German doctor who had spent the war in the Stenkovac refugee camp in

Macedonia … told *Die Welt*, 'It was very surprising that a large number of journalists either could not or would not perceive [that] the majority of the people in the refugee camps were men of military age. It was always represented as if there were no men in the camps at all. Even when the journalists were told this they refused to take account of it.'[31]

The Media and the Invasion of Iraq

The media legitimised the invasion of Iraq in 2003 in much the same way as it did the Gulf War—before the invasion it denied Iraq a voice that the world could hear; during the invasion the majority of the international media again tamely accepted the constraints of the pool system (now re-named 'embedding of journalists'); and after the war it studiously down-played any news that could cast doubt on the official explanation for what was happening, or not happening, in Iraq. Only when no weapons of mass destruction were found did it begin to suspect that its trust had been brazenly abused.

Bush was able to build an unshakable belief in the world that Iraq had hidden weapons of mass destruction and hoodwinked the UN weapons inspectors only because the media, almost without exception, repeated these assertions without once questioning them. Once again, as in the over-ture to the bombing of Serbia, not one newspaper or TV network allowed a representative of Iraq to have a voice. Instead correspondents sought Iraqi reactions, but only perfunctorily, and they or their editors decided what to report. Reports that devoted several hundred words to the accus-ations would only add phrases like 'the government of Iraq denied these allegations'. What it said beyond that denial—its explanation for what was being reported—was neither solicited nor published.

An excellent example of bias by omission was given, unintentionally, by Hans Blix when he repeated a remark made to him by Gen. Amir-el-Saadi, the chief scientific adviser to the Iraqi president, on Iraq's weapons of mass destruction: ' … But did they have weapons of mass destruction. Al Saadi had denied it and said that they would be "weapons of self destruc-tion".'[32] This and a host of other disclosures by him in his book are the first indications that the English-speaking world has received of the way that the Iraqi government viewed the gathering threat. During the entire build-up to war, not one print or media journalist tried to present the Iraqis' defence against the allegations that were being hurled against them. Had they done so they might have sowed doubt in the minds of the readers and viewers. That might in the end just have sufficed to avert a senseless and destructive war that had, by April 2004, cost up to 55,000 Iraqi lives.[33]

Any correspondent who had been asked by the newspaper or network to assess how serious a threat Iraq posed to its neighbours, and to Europe and the US, would have learned within hours that the economic sanctions had starved Iraq close to death; that more than half its people lived off food distributed by the World Food Program and other UN and international agencies under the oil-for-food programme;[34] that its per capita income had declined from $4,000 to $150;[35] that the child death rate had climbed from 50 per thousand in 1990 to 125 per 1,000 in 1998;[36] that its infrastructure had been so badly shattered that two-thirds of its people did not have safe drinking water, while a third did not have safe sanitation; and that its armed forces had not been able to purchase any modern tanks, field guns or aircraft in over a decade, and that attrition had reduced them to a third of their original size. The correspondent might have wondered whether a country in such dire straits had the capacity to even think of attacking its neighbours, and would have wondered whether even Saddam was capable of losing a quarter of a million persons in the 1991 war and learning no lessons from it. And the correspondent would definitely have noticed that even after war became inevitable, the Iraqi army did not carry out a single military exercise to hone its preparedness.

These were questions that needed to be asked of the Iraqi authorities, of Bush and his advisers, of the ordinary people of Iraq, and of its professors and analysts. In a domestic story, journalists would have raised these doubts as a matter of course, if for no other reason then to make their 'story' more interesting. But when it came to Iraq, these questions and doubts were never raised because no one thought it necessary to entertain any scepticism about the 'coalition's' claims. The golden rule of responsible journalism, the obligation to check a story with those whom it harms, was discarded as casually as a worn-out pair of shoes.

As a result, Iraq and its people were deprived of a voice with which to address the world when they needed it most. During nine long months of mounting tension, as they wondered whether the US and UK would unleash a war upon their tired and starved nation, and who would live and who would die if they did, they waited in silent impotence.

The pronounced bias that had developed in the visual media in particular was revealed by a study of media coverage in five countries commissioned by the *Frankfurter Allgemeine Zeitung*. This study showed that dissenting voices on Iraq were given only 2 per cent of the airtime on BBC. It was somewhat higher on ABC in the USA, but the improvement was only relative, for ABC aired dissent during only 7 per cent of its airtime.[37] BBC's senior management actually cautioned its staff in a confidential memorandum dated 6 February to 'be careful' about voicing dissent. The network's head of news justified this on the grounds that this was partly because 'there was a degree of political consensus within Westminster, with the Conservatives supporting the government's policy on the war and the Liberal Democrats, while opposed to the war, supporting the UK forces.'[38] The BBC later became a champion of the peoples' right to know the truth. But it did so in a succession of postmortems, after the war was over and thousands of Iraqis were dead. During the build-up to the war, its world service in particular did not believe that either Iraq or the 700,000 to a million protesters who marched through London on 15 February 2003 deserved a voice.

Perhaps the most brazen demonstration of Iraq's insignificance in a matter that meant life or death to its people was the way CNN and BBC aired the debates in the UN Security Council over the reports of UNMOVIC and IAEA. Both would transmit, in full, the speeches of Blix and Baradei, and the comments of the US, the UK, France, Russia, and China or a non-permanent member. Then, over silent footage of the remaining members' speeches, they would bring in a succession of 'experts', from previous American administrations, from think-tanks and former military officers, who would air their understanding of what Blix and Baradei *actually meant*, while the foreign ministers of half a dozen countries went on speaking in the background unheard. Among those who were thus reduced, literally, to performing puppets, was the permanent representative of Iraq, the country whose fate hung in the balance.

When the US and UK failed to get sufficient support for a second resolution in the Security Council authorising them to declare war on Iraq, and decided to invade the country without it, the need to manufacture consent gained a new importance. Rumsfeld immediately dismissed France and Germany as 'old Europe'—old meaning weak and spineless. Bush elaborated on this theme, contrasting 'old' Europe to the 'new' Europe, in which he included the ten East European states that were to join the EU in 2004, all of which supported the invasion of a country that they had barely heard of. In an interview to the *Guardian*, Richard Perle, one of the original neo-conservative cabal, lashed out at Europe and France and Germany: 'I think Europe has lost its moral compass. Many Europeans have become so obsessed by the prospect of violence they have failed to notice who we are dealing with.'

Perle reserved his most scathing comments for Germany and Chancellor Gerhard Schröder's new anti-war stance. 'Germany has *subsided* into a *moral numbing pacifism*.' In an extraordinary feat of intellectual gymnastics, he said: 'For the German chancellor to say he will have nothing to do with action against Saddam Hussein, even if approved by the United Nations, is unilateralism.' France fared little better. When asked whether the French might not have shown signs of moral fibre, Perle said: 'I have seen diplomatic maneuver, but not moral fibre.'[39]

But even Perle's attack paled into insignificance when compared to the diatribe launched on France, Germany and the European Union (excluding Britain) by the far right. 'To the list of polities destined to slip down the Eurinal of history,' wrote Mark Steyn of *Jewish World*, 'we must add the European Union and France's Fifth Republic. The only question is how messy their disintegration will be.'[40]

A new stereotype of Europe quickly emerged. No longer was it the original home of American culture. Instead Europeans rapidly came to be regarded as 'weak, petulant, hypocritical, disunited, duplicitous, sometimes anti-Semitic, and often anti-American appeasers'.[41] The US Congress passed a resolution requiring its cafeteria to rename French fries as freedom fries. Terms like 'cheese-eating surrender monkey' and 'Euroweenies' came into instant use. The leitmotif running through all this was surprise, outrage and disdain.

The xenophobic reaction of American leaders and opinion makers showed that they were perfectly aware of the implications of this development. For the first time since the end of the Cold War, the US found its claim to the moral leadership of the 'civilised' world being challenged directly by countries that it could not dismiss as being 'rogue states', heathens or atavistic dictatorships. Enlisting the media therefore assumed an unprecedented importance. The story of what the US was going to do, why it was doing it, and all the good things that would come out of it *had to be told, and had to be told in the right way*. This led to a further refinement of the 'pool' system. This was the 'embedding' of journalists with the military formations. According to the BBC's director of news, Richard Sambrook, it 'changed the face of war reporting forever', and not necessarily for the better.[42]

The US government made no secret of its reasons for offering the incomparable facilities of 'embedment' to journalists covering the war:

> Media coverage of any future operation will, to a large extent, shape public perception of the national security environment now and in the years ahead This holds true for the US public; the public in allied countries whose opinion can affect the durability of our coalition; and publics in other countries where we conduct operations, whose perceptions of us can affect the cost and duration of our involvement. ... we need to tell them the factual story—good or bad—before others seed the media with disinformation and distortions, as they most certainly will continue to do. Our people need to tell our story ...'[43]

Notwithstanding the pious intention to allow journalists to report 'the factual story—good or bad', the Pentagon in practice took no chances with the stories that actually got out. In exchange for the privilege of obtaining visuals and sound bytes of guns firing, buildings being blown up, and aircraft rocketing ground targets with all the accompanying din of battle, embedded journalists had to sign an agreement to submit their copy and footage to the army authorities for clearance before they sent it to their parent organisations for dissemination.

The language used to justify the practice of embedding also revealed the change of the context in which the control had to be established. Its purpose was to 'shape public perception of the national security environment'. This was a tacit admission that people were not already persuaded that Iraq presented a threat to the US' security and that the persuasion had to continue. This had hardly been necessary when the US entered the Second World War, when it sent its troops to Korea, and later to Vietnam. However disastrous the last intervention turned out to be, doubts about the need for it arose only years after the troops had already gone in, when Americans began to perceive the quagmire in which they were trapped.

This time, by contrast, the media had not simply to report a war but to help the government to persuade the American people that it was both just and necessary. And it was not only the American public but the public in allied and 'target' countries who needed to be persuaded. In short, the purpose of 'embedment' was to ensure that the media persuaded its readers and viewers that what was good for the US was good for the whole world, *including the country that was being invaded*! There could have been no clearer exposition of the hegemonistic purpose of the exercise.

In view of what happened during the war, the most disturbing feature of the 'guidelines' was their implicit separation of the media into 'the good guys' (i.e., the embedded journalists) and the 'others'—the 'bad guys'— who would definitely try to 'seed the media with distortions and disinformation'. Who could these 'others' be? They could hardly include Iraq's information minister, whose claims, in his daily briefings, of the number of American tanks, armoured personnel carriers, and helicopters destroyed became the subject of black humour as the war progressed. The only 'others' were the non-embedded journalists—the so-called 'independents' and the crews of the Arab TV networks, Abu Dhabi TV and the Qatar-based Al Jazeerah—who stayed in Basra and Baghdad and were at the receiving end of the missiles, bombs, artillery shells, cluster bombs and rockets, and could therefore not help seeing and reporting things in a different way.

Despite the experience of the pool system in Iraq and Kosovo in the past, the vast majority of American newspapers welcomed the system of embedding journalists with the frontline forces.[44] But not content with having ensured that journalists would not see what the invading forces did not want them to see, the US authorities decided to stage appropriate pieces of theatre for them to see and report home. Two such dramas were 'the saving of Private Jessica Lynch' and 'the toppling of Saddam's statue'.

The Saving of Private Lynch

The story of Private Jessica Lynch's rescue could not have come at a more opportune moment. After the euphoria of the war's first few days, the Allied military campaign appeared to have stalled. In place of 'shock and awe', the media had begun to carry stories of Iraqi women and children being gunned down at checkpoints and US prisoners of war being paraded in front of cameras by their captors. The American public needed a morale booster. The saga of Jessica Lynch's capture and heroic rescue was exactly what they needed. It was the story of brutal Iraqi captors gloating over the capture of a young and beautiful girl, and torturing her after they had killed, probably in captivity, her comrades-in-arms; and of a heroic mid-night rescue by the US marines using all the awesome power of American technology to effect a bloodless rescue. Each and every component of this story was crafted to reinforce the impression of America's moral superiority; its God-given right to assume the championship of civilisation against the barbarian, its awesome technology and consequent invincibility. Offering resistance to such an elemental force was not only futile, but also morally wrong.

Only after the war ended did the true story of her capture and rescue come out. Far from having been mistreated, Jessica Lynch had been cared for selflessly by the Iraqi doctors at Nasiriyah, who even denied critically important equipment to their own wounded in order to ensure her recovery. Her nine captured colleagues had not been killed by Fidayeen in the hospital. They had been brought in dead. Here is the unvarnished account of one of the journalists who visited the hospital at Nasiriyah.

> All Hollywood could ever hope to have in a movie was there in this extraordinary feat of rescue—except, perhaps, the truth.
>
> So say three Nasiriya doctors, two nurses, one hospital administrator and local residents interviewed separately last week in a *Toronto Star* investigation.
>
> The medical team that cared for Lynch at the hospital formerly known as Saddam Hospital is only now beginning to appreciate how grand a myth was built around the four hours the U.S. raiding party spent with them early on April Fool's Day.
>
> And they are disappointed.
>
> For Dr. Harith Houssona, 24, who came to consider Lynch a friend after nurturing her through the worst of her injuries, the ironies are almost beyond tabulation.
>
> 'The most important thing to know is that the Iraqi soldiers and commanders had left the hospital almost two days earlier,' Houssona said. 'The night they

left, a few of the senior medical staff tried to give Jessica back. We carefully moved her out of intensive care and into an ambulance and began to drive to the Americans, who were just one kilometer away. But when the ambulance got within 300 meters, they began to shoot. There wasn't even a chance to tell them "We have Jessica. Take her."'

One night later, the raid unfolded. Hassam Hamoud, 35, a waiter at Nasiriya's al-Diwan Restaurant, describes the preamble, when he was approached outside his home near the hospital by U.S. Special Forces troops accompanied by an Arabic translator from Qatar.

'They asked me if any troops were still in the hospital and I said "No, they're all gone." Then they asked about Uday Hussein, and again, I said "No,"' Hamoud said. 'The translator seemed satisfied with my answers, but the soldiers were very nervous.'

At midnight, the sound of helicopters circling the hospital's upper floors sent staff scurrying for the X-ray department—the only part of the hospital with no outside windows. The power was cut, followed by small explosions as the raiding teams blasted through locked doors.

A few minutes later, they heard a man's voice shout, 'Go! Go! Go!' in English. Seconds later, the door burst open and a red laser light cut through the darkness, trained on the forehead of the chief resident.

'We were pretty frightened. There were about 40 medical staff together in the x-ray department,' said Dr. Anmar Uday, 24. 'Everyone expected the Americans to come that day because the city had fallen. But we didn't expect them to blast through the doors like a Hollywood movie.'

Dr. Mudhafer Raazk, 27, observed dryly that two cameramen and a still photographer, also in uniform, accompanied the U.S. teams into the hospital. Maybe this was a movie after all ...

'The whole thing lasted about four hours,' Raazk said. 'When they left, they turned to us and said "Thank you." That was it.'

The Iraqi medical staff fanned out to assess the damage. In all, 12 doors were broken, a sterilized operating theatre contaminated, and the specialized traction bed in which Lynch had been placed was trashed.

'That was a special bed, the only one like it in the hospital, but we gave it to Jessica because she was developing a bed sore,' Houssona said.

What bothers Raazk most is not what was said about Lynch's rescue, so much as what wasn't said about her time in hospital.

'We all became friends with her, we liked her so much,' Houssona said. 'Especially because we all speak a little English, we were able to assure her the whole time that there was no danger, that she would go home soon ...'

A few days after her release, Lynch's father told reporters none of the wounds were battle-related. The Iraqi doctors are more specific. Houssona said the injuries were blunt in nature, possible stemming from a fall from her vehicle.

What the American military was up to was revealed by a BBC correspondent, who followed the story further a few days later:

The American strategy was to ensure the right television footage by using embedded reporters and images from their own cameras, editing the film themselves. The Pentagon had been influenced by Hollywood producers of reality TV and action movies, notably the man behind *Black Hawk Down*, Jerry Bruckheimer. Bruckheimer advised the Pentagon on the primetime television series 'Profiles from the Front Line', that followed US forces in Afghanistan in 2001. That approach was taken on and developed on the field of battle in Iraq.[45]

The Fall of Saddam's Statue

On 9 April, the war had been going on for three weeks. American forces were in Baghdad and were meeting little resistance. The only question that remained in people's minds was to what extent Saddam Hussein would resort to scorched-earth tactics in Baghdad, mining roads and blowing up bridges to kill as many Americans as possible before the inevitable end. Then suddenly the electrifying news flashed across the world that the war was over. The people of Baghdad had risen at last against the hated dictator, and themselves ended his regime. The symbol of their revolt was their pulling down of Saddam's statue in Firdous Square, at the heart of the city. According to the commentary carried by BBC and CNN, the crowds had come to the square, tried to pull down Saddam's statue and, when this proved difficult, had asked a US marine vehicle standing nearby to help them do so. They had then attached a cable to the statue, and the vehicle had obligingly pulled it down. The crowd had then attacked the head and body, broken it up and carried bits away.

The video footage of this event was flashed on television screens all over the world every few minutes till it became the icon of the war and perhaps the most frequently viewed teleclip in the world after the image of two aircraft hitting the World Trade Towers on 9/11 and bringing them down. The images exerted a powerful influence on peoples' minds. Most believed the commentary. Even the correspondent of the sober and anti-war *Guardian* felt obliged to endorse the view that people were at last coming out and expressing their joy at being liberated.[46]

In fact the crowd was small. And the entire event was staged by the US military authorities. Photographs taken from the adjoining Palestine Hotel, where nearly all the independent journalists in Baghdad were staying, show upon close examination that

- There had been no crowd in Firdous Square around the statue when a number of tanks, a US mechanised vehicle (MV) and several Humvees descended upon it.
- Three, possibly four, tanks took up positions around the square, guns facing *outwards*. Interspersed between them were American soldiers,

also facing outwards. They were clearly there to guard whatever was going on in the square and whoever was doing it.

- In the square there were only a handful of people, estimated at 150–200, including a large number of US soldiers. The Iraqis did not number more than a hundred. They were joined by the mechanised vehicle.
- The handful of Iraqis threw a rope over the statue for the MV to pull down. After some false starts, a US marine put an old Iraqi flag over Saddam's face. The Recovery Vehicle then pulled down the statue.[47]

An account given by Neville Watson, a clergyman from Australia and peace activist, who was less than 300 yards away, in a video-conferenced interview with Alan Sutherland of the *Information Clearing House* internet newspaper, tallied closely with the above reconstruction.[48]

Who were the members of this crowd? And who organised them? Two photographs, among the thousands taken during the war, exposed the entire episode as an American drama. The first, taken on 6 April, showed Ahmad Chalabi, the head of the Iraqi National Congress, arriving in Nasiriyah with 700 of his 'free Iraqi Forces' aboard four C-17 aircraft. Immediately behind him was an aide with a round face, receding hairline, arched eyebrows and a stylishly shaped beard and moustache. The second, taken on 9 April, showed the same aide raising his hand towards the camera in a V for Victory sign. This picture was taken at Firdous Square during the toppling of Saddam's statue and aired all over the world. How did a close associate of Chalabi travel from Nasiriyah to Baghdad in the middle of the war? And why did he do so? The answer is obvious: the Americans brought him to rent the crowd that toppled Saddam's statue.[49]

Good Journalists and Bad Journalists

Perhaps the worst long-term damage that the embedding system did was to create the belief in the minds of soldiers feeling the stress of battle that those who were not with them were against them. This led to independent journalists being shut out from contact with the soldiers and, more detrimentally, from entire areas under US or UK control. Not surprisingly, in view of their challenge to US hegemony, the prime sufferers were Arab journalists and correspondents from the European countries that had opposed the invasion. This led the European Broadcasters Union to accuse the Military Field Information Centre in southern Iraq of having created a caste system among war correspondents. One among several examples was its refusal to feed French footage out of its equipment to France-2 in Paris. According to Tony Naets, the EBU's head of news, 'They have created a caste system with embedded journalists—usually from countries in the so-called coalition who can associate with the troops—and the truly independent broadcaster who is prevented from coming anywhere near the news.'[50]

This feeling, at a subconscious level, may explain the repeated attacks that journalists came under from US forces in Iraq. In all 17 journalists lost their lives[51] in the three-week war. Almost half were killed not by the Iraqis but by the US military. This made the death rate among journalists, despite their non-combatant status, about 20 times higher than among the American and British armies.[52] The casualties began with three reporters and camera crew of the British television network ITN. It climaxed with an American tank firing a shell deliberately into the Palestine hotel, an attack with two missiles on the offices of Al Jazeerah, and another on Abu Dhabi TV, in two separate buildings. The Palestine Hotel was where all the independent journalists in Baghdad were staying. By the last days of the war it had become one of the best-known buildings in the world because it was the location from which the BBC and other independent channels were sending their telecasts. Two cameramen of Reuters were killed at the hotel. Al Jazeerah lost its chief reporter, Tarek Ayoub, who had just taken over the Baghdad office and was in the middle of a broadcast when he died. Of the 15 officially declared dead at the end of April, three had been killed by the Iraqis; five died in genuine accidents and seven were killed by Americans.[53]

Notes

1. Timothy Garton Ash, 'Anti-Europeanism in America', *The New York Review*, 13 February 2003.
2. This was rather obviously the reason why Saddam Hussein continued to pretend that he might still have some weapons of mass destruction, when in fact he had none. It is almost certainly the reason why North Korea and possibly Iran are racing to acquire nuclear weapons capability. Neither country believes that it can survive a nuclear exchange with the US or Israel. But both believe that possession of nuclear weapons and a willingness to use them if attacked will prevent the kind of aerial attacks that Iraq had been subjected to ever since 1981.
3. Peter Galbraith, *The Guardian*, 11 October 2004.
4. Lake reserved for the United States alone the right to decide when it would use force and how it would do so: 'When we do act, we will do so with others when we can, but alone when we must.' He also rejected the proposition that the US should assert a sphere of influence in its own hemisphere and in limited areas abroad, and leave to others the task of maintaining stability and order in their own spheres. 'We recognise that all nations have greater concerns for their immediate surroundings than they do for distant regions. *But as a great nation whose interests and ideals are global in scope*, we cannot—and will not—cede to others a right to intervene as they wish in the affairs of their neighbours without regard to international norms (Speech at the Kennedy School of Government, October 1994).

5. C. Boggs, *Gramsci's Marxism* (London, Pluto Press, 1976). This definition of the term is by Antonio Gramsci.
6. Giovanni Arrighi, *The Long Twentieth Century. Money, Power and the Origins of our Times* (London and New York, Verso, 1994), pp. 27–29 (emphasis added).
7. Associated Press, 'Poll: Bush should wait on Iraq', 7 October 2002.
8. The opinion polls were tracked religiously by the *Economist* in various issues in late 2002 and 2003. Only in Britain did the opposition weaken and turn into a lukewarm support for 'our boys in uniform' when it became apparent that war was only days away.
9. Ignacio Ramonet, 'Illegal Aggression' (*Le Monde Diplomatique*, April 2003).
10. Appeal by eminent jurists on international law concerning the recourse to the use of force against Iraq (Universite Libre de Bruxelles, *Le Monde Diplomatique*, April 2003).
11. This definition is taken from Gramsci. By hegemony, Gramsci meant the permeation *throughout* society of an entire system of values, attitudes, beliefs and morality that has the effect of supporting the status quo in power relations. (Boggs, *Gramsci's Marxism*). Drawing on this, Giovanni Arrighi has defined international hegemony as follows:

> The concept of world hegemony adopted here ... refers specifically to the power of a state to exercise the functions of leadership and governance over a system of sovereign states. In principle this power may involve just the ordinary management of such a system as instituted at a given time. Historically, however, the government of a system of sovereign states has always involved some kind of transformative action, which changed the mode of operation of the system in a fundamental way.

Arrighi distinguished sharply between 'hegemonic power', and 'dominance'. The former was

> something more and different from 'dominance' pure and simple. It is the power associated with dominance *expanded by the exercise of intellectual and moral leadership* ... Whereas dominance will be conceived of as resting primarily on coercion, hegemony will be understood as the *additional* power that accrues to a dominant group by virtue of its capacity to place all issues around which conflict rages on a 'universal' plane.

The claim of a dominant group to represent the general interest is always more or less fraudulent. Nevertheless ... we shall speak of hegemony only when the claim is at least partly true and adds something to the power of the dominant group. *A situation in which the claim of the dominant group to represent the general interest is purely fraudulent will be defined as a situation not of hegemony but of the failure of hegemony* [emphases added] (Arrighi, *The Long Twentieth Century*, pp. 27–29).

12. The phrase was coined by Walter Lippman who argued that a 'revolution in the art of democracy' could be used to manufacture consent. See Noam Chomsky, *Media Control. The Spectacular Achievements of Propaganda*, 2nd Edition (New York, Seven Stories Press, 2002), p. 14.
13. Chomsky, *Media Control*, p. 12.
14. For a detailed description of the way in which the US and UK sought to manufacture consent for their invasion of Iraq, and the way this unravelled in the months after the war, see Prem Shankar Jha, *The End of Saddam Hussein: History Through the Eyes of the Victims* (New Delhi, Rupa Books, 2003). For an updated account, see Prem Shankar Jha, *A Pawn of Empire: The Tragedy of Iraq* (London, Pluto Books, forthcoming).

15. See Chapter 11 for details of the Niger uranium story, and Chapter 13 for the '45 minutes' story.

16. For details of the agreement and its clandestine nature, see the official transcript of Ambassador April Glaspie's last interview with Saddam Hussein (*New York Times*, Sunday, 23 September 1990). One presumes that the *New York Times* checked the authenticity of the transcript with the State Department before publishing it.

    For the sharing of battlefield intelligence, see Richard Sale, 'Saddam was key in early CIA plot', *Information Clearing house* (e-newspaper), 11 April 2003, available at: www.informationclearinghouse.info/article2849.htm. UPI interviewed almost a dozen former US diplomats, British scholars and former US intelligence officials to piece together the above account. The CIA declined to comment on the report.

    For the supply of weapons, dual-use equipment and bacterial strains, see Joyce Battle (ed.), 'Shaking Hands with Saddam Hussein: The U.S. Tilts toward Iraq, 1980–1984 (National Security Archive Electronic Briefing Book No. 82, 25 February 2003, available at: www.gwu.edu/~nsarchiv/NSAEBB/NSAEBB82/index.htm). For a detailed analysis of the credibility and importance of the Iraqgate story, see article in the *Columbia Journalism Review*, March-April 1993, available at: www.cjr.org/year/93/2/iraqgate.asp. See also Prem Shankar Jha, *The End of Saddam Hussein*.

17. Stephen C. Pelletiere, 'A war crime or an act of war', *New York Times*, 31 January 2003.

18. Brian Appleyard, 'Blair demands overthrow of Saddam as millions march. Streets of London paved with protest', *Sunday Times*, 16 February 2003.

19. Ibid.; Tony Allen-Mills, David Cracknell and Sarah Baxter, 'The Other Man Under Siege', *Sunday Times*, 16 February 2003.

20. Jane Morse, 'U.S. Sees Political, Religious Freedom Growing Quickly in Iraq State Dept. spokesman discusses Iraq, France' (US Department of State International Information Programs, 23 April 2003).

21. In the Iraqi official transcript of Saddam Hussein's talks with US Ambassador April Glaspie on 25 July 1990, Saddam reminded Glaspie, 'The decision to establish relations with the U.S. were [sic] taken in 1980 during the two months *prior* to the war between us and Iran.' His next sentence gave away the reason for the concealment: 'When the war started, and *to avoid misinterpretation*, we postponed the establishment of relations hoping that the war would end soon.' Why did the US choose this moment to re-establish relations with Iraq? And why, if it was not related to the war with Iran, had it to be covert? What misinterpretation was the US so anxious to avoid? These questions were never asked.

22. There were notable exceptions, like John Pilger of the *Guardian* and Robert Fisk of the *Independent*, but these were few and far between and their voices were drowned in the tidal wave of skilfully orchestrated condemnation.

23. John Pilger, *Hidden Agendas* (New York, Vintage Press, 1998), p. 44.

24. This perceptive comment was made by Greg Philo and Greg McLaughlin, in a review of the reporting of the war quoted in Pilger, *Hidden Agendas*, p. 45.

25. Pilger, *Hidden Agendas*, p. 48.

26. Ibid.

27. Ibid., p. 46.

28. Robert Fisk, 'Journalists must always fight spin', *The Independent*, 17 January 2003.

29. Tim Laughland, 'The massacres that never were', *The Spectator*, October 1999.

30. Press release by the IWCTY on or around December 10, carried by National Public Radio in the US. George Robertson, Secretary-General of NATO, also gave the figure of around 2,000 on 3 December (see George Robertson, 'Things are getting better in

Kosovo so don't pick holes in its reconstruction', *The Independent*, 3 December 1999). See also Chapter 10 of this book.

31. Laughland, 'The massacres that never were'.

32. Hans Blix, *Disarming Iraq: The Search for Weapons of Mass Destruction* (Bloomsbury, 2004), p. 82.

33. This estimate has been given by John Pilger in *The New Statesman*, 15 April 2004.

34. Associated Press, 'Chronic poverty in Iraq may worsen', 19 June 2003.

35. Mona Megalli and Peg Mackey, 'US says donors must come to the aid of Iraq', Reuters, 21 June 2003.

36. UNICEF and Government of Iraq, Ministry of Health, 'Child and Maternal mortality Survey 1999. Preliminary report.' Available at: www.fas.org/news/iraq/1999/08/990812-unicef.htm.

37. David Miller, 'Taking sides', *The Guardian*, 22 April 2003.

38. Ibid.

39. Edward Pilkington and Ewen McAskill, 'Europe lacks moral fibre, says US hawk', *The Guardian*, 13 November 2002.

40. Garton Ash, 'Anti-Europeanism in America'.

41. Ibid.

42. Ciar Byrne, 'War reporting "changed forever", says BBC', *The Guardian*, 31 March 2003.

43. Memorandum containing guidelines for 'guidance, policies, and procedures on embedding news media during possible future operations/deployments in the CENTCOM AOR (issued by the US Secretary of Defense, February 2003), available at: www.defenselink.mil/news/Feb2003/d20030228pag.pdf.

44. Robert Fisk, 'How the news will be censored in this war', *The Independent*, 25 February 2003.

45. John Kampfner, 'Saving Private Lynch story flawed', BBC news programme 'Correspondent', 15 May 2003.

46. *Guardian*, 'The Toppling of Saddam – An end to thirty years of brutal rule', *Guardian*, 10 April 2003.

47. The photos were taken by a Reuters cameraman. These and the description given above are available at: www.informationclearinghouse.info/article2842.htm.

48. 'The Toppling Of Saddam Statue: An Eyewitness Report', SBS TV Australia, 17 April 2003, available at: www.informationclearinghouse.info/article3024.htm.

49. www.informationclearinghouse.info/article2842.htm

50. Ciar Byrne, 'Independents "frozen out" by armed forces', *The Guardian*, 3 April 2003.

51. Phillip Knightley, 'Turning the tanks on the reporters', *The Guardian*, 15 June 2003. At the time of writing two of them were still listed as 'missing'.

52. The total number of soldiers killed was less than 200 out of 200,000. But 17 out of less than 800 journalists were killed—more than one in fifty. If one calculates the ratio of independent journalists, it would be many times higher still.

53. Ciar Byrne, 'US soldiers were main danger to journalists, says Simpson', *The Guardian*, 27 June 2003.

13

LOSS OF HEGEMONY

Two and a half years after the invasion of Iraq, it was apparent that the US' bid to replace the Westphalian international order with an empire on the basis of military might alone was in deep trouble. The insurgency in Iraq was out of control and a civil war was about to break out. Many reporters who had visited Iraq said that it had already begun.[1] A clear majority of the American public had realised the US was caught in a quagmire that was beginning to resemble Vietnam, and wanted the troops to leave as soon as possible. The US' preoccupation with Iraq had enabled North Korea to go nuclear and get away with it, and had reduced America's ability to stop Iran from following suit. But most importantly, the US had lost the hegemonic position it had occupied over six decades, from the start of the Second World War.

Until the attack upon Iraq, its claim to *hegemonic power* in the era of global capitalism was beyond challenge. The US already enjoyed the hegemony of the 'American century'. It had played a crucial role in defeating Germany and fascism in the Second World War. It had made generous use of Marshall Plan aid to put Germany and much of Europe back on its feet. It had protected Western Europe from the threat of a Soviet invasion during the immediate post-war years, and it had led the capitalist world during the Cold War.

It was therefore the one country that could play the transformative role of the hegemonic power during capitalism's fifth cycle of expansion. In 1982 it led the shift from trade liberalisation by consensus to liberalisation through coercion, which characterised the Uruguay round of GATT. After the Cold War, the US again took the lead, this time in restricting the sovereignty of nation states.

The crusading role that the US began to carve for itself created a great deal of unease in Europe. But American hegemony remained intact so long as the US worked through the UN Security Council. It even survived the aerial bombardment of Serbia and the invasion of Afghanistan because the world accepted the moral justification it gave for it, and because the attack was endorsed by all the members of the Atlantic Alliance. But, in a single stroke, its unilateral decision to invade Iraq split the Alliance and destroyed the hegemony it had built over the previous six decades. This was not only because the action was taken in the face of unambiguous opposition in the Security Council but because this was the second application of the Bush National Security Doctrine of preventive (not pre-emptive) intervention in just three years, and one for which no other justification (such as bringing retribution down on Al Qaeda) could be found. Its allies could not therefore pretend not to notice the longer-term consequences of the new security doctrine. When peace was maintained through deterrence, a state could maintain its independence by not disturbing the status quo. By taking away this option, Bush's new security doctrine deprived a country of control over it's own destiny. It also wiped out the hard line that had divided war from peace in the past. As a result, even the US' closest former allies began to feel like bullfighters who were no longer sure that their capes would distract the bull.

Despite this the US may have been able to re-establish its hegemony if the coalition forces had found weapons of mass destruction in Iraq. But they did not. And as week followed week without any discovery of secret arms caches, even the tepid consent that Bush and Blair had managed to build for the invasion began to unravel.

The Unravelling of Consent

Where are the Weapons of Mass Destruction?

Thanks to the US Secretary of Defense Donald Rumsfeld's addiction to plain speaking, it is possible to put a precise date to when that consent began to unravel. This was 27 May 2003, just 48 days after the fall of Baghdad. On that date, Rumsfeld admitted that the US inspectors had not found any weapons of mass destruction and *might never find them* because *they may have been destroyed before the war*.[2]

Rumsfeld's admission let the genie out of the bottle. Within days intelligence agencies on both sides of the Atlantic disclosed that their reports had been deliberately distorted by their political masters to create the impression that Iraq definitely had weapons of mass destruction, and thereby create a case for an invasion of the country.

In Britain the first rumblings of discontent had surfaced before the invasion on 7 February 2003, when Whitehall officials protested that the intelligence material being provided by MI6 and other agencies was being used selectively by Downing Street to make a case for invasion. This had been provoked by the disclosure the previous day that a British 'intelligence' report handed to the Americans a few days earlier, and cited with approval by Colin Powell in his speech to the Security Council two days earlier, had been cobbled together from bits and pieces of published material including a 1999 Ph.D. dissertation by an American student named Al Marashi. Other parts had been lifted from a book published in 1999, titled *Saddam's Secrets*, by one Tim Trevan. The entire paper had been concocted in the same Coalition Information Centre in the prime minister's office, headed by his media adviser, Alastair Campbell, which had disseminated the story about Iraq's purchases of uranium yellow cake from Niger. Downing Street was in such haste to keep up with the Bush administration in the making of a case for invasion that it was not dissuaded from using El Marashi's piece, even though it very obviously referred to Iraq's activities a decade earlier. This disclosure prompted several MPs including Glenda Jackson, a former Labour minister, to protest that the government was misleading parliament and the public. 'And of course to mislead,' Jackson told Radio 4's *Today* programme, 'is a parliamentary euphemism for lying.'[3]

Rumsfeld's admission unleashed another attempt by the British intelligence agencies to protect their tarnished reputations. Through unsourced leaks in the media they made it known that MI6 and GCHQ, Britain's eavesdropping centre, had as long back as autumn 2002 opposed the misuse of their intelligence inputs to push the case for war. A key example was the assertion in the dossier presented to parliament on Iraq's weapons of mass destruction—that Iraq had, and could deploy chemical weapons within 45 minutes of being ordered to do so. The body of the report was guarded in its conclusions: 'intelligence indicates that the Iraqi military are able to deploy chemical or biological weapons within 45 minutes of an order to do so'. This was converted by Prime Minister Tony Blair in the foreword to the September 24 report into 'discloses that *[Saddam's] military planning allows* for some of the WMD [weapons of mass destruction] to be ready within 45 minutes of an order to use them'. The prime minister's office had changed an estimate of capability into evidence of concrete military planning for the use of weapons of mass destruction. As later disclosures proved, even the original assessment had been virtually forced into the report by relentless cajoling from the prime minister's office.

The first serious allegation of deceit to appear in the British media came from Andrew Gilligan, defence correspondent of the BBC. In BBC's *Today* programme at 6:07 am on 29 May 2003, in response to a question about Tony Blair's assertion that Iraq had WMD that would be 'ready to go in 45 minutes', Gilligan said the following:

> ... what we've been told by one of the senior officials in charge of drawing up that dossier was that actually the government probably knew that the 45-minute figure was wrong even before they decided to put it in. What this person says is that a week before the publication date of the dossier it was actually rather a bland production. ... The draft prepared for Mr. Blair by the intelligence agencies actually didn't say very much more than was public knowledge already and Downing Street, our source says, ... ordered, a week before publication, ... it to be sexed up, to be made more exciting and ordered more facts to be discovered.[4]

In response to a question about what facts were to be 'discovered', Gilligan went on to elaborate as follows:

> Well, our source says that the dossier, as it was finally published, made the Intelligence Services unhappy, because ... it didn't reflect, the considered view they were putting forward ... The forty-five minute point ... was probably the most important thing that was added. And the reason it hadn't been in the original draft was that it ... only came from one source and most of the other claims were from two, and the intelligence agencies say they don't really believe it was necessarily true because they thought the person making the claim had actually made a mistake ... had got mixed up.[5]

The allegation brought a blistering response from the government within minutes to the effect that 'not one word of the dossier was not entirely the work of the intelligence agencies.'[6] On 25 June, testifying before the Foreign Affairs Select Committee of parliament, Campbell said with a flourish: 'I simply say in relation to the BBC story: it is a lie, it was a lie, it is a lie that is continually repeated and until we get an apology for it I will keep making sure that parliament, people like yourselves and the public know that it was a lie.'[7] On 25 June Campbell did not know that 22 days later David Kelly would commit suicide, and that in the inquiry that followed, the murky role that the Prime Minister's office played, first in the preparation of the dossier and then in the 'outing' of David Kelly, would get fully exposed.

In the inquiry that followed Kelly's suicide, although Lord Hutton fully exonerated the government and the prime minister's office of Gilligan's 6:07 am charge of having 'sexed up the dossier by adding the 45 minute claim', the wealth of detail that emerged convinced all but a minority of the British public that it had been knowingly misled to by its government.

All that Lord Hutton did was to exonerate the prime minister's office of the charge of having concocted the 45-minute claim in Downing Street.

A close look at the documents that Hutton himself saw leads to the conclusion that the prime minister's office had gone much, much further than giving John Scarlett 'drafting suggestions'. They revealed that Tony Blair had not been satisfied with the first draft, because it contained nothing that would portray Saddam as an imminent threat, and a great deal that showed that he was not. The memos from the PM's office also showed that there was pressure upon the drafting team to find some 'real material', i.e., something new, that would give the dossier the sense of urgency that it lacked. The JIC did not have to insert a lie because a convenient piece of information, relayed by someone who might have been telling a lie, was conveniently at hand. All the JIC had to do, upon coaxing by the PM's office, was not to look too closely at its origin and reliability, and insert it. Thus while Lord Hutton rightly exonerated the prime minister's office of having *inserted* the 45 minute claim when it knew that it was wrong, his inquiry confirmed that Blair's office had indeed pushed and pushed the intelligence agencies till they used material they had initially rejected as worthless. In a broader sense, therefore, the PMO did indeed 'sex up' the report to make a case for war.[8]

The documents and e-mails unearthed by the Hutton Commission revealed precisely how this pressure was applied. On 17 September, seven days before the dossier was presented to parliament, the following e-mail was sent by Jonathan Powell, Blair's chief of staff, to John Scarlett, the chief draftsman of the dossier:

> The dossier is good and convincing for those who are prepared to be convinced. I have only three points ... First, the document does nothing to demonstrate a threat, let alone an imminent threat from Saddam. In other words it shows he has the means but it does not demonstrate that he has the motive to attack his neighbours let alone the west. We will need to make it clear in launching the document that we do not claim that we have evidence that he is an imminent threat. The case we are making is that he has continued to develop WMD since 1998 and is in breach of UN resolutions. The International community has to enforce those resolutions if the UN is to be taken seriously.[9]

Two days later Powell was still not satisfied with Scarlett's revisions:

> Found my copy. ... I think the statement on p. 19 that 'Saddam is prepared to use chemical and biological weapons if he believes his regime is under threat' is a bit of a problem. It backs up the Don MacIntyre argument that there is no CBW threat and we will only create one if we attack him. I think you should redraft this para. *My memory of the intelligence is that he has set up plans to use CBW and that these weapons are integrated into the military planning.*[10]

Those familiar with the rituals of bureaucratic communication know that phrases like 'I think you should', and 'my memory of', coming from the prime minister's chief of staff, are not suggestions but instructions on what to do and what to remember.

Hutton's verdict, delivered in January 2004, gave the Blair government a reprieve but the British public did not prove so easy to mollify. Two opinion polls, carried out hours after the verdict, showed that in one case 50 per cent of Britons thought Hutton's conclusions were unconvincing (49 per cent considered it a whitewash job), and in the other case 67 per cent thought that it had not got to the truth.[11]

Kelly's suicide proved a turning point for Blair. In a rowdy House of Commons session on 16 July 2003, the Conservative leader, Ian Duncan Smith, told Mr. Blair, 'You are rapidly becoming a stranger to the truth … You have created a culture of deceit and spin at the heart of government.' Other MPs bellowed disapproval, waved their papers in the air and accused him of having 'duped' them into going to war.[12] By mid-August, only four months after the invasion, Blair's credibility had sunk even further to the lowest point in his six years in office. An opinion poll showed that two out of three Britons believed that Blair had deceived Britain about Iraq's weapons of mass destruction.[13]

Growing Scepticism in America

The absence of WMD in Iraq also came as a shock to the American public. Mohammad El Baradei's decisive refutation of the Niger uranium story on 7 March had touched off a wave of investigations by journalists. Unfortunately for Iraq, the reports came out after the invasion was over, but they showed that the forgery may have originated in a British programme on spreading disinformation called the Information Operations (I/Ops). When the British report on Iraq's WMD came out, the IAEA had repeatedly asked the British government for copies of the concerned letters, but had been refused. The Americans had however obtained them, and the IAEA eventually obtained them from the Iraq Nuclear Verification Office in the Bush administration.[14]

Seymour Hersh, who first broke the story, left open the possibility that the US had been duped. But a subsequent news report filed by Nicholas Kristoff in the *New York Times* disclosed that the US had known that the documents were fakes at least since February 2002, but had still decided to use the canard to persuade Congress to declare war on Iraq.[15] This was confirmed first in a book and then in an op-ed page article in the *New York Times* on 6 July 2003 by Joseph Wilson, a former US ambassador who had served in Africa, and had been asked by the vice-president's office to visit

Niger and investigate the allegation. Wilson disclosed an even more damning fact: there had been two previous investigations by Barbro Owens-Kirkpatrick, an American ambassador to Niger, and Carleton Fulford, a Marine Corps general. Both had found that the Iraq-Niger story was not credible.[16]

Rumsfeld's admission, which coincided with Hersh and Kristoff's revelations, triggered a burst of anger in Washington among senior former members of the CIA and the military's Defense Intelligence Agency. Patrick Lang, a former head of worldwide human intelligence gathering for the Defense Intelligence Agency, believed that the DIA was 'exploited and abused and bypassed in the process of making the case for war in Iraq based on the presence of WMD.' He said that the CIA had 'no guts at all' to resist the deliberate skewing of intelligence by a Pentagon that was now dominating US foreign policy. Vince Cannistraro, a former chief of Central Intelligence Agency counter-terrorist operations, said that serving intelligence officers blamed the Pentagon for playing up 'fraudulent' intelligence, 'a lot of it sourced from the Iraqi National Congress of Ahmad Chalabi.' 'There are current intelligence officials who believe it is a scandal,' he said, and who believed that the administration, before going to war, had a 'moral obligation to use the best information available, not just information that fits your preconceived ideas.'[17]

The most direct and damaging attack came from Ray McGovern, a former CIA analyst with 25 years experience, who headed an organisation of former intelligence officials that had written both to President Bush and Kofi Annan protesting against the abuse of intelligence to start a war against Iraq. In a news analysis programme on BBC World Service TV news on 3 June 2003, McGovern accused the Bush administration of lying to Congress to hustle it into passing the war powers resolution on 11 October 2002. The brazen doctoring of intelligence inputs to force the country to arrive at a pre-determined conclusion was done by a group of persons at the Department of Defense, whom he referred to derisively as 'the cabal'.

Bush did his best to turn attention away from the storm that Rumsfeld had kicked up by asking to public to turn its attention to the future. 'My opinion is that we must work together to improve the lives of the Iraqi citizens, that we must cooperate closely to make sure that the Iraqi infrastructure is in place so that Iraqi citizens can live decently.'[18] But by then the damage had been done. Congressmen had become deeply uneasy about the possibility that they might have been knowingly duped by the administration. Henry Waxman, a Democratic senator from California, wrote a 40-page letter to President Bush making the same charges and demanding the same explanations as McGovern.[19]

Trust in the Bush administration received another blow when it became known that shortly after Wilson wrote his article in the *New York Times* on 6 July 2003, in an act of distilled vindictiveness, Cheney's office leaked it to the press that his wife Valerie Plame was an undercover CIA agent, and thereby ended her career and, to some degree, endangered her life.[20] Two years later. Judith Miller, the correspondent of the *New York Times* who had published the story, finally revealed the name of her informant. It turned out to be 'Scooter Libby', chief of Cheney's office. But Libby in turn revealed that he had been prompted to take this action by none other than Bush's closest political adviser, the *eminence grise* of the White House, Karl Rove.[21] The only conceivable rationale for such a vindictive act was that it was intended to serve as a warning to other potential whistleblowers of the punishments that they could bring upon themselves and their families if they followed the dictates of their conscience. It underlined the desperation that was seizing the White House as the fabric of half-truths, exaggeration and outright lies that it had built to make the case for invasion began to unravel.

Trust in Bush waned further when the Iraq Survey Group chief, David Kay, admitted that there probably were no WMD to be found in Iraq. The first intimation that a quiet burial was in the offing came at the end of August, when a senior member of the team admitted to the *Los Angeles Times* that the Group did not expect to find anything. 'We were prisoners of our own beliefs,' he told the *LA Times*. 'We said Saddam Hussein was a master of denial and deception. Then when we couldn't find anything, we said that proved it, instead of questioning our own assumptions.'[22]

On 2 October 2003, David Kay, the chief of the Iraq Survey Group (ISG), submitted an 'interim' report to the intelligence committees of both houses of the US Congress, stating that the Group had not found any weapons. However carefully it left the possibility of future finds open, the report hinted that there might be no weapons to find. On biological weapons it claimed to have unearthed a network of clandestine laboratories which seemed to be designed to preserve the expertise needed to resume production of biological weapons, but no such weapons had been found.[23] On chemical weapons Kay said that with 600,000 tons of munitions to be checked, the ISG had not had the time or the manpower to come to a definite conclusion either way about whether any weapons still existed. But the report inadvertently conceded that in the autumn of 2002, Iraq had neither mustard gas nor Sarin for use in weapons in case it was invaded.[24]

The ISG's report was however rich in innuendo, e.g., 'We have been struck that two senior Iraqi officials volunteered that if they had been ordered to resume CW production Iraq *would have been willing* to use stainless steel systems that would be disposed of after a few production runs, in place of corrosion-resistant equipment which they did not have.'[25] The obvious conclusion to be drawn from this report was that they had not been asked to go ahead with chemical weapons production. But Kay chose to emphasise the opposite, i.e., that the capability was present in Iraq to do so if it wanted to.

The report thus gave the impression that while Iraq did not have any WMDs, it had had every intention of developing them once again, whenever the opportunity arose. President Bush capitalised upon this 'open window' to assert that the ISG had found definite proof of Iraq's intention to violate the ban on the production of WMD, and so the invasion was justified. 'The report (by Kay's team) states that Saddam Hussein's regime had a clandestine network of biological laboratories, a live strain of deadly agent botulinum, sophisticated concealment efforts and advanced design work on prohibited longer-range missiles,' Bush said on 4 October, before starting a day-long trip to Milwaukee.[26]

But the report has to be seen against the circumstances in which the ISG had been set up, and Kay's own background. First, the credibility of the US and its claim to hegemony hung on David Kay finding these weapons. Telling the government and Congress that they had been wrong all along, and that thousands of people, including hundreds of Americans, had died for nothing because of their faulty decisions was not easy.

Second, David Kay's own past history made recantation exceptionally painful for him. Kay had been a tough, aggressive weapons inspector with IAEA in 1991–92, and had, through his confrontational style of working, unearthed Iraq's clandestine uranium enrichment programme, for which he had been awarded the IAEA's Distinguished Service Award. But through the 1990s, after leaving the IAEA in January 1992, Kay had become a vehement critic of the UN's inspection process, and systematically belittled its capacity to find the 'smoking guns'.

In January 2003, in an article in the *Washington Post*, Kay wrote: 'When it comes to UN inspections in Iraq, looking for a smoking gun is a fool's mission. That was true 11 years ago when I led the UN inspections there. It is no less true today. ... The answer is already clear. Iraq is in breach of UN demands that it dismantle its weapons of mass destruction.' Kay concluded by asserting that the only way to make sure Iraq had no more WMDs was to invade and occupy it. 'Let's not give it more time to cheat and retreat.'

This was the erstwhile warmonger who later had to admit that even with 1,400 inspectors and complete ownership of the bodies and souls of the Iraqi scientists involved in the WMD projects, he had found nothing but a few dual-use items of equipment that should, but had not been, declared, and some laboratories that might have been used to preserve bio-weapons know-how.

Kay was more forthright in his verbal declarations. When he announced his resignation as head of the ISG, he said that he did not want to continue searching for weapons of mass destruction because 'I don't think they existed'. When asked by the Senate Armed Services Committee to explain his resignation, he said, 'It turns out that we were all wrong, probably, in my judgment. And that is most disturbing.' This, and not the carefully qualified formal report of the ISG is what stayed in the minds of the public all over the world.[27]

No Link with Al Qaeda

America's attempt to re-establish its hegemony was further damaged when its investigators and the Coalition Provisional Authority failed to establish any link between Saddam and Al Qaeda. The media had become sceptical when reporters unearthed the fact that even while Bush had been instilling fear in the American public in speech after speech, saying that Iraq was on the point of handing over its weapons of mass destruction to Al Qaeda, he had all along been in possession of a national intelligence estimate that had concluded that there was no credible evidence of any link between Saddam and Al Qaeda.[28]

This scepticism deepened further after the publication of Ron Suskind's book, co-authored with former treasury secretary Paul O'Neill, *The Price of Loyalty*, and Richard Clarke's book, *Against All Enemies, Inside America's War on Terror*. Both O'Neill and Clarke's revelations showed beyond serious doubt that regime change in Iraq had been at the top of the Bush administration's agenda from virtually the day he became president. This reinforced the growing suspicion that the Al Qaeda link might also be as spurious as the attempt to buy uranium yellow cake from Niger. In an interview on the program 'Fresh Air', broadcast by National Public Radio on 14 January 2004, O'Neill said that Iraq had come up at the very first meeting of the National Security Council in January 2001. What had surprised him was not that it had come up but the relative placement of priority. 'I was surprised that Iraq had the highest priority. There were a lot of other things going on in the world, including the 50-year struggle in the Middle East (between Israel and Palestine).'

On the same programme, Ron Suskind, who wrote the book based upon his interactions with O'Neill, stated that Rumsfeld's notes to various people at that time justified the concentration on Iraq on the grounds that 'we need to make an example of Saddam to help guide the behaviour of other states.'[29]

Clarke's revelations were even more damning. His office had known that Al Qaeda was preparing to attack the United States ever since the 'millennium alert', when US intelligence agencies picked up signals that it was likely to plant bombs in hotels and other public places on New Year's Eve. The warning enabled US agencies to prevent two attacks and possibly disrupt plans for more. But Clarke was convinced that more was to come. Unfortunately he was unable to get anyone in the Bush White House to take him seriously. Instead, from the very beginning the Bush team was fixated on Iraq and belittled the threat from Al Qaeda. Cheney, whom he briefed that Al Qaeda was preparing an attack on the US, listened, and took several trips to the CIA headquarters, but spent most of his time there discussing Iraq. Clarke asked for a principals' (secretaries-level) meeting to brief the new team about Al Qaeda, but was told that in future he would not be dealing with the principals but would have to present his findings to a deputies (deputy secretaries) committee, which would brief the principals. Even the deputies meeting on Al Qaeda did not take place till April, after being scheduled and cancelled in February and March. At that meeting he met a wall of disinterest from the new team. Wolfowitz actually took offence at a comparison of Al Qaeda with the Holocaust, and referred to bin Laden as 'this little terrorist in Afghanistan'. National Security Adviser Condoleeza Rice asked Clarke to prepare a plan for shifting some of the anti-terrorism operational functions of his unit to a new agency that would be outside the National Security Council. The principals' meeting that Clarke had been asking for finally took place on 4 September 2001. By then it was far too late to avert the tragedy that was about to unfold. In any case, the meeting was a non-event.[30]

The absence of links between Saddam and Al Qaeda was finally confirmed by the 9/11 Commission, which presented its report in August 2004. But by then the rest of the world had already made up its mind that Iraq had no proscribed weapons and had not been building any. On the contrary, its armed forces had been so starved of conventional weaponry, and so low in morale, that they had chosen not to fight the invaders. It had made no plans to invade any neighbouring country, and had no connections with Al Qaeda.

Hegemony Cannot be Built Upon Failure

The rest of the world, and even the Iraqis, might have accepted this version of events over time if the American invasion had led to a distinct improvement in the lives of the Iraqis. Instead, what the invasion brought them was anarchy, misery and terror. During Saddam's reign, despite 12 years of sanctions, Iraqis had electric power, an abundant supply of gasoline, and, thanks in part to the UN's oil-for-food programme, enough to eat. Their streets were safe, their salaries and incomes were meagre but assured, and their currency, although depreciated, was stable. Schools and colleges were open, and girls attended them as freely as boys. There was not a hint of Islamic fundamentalism and the state, for all its oppressiveness, was un-flinchingly secular. In short, although Saddam's folly and the UN sanctions had dragged Iraq down from first-world affluence to third-world poverty, Iraq was still a functioning state. Most important of all, the system of financial circulation, which is the lifeblood of a market economy, had re-mained intact. People received their salaries and spent them. This created demand and income for others. The market economy, in short, flourished.

All this changed with the Americans' arrival. Within hours the central nervous system of the Iraqi state turned into mush and chaos reigned. Rioting and looting broke out immediately. In the first two days after Saddam's statue was pulled down, every one of the government's 139 or so public buildings, housing all its records and files, was swept clean. The poor erupted from the slums and began to systematically ransack the homes of the rich and the middle classes. Old scores began to be settled and the murder rate rocketed.

What caught the world's attention was the destruction of the Baghdad Museum of Archaeology, one of the greatest repositories of human anti-quities in the world. Ironically, the museum had only been reopened a year earlier, after the government decided that the threat of aerial bombard-ment by the Americans and British had receded! Robert Fisk's descrip-tion of the destruction epitomises the way in which Iraq itself has been destroyed:

> They lie across the floor in tens of thousands of pieces, the priceless antiquities of Iraq's history ... Our feet crunched on the wreckage of 5,000-year-old marble plinths and stone statuary and pots that had endured every siege of Baghdad, every invasion of Iraq throughout history—only to be destroyed when America came to 'liberate' the city.[31]

The looting and destruction of the Baghdad Archaeological Museum rivalled what the Taliban had done to the Kabul museum. In the worldwide outrage that followed, it turned out that American archaeologists and cur-ators of museums had warned the government of the danger of losing the priceless artefacts in the Baghdad museum, and urged it to prepare plans to protect it as soon as the troops entered Baghdad. Instead, as Fisk and other journalists reported, the American soldiers stood by as the museum was destroyed and ransacked, ignoring the agonised pleas of its staff to station at least one tank at the entrance. Instead, throughout the ensuing chaos, the building that the American troops guarded assiduously was the oil ministry.

But it was the country's descent into a state bordering anarchy that rapidly eroded whatever goodwill the Americans had garnered from over-throwing the Baathist regime. For months afterwards, the queues for gasoline even in Baghdad were often three miles long, with a waiting period of 8 hours to 24 hours. Power supply was intermittent, more off than on. Between 4 June and 19 June, delivery to Baghdad actually fell from 1300 MW to 800 MW.[32] The police simply vanished. As a result, within days all government buildings in Baghdad had been looted bare, as were all the hospitals and thousands of private homes. As for public safety, in the last week of May there were 70 murders in Baghdad—ten a day![33]

The most striking change was the insecurity that women had begun to feel in Iraqi cities. Kidnapping, rape and, for some, execution by their own relatives for having been raped (so-called 'honour killing') became their fate. 'Under Saddam we could drive, we could walk down the street until two in the morning,' a young designer told Lauren Sandler of *the New York Times*. 'Who would have thought the Americans could have made it worse for women? This is liberation?'[34]

A first-hand account of his feelings given to Medea Benjamin of the NGO 'Occupation Watch' by 'Mohamad' (a fictional name), an Iraqi army deserter who welcomed the Americans and was plying a taxi in Baghdad at the time of this interview, provides a flavour of what life had become in post-war Baghdad:

> No electricity means no traffic lights, so drivers do whatever they please. The few police back on the streets have no authority to enforce traffic regulations and no weapons to stop the carjackers. Entire sections of the city have been taken over by gangsters. And on top of it all, there are the US soldiers who block off streets with their tanks and cause huge traffic jams, or set up check points throughout the city and harass the drivers.[35]

The damage and misery could have been avoided if the Bush Adminis-tration had run a check with history. The neo-conservatives in the Pentagon were fond of citing Macarthur's transformation of Japan into a democracy. What they forgot was that Emperor Hirohito legitimised the American occupation for the Japanese people. In return, the Americans left the Japanese state structure largely intact, and worked through it to transform the country.

Nor did they learn from their own country's experience in Germany where, from Chancellor Adenauer downwards, the allies re-employed a large proportion of the administration of the Third Reich, not excluding the entire Gehlen organisation, which was made up almost entirely of former members of the Nazi intelligence apparatus. In Iraq, by contrast, the Americans made every mistake it was possible to make. Instead of reassuring people that their jobs were safe, and that they should come to work as usual and collect new identity papers in due course, even before they arrived in Baghdad they issued a list of nine top members of the Saddam regime whom they intended to try for war crimes. They also let it be known that they intended to purge the administration completely of all Baath party members, and that a list of around 2,000 officials had been prepared for this purpose.[36] The twin threats were enough to dismantle the entire administration of the country overnight, for in a country where the Baath party had for 35 years been the only avenue to power, this spelt the end of the bureaucracy. The police were similarly warned that they too would be purged. That was the end of the police. Reconstituting a new police and administration proved difficult and time-consuming. Till the end of May, the US authorities were running Baghdad with a mere 8,000 policemen. Not surprisingly, chaos prevailed.[37]

As for the army, it too was disbanded wholesale. In July, after two months of suspense over its fate, the L. Paul Bremer government announced that soldiers should collect $50 as severance pay and apply for reinduction. But when they turned up for their severance pay, there was no money. Protests were met with bullets and death. All in all, overnight there were 10 million unemployed Iraqis.[38]

By disbanding the bureaucracy and the army, the Americans disrupted the cash flow in the economy. Since they also did not peg the value of the dinar, no one knew whether to accept dinars and, if so, what they were worth. The value of the dinar crashed, and the few savings that Iraqis had managed to hold on to evaporated overnight.

There was also almost nothing to buy. Even if the US had intended to make Iraqis pay eventually for the damage the 'coalition' had inflicted on their country, it should have announce a loan to the new administration to meet essential needs till the oil revenues reappeared, in order to maintain the flow of purchasing power in the economy. This would have been a drop in the bucket compared to the Marshall Plan, and a short-term loan, not a grant. But no such step was taken. Instead whatever loans the US was prepared to make went to American companies, mostly belonging to President Bush's friends, who were awarded lucrative contracts to rebuild Iraq's infrastructure and service the army of occupation.[39]

The signs that Iraqis were not exactly welcoming the Americans came in the first weeks of the occupation. The coalition authorities had declared a general amnesty and given the people till 15 June to surrender their arms. But almost no one complied. As the deadline passed, the U.S. army conceded that during the amnesty Iraqis had handed in only 123 pistols, 76 semi-automatic rifles, 435 automatic rifles, 46 machine guns, 11 anti-aircraft weapons and 381 grenades and bombs—a drop in Iraq's ocean of weaponry.[40]

Attacks on US soldiers were not long in coming. Between 1 May and 27 September, 169 American soldiers lost their lives in Iraq. This was 31 more than the 138 that they lost in combat till April 30. The rate of attrition then was about 400 per year. By 14 October 2005 the American death toll had risen to 1,970 and that of the injured to more than 14,000. The number of daily attacks had risen from about 25 to 80.[41]

Bloodbath in Iraq

What hurt US hegemony the most was that the killing did not stop. The longer it went on, the more the world saw the US not as a torchbearer of freedom but as just another colonial power, and an inept one at that. The conquerors had been prepared to wade in blood to bring the fruits of European enlightenment to Iraq, but all over the world people had begun to ask how much blood anyone is justified in shedding in the name of democracy? How long will the killing go on? At what point will the cumulative total of Iraqi deaths—from the repeated bombing of the country, the killing of soldiers and civilians during the invasion, the scatter-gun tactics used by the American soldiers in their anti-insurgency operations, and the daily quota of bombings, murders, rapes and looting—add up to more than the number of people that Saddam Hussein's regime had killed and savaged during his 35-year reign?

Neither the US army nor the Coalition Provisional Authority (CPA) had any intention of letting people know. In sharp contrast to the painstaking tally of deaths of American soldiers kept and publicised by the US Defense Department, the US army and the CPA deliberately kept no tally of the number of Iraqis that had been killed. But during a trip in March 2004, in which he covered the whole of Iraq from the far north till Basra in the south-east, John Pilger estimated that, including civilians, regular soldiers, *fidayeen* and Iraqi conscripts, approximately 55,000 Iraqis might have lost their lives since the invasion began.[42]

Worst of all, far from diminishing, the death toll was rising. The Associated Press, which made a determined effort to estimate the number of Iraqi civilian casualties, reported that in just four provinces—Baghdad, Najaf, Karbala and Tikrit—5,558 bodies had been brought into the morgues between 1 May 2003 and 30 April 2004. Of these Baghdad alone accounted for 4,279. The survey showed that between May 2003 and April 2004, 25 times as many Baghdadis died violent deaths every month as in 2002. The death toll was 20 times as high as for New York (although the population was less than half) and 32 times higher than for the whole of Jordan in 2003.[43] All this was before the insurgents turned their guns on Iraqis in a calculated manner.

The above estimate did not include the most troubled province, centred on Fallujah, a city in the Sunni belt north-east of Baghdad, which had been particularly hostile to the US forces ever since US marines had killed 13 residents during a peaceful demonstration shortly after the conquest of Iraq. According to another AP survey, 1,361 Iraqis had been killed in April after the Sunni-Shia uprising began, more than 1,250 of them by American soldiers. The bulk of these casualties occurred in Fallujah. The head of Fallujah's hospital, Rafie al-Issawi, said that his records showed 731 killed and around 2,800 wounded since the Marines' siege began on 1 April, though he could not immediately provide a breakdown on how many were women or children.[44]

The AP estimate for April was by far the highest of an already disturbingly high monthly toll. An estimate by the Brookings Institution for March 2004 showed that 301 Iraqis had been killed, *excluding* insurgents and Iraqi police.[45] There was no tally of the number of insurgents killed and, more important, of the number of dead civilians who had been described as insurgents. This figure could be large, for on 20 April, Lieutenant General Ricardo Sanchez, the commander of U.S. forces in Iraq, said his troops had killed 1,000 insurgents in April.[46] This was not far short of the total number of deaths reported by Associated Press for the same period. In other words, the coalition authorities were describing virtually every person their armed forces killed in anti-insurgency operations as a combatant.[47]

By then every Iraqi, and most people elsewhere, knew that the US' claim of deadly accuracy in picking off insurgents was patently false. Its forces were using tanks, armoured personnel carriers, rockets fired from helicopters, mortars and 500-lb bombs. Large numbers of the troops were reservists who had had little experience of combat and absolutely none of counter-insurgency. What they were actually doing was described in vivid detail by Jo Wilding, a human rights activist who took medical supplies into the besieged town of Fallujah during the first American attack upon the city in April 2004.[48]

The True Face of Empire: Jo Wilding's Tale

April 11th, Falluja: Trucks, oil tankers, tanks are burning on the highway east to Falluja. A stream of boys and men goes to and from a lorry that's not burnt, stripping it bare. We turn onto the back roads through Abu Ghraib, Nuha and Ahrar singing in Arabic, past the vehicles full of people and a few possessions heading the other way, past the improvised refreshment posts along the way where boys throw food through the windows into the bus for us and for the people still inside Falluja. The bus is following a car with the nephew of a local sheikh and a guide *who has contacts with the Mujahedin and has cleared this with them*. The reason I'm on the bus is that a journalist I knew turned up at my door at about 11 at night telling me things were desperate in Falluja. He'd been bringing out children with their limbs blown off, the US soldiers were going around telling people to leave by dusk or be killed, but then when people fled with whatever they could carry, they were being stopped at the US military checkpoint on the edge of town and not let out, trapped, watching the sun go down.

He said aid vehicles and the media were being turned away. He said there was some medical aid that needed to go in and there was a better chance of it getting there with foreigners, westerners, to get through the American checkpoints. *The rest of the way was secured with the armed groups who control the roads we'd travel on.* We'd take in the medical supplies, see what else we could do to help and then use the bus to bring out people who needed to leave …

We pile the stuff in the corridor and the boxes are torn open straightaway, the blankets most welcomed. It's not a hospital at all but a clinic, a private doctor's surgery treating people free since air strikes destroyed the town's main hospital. Another has been improvised in a car garage. There's no anesthetic. The blood bags are in a drinks fridge and the doctors warm them up under the hot tap in an unhygienic toilet. Screaming women come in, praying, slapping their chests and faces. Ummi, my mother, one cries. I hold her until Maki, a consultant and acting director of the clinic, brings me to the bed where a child of about ten is lying with a bullet wound to the head. A smaller child is being treated for a similar injury in the next bed. A US sniper hit them and their grandmother as they left their home to flee Falluja. The lights go out, the fan stops and in the sudden quiet someone holds up the flame of a cigarette lighter for the doctor to carry on operating by. The electricity to the town has been cut off for days and when the generator runs out of petrol they just have to manage till it comes back on. Dave quickly donates his torch. The children are not going to live.

'Come,' says Maki and ushers me alone into a room where an old woman has just had an abdominal bullet wound stitched up. Another in her leg is being dressed, the bed under her foot soaked with blood, a white flag still clutched in her hand and the same story: I was leaving my home to go to Baghdad when I was hit by a US sniper. Some of the town is held by US marines, other parts by the local fighters. Their homes are in the US controlled area and they are adamant that the snipers were US marines.

Snipers are causing not just carnage but also the paralysis of the ambulance and evacuation services. The biggest hospital after the main one was bombed is in US territory and cut off from the clinic by snipers. The ambulance has been repaired four times after bullet damage. Bodies are lying in the streets because no one can go to collect them without being shot ...

...

We wash the blood off our hands and get in the ambulance. There are people trapped in the other hospital who need to go to Baghdad. Siren screaming, lights flashing, we huddle on the floor of the ambulance, passports and ID cards held out the windows. We pack it with people, one with his chest taped together and a drip, one on a stretcher, legs jerking violently so I have to hold them down as we wheel him out, lifting him over steps.

The hospital is better able to treat them than the clinic but hasn't got enough of anything to sort them out properly and the only way to get them to Baghdad on our bus, which means they have to go to the clinic.

We're crammed on the floor of the ambulance in case it's shot at. Nisareen, a woman doctor about my age, can't stop a few tears once we're out. The doctor rushes out to meet me: 'Can you go to fetch a lady, she is pregnant and she is delivering the baby too soon?'

Azzam is driving, Ahmed in the middle directing him and me by the window, the visible foreigner, the passport. Something scatters across my hand, simultaneous with the crashing of a bullet through the ambulance, some plastic part dislodged, flying through the window.

We stop, turn off the siren, keep the blue light flashing, wait, eyes on the silhouettes of men in US marine uniforms on the corners of the buildings. Several shots come. We duck, get as low as possible and I can see tiny red lights whipping past the window, past my head. Some, it's hard to tell, are hitting the ambulance. I start singing. What else do you do when someone's shooting at you? A tyre bursts with an enormous noise and a jerk of the vehicle.

...

Azzam grabs the gear stick and gets the ambulance into reverse, another tyre bursting as we go over the ridge in the centre of the road, the shots still coming as we flee around the corner. I carry on singing. The wheels are scraping, burst rubber burning on the road.

The men run for a stretcher as we arrive and I shake my head. They spot the new bullet holes and run to see if we're OK. Is there any other way to get to her, I want to know. *La, maaku tarieq*. There is no other way. They say we did the right thing. They say they've fixed the ambulance four times already and they'll fix it again but the radiator's gone and the wheels are buckled and she's still at home in the dark giving birth alone. I let her down.

...

We can't go out again. For one thing there's no ambulance and besides it's dark now and that means our foreign faces can't protect the people who go out with us or the people we pick up. Maki is the acting director of the place. He says he hated Saddam but now he hates the Americans more.

We take off the blue gowns as the sky starts exploding somewhere beyond the building opposite. Minutes later a car roars up to the clinic. I can hear him screaming before I can see that there's no skin left on his body. He's burnt from head to foot. For sure there's nothing they can do. He'll die of dehydration within a few days.

Another man is pulled from the car onto a stretcher. Cluster bombs, they say, although it's not clear whether they mean one or both of them. We set off walking to Mr Yasser's house, waiting at each corner for someone to check the street before we cross. A ball of fire falls from a plane, splits into smaller balls of bright white lights. I think they're cluster bombs, because cluster bombs are in the front of my mind, but they vanish, just magnesium flares, incredibly bright but short-lived, giving a flash picture of the town from above ...

The planes are above us all night so that as I doze I forget I'm not on a long distance flight, the constant bass note of an unmanned reconnaissance drone overlaid with the frantic thrash of jets and the dull beat of helicopters and interrupted by the explosions.

...

... The doctors look haggard in the morning. None has slept more than a couple of hours a night for a week. One has had only eight hours of sleep in the last seven days, missing the funerals of his brother and aunt because he was needed at the hospital.

'The dead we cannot help,' Jassim said. 'I must worry about the injured.'

We go again, Dave, Rana and me, this time in a pick up. There are some sick people close to the marines' line who need evacuating. No one dares come out of their house because the marines are on top of the buildings shooting at anything that moves. Saad fetches us a white flag and tells us not to worry, he's checked and secured the road, no Mujahideen will fire at us, that peace is upon us, this eleven year old child, his face covered with a keffiyeh, but for his bright brown eyes, his AK47 almost as tall as he is.

We shout again to the soldiers, hold up the flag with a red crescent sprayed onto it. Two come down from the building, cover this side and Rana mutters, 'Allahu akbar. Please nobody take a shot at them.' We jump down and tell them we need to get some sick people from the houses and they want Rana to go and bring out the family from the house whose roof they're on. Thirteen women and children are still inside, in one room, without food and water for the last 24 hours. ...

First we go down the street we were sent to. There's a man, face down, in a white *dishdasha*, a small round red stain on his back. We run to him. Again the flies have got there first. Dave is at his shoulders, I'm by his knees and as we reach to roll him onto the stretcher Dave's hand goes through his chest, through the cavity left by the bullet that entered so neatly through his back and blew his heart out. There's no weapon in his hand. Only when we arrive, his sons come out, crying, shouting. 'He was unarmed,' they scream. 'He was unarmed. He just went out the gate and they shot him.' None of them have dared come out since. No one had dared come to get his body, horrified, terrified, forced to violate the traditions of treating the body immediately. They couldn't have known we were coming so it's inconceivable that anyone came out and retrieved a weapon but left the body.

He was unarmed, 55 years old, shot in the back. We cover his face, carry him to the pick up. There's nothing to cover his body with. The sick woman is helped out of the house, the little girls around her hugging cloth bags to their bodies, whispering, 'Baba, Baba.' Daddy. Shaking, they let us go first, hands up, around the corner, then we usher them to the cab of the pick up, shielding their heads so they can't see him, the cuddly fat man stiff in the back.

The people seem to pour out of the houses now in the hope we can escort them safely out of the line of fire, kids, women, men, anxiously asking us whether they can all go, or only the women and children. We go to ask. The young marine tells us that men of fighting age can't leave. What's fighting age, I want to know.

He contemplates. Anything under forty-five. No lower limit.

It appals me that all those men would be trapped in a city which is about to be destroyed. Not all of them are fighters, not all are armed. It's going to happen out of the view of the world, out of sight of the media, because most of the media in Falluja is embedded with the marines or turned away at the outskirts. Before we can pass the message on, two explosions scatter the crowd in the side street back into their houses ...

...

The bus is going to leave, taking the injured people back to Baghdad, the man with the burns, one of the women who was shot in the jaw and shoulder by a sniper, several others. Rana says she's staying to help. Dave and I don't hesitate: we're staying too.

If I don't do it, who will?' has become an accidental motto and I'm acutely aware after the last foray how many people, how many women and children, are still in their houses either because they've got nowhere to go, because they're scared to go out of the door or because they've chosen to stay ...

It hurts to climb onto the bus when the doctor has just asked us to go and evacuate some more people. I hate the fact that a qualified medic can't travel in the ambulance but I can, just because I look like the sniper's sister or one of his mates, but that's the way it is today and the way it was yesterday and I feel like a traitor for leaving, but I can't see where I've got a choice. ...

Saad comes onto the bus to wish us well for the journey. He shakes Dave's hand and then mine. I hold his in both of mine and tell him 'Dir balak,' take care, as if I could say anything more stupid to a pre-teen Mujahedin with an AK47 in his other hand, and our eyes meet and stay fixed, his full of fire and fear. ...

And the satellite news says the cease-fire is holding and George Bush says to the troops on Easter Sunday that, 'I know what we're doing in Iraq is right.'

Shooting unarmed men in the back outside their family home is right. Shooting grandmothers with white flags is right? Shooting at women and children who are fleeing their homes is right? Firing at ambulances is right?

Well George, I know too now. I know what it looks like when you brutalise people so much that they've nothing left to lose. I know what it looks like when an operation is being done without anaesthetic because the hospitals are destroyed or under sniper fire and the city's under siege and aid isn't getting in properly. I know what it sounds like too. I know what it looks like when tracer bullets are passing your head, even though you're in an ambulance. I know what it looks like when a man's chest is no longer inside him and what it smells like and I know what it looks like when his wife and children pour out of his house. It's a crime and it's a disgrace to us all.'

Six months later Fallujah was razed to the ground. Fallujah was followed by Ramadi, Samarra and Tal Afar. No one pretended they were liberating the Iraqis any more.

Torture at Abu Ghraib

The final nail in the coffin of American hegemony was hammered by photographs of sexual molestation and abuse of Iraqi male (and occasionally female) prisoners in Abu Ghraib prison, which were shown on CBS' *60 Minutes* programme in the US at the beginning of May. Saddam's treatment of his political prisoners at Abu Ghraib prison had been one of the horror stories that Bush and Blair had used to justify their invasion of Iraq. The shock that world opinion received when it found that the American guards were systematically stripping Iraqi prisoners naked, making them masturbate in front of women soldiers and taking photographs for general distribution via CD-ROM to bored soldiers with nothing better to entertain them was therefore indescribable. These photographs immeasurably strengthened the growing opposition to *Pax Americana* in the rest of the world, for they reaffirmed Lord Acton's observation that if power corrupts, absolute power corrupts absolutely. But their impact on the majority of the American public was equally momentuous. It was summed up by Phillip Kennicott, staff writer of the *Washington Post*, as follows:

> Among the corrosive lies a nation at war tells itself is that the glory—the lofty goals announced beforehand, the victories, the liberation of the oppressed—belongs to the country as a whole; but the failure—the accidents, the uncounted civilian dead, the crimes and atrocities—is always exceptional. Noble goals flow naturally from a noble people; the occasional act of barbarity is always the work of individuals, unaccountable, confusing and indigestible to the national conscience ... This belief, that the photographs are distortions, despite their authenticity, is indistinguishable from propaganda. Tyrants censor; democracies self-censor. Tyrants concoct propaganda in ministries of information; democracies produce it through habits of thought so ingrained that *a basic lie of war—only the good is our doing—becomes self-propagating.* ...
> But these photos are us. Yes, they are the acts of individuals. But armies are made of individuals. Nations are made up of individuals. Great national crimes begin with the acts of misguided individuals; and no matter how many people are held directly accountable for these crimes, we are collectively responsible

for what these individuals have done. We live in a democracy. Every errant smart bomb, every dead civilian, every sodomized prisoner, is ours.[49]

Both in Baghdad and Washington, the Bush administration attempted to minimise the impact of the photographs by claiming that it was the handiwork of a handful of perverts. But as the information poured out, it became apparent that the abuse had been systematic and that for understandable but hardly reputable reasons of its own, the Pentagon had attempted to keep it under wraps. For instance, Associated Press had filed a detailed report on the abuse of prisoners in Abu Ghraib as far back as October 2003. Freed prisoners told AP about detainees punished by being forced to spend hours lying bound in the broiling summer sun; being attacked by dogs; being deprived of sufficient water; spending days with hoods over their heads. One told AP of seeing an elderly Iraqi woman tied up and lying in the dust; others told of ill men dying in crowded tents. They spoke repeatedly of being humiliated by American guards. In October none mentioned the sexual humiliation that later came to light but this may have been because Arab culture kept Iraqis from describing such mistreatment. But in a typical act of self-censorship, the mainline Anglo-Saxon media had ignored the AP report.[50]

The investigation that followed the airing of the pictures revealed that:

- The Red Cross first warned the Coalition Provisional Authority of prisoner abuse at Abu Ghraib as far back as spring 2003, within weeks of the conquest of Iraq. It continued to do this both verbally and in written submissions right through November. But these complaints had little effect. According to the Red Cross, the US authorities accepted some of its recommendations and ignored others.
- Between 31 August and 9 September, Major-General Geoffrey Miller, the head of the prison at Guantanamo Bay, conducted an inquiry into interrogation and detention procedures in Iraq. He is reported to have said that prison guards could 'set conditions' for the interrogation of prisoners. When the scandal came to light, the guards and the indicted guards and prison authorities claimed that this was the recommendation they were following when they humiliated and brutalised the prisoners. The purpose was to soften them up for interrogation by Military Intelligence.
- The first report on prison conditions and prisoner abuse was submitted by Major-General Donald Ryder on 5 November 2003. Its main finding was that the US 800th Military Police Brigade had not received specific training for their job. This was a tacit admission that they were running riot with their prisoners.

- Private Joseph Darby formally reported the abuse of prisoners to his superior officers on 13 January. He first slipped an anonymous note under the door of one of them, but later decided to make a formal complaint. The fact that over a thousand photos were loaded on the CD he received and surrendered shows that the torture was not only widely known and approved of, but was vicariously enjoyed. His desire to hide his identity reveals his fear of being ostracised or, worse still, victimised for having followed the dictates of his conscience. In other words, what was being done to the prisoners had the general approval of the soldiers guarding Abu Ghraib and other prisons in Iraq.
- The army launched a criminal investigation the very next day, and two days later made a carefully sanitised reference to it in a press briefing. It also informed the CPA chief, Paul Bremer, of what had happened.
- By the end of the month, it had relieved the head of the 800th MP brigade of command and placed her under investigation. Presumably based upon her defence, the Army Central Command ordered another inquiry by General Antonio Taguba. About this time, President Bush was also informed of the abuse and the inquiry that had been ordered.
- Taguba presented his report on 12 March, highlighting that the abuse was widespread and systemic, but a month earlier the Red Cross had submitted a 24-page formal report to the CPA summarising all of its findings in 2003.
- Based on these reports, Central Command made changes in training methods and accepted the recommendations of Taguba and Ryder to give prison guards no role in the interrogation of prisoners.[51]

But the most extraordinary feature of the scandal was that seven weeks after Taguba presented his report, neither Rumsfeld nor Wolfowitz, nor perhaps any senior member of the policy-making cabal, had found time to read the report.[52] The reason became apparent as journalists burrowed away, trying to find out just how far up the decision-making chain the responsibility for Abu Ghraib actually went. It turned out that both Donald Rumsfeld and Bush knew that 'unorthodox' methods were being used to extract information from prisoners taken during the invasion of Afghanistan. These had been sanctioned by none other than President Bush. A secret memorandum that he signed on 7 February 2002 contained a loophole that applied worldwide: 'I determine that none of the provisions of Geneva apply to our conflict with al-Qaeda in Afghanistan or *elsewhere throughout the world.*' This became the loophole through which Military Intelligence transferred the inhuman practices of Guantanamo to Iraq.[53]

Seymour Hersh's investigations after the Abu Ghraib scandal broke showed that Rumsfeld was directly responsible for extending to Iraq the scope of a highly secret interrogation-assassination programme developed for suspected members of Al Qaeda. It specifically involved torturing and sexually humiliating male prisoners to extract information.[54]

The Failure of Empire

With the unravelling of the consent that the US and UK had tried so hard to manufacture, the US lost the hegemony it had enjoyed for the previous six decades. The US' loss of hegemony was reflected by a Pew survey of 21 nations released on 3 June 2003. It showed a deepening scepticism toward the US. The survey found that

> the war has widened the rift between Americans and Western Europeans, further inflamed the Muslim world, softened support for the war on terrorism, and significantly weakened global public support for the pillars of the post-World War II era—the U.N. and the North Atlantic alliance. Majorities in five out of seven NATO countries surveyed favoured a more independent relationship with the US on diplomatic and security affairs. Fully three quarters in France (76%) and solid majorities in Turkey (62%), Spain (62%), Italy (61%) and Germany (57%) believe Western Europe should take a more independent role than it has in the past.[55]

All through the ensuing months fresh evidence of the US' loss of hegemony continued to accumulate. In July 2003, India, upon whom the Bush administration had banked to send a division (20,000 personnel) of troops, informed the US that it could not do so. Pakistan, which had half-committed itself to providing three brigades, also pleaded inability to do so. For the first time in the history of peacekeeping operations, no third-world country offered its troops for the 'stabilisation' of Iraq. The fissure between the US and 'Old Europe', reinforced by Russia and China, remained as wide as ever. But now the developing countries, with only a handful of exceptions, were lining up with 'Old Europe'.

India and Pakistan had said that they might reconsider their decision if there was a second UN resolution. In August, the US decided to go for a second resolution, offering to increase the role of the UN substantially. But it baulked at meeting the demand of France, Germany and Russia that it hand over control of Iraq to the UN. As a result, more than two months after the US had agreed to secure a second resolution from the UN, the issue remained deadlocked. By then it had become evident that the writ of the US had ceased to run. In future it would have to be imposed by force.

The question of obtaining another UN resolution came up once more in April 2004, when the US and UK began to make concrete plans for the transfer of authority to an Iraqi government formed by enlarging the US-nominated Iraqi Governing Council. This time, when asked whether the European Union would send troops to aid the Iraqi government after power was handed over, European Union Secretary-General Jaap de Hoop Scheffer said, 'If there is a sovereign, legitimate Iraqi government with full powers after June 30, and that government would direct a request to NATO, and if that request would be made on the basis of a new [UN] Security Council resolution, giving a specific mandate to a stabilization force, then I think NATO allies could enter in that discussion.' He continued, 'But I say sovereign, legitimate and credible Iraqi government and a new UN Security Council resolution. Those are the all-important yard-sticks.'[56] On the same day, Colin Powell, possibly reacting to Scheffer's statement, said that the government due to take power in Iraq on 1 July would have to give back some of its sovereignty to US-led military forces.[57] The divide between the European Union (minus Britain) and the US thus remained as wide as ever.

Retreat from Empire

In the end, as Hardt and Negri had foreseen, a world order organised as an American empire is proving virtually impossible to build and sustain.[58] Its weakness is that since it relies mainly on coercion, it shows little interest in accommodation or co-optation as tools of consensus building. The only language in which empire builders speak to those whom they wish to subjugate is force. Their only way of looking at other human beings is as subjects, not as equal citizens. The only moral base from which they can operate is the belief that the subject peoples are inferior to them, treating them as the 'Other' and discounting, if not denying, their humanity. The use of force becomes morally justifiable because its purpose is to lead the savage into enlightenment and give him a better life.[59]

Such a combination of arrogance, self-righteousness and messianism cannot fail to arouse violent opposition. In Iraq, the Americans have learned that superior force can win wars but cannot subjugate peoples. Even less can it be used to impose Western enlightenment from above.

By the early months of 2004, the more thoughtful members of the neo-conservative camp had become aware of the limits of military power. One of the more honest efforts at soul-searching came from Robert Kagan, who had written a closely reasoned justification for the use of force by the US to oust Saddam Hussein only 18 months earlier, in November 2002.[60] In his earlier article, Kagan had taken the common-sense observation that it is the weak who have the strongest interest in the observance of laws and the strong who are most strongly tempted to break them, and turned this into an explanation of both the European preference for a world ruled by law and the American preference for a world reorganised through the use of power:

> Most Europeans do not see the great paradox: that their passage into post-history depends upon the United States not making the same passage. Because Europe has neither the will nor the ability to guard its own paradise, and keep it from being overrun, spiritually as well as physically, by a world that has yet to accept the rule of 'moral consciousness', it has become dependent on America's willingness to use its military might to deter or defeat those around the world who still believe in power politics.[61]

To create a justification for unilateral military action, Kagan exaggerated European military impotence in the face not only of the US but of third-world and post-communist countries; exaggerated the threat that the latter could pose; and completely ignored the effectiveness of deterrence, especially in an age when all West European countries had nuclear weapons, or were capable of producing them at short notice. But the crucial under-lying premise of his argument was the moral infallibility of the US' judge-ment of when force had to be used. 'The day could come, if it has not already, when Americans will no more heed the pronouncements of the EU than they do those of ASEAN or the Andean Pact.'[62]

It was this belief in the US' moral infallibility that was lacking in his article 16 months later. Gone was the condescension of the 2002 article. Gone also was his belief that the source of Europe's respect for law was its military weakness. Acknowledging that a 'great philosophical schism has opened within the West', and that 'for the first time since World War II, a majority of Europeans has come to doubt the legitimacy of US power and US global leadership', Kagan candidly admitted, 'Invading Iraq and trying to reconstruct it without the broad benediction of Europe has not been a particularly happy experience *even if the United States eventually succeeds*. It is clear that Americans cannot ignore the question of legitimacy, *and it is clear that they cannot provide legitimacy for themselves.*'[63] Thus did Kagan begin the job of giving neo-conservative unilateralism a quiet burial.

As for Bush's doctrine of preventive intervention, upon which the bid for empire was, and still remains, built, this was rubbished decisively by the *New York Times*. In an editorial opinion titled 'Preventive War: A failed doctrine' published on 12 September 2004, it wrote:

> Before the Iraq fiasco, American leaders rightly viewed war as a last resort, appropriate only when the nation's vital interests were actively threatened and reasonable diplomatic efforts had been exhausted. That view always left room for pre-emptive attacks; America is under no obligation to sit and wait, if it is clear that some enemy is actually preparing to strike first. But it correctly drew the line at preventive wars against potential foes who might, or might not, be thinking about doing something dangerous. As the administration's disastrous experience in Iraq amply demonstrates, that is still the wisest course and the one that keeps America most secure in an increasingly dangerous era.[64]

Notes

1. 'Is it Too Late to Win the War?', *Time*, 26 September 2005.
2. Julian Borger, 'Pentagon cools on finding weapons', *The Guardian*, 29 May 2003.
3. Michael White, Ewen MacAskill and Richard Norton-Taylor, 'Downing St admits blunder on Iraq dossier. Plagiarism row casts shadow over No. 10's case against Saddam', *The Guardian*, 8 February 2003.
4. *The Guardian, The Hutton Inquiry and its Impact* (London, Politico's Guardian Books, 2004), p. 370.
5. Ibid., Chapter 2.
6. Ibid., p. 48.
7. Ibid., pp. 51–52.
8. Ibid., pp. 5, 19, 128–129.
9. Ibid., p. 128.
10. Ibid., p. 129 (emphasis added).
11. Claire Cozens, 'Widespread scepticism to Hutton whitewash', *The Guardian*, 29 January 2004.
12. Warren Hoge and Don Van Natta Jr., 'Blair heads for the US, trailing controversy over Iraq', *New York Times*, 17 July 2003.
13. Beth Gardiner, 'Memo: Blair urged to defend war in Iraq', Associated Press, 23 August 2003.
14. Ibid.
15. Nicholas D. Kristoff, 'Missing in Action: The Truth', *New York Times*, 6 May 2003.
16. David Johnston and Richard W. Stevenson, 'Former envoy talks in book about source of CIA leak', *New York Times*, 30 April 2004.
17. Jim Wolf, 'US insiders say Iraq intel deliberately skewed', *Reuters*, 30 May 2003.
18. 'Bush Plays Down Iraq WMD Hunt', *Reuters*, St Petersburg, 1 June 2003.
19. 'US Senate opens Iraq weapons probe', *BBC News*, 3 June 2003.
20. David Johnston and Richard W. Stevenson, 'Former envoy talks in book about source of CIA leak', *New York Times*, 30 April 2004.
21. Matthew Cooper, 'What I told the Grand Jury', *Time*, 25 July 2005. Libby was formally indicted and Rove became the subject of an intense investigation.
22. Robert Scheer, 'Bush was all too willing to believe émigrés' lies', *Los Angeles Times*, 2 September 2003.

23. Interim Report of David Kay to the US Congress, 2 October 2003. His precise finding was: '… this clandestine capability was suitable for preserving BW expertise, BW capable facilities and continuing R&D—all key elements for maintaining a capability for resuming BW production.'

24. Ibid. 'When Saddam had asked a senior military official in either 2001 or 2002 how long it would take to produce new chemical agent and weapons, he told ISG that after he consulted with CW experts in OMI he responded it would take six months for mustard. Another senior Iraqi chemical weapons expert in responding to a request in mid-2002 from Uday Husayn for CW for the Fedayeen Saddam estimated that it would take two months to produce mustard and two years for Sarin.'

25. Ibid. (emphasis added).

26. John J. Lumpkin, 'Numerous ideas cited for not finding WMD', Associated Press, 4 October 2003.

27. Jonathan Freedland, 'Tugging back the veil', in The Guardian, The Hutton Inquiry, p. 353. In his final report, dated 30 September 2004, Kay's successor, Charles Duelfer, confirmed that while Iraq had tried to maintain the scientific knowledge needed to make WMD, it had not stored or produced any since the early 1990s.

28. Walter Pincus, 'Report casts doubt on Iraq-Al Qaeda connection', Washington Post, 22 June 2003.

29. NPR interview on programme 'Fresh Air', 14 January 2004. Available at: www.npr.org/features/feature.php?wfld=1596972.

30. Richard A. Clarke, Against All Enemies: Inside America's War on Terror (New York, Free Press, 2004), pp. 227–238.

31. Robert Fisk, 'A Civilisation Torn to Pieces', The Independent, 13 April 2003.

32. Tareq Al Issawi, 'Sabotage knocks out power in Iraqi town', Associated Press, 20 June 2003.

33. Robert Fisk, 'And the truth the victors refuse to see', The Independent, 1 June 2003.

34. Lauren Sandler, 'Veiled and worried in Baghdad', New York Times, 16 September 2003.

35. Medea Benjamin, 'Open arms may turn into fire arms, says Iraqi soldier turned taxi driver', International Occupation Watch Center—Iraq, http://OccupationWatch-conditionsinIraq.htm, 4 August 2003.

36. Elizabeth Bumiller, 'U.S. names Iraqis who would face war crimes trial', New York Times, 16 March 2003.

37. It took the American Foreign Policy establishment more than a year to admit to the colossal blunders that the Coalition Provisional Authority had committed (see Larry Diamond, 'What went wrong in Iraq?', Foreign Affairs, September–October 2004.

38. E.A. Khammas, '10 million unemployed: The forgotten issue', International Occupation Watch Center – Iraq, http://Occupation Watch-conditions in Iraq.htm, 9 August 2003).

39. David Pace, 'Halliburton's contracts total $600 million', Associated Press, 30 May 2003.

40. Khaled Yacoub Oweis, 'US troops ambushed in Iraq as new raids launched', Reuters, 15 June 2003.

41. 'Is it Too Late to Win the War?', Time, 26 September 2005.

42. John Pilger, 'This Is A War Of Liberation And We Are The Enemy', The New Statesman, 15 April 2004. For months this figure sounded far too high, especially because estimates of the number of civilians killed made by private NGOs such as 'Iraq Body Count' were much lower. But in October researchers from Johns Hopkins University and Columbia University in the US and the Al-Mustansiriya University in Baghdad conducted a sample survey of 808 households in 33 areas, all randomly selected, and concluded that the Iraqi death toll after the invasion ended had exceeded 100,000. The researchers concede that their data were of limited precision, but their method of sampling was accepted by other scientists who pointed out that it had been used in

Kosovo in the late 1990s (Jane Perron, 'Iraqi civilian deaths now 100,000', *The Guardian*, 29 October 2004). It must be conceded though that the Kosovo estimates turned out to somewhat high. However, if the real count is even half this figure, it more than vindicates Pilger's estimate.

43. Ibid.
44. Lee Keath, 'AP toll says 1,361 Iraqis killed in April', Associated Press, 30 April 2004.
45. Ibid.
46. Ibid. Strictly speaking, the figure is for 5–20 April.
47. Suleiman al-Khalidi, 'US forces renew holy city battles in Iraq', *Reuters*, 15 May 2004.
48. This is extracted from Jo Wilding's complete account of what she witnessed at Fallujah. It is available at www.indymedia.co.uk (all emphases added). A shorter version was published in *The Guardian*, 'Getting Aid past US snipers is impossible', 17 April 2004.
49. Philip Kennicott, 'A wretched new picture of America: Photos from Iraq prison show we are our own worst enemy', *Washington Post*, 5 May 2004 (emphasis added).
50. Charles J. Hanley, 'Early Iraqi abuse accounts met with silence', Associated Press, 8 May 2004.
51. CBS News, 'Abuses at Abu Ghraib: Timeline of events'. Available at: www.cbsnews.com/stories/2004/04/27/60II/main614063.shtml.
52. Maureen Dowd, 'Shocking and awful', *New York Times*, 6 May 2004.
53. Seymour Hersh, 'Rumsfeld's dirty war on terror, Part 1', *The Guardian*, 13 September 2004.
54. Seymour Hersh, Rumsfeld's dirty war on terror, Part 2' *The Guardian*, 14 September 2004.
55. Pew Research Center, 'Views of a changing world 2003. War with Iraq further divides global politics', 3 June 2003, available at www.pewglobal.com.
56. 'Europe sees no Iraq role unless many conditions met', *Reuters*, 26 April 2004.
57. 'Powell sees limits on Iraq sovereignty post June 30', *Reuters*, 26 April 2004.
58. Hardt and Negri wrote: 'Many locate the ultimate authority that rules over the processes of globalisation and the new world order in the United States ... Our basic hypothesis, that a new imperial form of sovereignty has emerged, contradicts ... these views. The Unites States does not, and indeed no nation state today can form, the center of an imperialist project.' What makes this observation prophetic is that it was made four years before the Iraq war, and at a time when even Kosovo had only just taken place (Michael Hardt and Antonio Negri, *Empire* (Cambridge Ma., Harvard University Press, 2000), pp. xiii–xiv).
59. David Sanger, 'President Makes a Case for Freedom in the Middle East', *New York Times*, 14 April 2004. Sanger's article throws some light on this mindset:

> On April 14, 2004, facing a moment of political peril unlike any in the more than one thousand days of his presidency, George W. Bush made the case on Tuesday night for staying the course in Iraq with the language and zeal of a missionary and combined it with a stark warning that failure would embolden America's enemies around the world.

> *'We're changing the world,'* Mr. Bush said halfway through a speech and news conference that was largely an hour-long justification for holding fast in Iraq, no matter how the casualties mount, no matter how chaotic the process of forming a new government ... Drawing later on a line he often slips into his campaign speeches, he reminded a global audience that 'freedom is the Almighty's gift to every man and woman in this world. *And as the greatest power on the face of the Earth, we have an obligation to help the*

spread of freedom ... I hope today you've gotten a sense of my conviction about what we are doing,' he said at the end of the press conference. 'I feel strongly that the course this administration has taken will make America more secure and the world more free, and therefore the world more peaceful. It's a conviction that's deep in my soul' (emphasis added).

60. Robert Kagan, 'America's Crisis of Legitimacy', *Foreign Affairs*, March-April 2004.
61. Robert Kagan, 'Power and Weakness', *Policy Review*, No. 113, June and July 2002.
62. Ibid.
63. Kagan, 'America's Crisis of Legitimacy'.
64. 'Preventive war: A failed doctrine', *New York Times*, 12 September 2004.

14

Towards Darkness

In the closing pages of *The Age of Extremes*, Eric Hobsbawm made a prophetic observation:

> The twentieth century ended in a global disorder whose nature was unclear, and without an obvious mechanism for either ending it or keeping it under control ... The future cannot be a continuation of the past, and there are signs, both externally and, as it were, internally, that we have reached a point of historical crisis.[1]

His pessimism was well-founded, for it has taken barely a decade since he wrote his seminal work to bring the world to that point of historical crisis. In that decade, trade unions, the welfare state, the nation state and the Westphalian international order—economic and political institutions that were the bedrock of civilised life and took four centuries to build—have been severely undermined. Not only has nothing taken their place, but the destruction continues mindlessly under the spur of the 'titanic forces' of a new capitalism, whose destructive power few have yet understood and none know how to control.

In the global economy, the disarray that began three decades ago has grown steadily more pronounced. In the industrialised nations, the flicker of hope generated in America by the 'roaring nineties'—that a new era had dawned in which inflation and the trade cycle had both been banished—has been extinguished.[2] As Krugman had predicted, it turned out not to be the advent of a 'new economy', but simply an unusually long upswing of the old, cyclical kind.[3] The industrialised nations therefore continue to experience chronic unemployment, erosion of the welfare state through the restriction of benefits and the privatisation of public services, widening of income disparities, deregulation of working conditions, and a consequent 'race to the bottom' in both wages and the work environment.

The industrialising world has been split in two. A part has been incorporated into the expanding global capitalist system and has experienced rapid although uneven increases in income. At its leading edge, island enclaves and states like Hong Kong and Singapore have attained the living standards of Europe and the USA in as little as three decades. These have been held out to the rest of the developing world as the examples to be emulated, living proof that a free global market economy will deliver them from poverty. But at the trailing edge, the number of failed, or failing, states is steadily rising. Over a vast swathe of the world, which houses a quarter of the world's inhabitants, country after country is facing the threat of exclusion from the global economic system. This is creating political forces within them that are steadily reinforcing that exclusion. Predatory elites that base their power upon clientelist relationships have perpetuated misery, violence and civil war. More and more of these countries are becoming failed states. In between these extremes fall a large number of countries whose economies are increasingly linked to the rest of the world, but whose fate nevertheless remains uncertain. These include some of the most populous countries of the world: China, India, Indonesia, Russia, Brazil, Argentina, Mexico and Turkey.

Children have been among the worst-hit, albeit silent, victims for they have not even understood why they have had to leave a school, a neighbourhood, friends and the homes they grew up in, or why they have to starve. For all except the gilded few who own most of the wealth in the industrialised nations, the future has become utterly unpredictable and therefore indescribably threatening. Unable to plan for the future, young people in particular have taken to living in a never-ending present. History is being forgotten and planning is at a discount.

The historical crisis point has been reached even more rapidly in the international political system. Six years into the new millennium, the Westphalian state system is in tatters. Its central principles—respect for the sovereignty of nation states and non-interference in the domestic affairs of any state—are now observed mostly in the breach. The US' response to the growing chaos has been to try and resolve it by creating an empire. Such an attempt was inevitable, because it was the only way of reconciling global governance with its own search for nationhood. But the American empire that the Bush administration has sought to put in place of the Westphalian order is also proving unviable. Kosovo, the precursor to empire, and Iraq, the first ambitious essay in creating it, have both ended in heightened chaos.

Five years after its 'liberation', Kosovo is a failed state by any definition of the term. The last-minute ethnic cleansing of the Albanians that so angered the world in March 1999 has been replaced by a sporadic ethnic cleansing of the remaining Serbs; Serbian orthodox churches and monasteries continue to be destroyed. Kosovo is, if anything, even poorer and more miserable than it was in the days of its parallel government within Serbia. It is barely able to finance 4 per cent of its imports, and has an unemployment rate of over 50 per cent of the adult population. Inevitably, a large part of the former Kosovo Liberation Army has gravitated into smuggling, the international narcotics trade and other forms of organised crime.[4] Kosovo is now a nodal point in the international supply route for opium derivatives from Afghanistan to Europe.

What is still more inexcusable is that a good part of the misery has been directly inflicted upon the Kosovars—Serbs and Albanians alike—by the indecision of its liberators. After snatching Kosovo from Serbia by force, they have baulked at giving it full freedom, and left the decision to a referendum, to be taken when peace returns. This provision has ensured that peace does not return, for it has created the motivation for Albanians to keep driving Serbs out of Kosovo in order to make a return to Belgrade's rule more and more impossible, and effectively prevented foreign investment from coming into this half-born state. Not surprisingly, in March 2004, almost five years to the day after the intervention, Kosovo erupted in an orgy of violence that left 19 dead and 900 injured, 700 of them Serbs. It also destroyed 4,500 Serb homes and sent their residents streaming across the border into Serbia. In those 48 hours Albanians added 30 more churches and 2 more monasteries to the 112 that they had already damaged or destroyed; 33 of these dated from the fourteenth to sixteenth centuries.[5]

The aftermath of invasion has been eerily similar in Iraq. A life that had been rendered miserable and insecure by 12 years of economic sanctions has become even more so. Iraq has also vividly demonstrated the limits of American military power. As Jo Wilding's description of the road between Baghdad and Fallujah showed (see Chapter 13 of this book), by early April 2004 the US had all but lost control of the central part of the country. Attempts to re-establish it by force had given it only a fleeting respite. In the closing months of 2004, the US forces and the 'transitional' Iraqi regime under Iyad Allawi found themselves besieged in ever more heavily fortified 'green' zones, pretending to rule the country, while the bulk of the central zone was in the hands of local militias. These and, more dangerously, a rapidly growing volunteer force of suicide bombers were following an increasingly coordinated policy of bombings designed to kill Allawi's token police and security forces, and kidnapping civilian workers and journalists to discourage contractors from accepting repair contracts in Iraq. By January 2005 Baghdad itself was under siege. The insurgency was coordinated to the point where it was systematically attacking the infrastructure of oil pipelines, water mains, and power transformers and cables that kept Baghdad functioning.[6]

The US forces' forays into 'enemy'-held towns led to short-term victories, which were reversed once the troops left. Their methods of fighting the terrorists, which relied heavily on electronic intelligence and the use of bombs, rockets and tanks from safe distances, killed without discrimination. Inevitably large numbers of innocent civilians were killed, including women and children, and this only fuelled the hatred among Iraqis and their desire for revenge. In 2005 Iraq was not only in acute danger of becoming the world's next failed state, but, as the regular use of suicide bombers showed, had also become a base for the recruitment of fanatics to Al Qaeda.[7]

Iraq has also demonstrated the limits of Bush's doctrine of preventive military intervention, as, with the bulk of its troops committed there, the US has lost much of its capacity to dissuade Iran and North Korea from pursuing a nuclear weapons programme.[8]

Above all, the failure of the American bid for empire is reflected by its international isolation. The American bid to retain the hegemony that it acquired during the Second World War has failed. On 21 September 2004, when George Bush addressed the UN for the fourth time, several European heads of state who were attending the UN General Assembly stayed away and sent their foreign ministers to attend the UN plenum.[9] Two years after the invasion, only South Korea had fulfilled an earlier promise to send its troops to Iraq. Not a single additional country had responded to the US' pleas to help it restore peace in Iraq, which had become the quagmire that everyone dreaded.

Why Chaos will Worsen

Will the descent into systemic chaos that has been described in this book cease soon? Have we reached its nadir? Is a new global political and economic system being born, which will regain the capacity for equilibrating responses that nation state-based capitalism lost three decades ago? The answer to both questions must be 'no'. The 'titanic force' that is driving the world steadily deeper into chaos is fear. That fear is not only alive and well, but is constantly being nourished by acts of terror on the one hand and disproportionate responses on the other. But its roots lie in the globalising economy, not in the polity. Fear is an inevitable by-product of the rapid increase in economic interdependence brought about by the globalisation of capitalism. And that interdependence is still increasing.

Economic interdependence has been portrayed on innumerable occasions as a force for peace. Polanyi highlighted this as the main cause of the Hundred Years' Peace in the nineteenth century. A host of authors, ranging from Fukuyama and Huntington to Thomas Friedman, have repeated the argument in recent years.[10] But there is a fundamental weakness in this argument. Interdependence *maintains* peace, once it has been established. In other words, it does so in settled polities. Interdependence does not *create* peace. On the contrary, during periods of transition, growing economic interdependence can be a potent cause of war, for it creates vulnerability—and vulnerability gives birth to a desire for control. It is the attempt to re-establish control in the shortest possible time and by the most direct route that leads to war.[11]

Interdependence was very limited in the days before the industrial revolution. In the fourteenth and fifteenth centuries, for instance, most of the long-distance trade between nations was in finished products. Trade between Europe and the Orient, between Northern Europe and the Italian city states, and between South and Central America and Spain, took place in consumer goods such as cotton textiles, silks, processed and semi-processed woollens, spices, jewellery and bullion.[12] There was thus relatively little interdependence. Trade provided goods that enhanced the quality of life, especially of the aristocracy and the emerging mercantile middle class, but its disruption did not cause severe dislocation of what were then self-sufficient, subsistence economies.

Interdependence began to generate anxiety, and therefore became a significant determinant of policy, only when technological progress increased the scale of production to the point where industry became dependent for its raw materials and markets upon lands that it did not control. This happened with dramatic suddenness during the industrial revolution. Britain ceased to be self-sufficient in foodgrains as early as 1760. The industrial revolution began in the textiles industry, but it depended on imports for the entire supply of raw cotton. As if this did not create enough uncertainty, its output of textiles outgrew the British and West European markets at least as early as 1813. By 1840 it had become dependent on exports for the growth of its capital-goods industries as well.[13]

Industrialisation therefore linked the fate of the industrial working class in the industrialised countries with events abroad that it could not control, and it did so in a much more vital manner than trade in luxuries and exotic consumer goods had linked the mercantile class and the aristocracy in earlier epochs of capitalism. Quite suddenly, as much as half the population of the industrialised countries felt vulnerable, and backed moves by their governments to establish control over other nations. Colonialism was the inevitable response and reached its apogee in the British Empire. While Britain, France and Holland had established small trading colonies before the full onset of the industrial revolution, their rapid expansion and consolidation in the nineteenth century, and especially the scramble for empire among the industrialised nations in the 1870s, can be directly traced to the attempt to reduce the uncertainty that interdependence had created.

Globalisation is causing another quantum jump in interdependence. On the one hand it has added the entire shareholding class in the industrialised countries to the list of social groups that are directly threatened by upheavals in distant lands, and on the other it has linked their fate even more intimately to that of the newly industrialised countries than trade had linked the metropolitan nations to their dependencies in the nineteenth century. War, ethnic conflict or even an unexpected change of government in a newly industrialised country now threatens to disrupt not only trade but the global manufacturing chain. This threatens the profits of not only the TNCs that are directly affected because they have manufacturing or service units in those countries, but, thanks to the interlocking of shareholdings, a vast penumbra of other stakeholders as well. The shares in these companies are held by hundreds of millions of shareholders.

The vulnerability of these shareholders is beyond anything that could have been imagined as little as three decades ago. With financial globalisation, even the rumour of a natural catastrophe, a political coup or an economic set-back in a faraway country sends share markets plummeting and wipes out billions of dollars of paper wealth in moments. Since people live longer and pension plans are being privatised, it is not only security in the present but security in their old age that has come to depend upon stability and predictability in the newly industrialised countries. In sum, in capitalism's latest *avatar*, virtually the entire population of the metropolitan countries has developed a vital interest in controlling not only economic policies but also political events in the dependencies.

The primary agents of globalisation are the transnational corporations (TNCs). In 1970 there were about 7,000 non-financial TNCs investing directly in other developed or developing countries. By 1992 there were 37,000, with about 170,000 foreign affiliates. By the end of 1998 there were 60,000 parent companies with more than 500,000 affiliates. The latter accounted for $11 trillion worth of output. Against this, the total world trade amounted to $7 trillion. In a short period of 30 years, therefore, transnational production had become a far more important way of reaching goods and services to foreign lands than international trade.[14] The rise of the TNCs has also transformed world trade. A third of what is still classified as international trade is actually intra-firm sales within the TNCs, across national boundaries. Another third of international trade results from the 'arm's-length' activities of the TNCs, such as sub-contracting, licensing, franchising and the formation of strategic alliances, which do not involve equity participation by the parent TNC.[15] The TNCs thus control two-thirds of international trade. Today a country left out of their loop can at most sell agricultural products such as cereals, flowers and vegetables, poultry and dairy products, minerals, and 'undifferentiated' basic and intermediate manufactured goods such as steel, non-ferrous metals and bulk chemicals. These are all products in which the value added is low. The exporting country is therefore doomed to remain poor.

The political power of the TNCs does not stem from numbers alone, but from the concentration of economic power, even within this universe, in a handful of giant concerns. Of the 60,000 TNCs, the top 100 accounted for 2.1 trillion dollars worth of sales and employed six million persons. Only two of these companies were from the developing countries. Ninety were from the triad of the EU, Japan and the US. Twenty-seven out of the top 100 firms, including five of the top seven were American firms. UK-based firms accounted for another nine. Japan, another silent ally of the US in its drive towards empire, accounted for 17 firms. Eighty-five of the firms among the top 100 in 1998 had been on the list for more than five years.[16] Add to these goods and services providers, several hundred giant international banks, pension funds, mutual funds, hedge funds and insurance corporations, which move trillions of dollars across national frontiers everyday, and hold shares in these TNCs on behalf of hundreds of millions of shareholders, and one begins to see the outlines of both the economic power and the economic vulnerability that is driving the attack on the Westphalian state system.

Given the stakes involved, it is hardly surprising that politics has once again become the servant of economics. The driving force behind the trans-nationalisation of production is competition. The TNCs therefore need not only to move production to where the wages are lowest, but also to ensure that there are as few other hurdles to efficient production as possible. In other words, they need to 'persuade' the host country to do away with protectionism, high taxes, an opaque tax system, and non-tariff barriers to imports. To do this they have sought the help of their own governments. This is the probable origin of the shift in the US' trade negotiation strategy, in 1982, at the beginning of the Uruguay round of trade negotiations, from the building of consensus to the employment of coercion. Coercion, backed by the threat of exclusion from the global trading system, has remained the rich nations' weapon of last resort, even under the World

Trade Organisation, where it is enshrined in articles that permit cross-retaliation, i.e., retaliation against a state not fulfilling its obligations in one area of trade with economic sanctions in another.

The resort to coercion in order to break down the barriers of national economies has led seamlessly to its use to obtain—or, when needed, to block—political change in the host countries as well. The need arises because the policy changes that the transnationals and their parent governments expect the host government to make create millions of new losers in the host economy—workers who lose their jobs, shopkeepers who fall victim to the supermarkets, fixed income groups that find their real incomes and status seriously reduced, and so on—and therefore generate resistance and political unrest. The TNCs cannot afford the uncertainty that the potential for political unrest contains, for it makes it impossible for them to make accurate forecasts of costs, prices, demand, supply and production schedules. Their need for security has therefore created the conditions for coercive regimes to flourish. It explains why the champions of globalisation advocate democracy but hail the economic achievements of the authoritarian regimes in Southeast Asia. It was not by accident that Southeast Asia became the prime destination for such foreign direct investment in the 1970s and 1980s, followed by China in the 1990s. All these countries had authoritarian regimes and, to varying degrees, a Confucian tradition of state-society relations. Their elites were therefore more than ready to substitute economic freedom—the freedom to consume—for political freedom. All of them were therefore willing to persuade their people to 'defer' democratisation in order to promote economic development.

The Drive Towards Empire

It is therefore the globalisation of manufacturing over the past four decades that has provided the essential impetus for the US to abandon first its isolationism, then its multilateralism, and finally to opt for an aggressive, unilateral attempt to reshape the international order as an American empire. If globalisation is to continue unimpeded, all nations must eventually become part of a single integrated marketing and manufacturing system. This requires not only that the turmoil unleashed by the end of the Cold War be brought under control as rapidly as possible, but that this be done without restoring the sovereignty of the nation state. The UN Security Council was proving too cumbersome an instrument, and its members were predisposed to preserving the nation state, albeit with a progressive modification of its powers. The European members of NATO were opposed to letting NATO take on a peacekeeping role outside Europe.

To conservative policymakers in the US, unilateral action to destroy obstructionist regimes—using democracy as an ideological pretext for turning them into vassal states—seemed the only way to fill the vacuum. It was one that fitted in well with their inherited notions of American exceptionalism and manifest destiny.

Americans do not like to think of themselves as imperialists. As a result, the rejection of global democracy in favour of global empire has been swaddled in euphemisms like 'multilateralism' and 'unilateralism'. But their gradual acceptance of an imperial role for themselves is visible in the change of values and norms to which they subscribe. These internalise 'a new notion of right', and a 'new design for the production of norms and legal instruments of coercion that guarantee contracts and resolve conflicts'.[17]

The shift towards norms suited to a world organised as an empire without boundaries is most clearly visible in the gradual change of terminology, surrounding military intervention. The first casualty has been Grotius' notion of a just war as a response to 'injury received'. This has been set aside in favour of a much more ambitious justification that turns war into a police action and makes it obligatory for the hegemonic power to unleash it pre-emptively to serve the common good. The justification for such 'police action' has been expanding continuously and now encompasses the protection of the people of the country being invaded from repression by their own rulers; the elimination of threats to neighbours and to the rest of the 'civilised' world; the implanting of democracy; and, in its most ambitious form, the creation of a brave new world in which everyone will live in peace.

Thus the purpose of the intervention in Kosovo was to liberate the Kosovar Albanians, who were being ground under the heel of that Serbian hypernationalist, Slobodan Milosevic. While this description still contained traces of the old concern for the right to self-determination of ethnic nationalities, it disappeared altogether in the invasion of Afghanistan, and conclusively in the intervention in Iraq, which was presented to the world as a giant hostage rescue operation in which the long-suffering Iraqis were to be liberated from the clutches of a criminal gang that had been holding them hostage for decades. This impression was strengthened by stern warnings to the Iraqi government against using civilians as human shields when the invasion began. Invasion thus turned into liberation, and death into redemption. There was a messianic cast in this new definition that closely paralleled the messianism of the Jesuit priests who accompanied the Spanish conquistadors to South America. Neither hesitated to wield the sword and spread death in the cause of ultimate peace and the salvation of the soul. These were the sentiments that prompted the political theorist, Michael Mann, to exclaim:

When I began to read their writings and speeches, I recognised immediately the mindset, for the notion of achieving morally desirable goals through violence—if necessary over piles of dead bodies—was familiar to me from all the Imperialists, Fascists, and ethnic cleansers it had been my misfortune to study in recent years. I fear politicians when they come bearing morality.'[18]

Another norm in the making is the new faultline dividing the nations of the world. In the past, world leaders talked of peace-loving nations and war-mongers; revisionist versus status quo powers, and so on. What was missing from these categorisations was the element of moral condemnation and self-righteousness. After the Cold War ended, a new distinction rapidly gained acceptance—that between the 'civilised' and the 'rogue' or 'backlash' states. This distinction was carried further by George W. Bush in 2002, when he formulated the concept of the 'axis of evil', although the term evil was admittedly first used by his father to describe Iraq in 1990. The moral opprobrium these terms carry imply that a new set of norms that distinguish law-abiding from lawless behaviour are in the making, and have already gained a wide measure of acceptance.

Third, if nations that defy the will of the new imperial power are rogue states, then individuals who do so are tyrants, hyper-nationalists, terrorists, fanatics, *fidayeen* or, when the revilers run out of words, simply criminals. These terms have been used to describe first Milosevic, then Saddam Hussein, and now all the Iraqis who are resisting the US-led occupation of their country. President George W. Bush's description of the uprising that began in Iraq on 5 April 2004 in his radio broadcast to the nation five days later said it all. 'A small faction is attempting to derail Iraqi *democracy* and seize power,' he said on 10 April 2004. They were 'Saddam supporters and terrorists'. The Shias, according to him, were 'incited by a radical named Muktada Al Sadr, *who is wanted for the murder of a respected Shia cleric.*'[19] In Bush's fantasy world, Iraq was already a democracy; there was no general uprising against the American occupation; and Sunnis and Shias were not joining hands. The miscreants were simply terrorists and mis-guided blind followers of a deposed tyrant, and Al Sadr was nothing more than a common criminal trying to avoid facing a charge of murder! A few days earlier, Defense Secretary Donald Rumsfeld had dismissed the uprising as the work of a few 'thugs, gangs and terrorists'.[20]

The words *resistance, revolt, uprising, insurgency, nationalism* or *patriotism* have not figured even once in any official American, British or coalition statements. Nor has anyone acknowledged that the Shia uprising that began on 5 April 2004 united not only Sunnis and Shias in the poorer quarters of Baghdad, but no fewer than 15 previously separate and often hostile groups and factions. To quote Hardt and Negri, 'War has been banalised ... and ... reduced to a police action, and the new power that can *legitimately exercise ethical functions through war* is sacralised.'[21]

The similarities between the lexicon of terms that the British and American administrations are using to describe their actions in Iraq and those of older Empire builders was underlined by John Pilger in one of his dispatches after a visit to Iraq in March and April 2004:

> 'The task to which we have set our minds,' declared the governor of Kenya in 1955, 'is to civilize a great mass of human beings who are in a very primitive moral and social state.' The slaughter of thousands of nationalists, who were never called nationalists, was British government policy. The myth of the Kenyan uprising was that the Mau Mau brought 'demonic terror' to the heroic white settlers. In fact, the Mau Mau killed just 32 Europeans, compared with the estimated 10,000 Kenyans killed by the British, who ran concentration camps where the conditions were so harsh that 402 inmates died in just one month. Torture, flogging and abuse of women and children were commonplace. 'The special prisons,' wrote the imperial historian V.G. Kiernan, 'were probably as bad as any similar Nazi or Japanese establishments.' None of this was reported. The 'demonic terror' was all one way: black against white. The racist message was unmistakable.[22]

In Iraq, Pilger estimated that, against the 700 Americans that had been killed by 18 April 2004, the Iraqi death toll, including civilians, and soldiers and conscripts killed during the war, was probably as high as 55,000.[23] Quoting Richard Falk, Professor of International Relations at Princeton, Pilger writes: 'What we do routinely in the imperial west, is propagate through a self-righteous, one-way moral/legal screen positive images of western values and innocence that are threatened, validating a campaign of unrestricted violence.' Thus, he concludes, 'western state terrorism is erased, and a tenet of western journalism is to excuse or minimize "our" culpability, however atrocious. Our dead are counted; theirs are not. Our victims are worthy; theirs are not.'

The Terrorist Response

The insecurity that drives the desire to homogenise and control the world is an irrational sentiment. It cannot be reasoned with, because it does not spring from reason. Its most willing servants have sought to cloak their motives in a self-serving mixture of ideology and dogma, reinforced by race and religion, and are using these to justify building an empire. It should not therefore come as a surprise that the resistance to them is also drawing on race, religion and messianism. These are the nutrients of global terrorism. Like globalisation, terrorism is another concept that does not have a universally accepted definition. Even the definition adopted by the United Nations after the 9/11 attacks, which made a determined bid to de-link it from the ends that terrorists espouse and sought to define it solely in terms of the means they use, has not ended the ambiguity. There is even less agreement on its causes. But there is an unspoken consensus, voiced most forcefully by Tony Blair nine days after the London Subway bombings of 7 July 2005, that global terrorism has its roots in a perversion of Islam.

> This is a religious ideology, a strain within the world-wide religion of Islam, as far removed from its essential decency and truth as Protestant gunmen who kill Catholics or vice versa, are from Christianity.[24]

The antidote, Blair asserted, lay not in getting out of Iraq or leaving the Muslim nations to themselves, but in 'joining with key members of the Islamic community ... to promote the true face of Islam world-wide.'[25]

Similar statements, voiced by rote by western leaders, rule out the possibility that the new global terrorists might have genuine grievances, and that if these are addressed, it might reduce their appeal and make it easier to identify and isolate the fanatical core among them. By refusing to recognise that terrorism might have a cause, such statements leave the world with no other option but to confront it with force. Tony Blair summed this up in the same speech:

> Their cause is not founded on an injustice. It is founded on a belief, one whose fanaticism is such it can't be moderated. It can't be remedied. It has to be stood up to. And, of course, they will use any issue that is a matter of dissent within our democracy. But we should lay bare the almost-devilish logic behind such manipulation.[26]

Such analyses serve no purpose, for they avoid asking the crucial question—granted that terrorism, especially the slaughter of innocent civilians, is repugnant, why is the number of terrorists multiplying, and why now? And why are the moderates with whom western governments would like to cooperate steadily being sidelined in democratically conducted elections, such as the one that brought President Ahmedinejad to power in Iran in June 2005, and the Hamas to power in Palestine in February 2006?

An analysis of the evolution of Al Qaeda suggests that global terrorism is rooted in a defence of nationalism and the nation state, against an assault by the West and by what the terrorists consider to be a betrayal of that nationalism by their own national elites. While different people have emphasised different aspects of the betrayal from religion, to culture to morals, the common thread that runs through them is the threat to identity. Today's 'Islamic' terrorism is therefore another reaction, albeit a perverted and ultimately impotent one, to the assault by globalisation upon the nation state.

Global terrorism has evolved through three phases. In each it has become more dangerous than it was before. Its origins lie in a revolt against authoritarian rulers that is not very different from the insurgencies that the world was familiar with during the age of the nation state. What made it different from those classical insurgencies was that it was not directed against oppression by a local tyrant or a colonial ruler, but against a betrayal of values and culture by its own ruling class. This 'revolt' first became international when it was channelled by these same rulers into the Afghan *Jihad* of 1980. Only after that was over—and the *jihadis* found that they were anything but welcome in their home countries—did it assume the stateless, globalised form with which we are familiar today.

Osama bin Laden's metamorphosis from playboy to messianic terrorist illustrates the evolution of the terrorist challenge to globalisation.[27] Osama bin Laden was a typical adolescent from a well-to-do Saudi family. Born in Riyadh in 1957, to a small-time builder whose fortune grew by leaps and bounds because of the oil bonanza, he was one of his father's more than 50 children. He attended good schools and in his teens, like many well-to-do Saudi families, went for his summers to the mountains above Beirut. There Osama frequented the coffee houses and night clubs of what was then considered the Paris of the east. There was nothing to distinguish him from thousands of other children of the new Saudi moneyed class.

He began to change only after the onset of the oil boom in the mid-1970s. Osama was then at the most impressionable age of 18. Enrolled in the prestigious King Abdul Aziz University, he came under the influence of prominent dissident intellectuals from many Arab countries, notably Egypt, who were Islamic fundamentalists. Slowly his worldview began to coalesce. He rejected western models of modernisation and advocated a return to a pure Islamic state. He regarded western incursions into the Arab and Islamic world as forms of aggression not much different from the crusades of a millennium earlier. And he regarded the US as the fountainhead of the cultural, economic and political onslaught on Islam.

By the early 1980s, Osama had already seen the wholesale dissolution of traditional societies and values that integration with the world economy brought to a traditional country. What he was no longer convinced of was that beyond the disruption there lay a better future. He was therefore in search of an alternate model. The first step in this search was to expel the new colonisers from the Islamic lands. That explains the ease with which he and his followers have been able to merge Islamic fundamentalism with sophisticated modern technologies in the deployment of terror. The fact that he was deeply enmeshed with the university intelligentsia and part of a dissident movement from well before the Afghan war helps to explain the ease with which he mobilised his Islamist network in later life.

Osama first worked closely with the Saudi government. At its behest, in the early 1980s he created a *'mujahideen* task force' to aid the anti-Communist guerrillas in South Yemen. The Saudi-sponsored insurrection did not succeed, but his energetic participation in it made him a favourite of the establishment, which showered construction contracts upon the family company.

Osama showed his full organising genius only after he joined the Jihad in Afghanistan. Not only was he among the very first Arab Islamists to join it, but with Sheikh Abdallah Yussuf Azzam, the founder of what became the International Army of Islam (the 'dedicated core of international Islamic terrorism'), he established the *Bait-ul-Ansar* (the first receiving centre for the Islamic fundamentalists from Arab countries who came to fight in Afghanistan) and the *Maktab-al-Khidmat*, the Mujahideen Services Bureau. These not only became the conduit for funnelling mainly Arab Islamists into Afghanistan but also for financing their travel to Peshawar. By the mid-1980s this bureau had cells in more than 50 countries. That is the network out of which Al Qaeda was ultimately born.

In 1989 he returned to Saudi Arabia a hero and would have retired into the family business had it not been for the Iraqi invasion of Kuwait. No sooner had this happened, than he went to the government with plans to recruit special legions of 'Afghans', as the returned Mujahideen were called, and to use his construction equipment to build the same kind of defensive fortifications against an Iraqi invasion that had served the Mujahideen in Afghanistan so well. But the Saudi government spurned him and opted for American troops. Under the Wahabi code, the mere entry of a non-Muslim into the holy land was sacrilege, but Osama remained loyal to the royal family because he believed its assurances that the US would leave the moment the war ended. It was only when US troops did not leave, and the bases became permanent, that he finally turned against the royal family.

Over the next three years Osama became one of the leaders of a new generation of young, grassroots clergy in Saudi Arabia, which openly preached the removal of the royal family and the establishment of an Islamist government. In 1994, when the threat of an Islamic jihad against the regime became serious, the government finally stripped him of his citizenship.[28] Osama first took refuge in Sudan, but returned to Afghanistan after the Taliban victory, this time to stay.

In the seven years that followed, he built the largest and most powerful international terrorist network the world has known. He formed close connections with Ayman al Zawahiri of Egypt and Hussein al Turaby of Sudan, and may have been involved in, and almost certainly knew of, the attempt on Hosni Mubarak's life in Addis Ababa. In 1998 when he issued his now famous *fatwa* against the United States, his Mujahideen fighting force in Afghanistan consisted of over 10,000 persons. According to an Egyptian estimate, 2,830 of them were Arabs. The rest were Pakistanis, Tajiks, Uzbeks, Chechens, Bangladeshis and others. His worldwide network consisted of three concentric rings—the innermost ring contained his closest associates, many going back two decades.[29] Through them he controlled or influenced a very large number of terrorist organisations in the countries mentioned above, and cells in as many as 50 countries. Beyond them were thousands of individuals who swore loyalty to him, but belonged to still other groups around the globe.

Terrorism and Islam

The question that begs for an answer is why these dissident intellectuals turned away from secular forms of dissent and towards fundamentalism. Why did they not follow an earlier generation of Arab scholars and intellectuals and become Nasserites or socialists or both? The probable answer is their perception, however intuitive or indistinct, that these ideologies had nothing to offer them. Modernising ideologies, like socialism, communism and the benign form of nationalism were nourished by the belief that science, technology and industrialisation—in short, modernisation—held the prospect of a better life for all of them in the future. By the 1980s this belief had been almost completely eroded. Instead more and more Arab intellectuals were convinced that the Islamic countries had been firmly cast in the role of losers in the modern world. Not only did they suffer from all the disadvantages of smallness of size and lateness in starting down the road to industrialisation, but in their special case modernisation and economic success were denied to them because of their possession of oil and because of Israel. The economic might of the industrialised nations was built upon a cheap and plentiful supply of energy. Oil had begun to replace coal shortly after the First World War, and had become the primary source of energy after the Second. Most of the oil reserves of the world were concentrated in the Islamic world. Both Nasserism and Ba'athism, the two main modernising currents in the Arab world after the Second World War, had been pan-Arab in their ideology. Both had therefore contained the potential for uniting the Arab world and increasing its economic bargaining power. Thus, not only the US but the entire industrialised world had a vital interest in keeping the Islamic world economically disunited and weak.

Israel also had every reason to fear the emergence of a rich, unified, modern and technologically advanced pan-Arab confederation, for only such an entity could pose an effective threat to it. Since Israel had a virtually indissoluble link with the US; this turned the US into an opponent of Arab modernisation and the supporter of every archaic monarchy and sheikh-dom in the Arab world. Finally, US military support to Israel ensured the crushing defeat of Egypt and Syria in the wars of 1967 and 1973. For the youth in particular, these defeats effectively discredited Nasser's pan-Arab nationalism and Ba'athist socialism. In the 1970s and 1980s they began to look for another sustaining ideology—another world to believe in.

It was with these eyes that the youth and the intelligentsia of the Islamic world viewed the changes unleashed in their societies by sudden oil wealth in the 1970s and 1980s. The new wealth led to a rapid breakdown of the traditional, austere Islamic way of life, and scandalised the majority of the people. Rapid urbanisation strengthened this perception by loosening the bonds of custom and tradition. It also gave birth to individualism and a new sense of freedom, which was often difficult to distinguish from license. This occurred most noticeably in the new moneyed elite, which came to be regarded as decadent, immoral and an active threat to Islam. Since oil was a state monopoly in all the Islamic countries, the new moneyed elite was closely associated with the state. As a result, the state and the system of government it represented came to be regarded as venal.

Possession of oil also turned out to be more of a curse than a blessing. By pushing up the exchange rate of the currencies of the oil-exporting countries, it effectively prevented the establishment of even the small indus-tries that cater to everyday needs in most countries. Importing was simply too easy and the imported products too cheap. Thus oil wealth co-existed side by side with very high levels of unemployment and a large floating population of educated youth with very uncertain job prospects. It was an explosive mixture.

Apart from the baleful impact of oil wealth, there were three reasons why the terrorist response to globalisation began in the Islamic world. The first was a profound sense of victimisation that went back to the fall of the Ottoman empire, but had crystallised around the forced creation of Israel in the choicest part of the Arab civilisational heartland, and the US' morally blind support of anything and everything that Israel had done since then. The second was the holistic nature of Islam, which claims to guide or, in the case of the fundamentalists, dictate every action of the individual from cradle to grave. This makes a separation of political from private life more than usually difficult. A perceived injustice in the former becomes a justification for opposition and, if necessary, martyrdom in the latter. The third was the exploitation of this sentiment by the US against the Russians in Afghanistan. This created the infrastructure that was required by the terrorist movement in a remarkably short time. The Afghan jihad therefore did not create the terrorist challenge; it only facilitated its emergence.

Internationalising of Terrorism: The First Phase

The initial goal of most of the new Islamic warriors was not to attack the US but to overthrow their own heavily compromised governments. During the Afghan war, between 12,000 and 16,000 volunteers from Muslim countries all over the Middle East and Europe went to fight in Afghanistan. After the Afghan war ended, most of them returned to their countries. They returned changed into zealots for a new cause, the cause of international Islamic resurgence.[30] As early as 1996, there was evidence, painstakingly documented by a four-continent study of the *Los Angeles Times*, that these graduates of Afghanistan have given a violent and specifically anti-west, anti-modern edge to insurgencies and violent fundamentalist movements in Algeria, Tajikistan, Russia (Chechnya), Bosnia, Philippines, Egypt and India.[31]

The worldwide publicity given to the terrorist bombings of the US embassies in Nairobi and Dar-es-Salaam, in 1998, and the consequent highlighting of earlier attacks on US military and intelligence personnel,[32] created the impression that the terrorist attacks were aimed solely at the US. But in fact the attacks were far more diffused, and only later did they acquire their concentrated focus on the US. Perhaps the bloodiest intervention by the 'Afghanis', as they came to be called, occurred in the early and mid-90s in Algeria, where by the late 1990s they had killed a minimum of 2,000 villagers in remote parts of western Algeria. Most were killed in 'orthodox Islamic' ways, by having their arms and legs, and eventually their heads, chopped off.[33]

Egypt too bore the brunt of this type of terrorism.[34] The first fundamentalist group—the mother of all groups—was Al-Jihad, also called Islamic Jihad (IJ), which was headed by Abbud-al-Jumar. This was formed in the late 1970s. In 1981, it succeeded in assassinating President Anwar Sadaat while he was reviewing his troops at a ceremonial march past. Thereafter, there was a lull in terrorist violence. The IJ split in two. Terrorist violence however, revived sharply in 1992. Another group, called the Islamic Group, *Al Gamma'a al Islamiyya* (IG), emerged and seized the centre of the Islamic militant stage. In no time at all the IG became the most feared and despised group in the country. Although also formed in the late 1970s, it began to make a name for its insensate xenophobia. It came into the news when it began to attack and kill foreign tourists, bomb foreign institutions like banks and airline offices, and, among Egyptians, target middle-level security personnel and Coptic Christians. The IG's attacks reached a crescendo in 1993. In one such attack in April they succeeded in injuring the Egyptian information minister. In 1994, they killed another five foreign tourists and more than 20 Egyptians. But that was enough for the Egyptian authorities. In 1994, they began to use some of the same methods for dealing with their terrorists as the Punjab police. By the time of the Population Conference in October, the immediate threat from the IG had been largely contained.

The IG was not the only group to espouse extreme violence. A splinter group of the original Islamic Jihad, The Vanguards of Conquest, was responsible for a huge car bomb blast in Cairo in August 1993, which injured the interior minister, Hassan-al-Alfi. In November of the same year there was another car bomb attack on the foreign minister, Asif Sedki. In all six people were killed and 43 injured in these bomb blasts.

The attacks on the government climaxed in July 1995, when President Mubarak came within a hair's breadth of losing his life in Addis Ababa. Thus, between 1992 and 1995, as many as four members of the Egyptian cabinet had faced death by assassination, and three of them had been injured in the *attentats*. The root cause of the sudden spurt in violence that took place from 1992 onwards was the return to Egypt, Sudan, Libya and elsewhere in the Middle East, of Islamic fundamentalist Mujahideen who had gone to Pakistan to fight against the Soviet Union in Afghanistan. But the Mujahideen who returned had not simply merged themselves into local movements. Instead they were working to stitch these together into the new pan-Islamic fundamentalist movement. And the controls were being operated from Peshawar in Pakistan.

Immediately after the assassination attempt on their Foreign minister, when they intercepted a telegram to the terrorists of the Islamic Group from Peshawar in Pakistan in 1993, the Egyptians found clinching evidence that some if not all the attacks were being masterminded by terrorists still based in Pakistan. The contents of the telegram showed enough of an official Pakistani hand shielding and nurturing the terrorists to make President Mubarak cancel a proposed visit to Pakistan at the last minute. This forced the Pakistani government to finally get off the fence and sign an extradition treaty with Egypt and to extradite six persons suspected of being involved in the attack on Mubarak.[35] On 19 November 1995, not long after Pakistan took this decision, terrorists bombed the Egyptian embassy in Islamabad, killing three diplomats and a large number of Pakistani staff. The ambassador escaped.

Internationalisation of Terrorism: The Second Phase

By the mid-1990s, the 'Afghans' had become a floating, increasingly internationalised army of Islam. At least a thousand of them went to Bosnia, aided and abetted overtly by the US, and stiffened the resistance of the Bosnian Muslims fighting the Serb militias. A fair number appeared in Kosovo as part of the Kosovo liberation Army. The Russian government repeatedly asserted that Islamists from the Middle East had joined the Chechen insurgents, but the Western media treated these with some scepticism till the massacre of schoolchildren at Beslan in September 2004.

Only gradually did the focus narrow down to the US. The catalytic role in this transition was played by the Saudi religious establishment, which was furiously opposed to the continued presence of US troops on Saudi soil, and, more specifically, by Osama bin Laden. This sharpened the perception of the US as a hegemonistic power that was intent upon foisting its own brand of modernisation on the world, and was propping up the puppet regimes that were allowing the pure values of Islam to be corrupted.

This view of the US was crystallised in Bin Laden's *fatwa* of June 1998. Only after that did the US and its close allies become the prime targets of terrorist attack. Bin Laden demonstrated his intent by bombing the US embassies in Nairobi and Dar-es-Salaam. He followed it up with the suicide bombing of the USS Cole in 1999. Both were purely destructive acts that virtually shouted out the impotent rage of the opponents of globalisation and its assault upon Islam. It was not till 9/11 that the new terrorism made a significant impact upon public perceptions in the US. Bush took advantage of the resulting fear to implement the neo-conservative empire project to which he was already greatly attracted. But in doing so, he elevated what was (and, despite 9/11, still remains) a demonstration of impotence that costs at most a few score lives every year and changes nothing, to the status of the prime enemy of the empire project. In doing so he exposed the world to the risk of attracting other enemies of globalisation to the terrorist cause.

Till (and including) the 9/11 attacks, the new global terrorism had displayed the following characteristics:

- It was perpetrated by a new generation of modern and often technically qualified young persons who were reacting to what they considered a cultural and economic invasion of their country by the forces of globalisation.
- These were not religious in the traditional sense of the term. To them Islam was a banner to mobilise under, and shorthand for an entire way of living and thinking that was now under attack.

- The first targets of these new terrorists were their own governments, whom they accused of betraying their culture by bowing to or being seduced by the West, especially the USA.
- Their second target was the industrialised West, and particularly the USA, which they regarded as the most aggressive agent of globalisation, and therefore the fountainhead of the corruption that was eroding their societies and their values.

Till 9/11, terrorist acts in the west were perpetrated almost entirely by terrorists who had flown in from the Middle East. But after the invasion of Afghanistan and Iraq, a new kind of terrorist emerged. This was the suicide bomber. Immigrants and their children living in the West—fired by a sense of outrage and inflamed by daily reports of an indiscriminate killing of civilians by 'Coalition' forces firing rockets and missiles into buildings suspected of harbouring insurgents—have taken to attacking the societies in which they live. The first attack took place in Madrid, whose conservative prime minister Jose Aznar had been an active participant in the decision to invade Iraq. Two hundred Spanish civilians, probably nine-tenths of whom had vigorously opposed the invasion of Iraq, died in a succession of blasts in a Madrid suburban train on 11 March 2004. The second terrorist outrage occurred in London on 7 July 2005. Three blasts on the underground rail and one in a bus left 56 persons dead and 700 injured.

The London bombing threw a flood of light on the way in which terrorism was mutating into an attack on civil society itself. Three of the four terrorists—Haseeb Hussain, Shahzad Tanveer and Mohamed Siddique Khan—were born in Britain. One was not even born a Muslim but had converted to Islam some time earlier. All were fully integrated into British society. Hussain had dropped out of high school, but Khan had a wife and a child, and Tanveer was a 'promising cricketer'. Lindsay Germaine had married only a year earlier and his wife was four months pregnant. All consciously decided to lose their lives attacking the country and society in which they had been born and educated.

Statements by the British police and intelligence officials showed that they had been expecting a terrorist attack on Britain for some time. The alarm was first sounded not by MI5 or Scotland Yard but by the CIA. In a report completed at the end of May, it warned the US government that Iraq was breeding a new generation of terrorists who were likely to fan out into Europe and America after the war there ended. British intelligence officials took the warning seriously, but initially believed that the return flow would not seriously affect Britain, as not more than 200 Britons had taken part in the Afghan war and very few had gone to Iraq.[36] Their anxiety went up a notch when the collation of intelligence information with other European countries showed that a large number of dormant Islamic recruitment rings had come to life again. As many as 21 such rings had been identified.[37] These admissions implied that the former *jihadis* were kept under surveillance, and that most if not all the old recruitment rings were known and were being closely monitored.

British intelligence also routinely keeps a watch on mosques, and monitors visitors to the UK. Despite all this, the suicide bombers turned up nowhere on their radar screen. The only possible explanation even then was that none of the bombers were religious fanatics. This was later vindicated by the statements of the families of two of the four who had been identified.[38] From what they told the police, a clear pattern has emerged: they came from perfectly ordinary immigrant families where religion was about as important as it is in a traditional Christian, Hindu or Jewish family. Religion played no significant part in their decision. Had it done so, they would have been visiting mosques regularly, and their families would have been aware of the gradual rise of extremism in their make-up. Two of them at least had gone, or been sent, to *madrassas* in Pakistan. But it is possible that this happened only after they had been recruited, in order to help them develop the spiritual fortitude they needed for the extreme act of suicide.

If religion was not the primary motivation, then what was? One answer was given by five Muslim youth interviewed on 13 July by the BBC in Leeds. 'You have come to ask us how we feel when 50 people have died in London,' said one young man just out of his teens. 'This should never have happened, but why did you not come to us when thousands of Afghans were being killed and a hundred thousand Iraqis died? The others echoed his sentiments.'[39] The BBC dropped this particular line of inquiry from its subsequent telecasts, partly because the government had by then launched a concerted drive to deny any link with Iraq.[40]

The London bombings underlined the threat that the emergence of the suicide bomber posed to civil society. Suicide is the most extreme form of protest human beings are capable of—the final rebellion against a world they cannot change but also cannot continue to live in. Admittedly, something has to snap inside a person to make him or her want to commit suicide, and mental fragility makes the breakdown easier. Brainwashing then becomes much easier. But one does not have to be psychotic or brainwashed to choose this form of protest. On 6 May 1998, Bishop John Joseph ended his own life in a courthouse in Sahiwal, Pakistan when Ayub Massih, a 25-year-old Catholic was condemned to die for blasphemy against Islam.[41] On 21 January 2001, five members of Falun Gong tried to commit suicide in Tiananmen square by burning themselves. By then the Chinese government had jailed 450 of its members, sent 600 to mental hospitals, 10,000 to labour camps and 50,000 to detention centres.[42] In February 2003 five young Iranian women from villages near the city of Shiraz burnt themselves to death because their families refused to let them go out to work.[43]

Suicide is also an expression of helplessness. Writing about the prevalence of suicide among Chinese women, a Chinese writer, Si Si Lu, summed up the motive for suicide as follows:

> People who have the power and resources to make choices and changes in their lives are usually also able to express their views in a variety of moderate and socially acceptable ways. For those who lack the power or resources to address the sources of their discontent, however, suicide may provide a last resort.[44]

Had revenge for the invasion of Iraq been their sole motive, the bombers would have tried to set off the bombs without killing themselves. They may have chosen suicide because it also gave them an escape from a conflict that was tearing them apart but which they could not resolve. This was the conflict between their inherited Muslim identity and their acquired British one. Contrary to what most people believe, this conflict is virtually non-existent in those who make the decision to migrate. Their cultural identities are already fully formed and most of them ask for nothing more than a friendly reception from their host nation.

The confusion, and therefore conflict over identity, usually starts in the first generation born or raised from infancy in the host country. This new generation considers itself a part of the host nation, but has not severed its ties with its parent culture. It therefore actively seeks ways of fusing the two. Some of the most creative fiction, film and theatre in Britain is a fruit of this effort.

But the more successful this generation is in fusing its two inheritances, the greater is the potential for conflict if the still incomplete process is disrupted. That is what 9/11 did to the Muslim diaspora. The extravagant condemnation of Islamic fundamentalism, the thinly disguised distrust of Muslims and the heightened surveillance of Muslim youth that followed reversed the process of assimilation. Many reacted by rebelling against their host cultures. This took them back to the veil, the beard and skull-cap, the mosque and the *madrassa*.

But that road was not open to all. The further someone had gone down the road to assimilation, the more difficult did it become for him or her to choose this form of protest. Even the option that German Americans earlier had, of rejecting their German origin entirely because of Hitler's excesses, was not open to this group, because in the Iraq war and to some extent in

Afghanistan, it was the US and UK that had committed the aggression and many of the excesses that followed.

At its root, the conflict of loyalties is a product of the information revolution. The horrors of war and the meanness of the calculations that go into waging it can no longer be hidden from ordinary people. What is perceived as an unjust or unnecessary war creates a crisis of conscience that becomes very hard to bear. This explains the proliferation of anti-war NGOs all over the world, and the giant peace marches that preceded the invasion of Iraq. But the conflict is most acute among first-generation youth born of immigrant parents, who have developed a new identity and a new loyalty but have not yet shed their old ones. If the present chaos in the international state system continues, then, unable to turn back and unable to go forward, more and more of them will suffer a psychotic breakdown. Turning themselves into human bombs could become the revenge that a few take on a society that has left them with no psychological space to inhabit. It is an act not far removed, in its horrific intensity, from matricide. It may also explain why there seems to be an inexhaustible supply of suicide bombers for Iraq.

Everything that the British police came to know about the July 7 suicide bombers is explained by the predicament described above. Their sheer normality, their participation in team sports like cricket, and their lack of overt religiosity, reflected the level of their assimilation into British society. The fact that they kept their parents utterly in the dark about their intentions showed that the conflict they were unable to handle affected only their generation and not that of their parents. The fact that two of them were able to plan their own extinction despite having wives and children mirrored the acuteness of the struggle within them and, finally, the casual way in which they said goodbye to each other hours before their deaths, shows that they, at least, had resolved the conflict that had been tearing them apart.

There is a profoundly important moral in the London bombings. A globalised world, in which cultures will increasingly be intermixed, cannot co-exist with the amorality of the nineteenth- and twentieth-century nation state. The globalised world demands that host nations extend the same rule of law to the home countries of their immigrant populations as they live under themselves. The above-mentioned amorality exempts powerful nation states from the rule of law altogether. The new global terrorism is therefore as much an attack upon the untrammelled sovereignty of the nation state as are the military interventions in the name of human rights. The more it develops, the more will it hasten the end of the nation state. With no alternative global state system yet in sight, interventionism and terrorism will feed off each other to accelerate the descent into chaos.

Assault on Democracy

In the post-9/11 world, terrorism and empire have begun to feed off each other to destroy the democratic freedoms and institutions that are the world's inheritance from the days of the Westphalian international order. In the US, the Patriot and Homeland Security Acts have given law enforcement agencies draconian powers of arrest and almost indefinite detention without trial that make a mockery of the notion of habeas corpus. The US has violated the Geneva Convention on prisoners of war by unilaterally defining those captured in Afghanistan as *not* prisoners of war, and has kept them under indefinite detention at its military base in Guantanamo. Surveillance on visitors to America has increased to unheard-of levels. At immigration barriers, strip searches and incommunicado detention of visitors to the US have become common. Visitors are being routinely fingerprinted and new visas to the US are soon expected to include microchips containing the optical scans of the visa holders.

But the most continuously invasive attack on individual freedom has come from the further enlargement of the US' already comprehensive electronic spying capability. The US' eavesdropping infrastructure was born during the Cold War, out of a secret agreement in 1948 between the US, the UK, Canada, Australia and New Zealand to exchange intelligence information not only about target countries, i.e., the Soviet bloc and sundry 'neutrals', but also about each other. Until 1981 the five signatories exchanged only processed intelligence reports. From that year they also began to exchange raw intercepts under a programme code-named 'Echelon'. From then onwards, the US has had access to all communications intercepts all over the world, since Echelon consists of a network of satellites and computers designed to listen to all the non-military communications of governments, private organisations and individuals on behalf of the UK/USA signals intelligence alliance. In 2002 Echelon had 120 satellites in orbit and was monitoring over 180 billion minutes of international phone calls alone.[45] It also routinely monitored all internet communications. Even before 9/11 Patrick Poole, author of *ECHELON: America's Secret Global Surveillance Network*, had warned:

> What began as a noble alliance to contain and defeat the forces of communism has turned into a carte blanche to disregard the rights and liberties of the American people and the population of the free world. As has been demonstrated time and again, the NSA has been persistent in subverting not just the intent of the law in regards to the prohibition of domestic spying, but the letter as well.[46]

9/11 has given the US and its close allies the best of possible excuses to enlarge this system, with more listening posts, more powerful computers and a much-enlarged lexicon of key words to trigger the recording devices. The web page of the Global Communications Headquarters (GCHQ) of the UK government baldly claimed on 25 September 2002 that '*All traffic*, whether voice, fax or Local Area and Wide Area Networks (LANs and WANs) used for data communications are secured by state of the art cryptographic products—designed and manufactured internally.'[47] In October 2001, the US Defense Department publicly solicited offers for improving such capabilities to be created *within 12 to 18 months*.[48]

In one of those ironies of history where reality mimics fiction, George Orwell's *1984* has finally been born. Human beings increasingly enjoy freedom only so long as they stay within lines drawn by an all-seeing, all-powerful, invisible authority. The only unfettered freedoms they have left are to consume and to make love. The only difference is that Big Brother is not preaching communism; he is preaching democracy.

The US' drift towards an Orwellian state is not rooted solely in its fear of terrorism, and the skilful use that the neo-conservatives have made of it to herd a panic-stricken public towards an authoritarian state. Its roots go all the way back to the de-industrialisation of America triggered by capitalism's jump from the nation state to the globe. The migration of manufacturing industry to the low-wage countries of Asia and South America has forced a vast proportion of the American industrial working class into the service sector and into part-time work. This has left it far poorer and more insecure than ever before.[49] At the same time, there has been an inflow of mainly Latin American immigrants into the American heartland states. These have competed, often successfully, for the service sector jobs that are still available. Over a quarter of a century, the dispossessed working class has reacted first with a sense of defeat, then anger, and, finally, after 9/11 with fear. That fear has fused with anger into a search for scapegoats, both within the US and abroad. This is fuelling the shift to the right that has been evident in American politics for the past quarter of a century. There has been a similar shift to the right in European politics, which has been fuelled by the same basic cause, the onset of de-industrialisation. This is evident in the resurgence of the far right in French, German, and Italian politics. But only in the US has this sentiment coalesced into a political force strong enough to capture the state.

The way in which globalisation has caused the shift to the right in American politics has been captured in poignant detail by Dale Maharidge, author of *Journey to Nowhere*, which documents the despair of ruined steel workers in Youngstown, Ohio, in the late 1970s and early 1980s. Maharidge returned to Youngstown a dozen years later in 1996 and found that the feeling of defeat he had encountered earlier had turned into anger. After 9/11 he returned again, and over two-and-a-half years travelled thousands of miles and interviewed hundreds of people. He found that the anger had combined with fear and become 'a dangerous brew'. The transformation of this brew into a serious threat to American democratic institutions is best captured in his own words:

> What I found was that anger had now combined with fear, and together they had become a dangerous brew. Fear alone, of another terror attack, is a strong force in American politics. But fear connected with anger is an especially volatile combination. The 9/11 attacks were not solely the genesis but an amplifier of pre-existing tensions—rooted in the radically transformed American economy, from a manufacturing dynamo to that of millions of jobs of the Wal-Mart variety. One cannot displace millions of workers from high-paying jobs to low ones without a sociopolitical cost. It's a fundamental reality that was ignored during the rise of the so-called new economy.
>
> Prick the anger whose surface may be pro-Iraq war and anti-Arab, dismissive of Abu Ghraib, and one hears of ruined 401(k)s, poor or no healthcare, lost work. There are 1 million fewer jobs today than when George Bush took office, and the loss of higher-paid manufacturing jobs has been stunning.
>
> Where this mood will lead is unclear, but it cannot be overlooked by anyone concerned about the future of the United States.
>
> ... On the eve of a presidential election seventy-two years after Roosevelt vs. Hoover, Americans are not rioting over food, and homeless veterans are not marching on Washington. But there are different ways for anger to erupt. An undercurrent has been building for three decades. Talk-radio is but one example of how the anger has grown. In 1980 there were about seventy-five stations in the nation that were all talk. There weren't that many conservative hosts. Now there are 1,300 all-talk stations, and conservatives rule. It's no coincidence that their popularity rose concurrent with the decline of the manufacturing economy, as anger deepened in American society. These shows were not a cause but a free-market response.
>
> How bad is it? During the 2000 election we went to Texas and Tennessee to find some of the 11.6 million impoverished children—77 per cent had at least one working parent, according to the Children's Defense Fund. Because their wages were Dickensian, many had to beg for charity food. During what was alleged the most booming economy in history, America's Second Harvest (the nationwide network of food banks) gave away 1 billion pounds of food in 2000, more than double the amount in 1990. Yet it wasn't enough—many food banks ran empty. The despair we saw in the homes of working Americans that election year was equal to that we saw among the homeless in the early 1980s. In many houses I peered into refrigerators and saw them empty. Never underestimate the anger of a parent who puts her child to bed hungry.

Many of the angry people I interviewed after 9/11, those who tune in faithfully to Rush Limbaugh or Bill O'Reilly, know their highly paid jobs are forever gone or threatened. Their mood, I imagine, is like those on the right during the 1930s who felt the economy would never again be fixed; Limbaugh, O'Reilly and others are their Father Coughlins.

And it's not just those on the bottom. A software engineer in Portland, Oregon, told me recently that some of his colleagues have turned hard right, are fearful for their jobs and are angry.

There are tens of millions of American workers living in a virtual depression, in a virtual Weimar. Their anger is real, as is their fear. Ignoring it is dangerous. The right has been addressing it in the form of appearing decisive with 'preventive war,' or by cranking up the xenophobia. When many of them go into the voting booth they will punch the card or pull the lever for a candidate who appears strong.[50]

Maharidge's article proved prophetic. Despite a record registration of new voters and a record turnout at the polls, both of which should have helped the Democrats, Bush won by 3.61 million votes and a clear 51 per cent of the vote. This was the largest margin in recent history. Bush won despite having the worst record of any president after the Second World War, perhaps of the entire twentieth century, because two new factors had decided the outcome.[51] These were renascent Christian fundamentalism and fear. Twenty-two per cent of the electorate considered moral values—abortion, gay marriages and the like—to be the most important issue. Another 19 per cent admitted that terrorism was their overriding concern. Eighty-two per cent of these two groups voted for Bush.[52]

President Bush did not win because Kerry could not bring out the Democratic voters; he won despite Kerry's success in doing so. He won because even larger numbers of new voters came out to vote for him. They belonged to the Christian evangelical right. They voted for Bush because they wanted to turn the clock back. They wanted to prevent abortion; to prevent same-sex marriages; and to allow Christian prayers in the state school system. They approved of the curtailment of the democratic rights of individuals if this was necessary to make the masses feel more safe. They did not mind that their President had lied to them, or at least allowed them to draw the wrong conclusions, in order to take them into war. They did not mind if habeas corpus had been diluted and new interpretations were being given to law by executive order, to permit torture and sexual molestation of prisoners who had not been charged with, let alone convicted of, anything.

They were, in short, people who were not guided by reason but swayed by passion. They were not looking forward to the technology-dominated future but yearning to go back to the God-fearing past. For them rationality was at a severe discount. Only blind faith in God, in Bush and in the American flag mattered. They hankered for a past when life was simpler, and values were more clearly defined. They yearned for simple solutions to intractable problems and did not mind of their government took short-cuts to get to them. They longed for the conformism of the past and the freedom from doubt that it gave them. They took shelter in religion from a world that they no longer understood. They distrusted the big cosmo-politan cities. They were, in sum, America's answer to Osama bin Laden. On 2 November they cracked the liberal foundations upon which American democracy had rested since the New Deal of the 1930s.

Towards Darkness

Since global capitalism is in the early stages of its development, economic interdependence will continue to deepen, and the desire for control will continue to determine the actions of transnational corporations and their parent governments for several more decades. The chaos we are now ex-periencing is therefore destined to grow worse. Economic interdependence will cease to grow only when all or nearly all the world is integrated into a single market and forms part of a single manufacturing system. The desire for control will therefore continue to propel political change till the inter-national order based on sovereign nation states is replaced by a single political entity.

The transformation that the world is going through is not only far, far bigger than any of the four that have preceded it, but is also profoundly different from them. Capitalism generated chaos in each of its previous births by destroying the institutions appropriate to its earlier incarnation. But on each occasion the creation of new institutions was made possible by the survival of key institutions from the previous phase of capitalism. The most important of these was the nation state. By the time capitalism entered its third cycle of expansion and made the nation state its container, the Westphalian State had already been in existence for two centuries. Capitalism transformed it, giving it a strong ethnic identity, suppressing ethnic minorities, hardening frontiers and eliminating intermediate centres of power within the state in order to bring the individual into a direct re-lationship with the state. But it did so from within.

So when the industrial revolution created new winners and new losers and set off a struggle between the two, the struggle occurred within the framework of authority of a pre-existent state. The object of the prot-agonists was to capture the institutions of the state with the purpose of put-ting them to their own use. The state in turn was not a passive institution, but played an active part in both hastening some aspects of the change and retarding others. The purpose of both sets of actions was to ensure its stability and enhance its power. Thus the Tudor monarchs in England both helped build the institutions of the future capitalist nation state, and opposed, thereby slowing down, the enclosure movement in agriculture which threatened to devastate the social structure of the country.[53] Two centuries later, while the Luddites reacted to the machines that were destroying their livelihood by smashing them, the Chartists attempted to capture the state through universal franchise and use its power to improve their condition. Social democracy and the welfare state were the end products of this century-long struggle. They harmonised the interests of the winners and losers from capitalism to give the industrialised counties a degree of social harmony that they had not known for at least two centuries.

The systemic chaos that the world is slipping into now is qualitatively different because it is eroding the institutions of the Westphalian state without creating anything else that can harmonise the interests of the winners and losers on a global scale. The losers from the current transformation therefore have no higher 'global' authority to which they can turn either to mitigate its rigours or obtain redress. They are therefore being thrown on the mercy of market forces in a way that pre-existent statutes in the European countries, like the Elizabethan Poor Law and the Statute of Artificers in England, had prevented two centuries ago. The destruction of the institutions of the nation state is therefore taking place in a political vacuum where there is no authority to moderate its pace or guide its direction. This virtually ensures that the future will remain a continuation of the present. It is the path that Hobsbawm identified as leading to 'darkness'.

At the Crossroads

If the descent into chaos described above is to be halted before it sweeps away every institution of civilised life that was designed to moderate social and political conflict, the future must not be a continuation of the past. But a change of direction is only possible if one has an idea of the alternate future towards which one wants to go. It is possible to outline such a future, but conjuring it up only underlines how far the world has moved in the wrong direction.

The initial chapters of this book were devoted to showing that the single autonomous force that has been shaping the development of political and economic institutions in the world since the dawn of capitalism is the development of technology. This has triggered the past four cycles of capitalism's expansion, and is behind the remorseless expansion of global capitalism today. This expansion will not stop till most of the world has become its new 'container'. It is therefore safe to conclude that capitalism, as it expands, will continue to reshape the political structure of the world to suit its new needs. The replacement of a system of sovereign, independent nation states by a single integrated political and economic system that recognises few boundaries between the erstwhile independent states, and in the end leaves very little room for independent decision making outside delegated areas of responsibility is therefore not only inevitable, but has already begun.

What remains undecided is how this integrated political and economic system will be built. In 2005 the world has arrived at a crossroads. One road leads to an empire built on force and sustained by paranoia. It requires an ever-mounting recourse to coercion, as a single dominant power attempts to impose an international order of its own making upon the world. That is the road the world is on today. The other road leads to the creation and strengthening of a 'Commonwealth'—government through consensus, however imperfectly it is forged; an attempt to minimise the disruption of human life caused by the emergence of global capitalism; and a conscious attempt to give the institutions of the nation state time to adapt or, where that is not possible, to give way for the creation of new global institutions.

The idea of the world as a commonwealth does not challenge the process of global integration. Nor does it deny the US a hegemonic role in shaping it. It only insists that the US' hegemony cannot be built by indefinitely expanding the ambit of the US' national interest and claiming that this represents the interests of the world as a whole. To re-establish its hegemony the US will have to temper its goals in the fire of other countries' aspirations and needs. This is the conservative alternative to the radicalism that now nests securely at the far right of the political spectrum and dominates the global agenda for change.

Ever since the end of the Cold War, the US has been moving further and further down the first road. Under the spur of neo-conservative exhortations and seductive appeals to fulfil America's manifest destiny, a large section of the American public has become enamoured by the idea of creating an empire that will far outshine the Roman and British empires. It first went part of the way in dispensing with consensus when it spearheaded NATO's attack on Serbia. It went the whole way when it invaded Iraq. The aftermath of that invasion has exposed the inherent impossibility of creating an empire, at least in any sense that the world has known it before. It has plunged the US into a quagmire in Iraq, exposed the limits of its military power, and underlined the near impossibility, in the age of information and of deadly, portable small arms, of relying on force alone to restructure the world.

This does not however mean that a future US administration will find it easy to change course. An imperial power that chooses to rule through force alone runs the risk of having nothing to fall back upon if it fails. It is therefore condemned to rely upon it more and more, regardless irrespective of whether it is achieving its goals or not. Unilateralism thus leads to an inexorable escalation of violence till it consumes all those who are touched by it. This is the Achilles' heel of the Bush Security Doctrine of preventive intervention.

The US cannot afford to pull out of Iraq before crushing all opposition to the Allawi regime, because of the victory that this would hand to Al Qaeda and other terrorist organisations. Signs are proliferating, therefore, that it plans to push ahead on the course it has embarked upon. In the beginning of October 2004, the *Wall Street Journal* reported that in order to increase the size of the standing army, it is considering introducing conscription from June 2005. Similar reports appeared in a number of other American newspapers. They sparked a vigorous debate on the merits and drawbacks of reintroducing the draft.[54]

Although the word is never uttered, the Bush administration knows that to stabilise empire it must recover its hegemony. It did not come as a surprise, therefore, that within weeks of his second inauguration Bush unveiled another hegemonic justification for the untrammelled use of force. In his speech to the UN General Assembly in September 2004 he unveiled the US' new global mission. This was to 'expand the circle of liberty and security and development ... that brought unity to Europe, self-government to Latin America and Asia, and new hope to Africa.' According to him, what the US had been doing in Iraq was to 'reaffirm the equal value and dignity of every human life'.

The speech contained a new and chilling expansion of the 'axis of evil': 'We know that oppressive governments support terror while free governments fight terror in their midst. We know that free peoples embrace progress and life instead of becoming the recruits for murderous ideologies.' Every 'oppressive', i.e., authoritarian government was thus a potential ally of global terror. It therefore had to be overthrown and its people set free. In his second inaugural address he spelt this out more forcefully:

> For as long as whole regions of the world simmer in resentment and tyranny—prone to ideologies that feed hatred and excuse murder—violence will gather, and multiply in destructive power, and cross the most defended borders, and raise a mortal threat. There is only one force of history that can break the reign of hatred and resentment, and expose the pretensions of tyrants, and reward the hopes of the decent and tolerant, and that is the force of human freedom.

We are led, by events and common sense, to one conclusion: The survival of liberty in our land increasingly depends on the success of liberty in other lands. The best hope for peace in our world is the expansion of freedom in all the world.

America's vital interests and our deepest beliefs are now one. From the day of our Founding, we have proclaimed that every man and woman on this earth has rights, and dignity, and matchless value, because they bear the image of the Maker of Heaven and earth. Across the generations we have proclaimed the imperative of self-government, because no one is fit to be a master, and no one deserves to be a slave. Advancing these ideals is the mission that created our Nation. It is the honorable achievement of our fathers. Now it is the urgent requirement of our nation's security, and the calling of our time.

'So it is the policy of the United States to seek and support the growth of democratic movements and institutions in every nation and culture, with the ultimate goal of ending tyranny in our world'.

And in his State of the Union address a few weeks later he said:

To promote peace in the broader Middle East, we must confront regimes that continue to harbor terrorists and pursue weapons of mass murder. Syria still allows its territory, and parts of Lebanon, to be used by terrorists who seek to destroy every chance of peace in the region. You have passed, and we are applying, the Syrian Accountability Act—and we expect the Syrian government to end all support for terror and open the door to freedom. Today, Iran remains the world's primary state sponsor of terror—pursuing nuclear weapons while depriving its people of the freedom they seek and deserve. We are working with European allies to make clear to the Iranian regime that it must give up its uranium enrichment program and any plutonium reprocessing, and end its support for terror. And to the Iranian people, I say tonight: As you stand for your own liberty, America stands with you.

Within days of these speeches, the US intervened robustly, though peacefully, to change (or to obtain governments of its choice) in Ukraine and Lebanon, and to nudge existing regimes towards greater democracy in Saudi Arabia and Jordan. Bush also sent Condoleeza Rice, his new Secretary of State, to Europe to rally support and rebuild the Trans-Atlantic Alliance around this new mission, and followed this up with a personal visit. During this visit, in his speech to the European Union in Brussels, he used the word 'freedom' 22 times. Three days later, in Bratislava, Slovakia, he used 'freedom' or 'liberty' 17 times, once in each paragraph of his speech.[55] Throughout his visit, his message remained unvarying: We may have differed over how to bring democracy and end tyranny in Iraq, but as the original home of modern democracy, Europe cannot object to our efforts to oust dictators and promote democracy throughout the world, especially if we do so peacefully. We should join hands once more to promote democracy, for it is as much in Europe's interest as America's.

Bush received a cautious welcome in Europe and promises of support in strengthening democratic forces and institution, including various forms of training for members of the new Iraqi government and security forces, but no endorsement of his right to take pre-emptive, unilateral action in the future.

Commonwealth: Outlines of a Different Future

The US' bid to build an empire based upon force alone is on the verge of failure. But failure, when it comes, will not solve the problems of governance that globalisation and the erosion of the nation state system have created. Regulating the pace of social, economic and political transition from national to global capitalism requires a regulator. In the absence of a supra-national authority, that function can only be performed by the nation states themselves. All of them face the common challenge of determining the pace and order in which they will cede their previously sovereign powers to a supranational authority. That is the moral and political foundation of the concept of a global commonwealth.

The alternative to a unipolar world is therefore a multi-polar one. The alternative to unilateral action is multilateral action, endorsed by a world body such as the United Nations Security Council. The alternative to empire is therefore 'commonwealth'. A commonwealth would serve not merely the interest of lesser powers, but that of the dominant power as well. Acceptance of a world order structured as a commonwealth would leave the dominant country with the option of exploring several avenues for resolving a problem and of withdrawing, regrouping, and launching a different form of assault if the first one fails. It will permit it to build a consensus on the steps that need to be taken and the circumstances in which the use of force would be justified. It will, in short, give it a chance to rebuild its hegemony on a sustainable basis.

Throughout the first years of the new millennium, while the US has been pushing hard towards empire, the UN Secretary-General Kofi Annan, under a mandate from the millennium session of the United Nations General Assembly, has been painstakingly working to create the framework of a viable multilateral world order that can cope with the many challenges of globalisation. Future historians may come to regard Annan as the prime architect of a yet-to-be-consolidated multilateral and therefore democratic international order. Annan was one of the first heads of the UN to state categorically, at the opening session of the UN commission on Human

Rights in April 1999, that states could no longer shelter behind the doctrine of absolute sovereignty to oppress their subjects. The fact that this coincided with and therefore seemed to vindicate the aerial attack in Serbia, which killed several thousand people on a pretext of pre-empting ethnic cleansing that was dubious to say the least, made his timing questionable. But Annan was not speaking of one but the entire series of crises that had racked the world after the end of the Cold War. His statement needs to be seen against the determined, and initially successful, effort he made to prevent the unilateral resumption of the bombing of Iraq in February 1998. These two actions drew the boundary lines around the central problems that the world faced. In his report to the millennium session, Annan urged the international community to forge consensus around three basic questions of principle and process: when should intervention occur, under whose authority, and how. Within days the Government of Canada announced that it would set up and fund an independent International Commission on Intervention and State Sovereignty to establish a set of guidelines by which nations could decide when intervention in the internal affairs of a sovereign state became justified, and how it was best undertaken. The commission was co-chaired by Gareth Evans, former foreign minister of Australia, and Mohamed Sahnoun, an eminent Algerian diplomat, who was then a special advisor to the UN Secretary-General. It had ten members, five drawn from the west, one from Russia and four from the developing countries.[56] Despite the fact that nearly all the members lived in the affluent countries, and were not therefore inclined to challenge the basic premise that military intervention was sometimes justified, their report, which was presented to the UN General Assembly in December 2001, only fourteen weeks after 9/11, unambiguously reasserted:

> State sovereignty implies responsibility, and the primary responsibility for the protection of the people rests with the state itself ... Military intervention for human protection is an exceptional and extraordinary measure. To be warranted, there must be serious and irreparable harm occurring to human beings, or imminently likely to occur, of the following kind:
> A. Large scale loss of life, actual or apprehended, with genocide intent or not, which is the product either of deliberate state action or state neglect or inability to act, or a failed state situation; or
> B. Large scale ethnic cleansing, actual or apprehended, whether carried out by killing, forced expulsion, acts of terror or rape.

As NATO's incursion into Kosovo had already shown, while the inclusion of the term 'actual or apprehended' gave a great deal of latitude for interpretation, and therefore for abuse of the 'Responsibility to Protect', the commission was absolutely adamant that the only body that had the right to sanction intervention was the United Nations Security Council:

> There is no better or more appropriate body than the United Nations Security Council to authorise military intervention for human protection purposes. The task is not to find alternatives to the Security Council as a source of authority, but to make the Security Council work better than it has.

The report was to have been presented to the UN at the beginning of the General Assembly session in 2001, but was overwhelmed by 9/11. It was only presented a few days before the session ended in December and therefore went almost unnoticed. But it drew the battle lines between the increasing unilateralism of the US, which had displayed its impatience with the UN and its penchant for direct action by bombarding Iraq in December 1998 and orchestrating the bombing of Serbia in 1999.

When the US unveiled its doctrine of pre-emptive (in reality preventive) intervention and thereby served notice that the 400 year-old Westphalian state system that formed the backbone of the UN Charter had become obsolete, Annan could simply have rolled over and allowed the US to plough the UN into the earth. But instead he once again took up the challenge of defining the new threats to human society, and rebuilding the case for collective—and only collective—action. To do this he set up another high-level panel, which presented a second report in December 2004, entitled *A More Secure World: Our Shared Responsibility*.

The panel not only broadened the concept of security to include protection against disease, economic want, environmental degradation and high-risk technologies, but also highlighted the fact that, like global terrorism and the trade in narcotics, these too were threats without borders. It concluded, 'No State, no matter how powerful, can by its own efforts alone make itself invulnerable to today's threats. Every State requires the cooperation of other States to make itself secure. It is in every State's interest, accordingly, to cooperate with other States to address their most pressing threats, because doing so will maximize the chances of reciprocal cooperation to address its own threat priorities.' It ended by giving a call for 'a new comprehensive collective security system that will commit all of them to act cooperatively in the face of a broad array of threats'.

On 21 March 2005, Annan distilled the essence of the two previous reports in a letter addressed to all the members of the United Nations, titled *In Larger Freedom*. It is Annan's legacy to the world, for, as he says in its introduction, 'In preparing the present report, I have drawn on my eight years' experience as Secretary-General, on my own conscience and convictions, and on my understanding of the Charter of the United Nations whose principles and purposes it is my duty to promote.'

When it was released, he drew strong criticism from a section of the international media for having downplayed economic development. But this perception was at least partly a product of ignorance, as the ILO had released another report in February 2004, titled *A Fair Globalization: Creating Opportunities for All*, under the auspices of the World Commission on the Social Dimension of Globalisation, which was set up by the ILO and chaired by President Tarja Halonen of Finland, and President Benjamin William Mkapa of Tanzania. The key finding of that report, from which all of the commission's many recommendations sprang, was:

> Globalisation is making multilateralism both indispensable and inevitable. The multilateral system of the United Nations and its related organisations provides the basis for the global policies which are needed in the areas of development, trade, finance, and international peace and security ... There is no durable alternative which can respond to the needs and aspirations of people in an interdependent world.[57]

In Larger Freedom reunited economic development with political stability and human security. In an address delivered a month later in New Delhi, Annan explained,

> ... you are not meaningfully free if you are exposed to arbitrary violence, whether inflicted by the security forces of other states, or of your own state, or by what we euphemistically call non-state actors ... That is why I see 'larger freedom' as an overarching concept which includes ... development, security and human rights. You cannot really enjoy any one of the three without the other two, and all three need to be underpinned by the Rule of Law.

The Rule of Law is the philosophical bedrock of all three reports. The bulk of *In Larger Freedom* is an impassioned plea to all countries to sign on to international conventions in order to make them truly universal. Without quite saying so, he leaves us in no doubt that if we do not do so—if we try to safeguard our individual national sovereignties by standing out—we run the risk of deepening chaos and making the entire international order prey to arbitrary unilateralism. Collective security and collective action to protect individuals from economic want, disease, oppression and death is the only long-term alternative.

In a world where the political and economic interdependence of nations and their common need to surrender a small part of their sovereignty for the larger good is readily accepted, reports such as the three cited above point the way towards a functioning commonwealth in little or no time.

But one has only to compare their unqualified endorsement of multilateralism (and that of the UN Security Council) with the way that the US has made coercion the preferred method of dealing with other nations in both economic and political relations, mocked and threatened the UN, and ignored the wishes of the international community as expressed in the Security Council, and finally set up a Congressional Commission[58] to smear Annan's reputation and make sure no one even thinks of re-electing him as the secretary-general, to realise how precipitously the world is moving in the opposite direction.

Notes

1. Eric Hobsbawm, *Age of Extremes* (London, Abacus, 1994), pp. 562, 584.
2. 'Let us celebrate,' wrote Mortimer B. Zuckerman, in an editorial in *US News and World Report*. 'The Mantra is privatise, deregulate and do not interfere with the Market.' America had thus entered the 'New Economy'. All it had to do is to leave business 'free to innovate, restructure and relocate. Those are essential ingredients for baking an ever larger pie, however distasteful the downsizing and wage inequality that are part of the process' (quoted in Louis Uchitelle, 'World Beaters: Puffed up by Prosperity', *New York Times' Week in Review*, 27 April 1997).
3. Paul Krugman, 'America the boastful', *Foreign Affairs*, May–June 1998.
4. International Crisis Group, 'Collapse in Kosovo', ICG Europe report no. 155, 22 April 2004.
5. Ibid.
6. James Glanz, 'Insurgents attacking Baghdad's lifelines', *International Herald Tribune*, 22 February 2005.
7. This possibility prompted the 9/11 commission to warn the US administration: 'If Iraq becomes a failed State, it will go to the top of the places that will become breeding grounds for attacks against Americans at home (p. 367).
8. Peter Galbraith, 'Bush's security plan now rests on nothing but hope', *The Guardian*, 11 October 2004.
9. Terence Hunt, 'Bush urges world leaders to unite with him on Iraq', Associated Press, 21 September 2004.
10. See Chapter 1.
11. Edward D. Mansfield and Jack Snyder, 'Democracy and War', *Foreign Affairs*, May–June 1995. Mansfield and Snyder's finding that it was only stable democratic states that tended not to go to war with each other, and that democratising states were if anything more warlike that stable authoritarian states, captures one facet of this larger truth.
12. The significant exception was the Baltic and the North Sea region, in which there was a great deal of trade in timber spars, salt, coal, grain and such basic goods.
13. See Chapter 1.
14. United Nations, *World Investment Report 1993* (Geneva, UNCTAD), pp. 1, 13; United Nations, *World Investment Report 1999* (Geneva, UNCTAD), pp. xvii–xix.
15. Ibid.
16. United Nations, *World Investment Report 1999*, pp. xvii, 78–80.

17. Michael Hardt and Antonio Negri, *Empire* (Cambridge Ma., Harvard University Press, 2000), p. 9.
18. Michael Mann, *Incoherent Empire* (London, Verso, 2003).
19. Saturday morning radio address, 10 April 2004 (emphasis added). Available at: www.whitehouse.gov/news/release/2004/04/print/200404-10.html.
20. Katherine Pfleger Shrader, 'Concern mounts over growing unrest in Iraq', Associated Press, 8 April 2004.
21. Hardt and Negri, *Empire* (emphasis added).
22. John Pilger, 'This is a war of liberation and we are the enemy', *The New Statesman*, 15 April 2004.
23. This estimate sounds high, but explains the surprising finding of a poll of Iraqi public opinion carried out by the American Enterprise Institute in December 2003, that 31 per cent of the respondents had lost a loved one or a friend in the war and its aftermath.
24. Tony Blair, speech delivered on 16 July 2005. Reported in the *New York Times*. Taken here from internet site 'American Future: Making sense of a world in turmoil' at: http://americanfuture.typepad.com/american_future/2005/07/tony_blair_on_t.html.
25. Ibid.
26. Ibid.
27. Yossef Bodansky, *Bin Laden, The Man who Declared War on America* (California, Prima Publishing Forum, 2001), Chapter 1.
28. Ibid., pp. 102, 120.
29. Ibid., p. 52.
30. Hasan Alfi, interior minister of Egypt was quoted by the *Los Angeles Times* as saying, 'Unfortunately some power took hold of these young men and changed their way of thinking. It changed their principles. Their way became violent and they tried to compel others to take Islam by force. They came home and started setting the fires of terrorism.' See John Dahlberg and others, 'The Islamic blowback', *Los Angeles Times*, 4–7 August, 1996.
31. Ibid., 4 August 1996.
32. These included the killing of five Americans in Riyadh; 19 Americans at the Khobar towers in Dhahran, Saudi Arabia; an attack on CIA personnel at the gates of its Langley, Va. Headquarters; the 1993 bombing of the World Trade Center; an abortive attempt to blow up 12 United Airlines jets in the far East on the same day; and the successful suicide bombing of the USS Cole in Yemen.
33. Report by an Eminent Person's Group to the UN Secretary-General. The description given here was provided at a closed-door meeting in 1998 by I.K. Gujral, former prime minister of India, who was a member of the group.
34. US State Department, *Patterns of Global Terrorism* (1994, 1995 and other issues). Unless otherwise indicated this is the source for the information given in the succeeding paragraphs.
35. Briefing notes given by the Indian Ministry of External Affairs to journalists who accompanied Prime Minister Narasimha Rao on a working visit to Cairo in September 1995.
36. Ewen MacAskill, Duncan Campbell and Richard Norton-Taylor, 'Iraq creating new breed of jihadists, says CIA', *The Guardian*, Thursday, 23 June 2005.
37. Peter Beaumont, 'Insurgents trawl Europe for recruits' (*The Observer*, 19 June 2005).
38. Hasan Suroor, 'London "Suicide Bombers" were of Pakistani origin', *The Hindu*, 14 July 2005. Suroor reported one of Hasib Hussain's family members as saying that after his visit to Pakistan, he had 'gone off the rails'.
39. BBC World News, 0400 GMT, 14 July 2005.

40. Seumas Milne, 'It's an insult to the dead to deny the link with Iraq', *The Guardian*, 14 July 2005.

41. *National Catholic Reporter*, 15 May 1998.

42. BBC World Service, 23 January 2001.

43. 'Iranian Women Burn to Death in Protest', *Telegraph*, 24 February 2003.

44. Si Si Lu, 'Suicide as Protest', *The China Rights Forum*, No. 1, 2005, available at: www.hrichina.org/fs/view/downloadables/pdf/downloadable-resources/1,2005SuicideAsProtest.pdf).

45. Chalmers Johnson, *The Sorrows of Empire: Militarism, Secrecy and the End of the Republic* (London and New York, Verso, 2004), pp. 161, 165.

46. http://home.hiwaay.net/~pspoole/echelon.html#FN17

47. www.gchq.gov.uk/about/technology.html. A recent European parliament report confirmed this, admitting that

> Within Europe, all email, telephone and fax communications are routinely inter-cepted by the United States National Security Agency, transferring all target information from the European mainland via the strategic hub of London then by satellite to Fort Meade in Maryland via the crucial hub at Menwith Hill in the North York Moors of the UK (Steve Wright, 'An Appraisal of Technologies of Political Control', European Parliament: Scientific and Technologies Options Assessment, Luxembourg, 6 January 1998).

48. Tender issued by the US government (these are called Broad Agency Announcements). The relevant portion of the text reads:

> WASHINGTON, DC—October 31, 2001—The Department of Defense (DoD) and the Research and Special Programs Administration (RSPA) of the Department of Transportation (DOT) have issued Broad Agency Announcements (BAA) on the topic of Homeland Defense and Security.
> The DoD's BAA seeks proposals by December 23, 2001 for technologies that could be deployed in the next year to 18 months to help in combating terrorism, defeating difficult targets, conducting protracted operations in remote areas and developing countermeasures to weapons of mass destruction (http://www.itsa.org/itsnews.nsf/key/686A?OpenDocument0).

49. For instance, while more jobs were created than were destroyed in Long Island in 1995, while the average salary in the fastest-shrinking industries on Long Island was $49,730 a year, it was $18,000 a year in the jobs that were being created (Kirk Johnson and Thomas F. Lueck, 'The Region's Economy in Fundamental Shift', *New York Times*, 19 February 1996).

50. Dale Maharidge, 'Rust and rage in the heartland', *The Nation*, 20 September 2004.

51. In Iraq, the US was caught firmly in a quagmire. It could neither defeat the insurgency nor pull out of the country without appearing defeated and further inflaming Islamist violence. At home the economic recovery had been weak and jobless. Income differentials had widened rapidly. Five million more Americans could not afford, and therefore did not have, health insurance. Two per cent more of the population had slipped under the poverty line. The budget deficit was out of control and foreign investors were no longer prepared to fund the balance of payments deficit, which exceeded half a trillion dollars a year. As a result the dollar had fallen by 40 per cent in the previous 30 months.

52. CNN.com, Election Results, 5 November 2004 (http://cnn.org/ELECTION/2004/pages/results/states/US/P/00/epolls.0.html).

53. Karl Polanyi, *The Great Transformation* (Boston, Beacon Press, 1957), p. 36.
54. *The Week*, 'Is there a plan to reintroduce conscription?', *The Week—The Best of the British and Foreign Media*, London, 16 October 2004, p. 15 (www.theweek.co.uk).

The alternative is to rely more and more heavily on technology. Since there is a marked reluctance in the American population to incur the cost of building and maintaining an empire, especially in human lives, the US military is once again pinning its hopes on the development of new technology. In July 2003, the Pentagon revealed to the media that it was developing an urban surveillance system that would use thousands of cameras and other surveillance equipment, hooked to extremely powerful computers, to track, record, and analyse the movement of every vehicle *in a foreign city*. Dubbed 'Combat Zones That See' (CZTS), its centre-piece was groundbreaking software that was capable of automatically identifying vehicles by size, colour, shape and license plate, and instantly alerting the 'authorities' the moment it spotted a vehicle on the watchlist. The system foresaw the possibility that 'terrorists' would change license plates or the colour of their vehicles frequently to avoid detection. The software was therefore capable of searching months of records of all vehicle movements to compare vehicles spotted near 'terrorist sites'. The project was only the most ambitious of several being developed by the Defence Advanced Research Projects Agency (DARPA). Others were intended to scan databases of everyday transactions and personal records worldwide to predict terrorist attacks and create a computerised diary that would record and analyse 'everything a person says, sees, hears and reads' (see Michael J. Sniffen, 'US develops urban surveillance system', *Associated Press*, 2 July 2003).

The crucial element in the CZTS project is that it can only be used *after* the thousands of interlocking cameras are installed. This means that the foreign city will have to be invaded and occupied first. Another defence research project with chilling implications is the Gamma ray bomb, a bomb that will blur the distinction between nuclear and conventional weapons, because it will kill by delivering intense bursts of gamma rays. The obvious advantage of this weapon, should it ever become operational, is that it will leave all inanimate objects untouched, and only clear the killing field of human beings. The gamma ray bomb is not the most futuristic of the projects that the Pentagon has authorised. Another is the development of fighting robots. These are already being used for clearing mines and other static surveillance work.
55. John Vinocur, 'Some in Europe shy from a Bush F-word', *International Herald Tribune*, 1 March 2005.
56. The members were:

> **Gisèle Côté-Harper** (Canada) is a barrister and professor of law at Laval University, Quebec.
> **Lee Hamilton** (United States) is director of the Woodrow Wilson International Center for Scholars, Washington DC, and director of the Center on Congress at Indiana University.
> **Michael Ignatieff** (Canada) is currently Carr Professor of Human Rights Practice at the Kennedy School of Government, Harvard University. He is also a senior fellow of the 21st Century Trust, and served as a member of the Independent International Commission on Kosovo.
> **Vladimir Lukin** (Russia) is currently deputy speaker of the Russian State Duma. He worked at the Institute of World Economics and International Relations, Moscow (1961–65) and the Institute of US and Canadian Studies of the USSR Academy of Sciences (1968–87).
> **Klaus Naumann** (Germany) served as chairman of the North Atlantic Military Committee of NATO (1996–99) and played a central role in managing the Kosovo crisis and in developing NATO's new integrated military command structure.

Cyril Ramaphosa (South Africa) is currently executive chairman of Rebserve, a major South African service and facilities management company. He was elected Secretary-General of the African National Congress in June 1991, but left politics for business in 1996.

Fidel Ramos (Philippines) served as president of the Republic of the Philippines from 1992–98, and has since 1999 been Chairman of the Ramos Peace and Development Foundation, which deals with Asia-Pacific security, sustainable development, democratic governance and economic diplomacy.

Cornelio Sommaruga (Switzerland) is currently president of the Caux Foundation for Moral Re-Armament as well as president of the Geneva International Centre for Humanitarian Demining.

Eduardo Stein (Guatemala) is currently working with UNDP in Panama and served as head of the OAS Observer Mission to Peru's May 2000 general elections. He was Guatemalan foreign minister (1996–2000), a position in which he played a key role in overseeing the Guatemalan peace negotiations, particularly in marshalling international support.

Ramesh Thakur (India) has been vice-rector of the United Nations University, Tokyo, since 1998, in charge of the University's Peace and Governance Program.

57. The World Commission on the Social Dimension of Globalisation, *A Fair Globalization: Creating opportunities for All* (Geneva, ILO, 2004), p. 6.

58. The Norman Coleman commission. This is a bipartisan commission whose ostensible purpose is to investigate corruption within the UN in the administration of the UN oil-for-food programme that Annan helped start up in 1998.

ACKNOWLEDGEMENTS

This book was made possible by four people: Ashutosh Varshney, then Assistant Professor at Harvard, who urged me in 1994 to come to the Centre for International Affairs, and sponsored my stay there as a Visiting Fellow; John Echeverri-Gent at the University of Virginia, who made it possible for me to go there first as a Visiting Professor and later as a Visiting Lecturer; Suzanne Rudolph at the University of Chicago, who pointed me in the direction of Karl Polanyi; and most of all to Sanjay Reddy, now Professor at Barnard College, Columbia University, who drew my attention to the work of Lash and Urry, Giovanni Arrighi and others, and was ever ready to listen to my first tentative conclusions as I felt my way into a new intellectual world. On a personal level I owe them a debt that I cannot repay.

Index